THEORIES OF HUMAN DEVELOPMENT

THEORIES OF HUMAN DEVELOPMENT

Barbara M. Newman

Philip R. Newman

Psychology Press
Taylor & Francis Group

New York   London

First Published by Lawrence Erlbaum Associates, Inc., Publishers
10 Industrial Avenue
Mahwah, New Jersey 07430

Reprinted 2009 by Psychology Press

Cover design by Tomai Maridou

Library of Congress Cataloging-in-Publication Data

Newmn, Barbara M.
   Theories of human development / Barbara M. Newman, Philip R. Newman.
p.   cm.
   Includes bibliographical references and index.
   ISBN 978-0-8058-4702-4 — 0-8058-4702-2 (pbk.)
   ISBN 978-1-4106-1772-9 — 1-4106-1772-6 (e book)
   1. Developmental psychology. I. Newman, Philip R. II. Title.

 BF713.N494 2007
155—dc22   2007033906
                                                            CIP

10   9   8   7   6   5   4   3   2   1

Contents

Preface   **vii**

1   Introduction   **1**

PART I: THEORIES THAT EMPHASIZE BIOLOGICAL FACTORS   **15**

2   Evolutionary Theory   **19**

3   Psychosexual Theory   **45**

4   Cognitive Developmental Theory   **81**

PART II: THEORIES THAT EMPHASIZE ENVIRONMENTAL FACTORS   **121**

5   Learning Theories   **125**

6   Social Role Theory   **159**

7   Life Course Theory   185

PART III: THEORIES THAT EMPHASIZE THE INTERACTION
          OF PERSON AND ENVIRONMENT   207

8   Psychosocial Theory   211

9   Cognitive Social–Historical Theory   241

10   Dynamic Systems Theory   269

      References   297

      Author Index   321

      Subject Index   331

Preface

Theories of Human Development

Theories are like fantasies; they offer ideas that can be far reaching and profound or misguided and misleading. Each theory draws you into a world of ideas, leading you to consider relationships, processes, time, culture, and self in new ways and suggesting methods for exploring human behavior. The focus of this book is to provide an engaging introduction to important theoretical perspectives about human development. The nine theories that are presented have guided research, intervention, and practice in numerous fields including developmental psychology, life span development, education, medicine and nursing, social work, human services, counseling, parenting, therapy, and mental health.

One weakness of several current books in this area is that they offer a "shotgun" approach to theory. Each chapter is typically devoted to a separate theory, but students have no idea why these theories were selected or how they relate to one another. This book is designed to focus on three major families of theories: those that emphasize biological systems in guiding the direction of growth; those that emphasize environmental factors in guiding the direction of growth; and those that emphasize a dynamic interaction between biological, environmental, and self-directed forces in guiding the shape and direction of development. Within each family, three specific theories are presented. These theories were selected to illustrate perspectives that have a long and productive history in human development and that continue to evolve because of new insights from contemporary scholarly work. As students become familiar with the three families of theories, they will have new resources to think critically about theoretical ideas, begin to assess the strengths and weaknesses of the theories, and gain a deeper understanding of how the particular emphasis of a theory guides research, application, policy and public opinion.

The book was written for upper division undergraduates and beginning graduate students who have already taken one course in human development or developmental psychology. It is comprised of 10 chapters: an introduction and nine theory chapters divided into three families. The introduction (ch. 1) reviews the role that theories play in guiding the development of knowledge and the design of interventions. It also highlights some of the challenges of understanding human development across the life span. Each family of theories is introduced with a brief interlude that provides some highlights of each theory and its unique perspectives, and some discussion of why the theories in that section have been grouped together.

The discussion of each theory includes the following sections:

A. The historical and cultural context in which the theory was developed.
B. An overview of key concepts and important ideas.
C. New directions in contemporary scientific work.
D. A research example that shows how the theory has been tested and modified.
E. An application that shows how the theory guided the design of an intervention or program.
F. An analysis of how the theory answers the basic questions that a theory of human development is expected to address.
G. A critique of the theory, pointing out strengths and weaknesses.

The book is written in a clear, comprehensible style without sacrificing the integrity and complexity of ideas. Concepts are explained so that students can grasp the underlying logic of the theory and its basic contributions. Each chapter follows the same organization to allow students to do their own comparisons and to learn to anticipate the issues that are likely to be raised. By emphasizing three families of theories and selecting a few examples within each family, we hope to help students begin to grasp the essential features of the family of theories and appreciate how new theories they will encounter fit within one orientation or another.

The book highlights the significance of theories in building a knowledge base by demonstrating the role of theory in guiding research, helping to interpret behavior, and shaping the nature of interventions. Students will appreciate how theories are revised and extended as new issues are brought to light. They will observe, through examples, how the research process contributes to the evaluation and modification of theories. They will also see how, over time, ideas that may have been introduced in one theory are revisited in another theoretical framework, or how an emerging societal issue brings back the relevance of a theoretical concept from the past. Students will also be encouraged to develop a critical perspective by understanding the historical and cultural context within which each theory was developed. This perspective suggests the inevitable biases that accompany any individual's efforts to explain and predict human behavior, situated as they are in the prevailing scientific environment as well as the theorist's particular scholarly training, values, and beliefs.

In conclusion, we hope the text will serve instructors well in bringing the realm of theory to life. We hope the content will encourage students to see the field of human development as a living science that invites their critical thinking and creative contributions.

ACKNOWLEDGMENTS

We have had continuing encouragement from the editorial staff of Lawrence Erlbaum Associates in the development of this book.

In addition to the staff of Lawrence Erlbaum Associates, we are grateful for the suggestions provided by academic reviewers including: Michael Mascolo, Merrimack College; Victoria L. Bacon, Bridgewater State College ; and Judy Blumenthal, Montgomery College.

Chapter 1

Introduction

CHAPTER OUTLINE

What is Human Development?

What is a Theory?

What Do We Expect from a Theory of Human Development?

What are the Challenges to Understanding Human Development Across the Life Span?

The Organization of the Text

Chapter 1

Introduction

The world of scientific inquiry can be divided into two related components: observation and theory. Scientific observations describe what happens; scientific theories offer explanations about "how" and "why" these things happen.

Imagine the following situation. You are babysitting for Clark, who is 2 ½. You are getting ready to go to the park, which Clark loves, and you tell Clark that he needs to get his shoes on before you can leave the house. Clark sits down on the floor, pulls his shoes on, and starts to tie his laces. You see that he is having trouble, so you offer to help. "No!" says Clark, "I do it." You wait a while, and then you say, "Let me get that so we can go to the park." "No!" says Clark again, and pulls away. "Don't you want to go to the park?" you ask. Clark takes his shoes off and says, "OK, park."

As a student of human development, you might begin to try to understand this situation by reflecting on what you observed. What did Clark say and do? What did you say and do? What was the context in which this interaction took place? Once you have taken careful account of the "what" of the situation, you will probably begin asking yourself some questions in order to understand the "why" of situation and how to cope with it. You may wonder about the meaning of the situation for you and for Clark. You might consider that since you are an adult and Clark is a young child, the meaning of the situation might be different for each of you. Why won't Clark accept your help? Does Clark understand why he has to wear shoes to the park? Why is Clark so set on tying his own shoes? What role did you play in this situation? Did you say or do something that made Clark reject your help? How can you intervene so that Clark puts his shoes on and gets to go to the park? In order to answer these questions, you need to link your observation of your behavior and Clark's behavior to ideas that explain them. These ideas are your theory of why things happened as they did for you, for Clark, and for you and Clark. The theory will lead you to a decision about what you might do next.

In the field of human development, theories play a powerful role by shaping our ideas about the meaning of behavior, expanding our understanding of the scope and potential of complex human functioning, opening the way to new research, and guiding interventions. There is no single, agreed on theory that all scholars of human development endorse. Yet, many of the theories have given us a new lens for observing and interpreting behavior. Jean Piaget's theory of cognitive development led to a new appreciation for the way children create meaning out of their experiences. Sigmund Freud's theory of psychosexual development provided insights into the unconscious, giving us a way of thinking about the tension between strong motives or desires and the constraints against expressing those desires. Albert Bandura's theory of social learning led to widespread use of the idea of modeling to characterize the social conditions under which children learn through observation and imitation of the behavior of others. His ideas about self-efficacy have pointed out the importance of confidence as a person strives to meet new and challenging standards for performance. Erik Erikson's psychosocial theory highlighted the concept of identity, a creative synthesis of self in society that emerges and then guides the direction of development over the life span. These are a few examples of how theorists have provided frameworks for identifying unobservable processes and mechanisms that account for behavior. In doing this, they have given us a new vocabulary for understanding and studying the dynamics of development.

This book is a selective introduction to nine theories that have inspired the study of human development and produced a rich heritage of research and intervention. Each theory has a distinguished history, but is also currently important in shaping the focus of the field and guiding approaches to both research and practice.

This introductory chapter will address the following questions:

1. What is human development?
2. What is theory?
3. What do we expect from a theory of human development?

4. What are some of the challenges to understanding human development across the life span?

The chapter closes with an overview of the organization of the text.

WHAT IS HUMAN DEVELOPMENT?

The term *human development* suggests a focus on the human species, not all life forms. This focus brings with it special considerations. First, humans have ideas and experiences that influence their outlook. Scientists and theorists are similar to other humans in this regard. Scholars of human development are humans studying their own species. They have their own thoughts and experiences that may serve as a basis for expectations about the direction and meaning of behavior. Often, these personal thoughts and experiences serve to give focus and direction to the scholar's work. For example, Freud's father died when Freud was a young boy. In his theory of development, understanding the relationship of a boy to his father played a pivotal role. Thus, special consideration number one reminds us that each theory of human development must be understood as reflecting the education and training, historical context, and personal experiences, values, and beliefs of the human beings who invented it.

A second special consideration in the study of human development is that humans enjoy a wonderful capacity for representational or symbolic thought. Thus, the study of human development must include more than a description of behaviors and explanations that account for these behaviors. It must also include descriptions of the nature of mental activity such as knowledge acquisition and use, imagination, aspirations and plans, emotions, problem solving, patterns of change and the direction of change in mental activity, and some suggestions about the relationships between mental activity and behavior.

A third special consideration in the study of human development is that humans have a comparatively long life span during which their capacities change dramatically. In contrast to many other species, humans are born in a relatively dependent state, and their daily survival depends on the care and nurturance provided by others. This dependent state continues for quite some time. Humans may live to an advanced age of 100 years or more, achieving many new levels of complex thought and behavior, participating in a wide range of social relationships, and adapting to diverse physical and social settings. The study of human development must address constancy and change of an organism that has an impressive capacity for change over a long period of time.

The study of human development focuses on describing patterns of constancy and change across the life span and identifying the underlying processes that account for these patterns (Kagan, 1991). The term *development* implies change that occurs over time and that has a direction. The direction is usually from simple to more complex, from less organized and coordinated to more organized and coordinated, or from less integrated to more integrated. In order to decide whether a particular change is developmental, one must ask if there is some pattern to the change that can be observed from one individual to the next, and if this change appears to have a direction that suggests a new level of complexity or integration. Consider the behavior of walking as an example. Walking is a new form of locomotion that can be observed from one child to the next. The change from crawling or scooting to standing and walking involves new levels of coordination in balance, and new integration of sensory and motor information.

WHAT IS A THEORY?

A formal scientific theory offers constructs that help explain the relationships among variables. We all have our informal, intuitive theories about why people behave as they do. For example, the adage "The acorn doesn't fall far from the tree," is an informal theory that predicts that children are going to grow up to behave a lot like their parents. A formal scientific theory is a set of interconnected constructs and hypotheses, the function of which is to describe unobservable structures, mechanisms, or processes and to relate them to one another in order to explain observable events. For example, in learning, the information or strategies that have been learned are not observable nor is the process of learning. The information becomes observable by asking questions, giving a test, or presenting a situation where the information must be used to solve a problem. However, the process of learning the information is not directly observable and our understanding of this process relies on theories that attempt to explain how new information is acquired, remembered, and produced when needed.

Theories are like short stories with a situation, main characters, and a plot. The theory identifies a *domain* such as cognition, language, learning, motivation, or identity development that will be the focus of explanation. This is the *situation*, or problem, the theory is attempting to address. In order to understand a theory, one must be clear about which phenomena the theory is trying to explain. A theory of intellectual development may include hypotheses about the evolution of the brain, the growth of logical thinking, or the capacity to use symbolism. Such a theory is less likely to explain fears, motives, or friendship. Understanding the focus of the theory helps to identify its range of applicability. Although principles from one theory may have relevance to another area of knowledge, a theory is evaluated in terms of the behavior it was originally intended to explain.

In reading about each theory, you will encounter certain *assumptions* about the scientific process, human behavior, or development. These assumptions may not be testable; they provide a platform upon which the theory is built. Assumptions are the guiding premises underlying the logic of a theory. In order to evaluate a theory, you must first understand what its assumptions are. Charles Darwin assumed that lower life forms "progress" to higher forms in the process of evolution. Freud assumed that all behavior is motivated and that the unconscious is a "storehouse" of motives and wishes. The assumptions of any theory may or may not be correct. Assumptions may be influenced by the cultural context that dominates the theorist's period of history, by the sample of observations from which the theorist has drawn inferences, by the current knowledge base of the field, and by the intellectual capacities of the theorist.

Each theory is comprised of key *constructs* that refer to certain unobservable relationships or processes. You might think of these constructs as the principle characters in the story. We use constructs such as intelligence, motivation, and goals to explain human behavior, just as we use constructs such as electricity, gravity, and momentum to explain the physical world. In each case, the construct is not observable directly, although in the case of the physical world, scientists often have reached agreement on ways of measuring these constructs. Developmental scholars work to measure explanatory constructs just as do physical scientists, but agreement about approaches to measurement is much slower. In theories of human development, the constructs may vary from those that are closely linked to an observation, such as the term *reinforcement*, to others that are very abstract and unlikely to be observed or measured, such as *equilibrium*.

Finally, theories offer *if–then* links or *testable hypotheses*. This is the plot. What does the theory predict? For example, Skinner's theory of operant conditioning offered the following testable hypothesis: "When a response is followed by a reward or reinforcement, the probability of its recurrence will increase." This means that successful actions (those that are rewarded) are more likely to be repeated than unsuccessful actions. From this single hypothesis, one can interpret many observations about human behavior and predict others.

Theories add new levels of understanding by suggesting causal relationships, by unifying diverse observations, and by identifying the importance of events that may have gone unnoticed. Theories of human development offer explanations regarding the origins and functions of human behavior and the changes that can be expected in behavior under certain conditions or from one period of life to the next. Once you agree to use the constructs of the theory as a way of talking about the domain, the theory takes you through a set of logical steps to predict the nature and direction of constancy and change.

Upon entering the world of a specific theory, it is easy to be caught up in its vocabulary and logic and to think of the theory as offering the truth about its domain. However, an important aspect of any scientific theory is that it is viewed as *tentative* and open to revision based on new observations. Scientific theories are different from beliefs. They are created with an understanding that new instrumentation, new observations, and new insights may result in new, integrative, and better explanation. Thus, in your study of scientific theories you must realize that you are dealing with works in progress, and always treat them as providing descriptions and explanations that are useful until a more inclusive, accurate analysis is available (Bordens & Abbott, 2002).

WHAT DO WE EXPECT FROM A THEORY OF HUMAN DEVELOPMENT?

A theory of development should help to explain how people change and grow over time, as well as how they remain the same (Thomas, 1999). We expect a theory of human development to provide explanations for six questions:

1. What is the *direction* of change over the life span? We assume that there is a direction to development, that it is not random. Development is not the same as changing one's hair style or deciding one day to play tennis and the next to play soccer. Theories of development offer some big ideas about maturity, and shed light on important ways in which thought, self-understanding, the capacity for social relationships, and/or the capacity for adaptation become increasingly complex and integrated as life goes along.
2. What are the *mechanisms* that account for growth from conception through old age? Do these mechanisms vary across the life span? Theories of development suggest kinds of processes or experiences that bring about systematic change. In this book, we will present and explain the variety of mechanisms theorists offer for how growth and development occur. For example, Piaget's theory suggests that change occurs when a person encounters discrepancy between what is experienced in the world and the mental representations of that experience. He assumed that there is a natural tendency for people to resolve this discrepancy and seek equilibrium. Another theorist might offer a different kind of mechanism for explaining how change occurs. And in some instances, a theory suggests that different kinds of processes are at work at different periods of life.
3. How relevant are early experiences for later development? The theories presented in this book offer different ideas about the significance of early experiences for the psychological and behavioral organization of later periods of life. Some theories suggest that incidents from infancy and child-

hood play a powerful role in guiding the direction of development well into adulthood. Other theories emphasize the influence of contemporary events in guiding development by viewing the person as continuously adapting to new demands and new opportunities.

4. How do *physical, cognitive, emotional,* and *social functions* interact? Most theories of human development focus on a specific domain such as cognition, learning, social relationships, or the expression and management of emotions. However, they also consider the interplay of other domains. For example, according to learning theories, unsatisfied physical needs may lead to a greater sensitivity to certain types of reinforcements. According to cognitive theory, emotions can contribute to attention and investment in the solution of certain problems. We will examine how the theories approach the integration of the physical, cognitive, emotional, and social aspects of behavior.

5. How do the *environmental* and *social contexts* affect individual development? Individuals develop in context. Theories of human development provide ways of conceptualizing context and of highlighting which aspects of context are especially important in shaping the directions of growth. Should we focus on mother as context? father? both parents? siblings? friends? spouse? school? work? the physical environment of home or neighborhood? How do social constructions, including social class, race, ethnicity and religion, become integrated into a person's life story? How and in what ways do they matter? We will analyze the salient aspects of each theory as they address the role of the environment in shaping development.

6. What factors are likely to place the person *at risk* at specific periods of the life span? Although humans have an enormous capacity for adaptation, some combination of conditions is likely to impede optimal growth. We look to theories of human development to help us understand how development might be disrupted. Each of the nine theories provides constructs that address vulnerabilities or risks and some predictions about the conditions that increase risk. Some of the theories also offer differentiated views of risk over the life span.

WHAT ARE THE CHALLENGES TO UNDERSTANDING HUMAN DEVELOPMENT ACROSS THE LIFE SPAN?

Take a moment to reflect on your own development over the past 10 years. Try to inventory all the ways that you have changed, including your physical self, your plans and goals, the quality of your relationships, the settings in which you participate, the roles you play, the tasks you try to accomplish and your ability to succeed at those tasks, the way you use your leisure time and the people you spend time with, and your level of self-insight. Now, consider the ways you experience a sense of self-sameness, such as a constant sense of "I" who guides and directs your behaviors, certain continuous roles and relationships, your assessment of your underlying temperament and personality, your strengths and special talents, and a basket of early childhood memories that come along with you into each new phase of your life. Theories of human development face tremendous challenges in trying to offer scientifically based, empirically testable frameworks to account for the nature of stability and change over the life span. A few of these challenges are identified below; you may think of others:

1. Change in the person is taking place in the context of a changing environment. We do not have the luxury of placing a person in a "petri dish" and watching how he or she grows. A person develops over a long period of time, and as he or she grows, the environment changes. New siblings are born; parents get older; the society's norms for social behavior may change; opportunities for education and employment may change; new technologies and medical interventions may provide new resources; diseases, disasters, and war may place the person at risk. A challenge for each theory is to conceptualize the reality of a changing person in a changing environment (Magnusson & Cairns, 1996).

2. Change is both quantitative and qualitative. Human beings grow by inches and pounds. But they also grow through transitions from lying, to creeping, to crawling, to walking. Some changes, like a person's vocabulary, can be thought of as additive. At age 8 months, most infants typically have no real words; by 16 months most babies have about 24 words, and by 30 months most toddlers have about 570 words. In contrast to vocabulary, which grows incrementally, the creation of two word sentences ("daddy bye-bye," "more juice") is a qualitative change in language use. At age 16 months, few infants make these primitive sentences, but by 30 months almost all children create them (Fenson et al., 1994). Two word expressions are an initial grammar through which children are able to convey their own complex meaning. The words "more" and "juice" have shared meaning, but by putting them together, the child makes a primitive sentence that conveys an idea that is more complicated than the words alone. Two word sentences are a qualitatively new language capacity that is a reorganization of vocabulary and meaning. Theories of human development face the challenge of accounting for both quantitative and qualitative changes and explaining how they operate together.

3. Human development is a product of the interaction of three dynamic systems: the biological, the psychological, and the societal. Each system is complex in its own right, and each has the potential for influencing the others (Erikson, 1963). The biological system includes all those processes necessary for the person's physical functioning, including genetic factors, physical maturation, vulnerability to disease, nutrition, exercise, sleep and

rest cycles, sexual functioning, and exposure to toxins. The psychological system includes all those mental processes needed to make meaning out of experiences, to learn, and to take action. Symbolic abilities, memory, language, the capacity for problem solving, emotion, coping strategies, and creativity are examples of components of the psychological system. The societal system includes all those processes through which a person becomes integrated into society. These include social roles, family, participation in social institutions such as school, work, and religion, cultural values and norms, and exposure to discrimination or intergroup hostilities. Theories of human development may emphasize one or two of these systems more than the others, but without some recognition of the interaction of these systems, the analysis of human development is incomplete.

4. Human beings are conscious and goal-directed. The final challenge we want to raise in this introductory chapter is the need to recognize that humans make choices that guide the direction of their own development. Often, the concepts of nature (a biological plan for development) and nurture (the environmental context of development) are presented as constructs that help account for the direction of growth. Current scholarly work emphasizes that these two factors interact with each other, so that we no longer seek a purely environmental or a purely biological explanation for human behavior. Rather, we look for evidence about how the expression of certain genetically guided patterns are mediated by environmental conditions. However, in these analyses, a third dimension, self-directed goal behavior, is often omitted.

The great variability and flexibility of human behavior and development are advantages in terms of enhanced adaptive potential. However, the organism needs to organize his or her resource investment by making choices and focusing resources accordingly. Thus, life-span development theory inherently raises questions of how individuals decide which domains or goals to select and how they remain focused on the domains or goals they have chosen (Heckhausen & Schulz, 1999, p. 70).

The challenge to theories of human development is to offer an explanation for the choices individuals make that ultimately contribute to the direction of their development.

THE ORGANIZATION OF THE BOOK

The remainder of this book focuses on nine theories divided into three families of theories. Part I includes evolutionary theory, psychosexual theory, and cognitive developmental theory, which place a comparatively strong emphasis on *biological factors* that guide the direction of development. Part II includes learning theories, social role theory, and life course theory, which place a comparatively strong emphasis on *environmental factors* that guide the direction of development. Part III includes psychosocial theory, cognitive social historical theory, and dynamic systems theory, which emphasize the ongoing *interaction of the person and the environment*. As an initial orientation to the book, Table 1 provides an overview of the emphasis of each theory, its primary domain and the methods it uses to gather information and evaluate its claims.

Of course, this division of the theories into three families is an overgeneralization. Each theory has something to say about biological factors, environmental factors, and person–environment interactions. However, we expect that this organization will help you recognize some of the common threads among the theories, compare and contrast them, and work out your own assessment of their strengths and weaknesses.

The presentation of each family of theories begins with a brief interlude or overview in which the issues that tie the theories together are introduced. The discussion of each theory includes the following sections:

A. The historical/cultural context within which the theory was developed.
B. An overview of key concepts.
C. Contemporary directions of the theory.
D. A research example that shows how some aspect of the theory has been tested.
E. An application that shows how the theory has been used to address a practical problem.
F. A review of how the theory answers the six questions discussed above that are expected to be addressed by a theory of human development.
G. A critique of the theory, pointing out its strengths and weaknesses.

As you read each theory, we encourage you to consider its broad impact as well as its scientific merit. You will be thinking about the contributions these theories have made to research and intervention, and their ability to shape the worldview of people outside the narrow circle of human development researchers and scholars.

TABLE 1.1
Overview of Nine Theories

Theory	Emphasis	Primary Domain	Unique Methods
Evolutionary Theory	Biological Evolution	Fitness; sexual reproduction	Ethology; observation of behavior in natural settings
Psychosexual Theory	The origins and development of mental life	Personality development, emotions, motivation, morality	Free association, dream interpretation, case analysis
Cognitive developmental theory	The origins and development of cognition	The development of reasoning and logical thought	Cognitive interview, problem solving tasks, observation
Learning Theories	The establishment of relatively permanent links between stimuli and responses	Learned behaviors, expectancies, vicarious learning-Changes in behavior as a result of experience	Laboratory experimentation
Social Role Theory	Socially constructed roles and role relationships	The development of the self in social life	Survey, interview, and case material
Life Course Theory	Individual life in social and historical time	Transitions and trajectories over the life course	Archival data, demographic data, longitudinal studies, intergenerational studies
Psychosocial Theory	The interaction of the individual and society	Stages of ego development, identity, world view, and social relationships	Case material, play analysis, narratives and life stories, and psychohistory
Cognitive Social Historical Theory	The social and cultural basis of thinking	Cognition, the relationship of speech and thinking, the nature of consciousness, learning and development	Experimental demonstrations that promote or include learning and development, double stimulation method
Dynamic Systems Theory	The function and change of complex systems	Emergence of novel patterns (e.g. motor behavior, skills, cognition, and social interactions)	Mathematical, multidimensional modeling; observation; experimentation

Part 1

Theories That Emphasize Biological Factors

How do human beings emerge from a fertilized egg into their full blown stature as an adult? In the 16th and 17th centuries, some scholars believed in the idea of an homonculous, a fully formed, miniature human believed to be contained in the spermatozoom. This theoretical construct helped to explain how the human body was guided toward its adult shape, structures, and functions. A more contemporary term that reflects this idea is epigenesis, the "approximately stepwise process by which genetic information, as modified by environmental influences, is translated into the substance and behavior of an organism" (Flexner, 1987, p. 653). You can think of this view as if humans were like plants. Seeds contain all the information necessary to grow into daisies, carrots, or marigolds. The role of the environment is to provide the basic, "just good enough," resources so that the potential embedded in the seed can reach its full expression. Just give seeds the correct amount of water, sun, soil, and the right temperature for their growing season, and the fate of the seeds is predetermined.

The three theories presented in this section are members of a family of theories that have a strong biological thread. In the literature about development, this is sometimes referred to as the *nature*, *innate*, or *nativist* camp. Of course, no theory of development claims that the story of growth is entirely about nature. No human, whatever his or her biological endowments, can live without oxygen, food, water, and shelter. We are increasingly aware that humans also require social contact and cognitive stimulation. However, when we ask about how development occurs, the theories presented in this section tend to give a strong role to biologically based capacities that guide the direction and nature of growth.

The three theories presented in this section are evolutionary theory, psychosexual theory, and cognitive developmental theory. Each of these theories addresses the process of adaptation. Evolutionary theory focuses on the long-term adaptation of the species over many generations. A primary issue in this theory is the importance of the reproductive process through which adaptive capacities are transmitted biologically from one generation to the next. The human beings alive today are a product of a long period of biological evolution, carrying with them the genes for specific physical structures, cognitive functions, and sensory capacities that allow them to find a mate, reproduce, and rear their young to reproductive age.

Psychosexual theory focuses on the psychological development that accompanies sexual maturation during a life time. The theory helps explain how sexual impulses and drives are experienced at the psychological level. The tension between individual survival and group survival is highlighted in this theory by constructing a model of the mind and its structures that allow some degree of impulse gratification within socially acceptable boundaries. The direction of development is predetermined and viewed as universal, from the oral-dependent status of the infant to the sexually mature, well-socialized status of the healthy adult.

Cognitive developmental theory focuses on the unfolding of cognitive capacities that accompany problem solving and adaptation to the challenges of coping with the physical and social worlds. The theory helps explain how the mind develops from the early reflexive capacities of the newborn to the abstract, hypothetical problem-solving capacities of the adult. Here, too, the direction of development is predetermined and viewed as universal, from reasoning that is based largely on direct interaction and manipulation of objects, to the capacity for mental representations of concepts, and finally the internal manipulation of variables guided by principles of logic.

The three theories are linked by their shared interest in the biological bases of behavior as a guide to development, and their focus on development from an immature to a mature state. They all suggest universal directions of development. The theories focus on different domains of development—evolutionary theory and psychosexual theory focus on cognitive and emotional capacities that accompany sexual maturation; cognitive developmental theory focuses on cognitive maturation as the primary adaptive capacity. The three theories differ in the mechanisms they suggest for change, and in the level of "conscious attention" they attribute to individuals in the process of change.

Chapter 2

Evolutionary Theory

CHAPTER OUTLINE

Historical Context

Stages of Development

Key Concepts

    Natural Selection

    Adaptation

    Evolution and the Human Species

        Humans are mammals

        Humans are primates

        Humans are a unique species

New Directions

    Ethology

    Evolutionary Psychology

A Research Example: Attachment

    Formation of Attachments with Mother, Father, and Others

    Patterns of Attachment

        The strange situation

        Four patterns of quality of attachment

    The Relevance of Attachment to Later Development

An Application: Balancing Work and Family Together

How Does Evolutionary Theory Answer the Basic Questions that a Theory of Human Development is Expected to Address?

Critique of Evolutionary Theory

    Strengths

    Weaknesses

Key Terms

Chapter 2

Evolutionary Theory

Humans are living beings, linked to all other forms of life through the process of evolution. The theory of evolution explains how diverse and increasingly more complex life forms come to exist. Evolutionary theory assumes that the natural laws that apply to plant and animal life also apply to humans. This theory is important in the study of human development because it integrates human beings into the vast array of life forms and suggests explanations for a variety of characteristics that we regard as essentially human. Evolutionary theory emphasizes the importance of biological forces in directing growth and the gradual modification of species as a result of adaptation to specific environments. The theory addresses change over many generations and thousands of years; it is not intended as a theory about how change and adaptation occur within short periods or even within one lifetime. This chapter focuses on the key concepts of evolutionary thought and their relationship to an understanding of human behavior through advances in the fields of ethology and evolutionary psychology.

HISTORICAL CONTEXT

Charles Darwin was born in Shrewsbury England in 1809. He was from an educated family with a long-standing tradition of belief in the concepts generated by the theory of evolution. Darwin's grandfather Erasmus Darwin was a pioneer in the development of evolutionary theory. His ideas about the topic were published in a book entitled *Zoonomia* in 1794–96. For example, in this book, Erasmus wrote about sexual selection: "The final cause of this contest among males seems to be that the strongest and most active animal should propagate the species which should thus become improved." However, the work was based largely upon speculation and generalizations, and Charles Darwin denied that it had any significant impact on his own thinking.

As a schoolboy, Darwin rebelled against the classical pattern of learning by rote memorization. He preferred to spend long periods of time outdoors, exploring nature and puzzling over its mysteries. Darwin recalls that as a young boy of about 8 or 9, he already had a strong interest in collecting all sorts of things, including shells, coins, and rocks, and was interested in learning the names of the plants he found in his wanderings (Barlow, 1958). As a young man, Darwin explored careers in medicine and theology, but he found those studies uninteresting. He continued to spend much of his time outdoors, exploring nature.

In 1831, an opportunity arose that allowed Darwin to indulge his passion for the outdoors in a professionally acceptable way: He became the resident naturalist on *H.M.S. Beagle*. The crew's mission was to sail to South America, surveying its coast and the islands of the Pacific, to map this region, and to document its plant and animal life. The voyage lasted from 1831 to 1836. During those years, Darwin demonstrated unbounded energy in his exploration of the natural phenomena that he encountered.

Returning to England, Darwin settled down to work on the samples he had collected and to reflect on his observations. With painstaking attention to details, over a period of 20 years he developed his theory of how species can change and evolve into new plant or animal forms. However, he postponed writing about his views while he searched for examples that would support his argument. Not until 1859, when he learned that another naturalist, Alfred Russell Wallace, was about to introduce a very similar argument, was Darwin compelled to publish *The Origin of Species*.

KEY CONCEPTS

Natural Selection

Charles Darwin has been credited with the discovery of the basic mechanism that could account for the transformation of species over long periods and in many different environments. In line with Charles Lyell's (1830/1833) idea of uniformitarianism, Darwin believed that unchanging laws of nature apply uniformly throughout time. The challenge posed by this assumption was to discover the basic mechanism that could account for species change from the beginnings of life to the present. The mechanism that Darwin (1859) discovered is natural selection.

The law of natural selection predicts that behavior is adapted to the environment in which it occurs. Natural selection operates, via an individual organism's reproductive success, from one generation to the next. Reproductive success, sometimes called fitness, varies among members of a species (Archer, 1991). Every species produces more offspring than can survive to reproduce because of limitations of the food supply and natural dangers. Darwin observed that there was quite a bit of variability among members of the same species in any given location. Some individuals were better suited than others to their immediate environment and were more likely to survive, mate, and produce offspring. These offspring were also more likely to have characteristics appropriate for that location. Over long periods of time, those members of the species that had the selective advantage would be more likely to survive and reproduce, thus passing their characteristics on to future generations. If the environment changed (in climate, for example), only certain variations of organisms would survive, and again new species would evolve. Forms of life that failed to adapt would become extinct. Thus, in the context of changing environmental conditions, the variability within a species ensures the species' continuation or its development into new forms. Darwin viewed evolutionary change as taking place slowly and incrementally as individual organisms adapt and populations with similar adaptive characteristics dominate an environment or ecological niche.

The concept of fitness has been expanded to consider the idea of inclusive fitness (Hamilton, 1964). This idea suggests that fitness is not only determined by an individual's reproductive success, but by promoting the survival and reproductive success of others who share one's genetic ancestry. In human groups, behaviors that support one's family members or that make it possible for one's kin to be more attractive in the mating process would be considered examples of inclusive fitness.

In the process of natural selection, new species may emerge, and existing species may become extinct. Extinction, just like the appearance of a new species, is a natural process. The size of the fertile, breeding population of a species becomes so small that it cannot be sustained. This may occur as the result of some catastrophe when many species that had been flourishing are destroyed in a relatively rapid climate change. Extinction can also occur when individuals in a specific species are reduced to a very small number so that inbreeding occurs and weakens the genetic strain. Genetic anomalies are transmitted more rapidly from one generation to the next, threatening survival or reproductive capacity. Changes in environmental conditions, such as disease, a rapidly growing predator, or climate, can result in extinction at the same time as it results in the formation of new species.

The law of natural selection has been referred to as the principle of *survival of the fittest*. Herbert Spencer (1864) first referred to it in this way. This phrase often calls up images of head-to-head combat between members of a species. This is not what Darwin's principle says. Darwin describes the process in the following way:

> It may metaphorically be said that natural selection is daily and hourly scrutinizing, throughout the world, the slightest variation; rejecting those that are bad, preserving and adding up all that are good; silently and insensibly working, whenever and wherever opportunity offers, at the improvement of each organic being in relation to its conditions of life. We see nothing of these slow changes in progress, until the hand of time has marked the lapse of ages, and then so imperfect is our view into long-past geological ages, that we see only that the forms of life are now different from what they formerly were. (Darwin, 1859/1979, p. 77)

In fact, it is reproductive advantage, not survival per se, that results in the continuation of certain characteristics. For example, if a characteristic resulted in a relatively early death for mothers but the survival of her offspring, that characteristic might have an adaptive advantage.

Darwin described two aspects of evolution (Mayr, 1991). One is the gradual change within a species over time from earlier to later forms. For example, even though they are the same species, modern chimpanzees alive today are not identical to the chimpanzees that lived thousands of years ago. They have had to adapt to changing environmental conditions, including alterations in food sources, landscapes, and threats. The second is the breaking away from an earlier evolutionary lineage and the establishment of a new branch in the phylogenetic tree. This is the process of speciation that contributes to biological diversity. For example, some combination of events led to the separation of the hominids from homo erectus to homo sapiens about 300,000 to 400,000 years ago.

Adaptation

Adaptation is the process that underlies evolutionary change—the process by which living things develop structures and problem-solving mechanisms that enable them to thrive in a particular environment. Adaptation is expressed in specific characteristics that are functional in the face of specific problems the organism must solve. For example, the need to distinguish edible from poisonous foods results in the adaptation of specific sensory capacities in taste, smell, and visual discrimination. The particular sensory abilities that evolve depend on the sources and variety of foods the organism encounters. Adaptation can operate at the biological level, as a change in some physical characteristic over generations. Adaptation can also operate at the behavioral level, as a change in some pattern of behavior.

Evolution and the Human Species

"If one sets January 1 as the origin of life on earth, marine vertebrates would then first appear on November 24, dinosaurs on December 16, and man at 10:15 P.M. on December 31" (Lerner & Libby, 1976). The evolution of the family of humans began only about 2 million years ago with the species homo habilis and homo erectus. Homo habilis lived between 1.9 and 1.8 million years ago, and fossil evidence of this species was found only in Africa. Homo erectus lived between 1.8 million and 300,000 years ago, with fossil remains discovered in Africa and throughout Europe and Asia. Modern humans, homo sapiens, most likely had their origins in Africa about 600,000 to 100,000 years ago. This group of advanced humans then dispersed throughout the Old World and replaced other human species. With techniques from molecular biology it is possible to trace characteristics of mitochondrial DNA that show that the modern humans found in various areas of Europe, Asia, and America are quite similar to one another, suggesting common genetic ancestry. The DNA would not be so similar if they had evolved independently from local primitive ancestors (Lewin, 1987; Tattersall, Delson, & Van Couvering, 1988).

Thus the picture that is taking shape is one of a common modern ancestor, whose offspring migrated throughout the world and dominated other human species. The question that continues to puzzle modern paleoanthropologists is how to account for the significant gap in capacity between the earlier species of humans and those of modern homo sapiens. The domination of modern humans was probably subtle, not a case of open warfare or competition. Some superiority in hunting skills, tool making, and planning could have given the modern species an evolutionary advantage by enabling them to establish dependable sources of high-quality food (Simons, 1989). This domination was comparatively rapid, fueled by enormously powerful mental evolution and the accompanying forms of cultural evolution that brought complex tool development, advanced techniques for hunting and gathering, the invention of agriculture, and the eventual growth of tribes, chiefdoms, and political states.

Wilson (1975) described the process through which humans achieved such a rapid and advanced level of functioning as the *autocatalysis model*. This term suggests that a capacity that emerged in the process of adaptation resulted in an acceleration of the change process itself.

> When the earliest hominids became bipedal as part of their terrestrial adaptation, their hands were freed, the manufacture and handling of artifacts was made easier, and intelligence grew as part of the improvement of the tool-using habit. With mental capacity and the tendency to use artifacts increasing through mutual reinforcement, the entire materials-based culture expanded. Cooperation during hunting was perfected, providing a new impetus for the evolution of intelligence, which in turn permitted still more sophistication in tool using, and so on through cycles of causation.... The autocatalysis model usually includes the proposition that the shift to big game accelerated the process of mental evolution. (pp. 567–568)

Humans are mammals.   Humans have characteristics that link them to the larger group of mammals from which they descended. Humans produce live young. The mothers feed their young on milk produced by the mammary glands. Their bodies are covered with skin, which is protected by hair.

Humans are primates.   Humans also have characteristics that link them to other primates, the class of mammals that includes humans, apes, monkeys, lemurs, and tarsiers. Primates share 10 major characteristics:

1. Progressive movement of the eyes toward the midline of the head and consequent development of stereoscopic (three-dimensional) vision.
2. Retention of 5-digit extremities and of the major bones of the arms and legs—clavicle, radius, and fibula.
3. Progressive development of the digits, particularly the thumb and big toe, which allows for increasing dexterity.
4. Development of flattened nails, instead of claws, and also of sensitive pads on the tips of the digits.
5. Progressive shortening of the snout, reduction in the size of the apparatus for smell, and consequent reduction in olfactory acuity.
6. Great increase in the size of the brain.
7. Prolongation of prenatal and postnatal development.
8. Decrease in the number of teeth and retention of a simple molar system.
9. Overall increase in body size, progressive development toward upright stature, and increased dependence on the hind limbs for locomotion.
10. Development of complex social organizations.

Humans are a unique species.   Humans also have some features which characterize human nature. All human beings, regardless of culture, share characteristics that tie them together as a species. They share a common body shape and specific organs such as eyes, nose, ears, hands and feet, which can be recognized as human despite individual differences. They can mate and produce living children who in turn are capable of reproducing. Critical among the characteristics of humans is bipedalism as a primary means of locomotion, which leaves the hands free for tool use, holding, carrying, and gesturing. The structure of human hands permits the flexible manipulation of objects as tools. Reduced reliance on smell and relatively greater reliance on vision influence the human mode of exploring the environment. Because of the prolonged period of prenatal and postnatal development characteristic of human infants, humans are highly social; they are oriented toward social stimuli and have highly developed capacities for solving social problems. Perhaps the most critical aspect of human nature is the size, structure, and complexity of the brain. As a result of this brain, humans have extensive symbolic capacities and a remarkable ability to learn. They produce spoken symbolic language. They store information and pass it on from one generation to the next. They are self-conscious; they raise questions about their origin and anticipate their death.

NEW DIRECTIONS

Ethology

Have you ever been to a park where a number of dogs are playing together? Have you noticed how they chase each other, engage in a form of rough and tumble play, and bite at each other's legs and neck without actually harming each other. Playfulness is an example of a topic that is of interest to ethologists. What is the adaptive value of playfulness? Why do animals play? Ethology is the study of the functional significance of expressive behavior in its social context from an evolutionary perspective (LaFreniere, 2000). Its roots lie in Darwin's ideas about behavioral adaptation. In addition to the evolution of physical organs and body structures, adaptation has produced patterns of motor activity, facial expressions, and emotional reactions. Darwin himself was very interested in the adaptive nature of emotions and wrote extensively about it in *The Expression of the Emotions in Man and Animals* (1872/1965).

Evolutionary theory focuses attention on those capacities and behavior patterns that contribute to the reproductive success and continued adaptation of the species. From this perspective, the study of individual behavior and development focuses on how a particular behavior contributes not just to the future growth and development of the individual but to the adaptation and continuation of the species.

The future of a species depends on the capacity of its individual members to survive, mate, reproduce, and rear their young. Some of the factors that contribute to the vigor and continuity of a species are the health of the individuals when they attain reproductive capacity, the characteristics of the environment that promote or inhibit procreation, and the capacity of sexually mature partners to rear their offspring.

From Darwin's interest in the evolution of species grew the ethologists' interest in those behaviors that are central to the species' survival, including feeding efficiency, competition among males for breeding females, and cooperation among males in warding off predators and competing primates. The field of ethology has emerged as the study of evolutionarily significant behaviors that appear to be innate and specific to a particular species. These behaviors are commonly associated with eating, mating, and protecting a species from harm.

Behaviors that are successful in coping with specific environmental conditions are supported by an integration of brain structures, physiological responses, and motivational underpinnings. Ultimately, those behaviors appear as spontaneous, unlearned actions that provide some type of adaptive advantage. An example is the infant's smile. Smiles occur early in the postnatal period. They function as a powerful signal that evokes a caregiving response. Over time, the infant's smile takes on more complex meanings within a social context. Yet, it begins as an unlearned behavior that has important adaptive value.

Ethology uses observation, experimentation, and the comparative method to investigate the proximal causes of behavioral acts, the relative contribution of inheritance and learning to these acts, and the adaptive significance and evolutionary history of various patterns of behavior within and across species. Ethologists emphasize the importance of studying behavior in natural settings (Blurton-Jones, 1972; Eibl-Eibesfeldt, 1975). Laboratory experiments may be used to discover answers to questions derived from these observations.

Two early contributors to the field of ethology, Konrad Lorenz (1935/1981) and Niko Tinbergen (1951), focused on *innate behaviors* and how they are expressed under natural conditions. Innate behaviors are present in some standard or shared form in all members of a species. They are expressed without previous learning and remain relatively unchanged by experience. Innate behaviors include *reflexes*, which are simple responses to simple stimuli. A baby's grasp of a finger or other object that is placed in its palm is a reflex. Many infant reflexes disappear by the end of the 1st year. However, some reflexes including sucking, creeping, stepping, and grasping are replaced by very similar behaviors that come under voluntary control.

Some innate behaviors, called *fixed* or *model action patterns*, are more complex than reflexes. Birds build nests, squirrels bury nuts, and goslings follow their mothers. These behaviors are genetically guided sequences that are prompted by a particular stimulus pattern that releases or signals the behavior. The *releasing stimulus* may be a certain odor, color, movement, sound, or shape. It may require a special relation between stimuli. For example, Lorenz (1943) first hypothesized that certain aspects of an infant's appearance stimulate positive emotional responses in adult caregivers. The quality of "cuteness" or "babyness" that Lorenz identified includes a head that is large in proportion to the body, large eyes, and round, pudgy cheeks.

John Bowlby (1958, 1988) was influential in bringing the ethological perspective to the study of child development through his observations of infant–caregiver attachment. Bowlby described the *attachment behavioral system* as a complex set of reflexes and signaling behaviors that bring about caregiving responses from adults. These responses in turn shape an infant's expectations and help to create an inner representation of the parent as a caring, comforting person.

The infant's innate capacities for smiling, cooing, grasping, and crying draw the adult's attention and provoke a sympathetic response. The adult's gentle cuddling, soothing, and smiling establish a sense of security in the child. Attachment, viewed in this light, is an innate behavior system that promotes the safety of offspring in infancy and provides the basis for the trusting social relationships that are necessary for mating and parenting in adulthood.

Bowlby argued that attachment behavior serves a basic survival function: protection.

> Whilst attachment behaviour is at its most obvious in early childhood, it can be observed throughout the life cycle, especially in emergencies. Since it is seen in virtually all human beings (though in varying patterns), it is regarded as an integral part of human nature and one we share (to a varying extent) with members of other species. The biological function attributed to it is that of protection. To remain within easy access of a familiar individual known to be ready and willing to come to our aid in an emergency is clearly a good insurance policy—whatever our age. (Bowlby, 1988, p. 27)

Subsequent research has demonstrated the importance of patterns of attachment in influencing adolescent and adult behaviors.

Focusing on a different behavioral system, William Charlesworth (1988) studied the importance of social interaction as a mechanism that allows humans to *obtain resources from the environment* at any point in the life span. He suggested that the resources required to resolve the crises of the psychosocial stages vary with the stage. The infant may require protection, food, or attention; the toddler may require a toy or someone to talk to; the child of middle school age may need tools and materials for work; and the early adult may need a mate. Strategies for obtaining resources change with development. Infants learn to signal their needs by crying or fussing. As they get older, children acquire an increasingly diverse set of strategies to use in their efforts to get the resources they need. Both aggressive and help-giving behaviors are strategies designed to elicit needed resources. Language strategies help people acquire needed resources of many kinds.

Many general areas of human behavior are functionally relevant to the fitness of individuals and groups (Charlesworth, 1992). They include:

Reproductive strategies, such as having few or many sex partners
Infant immaturity requiring prolonged care
Infant–caregiver attachment
Parent–child conflicts
Sibling rivalry
Peer group formation and functions, especially cooperation, competition
dominance, and submission
Pair-bonding and mate selection
Helping behavior and altruism
Learning as adaptive behavior
Individual creation and modification of the environment
Social evolution and the elaboration of rites, rituals, and religions

Evolutionary Psychology

Whereas ethology focuses on analyzing adaptive behavior patterns across species, the goal of evolutionary psychology is to draw upon principles of evolution to understand the human mind. "The mind is a set of information-processing machines that were designed by natural selection to solve adaptive problems faced by our hunter–gatherer ancestors" (Cosmides & Tooby, 1997). This focus takes us to a time when humans lived in small, nomadic groups traveling from place to place to find sources of food and trying to protect themselves from the dangers of predatory animals, weather, illness, and other humans. This way of life existed for over 2 million years, during which various human species (along with their human minds) emerged. From this perspective, the human mind is highly adapted to solve problems faced by these human ancestors, but it may not be well adapted to solve the new problems that have emerged in our recent industrial/post industrial way of life.

According to evolutionary psychologists, the human brain is a physical system that is designed to generate responses that are effective in dealing with the information being received from specific environmental situations. It is comprised of a large number of complex mini-machines or subsystems that have evolved in response to the specific problems that humans faced in the thousands of years during which modern humans emerged from their hominid ancestors (Buss, 1995). Evolutionary psychologists view adaptation as resulting in the formation of functionally specific capacities as well as structures that can integrate information from a variety of sources. You might think of each structure as a tool designed to perform a specific task. The brain has an optic nerve that coordinates visual information; an olfactory center that receives and interprets smells; and an auditory system that receives, integrates, and interprets sound waves. The optic nerve is not designed to receive sound waves, and the auditory system is not sensitive to light. In this same sense, evolutionary psychologists seek to discover mental structures that contribute to performing other information-processing tasks such as recognizing faces, detecting threats, or recognizing and producing spoken language.

According to evolutionary psychologists, through the process of natural selection, certain mechanisms developed that are sensitive to specific environmental conditions and, when activated by those conditions, these mechanisms function to produce an adaptive response or set of responses. The question of interest is "What are the psychological mechanisms that have emerged in this way?" In general, mechanisms of interest are linked to important adaptive functions (Buss, 1995).

Evolutionary psychology focuses on how the mind may have become structured to resolve adaptive problems. Adaptive problems have two essential qualities: (a) they are likely to have occurred repeatedly in human evolutionary history; and (b) the solutions to these problems influenced reproductive success (Cosmides & Tooby, 1997). Adaptive problems include: How to tell if someone is a friend or a threat, how to select a mate, how to select a good dwelling, or how to collaborate in order to hunt large game.

Buss (1995) provided a concrete example of how evolutionary psychology might lead to the formulation of logically deduced hypotheses and testable predictions. He begins with Triver's (1972) theory of parental investment and sexual selection. According to Triver's theory, which is derived from Darwin's theory of sexual selection, the sex that has the greater investment in the offspring will be more selective in choosing a mate; the sex that has less investment will be more competitive with others of the same sex for sexual access. Beginning with this midlevel theory, the following hypothesis emerges: Where males do contribute resources to the offspring, females select mates, in part, on the ability and willingness of males to contribute resources.

From this hypothesis, three specific predictions that can be tested emerge:

1. Women have evolved preferences for men who are high in status.
2. Women have evolved preferences for men who show cues indicating a willingness to invest in them and their offspring.
3. Women will divorce men who fail to contribute expected resources, or who divert their resources to other women and their children.

These three predictions can all be evaluated through traditional social science methods. If they prove correct, the theoretical hypothesis from which they were derived is supported; if the evidence does not support these predictions, the underlying theoretical assumption is likely to be rejected. Thus, even though evolutionary psychologists seek explanations for the origins of mental mechanisms in the long-distant past, they can use evidence from contemporary behavior to assess whether their explanations have merit.

From an evolutionary perspective, any behavior can be assessed by asking a few basic questions: What behavior is necessary to achieve a goal, how much energy is needed to achieve the goal, when should the organism stop the activity, and what should the organism do next (Neese, 2001). These questions suggest that the organism has to recognize the nature of a problem and bring to bear the best "tool" needed to solve the problem. There are start up costs to beginning any new behavior, so the most adaptive responses will contribute to long-term fitness. Once a behavior has been started, the organism has to assess how hard and long to persist at the task. There is risk in putting too much energy into one problem and ignoring other important tasks. There is also risk in giving up too soon before an important goal has been reached. Since environmental conditions fluctuate, the ability to make this assessment has to be flexible. Finally, once a goal has been achieved, the organism has to redirect energy to a new task. This suggests that the organism has a set of goals and has to direct energy to one or more of them in some priority. Fitness is enhanced when the organism is able to meet goals for health and safety, reproductive success, social allegiances, and care and nurture of the offspring as conditions require. Thus, while respecting the complexity of the human mind, evolutionary theory offers a context for focusing on a select group of problems and their adaptive solutions.

A RESEARCH EXAMPLE

With a focus on reproductive success, evolutionary theory highlights three phases of the life history: healthy growth and development leading up to the reproductive period, success in mating and the conception of offspring, and the ability to parent offspring so they can reach reproductive age and bear offspring of their own (Charlesworth, 1992). Primates, including humans, are most vulnerable during infancy and childhood; children require continuous care and protection if they are to survive to reproductive age.

John Bowlby's theory proposed the concept of an attachment behavior system as an organized pattern of infant signals and adult responses that form the basis of a relationship during the very earliest stage of development and a corresponding behavioral system referred to as the parenting or caregiving system that is made up of the responses of the caregiver to the infant's signals (Bowlby, 1988; Ainsworth, 1985). These theoretical concepts have stimulated an enormous body of research that addresses the dynamics of how infants survive in the early years of life and how those experiences are internalized to shape their expectations for subsequent intimate relationships.

Certain patterns of caregiver–infant interaction in the 1st months of life contribute to the formation of attachment. One of the most significant of these is synchrony of interaction (Isabella & Belsky, 1991). Parent–infant pairs that show positive attachment relations at 1 year have been observed to demonstrate interactions that are rhythmic, well timed, and mutually rewarding. When the caregiver is unresponsive to the infant's signals of distress, overly intrusive when the infant is calm, or underinvolved, a less positive attachment is formed. In addition to the quality of interactions, the quantity of interaction also plays a key role in establishing the infant's confidence about the caregiver's capacity to protect and comfort (Cox, Owen, Henderson, & Margand, 1992).

Evidence that an attachment has been formed has been demonstrated by the presence of at least three behaviors. First, infants try to maintain contact with the object of attachment (Ainsworth, 1973). Second, infants show distress when the object of attachment is absent (Schaffer & Emerson, 1964). Third, infants are more relaxed and comfortable with the object of attachment and more fretful with others (Bronson, 1973).

Formation of Attachments With Mother, Father, and Others

Most infants have more than one caring person with whom they form an attachment. Most commonly, the first object of attachment is the mother, but fathers, siblings, grandparents, and childcare professionals may also become objects of attachment. Several factors have been identified as important for predicting which people will form the infant's hierarchy or radius of significant attachment figures (Colin, 1996; Cassidy, 1999):

1. The amount of time the infant spends in the care of the person.
2. The quality and responsiveness of the care provided by the person.
3. The person's emotional investment in the infant.
4. The presence of the person in the infant's life across time.

Patterns of Attachment

Consistent with an evolutionary perspective, the fact that the capacity to form an attachment is part of human nature does not mean that the expression of the attachment response will be the same in all humans. According to attachment theory, if an adult is present to interact with the infant, an attachment will be formed. However, research has discovered that individual differences emerge in the quality of attachment, depending on the accumulation of information the infant gathers over many instances when the infant is seeking reassurance, comfort, or protection from threat (Weinfield, Sroufe, Egeland, & Carlson, 1999). The adults' acceptance of the infants and their ability to respond to the infants' varying communications contribute to the formation of a secure attachment. The caregivers' patterns of expressing affection and rejection influence how well babies can meet their needs for reassurance and comfort.

The Strange Situation. Differences in the quality of attachment have been highlighted by observations of babies and their caregivers in a standard laboratory procedure called the *strange situation* (Ainsworth, Blehar, Waters, & Wall, 1978; Bretherton, 1990). During an approximately 20-minute period, the child is exposed to a sequence of events that are likely to stimulate the attachment system. The situation introduces several potentially threatening situations including the presence of a stranger, the departure of the mother, being left alone with a stranger, and being left completely alone, all in the context of an unfamiliar laboratory setting. During this situation, researchers have the opportunity to make systematic observations of the child's behaviors, the caregiver's behaviors, and characteristics of their interactions, as well as to compare these behaviors across varying segments of the situation.

Four Patterns of Quality of Attachment. Four patterns of attachment behavior have been distinguished using the strange situation methodology: (a) secure attachment, (b) anxious-avoidant, (c) anxious-resistant, and (d) disorganized attachment.

Infants who have a secure attachment actively explore their environment and interact with strangers while their mothers are present. After separation, the babies actively greet their mothers or seek interaction. If the babies were distressed during separation, the mothers' return reduces their distress and the babies return to exploration of the environment. Infants who show an anxious-avoidant attachment avoid contact with their mothers after separation or ignore their efforts to interact. They show less distress at being alone than other babies. Infants who show an anxious-resistant attachment are very cautious in the presence of the stranger. Their exploratory behavior is noticeably disrupted by the caregivers' departure. When the caregiver returns, the infants appear to want to be close to the caregiver, but they are also angry, so they are very hard to soothe or comfort. In the disorganized attachment, babies' responses are particularly notable in the reunion sequence. In the other three attachment patterns, infants appear to use a coherent strategy for managing the stress of the situation. The disorganized babies have no consistent strategy. They behave in contradictory, unpredictable ways that seem to convey feelings of extreme fear or utter confusion (Belsky, Campbell, Cohn, & Moore, 1996).

The attachment behavioral system and the caregiving system have also been studied in the home environment. When observed at home, babies who have a secure attachment are observed to cry less than other babies (Tracy & Ainsworth, 1981; Ainsworth, 1985). They greet their mothers more positively upon reunion after everyday separations, and appear to respond more cooperatively to their mothers' requests. Attachment theorists hypothesize that securely attached babies have a working model of attachment in which they expect their caregiver to be accessible and responsive.

Mothers of babies who were characterized as anxious-avoidant seem to reject their babies. It is almost as if they were angry at their babies. They spend less time holding and cuddling their babies than other mothers, and more of their interactions appear to be unpleasant or even hurtful. At home these babies cry a lot, they are not readily soothed by contact with the caregiver, and yet they appear to be quite distressed by separations.

Infants who are characterized as anxious-resistant have mothers who are inconsistent in their responsiveness. Sometimes these mothers ignore clear signals of distress. At other times they interfere with their infants in order to make contact. Although these mothers appear to be able to enjoy close physical contact with their babies, they do not necessarily do so in ways appropriate to the baby's needs. The result appears to be the formation of an internal representation of attachment that is highly unpredictable. These babies try to maintain proximity and to avoid unfamiliar situations that increase uncertainty about accessibility to their caregivers.

Research suggests links between the disorganized attachment and serious mental health problems among mothers, including abusive tendencies, depression, and other mental illnesses. These mothers are likely to be psychologically unavailable and unpredictable (van Ijzendoorn, Goldberg, Kroonenberg, & Frenkel, 1992). Observations of mothers and infants who are described as having a disorganized attachment highlight two different patterns. Some mothers are negative, intrusive, and frighten their babies in bursts of intense hostility. Other mothers are passive, helpless, and rarely show positive or comforting behaviors. These mothers appear to be afraid of their babies, perhaps not trusting their own impulses to respond appropriately (Lyons-Ruth, Lyubchik, Wolfe, & Bronfman, 2002).

In U. S. samples, about two-thirds of the children tested have been characterized as securely attached. Of the remainder, more children fall into the anxious-avoidant category than into the anxious-resistant category (Ainsworth et al., 1978). Only a small percentage of infants show the disorganized pattern (van Ijzendoorn et al., 1992; Carlson, Cicchetti, Barnett, & Braunwold, 1989; Radke-Yarrow, Cummings, Kuczynski, & Chipman, 1985). This highly disorganized attachment is associated with very serious mental health problems in later childhood and beyond (Fonagy, 2003).

The Relevance of Attachment to Later Development

The nature of one's attachment pattern has been found to influence expectations about the self, others, and the nature of relationships. The formation of a secure attachment relationship is expected to influence the child's ability to explore and engage the environment with confidence, knowing that the protective "other" is near at hand. Children who experience a secure attachment are less likely to be exposed to uncontrollable stress. They experience rhythmic, meaningful, and predictable interactions that contribute to their social competences. As a result, they are hopeful about their ability to form positive relationships with others (Weinfeld et al., 1999).

Long-term benefits of a secure attachment have been documented. Secure attachments in infancy have been associated with positive adaptive capacities when the child is 3 to 5 years old. Securely attached infants become preschoolers who show greater resilience, self-control, and curiosity (Schneider, Atkinson, & Tardif, 2001). In contrast, infants who have a disorganized attachment are very hostile, aggressive preschoolers. A new clinical diagnosis, *reactive attachment disorder,* has been linked to serious disturbances in infant attachment. Two expressions of this disorder have been described: inhibited type, in which the person is very withdrawn, hypervigilant in social contacts, and resistant to comfort; and uninhibited type, in which the person shows a lack of discrimination, being overly friendly and attaching to any new person (DeAngelis, 1997).

From a life-span perspective, the quality of the attachment formed in infancy influences the formation of later relationships (Ainsworth, 1989). Children who have formed secure attachments are likely to find more enjoyment in close peer friendships during their preschool years. In an analysis of the results of over 60 studies of the relationship of parent–child attachment and peer relations, the quality of attachment with mother was consistently predictive of the quality of close peer friendships, well into middle school and early adolescence (Schneider et al., 2001). Children who have secure attachments are more likely to attribute positive intentions to peers, whereas children with anxious attachments are more likely to view peers with wariness.

The attachment construct has been useful in helping to explain the nature of adult love relationships. Romantic relationships can be characterized along many of the same dimensions as infant attachments, including the desire to maintain physical contact with the loved one, increased disclosure and responsiveness to the loved one, the effectiveness of the loved one in providing comfort and reassurance that reduce distress, and an element of exclusiveness or preferential response to the loved one (Hazan & Shaver, 1987). Fears about loss and abandonment, born from anxious-avoidant attachments, are likely to result in anxiety about one's contemporary relationships. People who are consistently anxious about their relationships tend to be more coercive and mistrustful, thus pushing their partners away (Feeney, 1999; Tracy, Shaver, Albino, & Cooper, 2003).

> I had a real problem trusting anyone at the start of any relationship. A couple of things happened to me when I was young, which I had some emotional difficulties getting over. At the start of our relationship, if P. had been separated from me, I would have been constantly thinking: 'What was he doing?'; 'Was he with another girl?'; 'Was he cheating on me?'; all that would have been running through my head. (Feeney, 1999, p. 365)

The parenting relationship can also be understood as an elaboration of one's childhood attachment. Adults who have experienced a secure attachment in their own infancy have been found to be more likely to be able to comfort and respond to their children. Adults whose childhood attachments were unpredictable or even hostile are more likely to have difficulty coping successfully with young infants' needs (Ricks, 1985; George & Solomon, 1999). For example, in one study, parents were observed while their infants were having inoculations. Those parents who had an avoidant attachment style were less responsive to their infants' distress in this context (Edelstein et al., 2004).

It would be a mistake to assume that the quality of adult love relationships or parental behavior is determined solely by the quality of childhood attachments. Many experiences intervene to modify the attachment representation and to expand one's capacity to love another person after infancy. However, a growing body of research links the quality of early attachments with a person's orientation to and capacity for social relationships within the context of friendships, intimate relationships, and parent–child relations.

AN APPLICATION: BALANCING WORK AND FAMILY LIFE

Evolutionary psychology leads us to consider the brain/mind as a highly adapted organ that has evolved over thousands of years as a result of being faced with a repeated set of problems to solve. One of those repeated problems is the protection and care of infants and young children. An application of this theoretical perspective allows us to understand some of the stressors that face contemporary families as they struggle to balance work and family life.

Thinking back to our hunting and gathering ancestors, human females invested more time and energy in their offspring than human males due to the long gestational period, the period of lactation, and the relative vulnerability of human infants in the first years of life. As a result, parental salience, including both worries and joys associated with parenthood, is likely to be greater for women than for men. This has been found to be the case across societies. In general, the parental role is more central to the identity of women than men, and, as a result, parenting is a greater source of role strain for mothers than fathers. Even though the dual-earner lifestyle is normative for contemporary families in the United States, including families with infants and young children, women and men continue to experience conflict in trying to balance work and family life. Women with young children who are in the labor market continue to experience guilt about not spending enough time with their children. Even when both parents are equally involved in the labor market, men and women tend to agree that child care and certain household maintenance tasks are primarily the wife's domain. What is more, some studies find that many couples still endorse the view that, all else being equal, they would prefer the husband to be in the labor force and the wife to be at home, caring for the children and maintaining the household.

From the perspective of evolutionary psychology, this struggle can be explained in the following way: Men and women have evolved to conceptualize their parental roles as reflected in an early hunting and gathering society where men were hunters and women were gatherers. Men left the family for long periods of time while women stayed near the cave or hut, protected and nurtured their family, and provided food stuffs from nearby plants.

The family was the primary group, extending into the clan and tribe. There were no other institutions such as schools, corporations, churches, or governments to place competing role demands on men or women. As a result, all the problem solving efforts were directed to the basic survival challenges for one's self, one's family, and one's clan.

Many of the adaptive problems that humans had to face were social: attracting a mate, forming an enduring bond between mates, identifying which people had important resources and building and preserving alliances and coalitions with those who had resources, protecting and caring for one's children, and encouraging others to care about and protect one's offspring. The extreme social nature of humans has led to a strong preference for people who are kind, cooperative, and trustworthy (Buss, 1995). At the same time, for women, a strong preference has been established for long-term sexual alliances with men who have status and control of resources. For men, a strong preference has been established for long-term sexual alliances with women who are sexually faithful. The threat of women's infidelity is especially troublesome for men since men have more uncertainty than women in confirming their parenthood.

Consider the implication of these adaptive mechanisms as they are carried out in contemporary society. The majority of married couples with young children are dual earner couples. The intense involvement of both partners in an institution other than home, family, and immediate community is a very recent demand for which neither men nor women are well adapted. Both partners seek kind, cooperative, collaborative qualities in each other and try to work out a satisfactory balance in caring for their children and meeting their needs for intimacy.

However, embedded in this desire for collaboration is a potential conflict. For a woman, the adaptive mental mechanisms that are likely to be called into play in this situation are thought systems that allow her to protect and safeguard her children, assessment abilities to be sure that her husband is able to have the resources necessary to provide for the safety and well-being of her family, and testing devices so that she can determine whether or not he is directing those resources to her and her children, not to others. For a man, the adaptive mental mechanisms that are likely called into play are techniques to restrict his partner's availability to other potential partners in order to prevent sexual infidelity. Thus, even though the partners may agree that they will both be in the labor force away from home, the arrangement is stressful for both partners and a continuous source of tension. From the perspective of evolutionary psychology, the dual earner family arrangement in which both partners are away from home for long periods each day is at odds with adaptive mechanisms that have been developed over thousands of generations of evolutionary history because they contributed to reproductive success.

HOW DOES EVOLUTIONARY THEORY ANSWER THE BASIC QUESTIONS THAT A THEORY OF HUMAN DEVELOPMENT IS EXPECTED TO ADDRESS?

What is the direction of change over the life span? How well does the theory account for patterns of change and continuity?   The direction of development from infancy through adulthood is guided by genetic information that has evolved over thousands of years. Humans share a common direction of biological development including the maturation of the nervous system, motor capacities, and the reproductive system. Infants are born with certain instincts or reflexes that can be considered a product of natural selection. Over the course of infancy and childhood, these reflexes either drop away or come under voluntary control. The critical points in the life span include survival of infancy and childhood to achieve reproductive age, finding a mate, reproducing, and rearing one's young to their reproductive age.

The process of natural selection focuses on species change over long periods of time. Change occurs as a gradual process of adaptation to changing environmental conditions over generations. Adaptation is a process by which living things develop structures and problem-solving mechanisms that enable them to thrive in a specific environment.

What are the mechanisms that account for growth? What are some testable hypotheses or predictions that emerge from this analysis?   The human genome includes a plan for the nature and direction of growth. This genetic plan is a product of thousands of years of evolution that links human beings to other mammals, especially the primates. The human genome, according to the theory of evolution, is a product of the mechanism of natural selection. The human beings that exist today, including their mind/brain, have evolved over time in the face of a repeated set of problems to solve. Testable hypotheses that emerge from this theory suggest that the human mind will approach specific adaptive problems with an eye toward how the solution contributes to their reproductive success. As an example, evolutionary psychology suggests that men and women have different reproductive goals. As a result, their preferences for mate selection will differ in order to support their reproductive goals.

How relevant are early experiences for later development? What evidence does the theory offer to support its view?   The concept of fitness includes the importance of the ability to survive the vulnerable period of infancy and childhood in order to reach reproductive age. For humans, the social and cognitive capacities that are established early in life have implications for subsequent ability to find a mate and rear one's children to reproductive age. The importance of the human brain for problem solving points to the significance of early childhood experiences, especially health, social interactions, and cognitive stimulation for later survival and reproductive success. The theory has led to the investigation of attachment as a primary behavioral system through which parents and children establish a close emotional bond. An enormous body of research evidence points to the contribution of the quality of attachment for later adaptive success.

How do the physical, cognitive, emotional, and social functions interact? How well does the theory explain these interactions?   Evolutionary theory focuses on behavioral systems that are central to species survival. These behaviors are often associated with obtaining resources, recognizing threat and defending one's self or one's family from threat, finding a mate, and rearing the young. These are all complex behavioral systems that involve physical, cognitive, emotional, and social functions. In Darwin's work on the expression of emotions, for example, he argued that emotions play a survival role by linking the recognition of a potential threat to preparation for action. Emotions also play a social role. They convey one's internal state to others through nonverbal communication including facial expressions and body posture.

How do the environmental and social contexts affect individual development? What aspects of the environment does the theory suggest are especially important in shaping the direction of development?   The basic mechanism of evolutionary change is natural selection, which predicts that behavior is adapted to the environment in which it occurs. Over long periods of time, those members of a species that have a selective advantage in a particular environment are more likely to survive, mate, and produce offspring. The field of ethology is focused on the study of the functional significance of behaviors that appear to be innate and specific to a particular species which are expressed under particular environmental conditions. Both reflexes and fixed action patterns require certain environmental cues in order to be expressed. At the level of the individual, survival continues to reflect the ability to resolve adaptive problems, including: recognition of threat, the ability to acquire needed resources, the ability to find a suitable dwelling, the ability to collaborate in order to protect one's territory, or the ability to attract a mate. Solutions to these adaptive problems depend on the specific resources and demands of the specific environment in which one lives.

According to the theory, what factors place individuals at risk at specific periods of the life span?   Evolutionary theory is quite specific about the importance of critical issues that threaten survival across the life span. Over the life span, fitness is enhanced when the person is able to meet goals for health and safety, reproductive success, social allegiances, and the care and nurture of his or her offspring. In infancy, protection from harm is especially important, thus generating the extensive focus on attachment and the complementary parenting behavioral system. At each stage of the life span, social interaction is required to obtain the necessary resources from the environment. Factors that interfere with the achievement of social competence, including physical characteristics that might lead to social rejection, parental abuse or neglect, dominance by others, or social alienation, are all relevant risk factors. Evolutionary psychology focuses on the ability of the human mind to solve adaptive problems. Factors that interfere with the person's adaptive problem solving capacity, including genetic anomalies, malnutrition, or lack of social or cognitive stimulation, could all place individuals at risk for survival.

CRITIQUE OF EVOLUTIONARY THEORY

From an evolutionary point of view, the future of a species depends on the capacity of its individual members to survive during infancy and childhood, mate, reproduce, and rear their young to reproductive age. The factors that contribute to the vigor and continuity of a species are the health of individual members when they attain reproductive capacity, an environment that is conducive to the formation of sexually mature dyads, and the capacity of sexually mature partners to rear their offspring. Among humans, the attachment-parenting systems are essential for an infant's survival and subsequent capacity to form enduring social bonds. During adolescence, when sexual activity emerges and attitudes about marriage and parenting are being formulated, the quality of life for young people of every cultural group is critical to the future of human beings. During adulthood, the ability to attract a mate, be fertile, and protect and nurture one's offspring are the signposts of fitness.

Strengths

The evolutionary perspective draws attention to the interconnection between an individual's life history and the long-range history of the species. Principles of natural selection operate slowly over generations. However the reproductive success of individuals over the course of their own life span will determine whether their genetic material continues to be represented in the larger population. The application of evolutionary theory to human motivation, mental processes, and behavior integrates information and observations from many fields, including developmental biology, paleontology (including paleobiology and paleozoology), paleoanthropology, population genetics, social psychology, developmental psychology, and cognitive psychology.

Evolutionary theory and its extensions into ethology and evolutionary psychology have stimulated investigation of the universal nature of human thought and behavior as well as the adaptive nature of individual differences. Beginning with the assumption that contemporary human beings share a common human ancestry, the theory inspires the investigation of a wide variety of topics including shared cognitive problem solving strategies, social competences, motives for mate selection and fidelity, reproductive strategies, and the role of emotions in guiding behavior to name a few. The theory has become a fertile heuristic in focusing inquiry on how humans assess critical features of their human social environment and how they make use of that information to guide action.

Evolutionary theory offers explanations for widely shared human behaviors, such as the tendency of men to show more evidence of intrasexual competition than women, or the tendency of parents to prefer a norm of equal distribution of resources across their offspring while children tend to compete with one another for resources. Evolutionary psychologists and ethologists do not assume that concerns about fitness are conscious. However, they do assume that motivation toward fitness ultimately shapes behavior in systematic directions as a result of a conscious assessment of one's situation. Thus, the theory helps to explain why behaviors that may appear to be risky, dangerous, or self-destructive may be preferred under conditions of low resources or low status if those behaviors offer some opportunity for increasing one's reproductive opportunities or the reproductive opportunities of one's offspring (Daly & Wilson, 2001).

The evolutionary perspective also draws attention to the importance of variability for a species to survive. Individual differences contribute to the vigor of a species. Human beings are genetically designed to permit wide variations in size, body shape, coloration, strength, talent, intelligence, and personality. This variability contributes to our capacity to adapt successfully to a wide variety of environmental conditions, thereby protecting the species as a whole from extinction.

Weaknesses

Evolutionary theory assumes that the human species that exists today is a product of the process of natural selection that took place over millions of years. Without denying the truth of that assumption, one is still left to puzzle about the adaptive requirements of life in that long-ago time. Evolutionary psychology suggests that mental mechanisms exist today because they solved problems our ancestors faced in the past. In identifying evolutionary hypotheses to explain contemporary behaviors, such as mate selection, risk taking, jealousy, cooperative behavior, or cheating, evolutionary psychologists consider a likely human and environmental landscape that faced ancestors in a hunter-gatherer society. The reconstruction of the nature of that society rests on evidence from paleontology and paleoanthropology. There are no written records of the conditions of life over the millions of years through which homo habilus, homo erectus, and homo sapiens evolved. Thus, the conceptualization of the specific conditions often referred to as the environmental stimuli to which the human mind had to adapt are the result of speculations drawn from fossil remains, the presence of tools and artifacts in the region where fossil skeletal remains were found, and the reconstruction of the landscape, climate, and plant and animal life likely to have lived at the same time. Assumptions about the kinds of problems men and women had to solve are based on an unverifiable construction of prehistoric life.

Evolutionary theory views the human mind as comprised of a large number of small specialized mechanisms. These mechanisms are primed to recognize a particular type of input, evaluating it for the relevant information, and passing it on or integrating it with other information to produce actions. Most of this takes place outside of conscious awareness and yet is essential for adaptive functioning. This view of the mind, coupled with the assumption about adaptation to an ancient past, fails to incorporate the flexibility and adaptive capacity of human cognition. The modern human brain has evolved with remarkable capacities for symbolic representation, including language, symbolic drawing, and symbolic play, extensive capacities to learn through imitation, guided instruction, trial and error, and repetition, and capacities for abstract thinking, including analysis and synthesis. As a result, we are a product of what Julian Huxley (1941) referred to as psychosocial evolution as well as natural selection. According to Huxley, the adaptive mechanisms that humans bring to bear in coping with modern day life are a result of information that is passed down across recent generations from parents, teachers, books, religious leaders, lawmakers, and philosophers, as well as the mental mechanisms that may have been inherited through natural selection. Adaptative responses can include "unconscious" orientations as well as conscious rules and insights about the current situation. The brain is not limited in its problem solving only to those mechanisms that may have been shaped by an ancient social and environmental landscape. It is also informed by information that is passed down from one generation to the next.

Evolutionary theory is primarily explanatory, not predictive. As Darwin noted in the quotation earlier in the chapter, the process of evolution is on-going. Although viewed as a process that takes place gradually over thousands of years, evolution can be altered by the emergence of mutations that are particularly suited to improve reproductive success in a specific environment, by some drastic environmental conditions that eliminate some variability from the gene pool, or by a prolonged physical separation of species (Gould, 2002). In modern times, the reproductive success of individuals can be altered through access to certain birthing practices, alternative reproductive technologies, genetic engineering, and genocide. The theory does not predict the direction of human evolution. Given the increasing capacity of humans to alter both the genome and the environment, one might ask whether the process of natural selection continues to be as relevant to the human species as it was in the distant past.

The focus of evolutionary psychology is on analyzing mental mechanisms that are primed to respond to specific cues or input. According to this theory, humans are not consciously striving for fitness or reproductive success. Their behavior is not guided by a general goal of wanting to ensure the continuation of their genetic material in future generations. Rather, their behavior is analyzed in terms of the natural or preadapted response of a mental mechanism to a specific cue: for example, the smell of meat stimulates salivation; the site of a beautiful face stimulates a positive attraction; the detection of cheating stimulates wariness. The environmental cues are proximal (immediate to the point of response), but the origins of the responses are distal (based on adaptive processes established in the ancient past).

One might say that evolutionary theory focuses on all that is important. As a species, we are here as a result of evolution. The kind of humans we are, our structures, our functions, our brains, are all a product of evolution. Yet, evolutionary theory focuses on a limited range of human behavior. The theory is an effort to explain how contemporary behavior is linked to adaptive processes that contributed to fitness. As discussed above, adaptive problems are those that our ancestors had to face over and over again. The solutions influenced the individual's reproductive success. According to this definition, not all human behavior falls into the classification of an adaptive problem. This is not a theory that will necessarily help explain the development of creative responses to novel situations; the emergence of higher-order abstract reasoning and its application in science, philosophy, and the humanities; personal development in later adulthood and very old age; the pursuit of long-term goals; the clarification of values; the desire to achieve new levels of intimacy in an ongoing relationship; or the desire to attain high levels of emotional balance or spiritual insight. This is not a theory to help us understand why some people are more adept in problem solving or social relations than others, or why some children have a more outgoing, sociable personality while others are more withdrawn and introspective. Finally, this is not a theory that can guide intervention about how to promote positive adaptation under various conditions. Guidance for how to help an aggressive child gain new levels of self-control, how to support a high school student who is experiencing social rejection, or how to counsel a college student who is confused about the choice of a major are not likely to be found within the realm of this theory.

KEY TERMS

natural selection

fitness

inclusive fitness

adaptation

extinction

ethology

innate behaviors

evolutionary psychology

adaptive problems

attachment behavior system

Chapter 3

Psychosexual Theory

CHAPTER OUTLINE

Historical Context

Key Concepts

   All Behavior Is Motivated

   Domains of Consciousness

   Three Structures of Personality

      Id

      Ego

      Superego

   Stages of Development

   Defense Mechanisms

   Identification and Transference

New Directions

   Ego Psychology

   Object Relations Theory

A Research Example: The Rediscovery of the Unconscious

   Perceptual Defense

   Selective Attention

   Neurological Damage

   Unconscious Insights

An Application: Psychosexual Theory and Parenting

How Does Psychosexual Theory Answer the Basic Questions that a Theory of Human Development Is Expected to Address?

Critique of Psychosexual Theory

   Strengths

   Weaknesses

Key Terms

Chapter 3

Psychosexual Theory

Evolutionary theory calls attention to the importance of the reproductive functions as they contribute to fitness and long-term species adaptation. Psychosexual theory focuses on the impact of sexual and aggressive drives on the individual's psychological functioning. It distinguishes between the impact of drives on mental activity and their effect on reproductive functions. The theory assumes that very young children have strong sexual and aggressive drives that find unique modes of expression through successive developmental stages. Throughout childhood, adolescence, and adult life, sexual and aggressive drives operate to direct aspects of one's fantasies, self-concept, problem-solving strategies, and social interactions.

A unique feature of psychosexual theory is the importance placed on childhood experiences for shaping adult thoughts and behavior. The theory focuses on both normative and pathological patterns of growth and development that result from the socialization pressures that act on biologically based drives. The theory highlights the relevance of certain primary social relationships, especially the mother–child and father–child dyads, for their role in determining the expression and gratification of needs and the internalization of moral standards. Many contributions of psychosexual theory continue to influence the study of development and approaches to therapeutic interventions.

HISTORICAL CONTEXT

Sigmund Freud was born in Freiberg (now Pribor), Czechoslovakia, in 1856. Both his grandfather and great-grandfather had been rabbis. He was the first son of his father Jacob's second or third marriage (Jahoda, 1977, p. 5). His family's business failed when he was 4 years old, and in 1860 his family moved to Vienna. His family remained poor. In 1873, he entered the University of Vienna and graduated in 1883 with a medical degree.

In school, he became interested in neurology and studied nerve tracts and the relationship of nerve cells. His early research focused on the functions of the medulla and the conduction of nerve impulses in the brain and spinal cord. He also did pioneering work in the use of cocaine as a local anesthetic, but he did not carry on with this work.

In 1885, Freud went to Paris to work with a French neurologist, Jean Martin Charcot, who specialized in treating hysteria using hypnosis. During his time in Paris, Freud became less interested in the physiological bases of neurological problems and more interested in their psychological bases. Freud began working on this problem in collaboration with a close friend and colleague, Josef Breuer. Freud and Breuer developed a theory of hysteria in which they attributed certain forms of paralysis to psychological conflict rather than to physiological damage (Breuer & Freud, 1895/1955).

In 1886, Freud returned to Vienna and opened up a private practice. He began using hypnosis as a therapeutic treatment. During this time he began to develop the idea that the human mind was made up of both conscious and unconscious components. He published *A Case of Successful Treatment by Hypnotism* in 1892–93 and *Studies on Hysteria* in 1893–95. In the 1890s he stopped using hypnosis and began using free association as a way of reaching the unconscious mind. In this technique, the patient was aware of what he or she said. The process of psychoanalysis focused on analyzing the material that was produced through association and areas of resistance to reveal the content of the unconscious.

In 1900, Freud published *The Interpretation of Dreams*, which includes substantial information from his own self-analysis. He believed that dreams gave more direct evidence of the contents of the unconscious mind than free associations even though the dream content was in symbolic form. Thus, free association and dream interpretation became established as two primary techniques of psychoanalysis.

In 1905, Freud published *Three Essays on the Theory of Sexuality*, which articulated his view that sexual conflict and expression of impulses existed in infancy and young childhood and influenced the formation of the adult personality. These ideas were met by a storm of anger, rejection, and protest by many within the medical community. His medical colleagues could not accept the idea of childhood sexuality. They considered his public lectures on the topic to be crude and distasteful. Freud was denied a professorial appointment at the University of Vienna primarily because of these lectures and writings. Even Breuer, his longtime colleague and collaborator, found Freud's preoccupation with sexual motives offensive and terminated their association.

But, at the same time, the new theory of infantile sexuality led a group of young followers to gather around Freud and pursue the implications of these ideas. Freud helped form the International Congress on Psychoanalysis. There, he developed his psychosexual theory and taught the principles of psychoanalysis to his followers. Freud demanded rather strict adherence to the basic principles and concepts of this theory, and some members of the analytic circle broke away to pursue their own versions of the theory. Most notable among these were Carl Jung and Alfred Adler, who broke with Freud in 1912 and founded their own schools of analytic thought that continue to be influential today.

Freud spent the last 25 years of his life lecturing, writing, teaching his theory to younger physicians, working with patients to gather supporting evidence for his theory, and conducting the business of the International Congress. He remained in Vienna during the rise of Naziism in Germany, but was spirited away to England by supporters in 1938 after the Nazis invaded Austria. In 1923, he developed cancer of the jaw, which was very painful. He underwent repeated surgeries and finally died of the disease in 1939.

Marie Jahoda (1977) noted that "there is virtually no aspect of Freud's work that has escaped becoming the subject of controversy; even some biographical details provided by him or his contemporaries are now open to doubt" (p. 5). Major biographers such as Jones (1953–57) and Ellenberger (1970) disagree about the facts of Freud's life and the factors that guided his thoughts and work. Freud was a very prolific writer and over the years he often revisited aspects of his theory and analytic techniques. Thus, when someone asks, "Did Freud believe this or that?" it is possible to find support for a variety of positions depending on which work one consults. This helps perpetuate the controversies over his ideas. However, there is no doubt that his ideas have been influential in determining how we think about the human psyche and the factors that shape it.

KEY CONCEPTS

All Behavior Is Motivated

Freud assumed that all behavior (except that resulting from fatigue) is motivated. He thought that all behavior has meaning; it does not occur randomly or without purpose. Many of the concepts of psychosexual theory attempt to describe the processes by which sexual and aggressive drives motivate behavior. A related assumption of psychosexual theory is that there is an area of the mind called the unconscious that is a storehouse of powerful, primitive motives of which the person is unaware. Unconscious as well as conscious motives may motivate behavior simultaneously. Thus, behaviors that may appear to be somewhat unusual or extremely intense are described as multiply determined—that is, a single behavior expresses many motives, some of which the person can recognize and control and others that are guided by unconscious thought. One of the most controversial aspects of Freud's psychosexual theory was the central role he gave to the unconscious as the guide or force behind most aspects of human behavior.

> In the course of centuries the *naïve* self-love of men has had to submit to two major blows at the hands of science. The first was when they learnt that our earth was not the center of the universe but only a tiny fragment of a cosmic system of scarcely imaginable vastness. This is associated in our minds with the name of Copernicus, though something similar had already been asserted by Alexandrian science. The second blow fell when biological research destroyed man's supposedly privileged place in creation and proved his descent from the animal kingdom and his ineradicable animal nature. This revaluation has been accomplished in our own days by Darwin, Wallace, and their predecessors, though not without the most violent contemporary opposition. But human megalomania will have suffered its third and most wounding blow from the psychological research of the present time which seeks to prove to the ego that it is not even master in its own house, but must content itself with scanty information of what is going on unconsciously in its mind.(Freud, 1917, pp. 1916–17)

Freud's analysis of normal development as well as his explanations for specific forms of mental illness are derived from his understanding of the ways that sexual and aggressive drives press for expression and are inhibited or given various outlets in thoughts, dreams, behaviors, and symptoms. The term *drive* is sometimes referred to as psychic energy, tension, instincts, or *libido.* Drives can be thought of as sexual and aggressive forces that have a biological or somatic origin—they are a result of some metabolic function, but they are also intimately linked to psychological processes. Freud envisioned a model in which the energy behind the drives builds up as it seeks satisfaction. The psychic energy that is embodied in these drives can be expressed in a variety of ways, but the energy itself will not be destroyed. Drives have a power or force. A person can experience a drive along a continuum from mild to strong. Drives have an aim—a desire to be satisfied that may be handled immediately, delayed, or possibly redirected so that it is only partly satisfied. When possible, drives are satisfied immediately to reduce tension and achieve a state of equilibrium. Drives have an object—a person or thing that allows the drive to achieve its aim. The object of the drive is closely linked to the specific environment in which the child functions. Thus, in order to understand how drives are satisfied one must have a concrete understanding of the social and physical resources that are available to a child at a specific developmental period (Ritvo & Solnit, 1995). Over time, a person becomes able to delay the satisfaction of the drives and finds increasingly flexible and socially appropriate ways to achieve satisfaction.

Five organizing concepts of psychosexual theory are discussed below: the domains of consciousness, the three basic structures of personality, five stages of development, the notion of defense mechanisms, and the processes of identification and transference.

Domains of Consciousness

One of the most enduring contributions of psychosexual theory is the analysis of the topography of mental activity (See Fig. 3.1). Freud thought the human mind was like an iceberg. Conscious processes are the tip that protrudes out of the water; they make up only a small part of the mind. Our conscious thoughts are fleeting. We can have only a few of them at any one time. As soon as energy is diverted from a thought or image, it disappears from consciousness.

The preconscious is analogous to the part of the iceberg near the waterline. Material in the preconscious can be made conscious if attention is directed to it. Preconscious thoughts are readily accessible to consciousness through focused attention. You may not be thinking about your hometown or your favorite desserts right now, but if someone were to ask you about either of them, you could readily recall and discuss them.

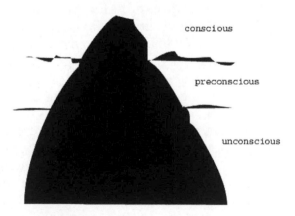

Figure 3.1.   Domains of consciousness.

The unconscious, like the rest of the iceberg, is hidden from view. It is a vast network of content and processes that are actively barred from consciousness. Freud hypothesized that the content of the unconscious, including wishes, fears, impulses, and repressed memories, plays a major role in guiding behavior even though we cannot explain the connections consciously. Behaviors that are unusual or extremely intense may not make sense if they are explained only in terms of conscious motives. However, through certain techniques used in psychotherapy, the link between unconscious wishes and fears and overt behaviors often can be established.

Here is an example of the complexity of the process. A patient of Freud's who had recently been married sometimes forgot his wife's name. Freud hypothesized that consciously the man felt he loved his wife and thought they were happy together. Freud thought that forgetting the wife's name provided a clue to the content of the man's unconscious. In his unconscious, the man had strong, negative feelings about his wife, feelings that were so unacceptable that they could not be allowed expression. By forgetting his wife's name, Freud reasoned that the young man could express some level of hostility toward her and, at the same time, punish himself for his unconscious anger toward her.

Three Structures of Personality

Freud (1933/1964) described three components of personality: the id, the ego, and the superego. In his writings about these structures, Freud suggested a developmental progression in which id exists alone at birth, ego emerges during infancy, and the superego takes shape in early childhood. In adulthood, the three structures must find an effective pattern of interaction in order to support adaptation.

Id. The id is the source of instincts and impulses. It is the primary source of psychic energy, and it exists from birth. Freud believed that newborn infants' mental processes were comprised completely of id impulses, and that the ego and superego emerged later, drawing their energy from the id.

The id expresses its demands according to the pleasure principle: People are motivated to seek pleasure and avoid pain. The pleasure principle does not take into account the feelings of others, society's norms, or agreements between people. Its rule is to achieve immediate satisfaction of impulses and discharge of energy. When you lie to a friend to protect your own image, or when you cut ahead of people in line so you won't have to wait, you are operating according to the pleasure principle.

The logic of the id is also the logic of dreams. This kind of thinking is called primary process thought. It is characterized by a lack of concern for the constraints of reality. In primary process thought, there are no negatives. Everything is yes. There is no time. Nothing happens in the past or in the future. Everything is now. Symbolism becomes flexible. One object may symbolize many things, and many different objects may mean the same thing. Many male faces can all represent the father. The image of a house may be a symbol for one's mother, a lover, or the female genitalia, as well as for a house.

Ego.   Ego is a term that has two related meanings. One is the idea of ego as a person's self including one's physical self, self-concept, self-esteem, and mental representations of the self in relation to others. This sense of ego emerges as psychic energy is directed toward the self—a process that is sometimes called primary narcissism. The idea is that the sense of self is born out of self-love, an enthusiasm and excitement for one's body, one's experiences, and one's emerging sense of agency. The second idea of ego refers to all mental functions that have to do with the person's relation to the environment. It includes a multitude of cognitive processes, such as perception, learning, memory, judgment, self-awareness, and language skills that allow a person to take in information, process it, assess its implications, and select a course of action. Freud thought the ego begins to develop in the first 6 or 8 months of life and is well established by the age of 2 or 3. Other scholars view the ego processes as present from birth (Moore, 1995). Of course, much change and growth occur over time as the ego responds to demands from the environment and finds strategies that support effective functioning. The ego also responds to the demands of the id and the superego and helps the person satisfy needs, live up to ideals and standards, and establish a healthy emotional balance.

The ego operates according to the reality principle. Under this principle, the ego protects the person by waiting to gratify id impulses until a socially acceptable form of expression or gratification can be found. In the ego, primary process thought becomes subordinated to a more reality-oriented process, called secondary process thought. This process begins to dominate as the ego matures.

Secondary process thought is the kind of logical, sequential thinking that we usually mean when we discuss thinking. It allows people to plan and act in order to engage the world and to achieve gratification in personally and socially acceptable ways. It enables people to delay gratification. It helps people assess plans by examining whether they will really work. This last process is called reality testing.

Superego.   The superego includes both a punishing and a rewarding function. The conscience, which includes ideas about which behaviors and thoughts are improper, unacceptable, and wrong, carries out the punishing function. The ego ideal, which includes ideas about what behaviors and thoughts are admirable, acceptable, and worthy of praise, carries out the rewarding function. Freud's work led him to conclude that the superego does not begin to develop until the age of 5 or 6, and probably is not firmly established until several years later. Other theorists have suggested that the roots of the superego emerge in infancy as the child becomes differentiated from the caregiver and aware of the possibility of disrupting the close bond with this loving object (Klein, 1948). Because it is formed during early childhood, the superego tends to be harsh and unrealistic in its demands. It is often just as illogical and unrelenting in its search for proper behavior as the id is in its search for pleasure. When a child thinks about behaving in a morally unacceptable way, the superego sends a warning by producing feelings of anxiety and guilt.

The superego is developed through a process called identification. Motivated by love, fear, and admiration, children actively imitate their parents' characteristics and internalize their parents' values. Through identification, parents' values become the ideals and aspirations of their children. In this way, the moral standards of a society are transmitted from one generation to the next.

The Relationship of Id, Ego, and Superego. Ego processes work toward satisfying id impulses through thoughts and actions without generating strong feelings of guilt in the superego. In one sense, the ego processes serve both the id and the superego, striving to provide gratification, but in morally and socially acceptable ways. In another sense, ego is the executive of personality. The strength of the ego determines the person's effectiveness in meeting his or her needs, handling the demands of the superego, and dealing with the demands of reality. If the ego is strong and can establish a good balance among id, superego, and environmental demands, the person is satisfied and free from immobilizing guilt and feelings of worthlessness.

When id and superego are stronger than ego, the person may be tossed and turned psychologically by strong desires for pleasure and strong constraints against attaining those desires. When environmental demands are strong and the ego is weak, such as when an adolescent is confronted by strong pressures for peer conformity and the threat of peer rejection, a person may also be overwhelmed. According to psychosexual theory, it is the breakdown of the ego that leads to mental disorder.

Much of the relationship of the id, the ego, and the superego is played out at an unconscious level. In the early years, aspects of basic drives and primary process thought are noticeable in a child's consciousness. This is an indication of the conscious presence of the id. As the ego grows stronger, it is able to push the id's desires and fantasies into the unconscious so the person can attend to the exploration and demands of the external world. Freud thought that the superego also operated mostly at the unconscious level, although the ego ideal is largely conscious. He thought the ego, however, functioned at both the conscious and unconscious levels.

The concept of achieving new levels of ego strength reflects the goal of development in psychosexual theory. Over time, the ego has to attend to pressures from the id and find acceptable outlets for drive satisfaction. The ego has to choose morally acceptable behaviors in order to avoid guilt from a punitive superego. Finally, the ego has to act in the real world, finding ways to protect the self and loved ones from real dangers as well as to find new sources of access to objects that will satisfy basic drives.

Stages of Development

Freud assumed that the most significant developments in personality take place during five life stages from infancy through adolescence, with the primary emphasis given to the first 5 or 6 years of life. After that time, according to Freud, the essential pattern for expressing and controlling impulses has been established. Later life serves only to uncover new modes of gratification and new sources of frustration.

The stages Freud described reflect his emphasis on sexuality as a driving force. Freud used the term sexuality quite broadly, referring to the full range of physical pleasure, from sucking to sexual intercourse. He also attached a positive, life-force symbolism to the concept of sexuality, suggesting that sexual impulses provide a thrust toward growth and renewal. At each stage, a particular body zone is of heightened sexual importance. The shift in focus from one body zone to the next is due largely to the biologically based unfolding of physical maturation. The five stages Freud identified are the oral, anal, phallic, latent, and genital stages.

During the oral stage, in the 1st year of life, the mouth is the site of sexual and aggressive gratification. Babies use their mouths to explore the environment, to express tension, and to experience pleasure. Freud characterized infants as passive and dependent. They take things in, absorbing experience just as they swallow milk. As infants learn to delay gratification, the ego becomes more clearly differentiated and they become aware of the distinction between the self and others. With this awareness comes the realization that all wishes cannot be satisfied.

In the anal stage, during the 2nd year of life, the anus is the most sexualized body part. With the development of the sphincter muscles, a child learns to expel or withhold feces at will. The conflict at this stage focuses on the subordination of the child's will to the demands of the culture (via parents) for appropriate toilet habits.

The phallic stage begins during the 3rd year of life and may last until the child is 6. It is a period of heightened genital sensitivity in the absence of the hormonal changes that accompany puberty. Freud described the behavior of children at this stage as bisexual. They direct sexualized activity toward both sexes and engage in self-stimulation. This is the stage during which the Oedipal or Electra complex is observed.

The Oedipal complex in boys and the Electra complex in girls result from ambivalence surrounding heightened sexuality. According to psychosexual theory, the child has a strong, sexualized attraction to the parent of the opposite sex. The child may desire to have the exclusive attention of that parent, and may fantasize that the other parent will leave, or perhaps die. In other words, the same-sex parent becomes a fantasied rival. At the same time, the child fears that amorous overtures toward the desired parent may result in hostility or retribution from the parent of the same sex. The child also worries that this beloved, same-sex parent will withdraw love. Parental threats intended to prevent the child from masturbating, and fantasies of the possibility of castration or bodily mutilation, may add to the child's fears that sexualized fantasies are going to result in punishment or withdrawal of love.

An important component of the Oedipal or Electra complex dynamic is the view of the young child as engaged in complex, conflicting wishes that involve the mother–father–child triad. Many competing impulses come into play: the conflict between wanting to satisfy sexual drives and the awareness that self-stimulation is not socially acceptable; the conflict between wanting to remain a child who is loved and cared for by both parents and the desire to assume a more mature role in the eyes of the opposite sex parent; the anger and rivalry experienced toward the same-sex parent and the desire to preserve that parent's love and admiration; the pressures to embrace one's own gender identity and the envy one feels toward the opposite sex. In a successful resolution of the Oedipal or Electra conflict, the superego emerges as a strong structure that aids the ego in controlling unacceptable impulses. Through a process of identification with one's parent's moral and ethical values, the child achieves a new level of autonomy, and at the same time receives the admiration and approval of both parents, who see the child as moving in the direction of maturity and self-control. Most of the intense and painful conflicts of this period are repressed, and the ego emerges with a new degree of self-esteem and confidence about his or her place in the family structure (Tyson & Tyson, 1995).

Freud believed that once the Oedipal or Electra conflict is resolved, the child enters a period of latency. During this stage, which lasts from about 7 years until puberty, no new significant conflicts or impulses arise. The primary personality development during this period is the maturation of the ego.

A final stage of development begins with the onset of puberty: the genital stage. During this period, the person finds ways of satisfying sexual impulses in mature, dyadic relationships. Adolescence brings about a reawakening of Oedipal or Electra conflicts and a reworking of earlier childhood identifications. Freud explained the tension of adolescence as the result of the sexual threat that the mature adolescent poses to the family unit. In an effort to avoid this threat, adolescents may withdraw from their families or temporarily devalue their parents. With the selection of a permanent sex partner, the threat of intimacy between young people and their parents diminishes. At the end of adolescence, a more autonomous relationship with one's parents becomes possible.

Freud believed that the psychological conflicts that arise during adolescence and adulthood result from a failure to satisfy or express specific childhood wishes. At any of the childhood stages, sexualized impulses may have been so frustrated or overindulged that the person continues to seek their gratification at later stages of life. Freud used the term fixation to refer to continued use of pleasure-seeking or anxiety-reducing behaviors appropriate to an earlier stage of development. Since no person can possibly satisfy all wishes at every life stage, normal development depends on the ability to channel the energy from those impulses into activities that either symbolize the impulses or express them in a socially acceptable form. This process is called sublimation. During adolescence and early adulthood, patterns of impulse expression, fixation, and sublimation crystallize into a life orientation. From this point on, the content of the id, the regulating functions of the superego, and the executive functions of the ego rework the struggles of childhood through repeated episodes of engagement, conflict, and impulse gratification or frustration.

Defense Mechanisms

Much of the ego's work involves mediating the conflicts between the id's demands for gratification and the superego's demands for good behavior. This work is conducted outside the person's awareness. When unconscious conflicts threaten to break through into consciousness, the person experiences anxiety. If the ego functions effectively, it pushes these conflicts into the unconscious and thereby protects the person from unpleasant emotions. The ego proceeds to satisfy desires in acceptable ways by directing behavior and social interaction.

Strong, unresolvable conflicts may leave a person in a state of constant anxiety and symptoms may emerge. A person who feels a desire that is thought to be very "bad," such as an unconscious wish to harm a parent or to be sexually intimate with a sibling, may experience anxiety without recognizing its source. The ungratified impulse continues to seek gratification. The superego continues to find the impulse unacceptable, and the conflict continues to produce anxiety in the person's conscious experience. The unpleasant emotional state may preoccupy the person and make it difficult to handle the normal demands of day-to-day life.

Defense mechanisms protect the person from anxiety so that effective functioning can be preserved. They distort, substitute, or completely block out the source of the conflict. They are usually initiated unconsciously. Often the defense mechanism used depends on a person's age and the intensity of the perceived threat. Younger children tend to use denial and repression (pushing thoughts from awareness). A more diverse set of defenses, requiring greater cognitive complexity, becomes available in the course of development. In situations of greatest threat, denial is often the initial defense used, regardless of age.

According to Freud, the basic defense mechanism is repression, a process whereby unacceptable impulses are pushed into the unconscious. It is as if a wall were constructed between the unconscious and the conscious mind so that anxiety-provoking thoughts and feelings cannot enter consciousness. With unacceptable thoughts and impulses far from awareness, the person is protected from uncomfortable feelings of anxiety and may devote the remaining psychic energy to interchange with the interpersonal and physical environments. This defensive strategy has two major costs. First, it takes energy to continue to protect the conscious mind from these thoughts, thereby reducing the amount of mental energy available to cope with other daily demands. Second, if too many thoughts and feelings are relegated to repression, the person loses the use of the emotional system as a means of monitoring and evaluating reality.

The following are defense mechanisms:

Repression: Unacceptable wishes are barred from conscious thought.
Projection: Unacceptable wishes are attributed to someone else.
Reaction formation: Unacceptable feelings are expressed by the opposite feelings.
Regression: One avoids confronting conflicts and stresses by reverting to behaviors that were effective and comforting at an earlier life stage.
Displacement: Unacceptable impulses are expressed toward a substitute target.
Rationalization: Unacceptable feelings and actions are justified by logical or pseudological explanations.
Isolation: Feelings are separated from thoughts.
Denial: Parts of external reality are denied.
Sublimation: Unacceptable wishes are channeled to socially acceptable behaviors.

According to Freud, all people resort to defense mechanisms at various times in their lives. These mechanisms not only reduce anxiety but may lead to positive social outcomes. Physicians who use isolation may be able to function effectively because they are able to apply their knowledge without being hindered by their feelings. Children who rationalize defeat may be able to protect their self-esteem by viewing themselves favorably. The child who projects angry feelings onto someone else may find that this technique stimulates a competitive orientation that enhances performance.

One of the goals of psychotherapy is to help people recognize and admit into consciousness deeply troubling fantasies, beliefs, wishes, or impulses that are repressed or transformed through other types of defenses. Often these unconscious thoughts are linked to strong feelings of shame, guilt, humiliation, or fear of loss of love. During psychotherapy, the patient gradually tests the therapist in order to determine whether these unconscious thoughts can be expressed without experiencing these negative feelings. At the same time, the analyst helps the patient move closer and closer to recognizing these thoughts in the conscious domain (Weiss, 1990). Once the analyst can help the patient bring this highly blocked material into consciousness, the patient can begin to understand and manage both the thoughts and the anxiety they produce and gradually the material becomes less troubling.

Regression is an especially important defense when considered from a developmental perspective. Many theorists suggest that development is a *spiraling* process in which forward movement and increased integration of complex functions may alternate with temporary backsliding or return to a more comfortable, less demanding position. In psychosexual theory, regression may occur when a person (child or adult) reverts to an earlier form of drive satisfaction, immature forms of relationships with others, lower moral standards, or more simplistic ways of thinking and solving problems. Anna Freud (1965) and Peter Blos (1967) both wrote about the idea that regression can serve ego development if it is not met with extreme disapproval. Sometimes it is necessary to return to an earlier mode of functioning in order to resolve conflicts that were inadequately resolved at that time, or to engage in a kind of playful childishness in order to achieve a new level of mastery. Most obviously, in the creative process, a certain amount of regressive fantasy thought can unlock possible associations that make sense according to primary process thinking but are censored in secondary process thinking (Tyson & Tyson, 1995).

Some people rely more on one or two defensive techniques than on the others. The resultant defensive style becomes part of an overall personality pattern. It permits one to regulate the impact of the environment and to perceive experiences in ways that are compatible with one's needs. When defense mechanisms are used to excess, however, they may indicate a deeper psychological problem. The use of defense mechanisms draws psychological energy from the ego. Energy that is used to prevent certain wishes from entering conscious thought is not available for other life activities. A person whose energy is devoted to defensive strategies may be unable to develop other ego functions and to use those functions adequately.

Identification and Transference

Psychosexual theory suggests that beginning in childhood and continuing through adulthood, we incorporate the observable characteristics and personal values of people whom we either love, admire, or fear. This process is referred to as *identification.* We modify our own behaviors and beliefs in order to become more similar to significant others. Identification plays a key role in the process of ego development and socialization in early childhood. Through this process, significant components of gender identity and morality are incorporated into the self. Identification may begin in a wishful fantasy to become like someone else or to merge with a love object. However, over time the content of these identifications becomes integrated into the person's stable character. The source of the identification may become repressed or detached from its origin. A teenage boy who is trying to negotiate with his parents to let him go on a weekend trip with his friends may try to argue that by going away he will be showing his parents just how responsible he can be. He may be surprised when his mother tells him that he is acting just like his father in the approach he is taking to make his case.

Identification begins in early childhood and continues throughout life. It may be both a conscious and an unconscious process. For example, a young adult may perceive that a coworker is especially successful in the work setting, and may begin to identify with some of that person's actions or attitudes thinking, "If I am more like my coworker, perhaps I will be more highly valued in the work setting." The motivation to identify with the coworker may also originate from unconscious anger or envy of the coworker's success. In order to defend against these unacceptable aggressive drives, the person may take on characteristics of the coworker. This conflicted motivation for identification may create anxiety for the person as he or she manifests attitudes and behaviors that are at some level attached to aggressive fantasies (Schafer, 1968; Abend & Proder, 1995).

In identification, a person incorporates characteristics of a valued object. In *transference,* a person projects the characteristics of an internalized identification onto another person. The person repeats feelings or desires that had been directed to an important object in an earlier time of life to a new, contemporary relationship. So, for example, a student may transfer characteristics of his or her mother onto a teacher, acting toward the teacher as if that person were his or her mother, and expecting the teacher to treat him or her the way the student's mother treated him or her. The motivation for the transference may be to satisfy an unfulfilled wish or to reconstruct an unfulfilled relationship. A contemporary object becomes a symbolic substitute for the person who was important in childhood. From the psychosexual perspective, some amount of transference becomes integrated into every adult's character. The unmet, repressed wishes toward significant childhood figures, including parents, siblings, teachers, or religious leaders, are carried forward into adulthood. Transference can occur when the contemporary relationship has some real or symbolic equivalence or resemblance to the earlier object.

The concepts of identification and transference are important not only because children and adults experience them, but because adults are often the objects for these processes in others. As teachers, community leaders, therapists, human service professionals, supervisors, and parents, adults are the significant others who provide the content for identification and may become the object of transference.

NEW DIRECTIONS

In much of his writings and in his approach to psychoanalytic therapy, Freud concentrated on the nature of unconscious conflicts, their sources, the way they found expression, and the ways in which they operated to rob the ego of energy or disrupt adaptive functioning. One direction that emerged in the elaboration of psychosexual theory was the importance of the ego, including a more detailed description of ego development, ego functions, and the ability of the ego to assess and manage threats. This direction is referred to as ego psychology. Another direction focused on the centrality of early object relations, that is the interpersonal sphere in which self and other are co-constructed, as the context for ego development and as prototypes for shaping subsequent object relations. This direction is referred to as object relations theory.

Ego Psychology

In his structural theory, Freud introduced the concept of ego and its *executive* functions in managing the expression of impulses, negotiating between the id and the superego, striving to attain goals embedded in the ego ideal, and assessing reality. His daughter, Anna Freud, took these ideas further in her important book, *The Ego and the Mechanisms of Defense,* (1936/1946), outlining new ego capacities that emerge from infancy through adolescence. In this work, she highlighted the various threats that the id poses to the ego at each stage of development, and provided a classification of the defense mechanisms the ego uses to protect itself from unruly and unacceptable impulses.

Anna Freud gave special attention to the period of adolescence as a time of increased sexual and aggressive energy that is linked to the biological changes of puberty. At this time, children are likely to be overwhelmed by libidinal energy and the ego is more or less fighting for its life. Anger and aggression become more intense, sometimes to the point of getting out of hand. Appetites become enormous. Oral and anal interests come to the surface again expressed as pleasure in dirt and disorder, exhibitionistic tendencies, brutality, cruelty to animals, and enjoyment of various forms of vulgarity. In her clinical cases, Anna Freud observed that previously successful defense mechanisms threatened to fall to pieces as intense sexual impulses emerged. During this period, the ego may employ very rigid defenses in order to deny the instinctual drives. Adolescents may vacillate in their behavior from loving to mean, compliant to rebellious, or self-centered to altruistic, as the ego tries to assert itself in the midst of conflicting and newly energized libidinal forces.

Elaborating on Anna Freud's view of adolescent development, Peter Blos (1962) expanded the concept of ego and the mechanisms of defense by identifying the coping mechanisms that emerge in adolescence as young people find ways of adapting psychologically to the physical transitions of puberty. By the end of adolescence, those ego conflicts present at the beginning of puberty are transformed into more manageable aspects of identity construction and expression. Blos noted five major accomplishments of ego development for young people who navigate adolescence successfully:

1. Judgment, interests, intellect and other ego functions emerge that are specific to the individual and very stable.
2. The conflict-free area of the ego expands, allowing new people and experiences to acquire psychological importance.
3. An irreversible sexual identity is formed.
4. The egocentrism of the child is replaced by a balance between thoughts about one's self and thoughts about others.
5. A wall separating one's public and private selves is established.

The prominence of ego psychology was enhanced through the work of Heinz Hartmann. In his book, *Ego Psychology and the Problem of Adaptation* (1939), Hartmann suggested that not all aspects of the ego's functioning arise out of conflict with the id and the superego. He introduced the concept of the conflict-free sphere of the ego, including basic adaptive functions such as perception, recognition of objects, the development of problem solving, motor development, and language. Hartmann thought that the concepts of ego, id, and superego were more accurately viewed as three interrelated components of mental functioning that could expand or contract under the influence of one another. He offered a developmental picture of the ego beginning with early differentiation and distinction between id and ego, a process of growing clarity between self and the external reality, a shift from early narcissism to investment in others, and to the eventual achievement of adaptive, secondary process thinking (Boesky, 1995). Hartmann expanded the scope of interest within psychotherapy to include more attention on problem solving and the goal-oriented nature of thought and behavior.

Building on Hartmann's work, Edith Jacobson (1964) described how the self is shaped through identification with others and achieves new levels of autonomy through the incorporation of moral codes and ethical values. According to Jacobson, the superego is not always a threat to the ego. It can become a stimulus for new levels of ego development when anxiety or guilt signal a need for a new standard of moral behavior. In their extension of the concept of ego, Rubin and Gertrude Blanck (1986) moved from a view of many ego functions to a more executive, integrated analysis of ego:

> We suggested that the ego is the overall organizing process. Instead of defining it by its functions (Hartmann), we proposed that it be defined by its func-tion*ing*—that is, we now focus attention upon the total person who functions, rather than upon the separate functions. (Blanck & Blanck, 1986, p. 88)

Thus, ego psychology became a study of the development and differentiation of the ego as integrative, adaptive, and goal directed. The ego is at once an intricate composite of multiple capacities, including planning, assessing, defending, coping, and mediating, and the integration of these with other aspects of self-concept, self-esteem, and personal identity that give the person substance, individuality, and location in the social world.

Object Relations Theory

The relational paradigm emerged and has been consolidated within psychoanalytic thought over the past 70 years (Borden, 2000). Theorists such as W. R. D. Fairbairn, Melanie Klein, Harry Stack Sullivan, Donald Winnicut, and Heinz Kohut are forerunners in this perspective. They stress that humans have basic needs for connection, contact, and meaningful interpersonal relationships throughout life. According to this view, the self is formed in an interpersonal context, and emerges through interactions with others. The path toward maturity requires that the person achieve a sense of vitality, stability, and inner cohesiveness which are formulated through interpersonal transactions. In the relational perspective, psychopathology or dysfunction arise when a person internalizes rigid, rejecting, or neglectful relational experiences and then uses these internalizations to anticipate or respond to real life social encounters. Since the internalized relational pattern is familiar and well learned, the person is reluctant to give it up even if it leads to feelings of isolation, anxiety, or self-loathing (Messer & Warren, 1995).

One of the leading theorists in the elaboration of object relations theory was Margaret Mahler. Her work grew out of the study of psychoses in children, especially infantile autism and what was referred to as symbiotic psychosis. In an effort to understand how the self emerges, she carried out detailed studies of mother–child dyads. Based on her observations, she identified three phases in the emergence of a balanced, integrated sense of self and other: the autistic phase, the symbiotic phase, and the separation–individuation phase. Underlying her theorizing is a view that the infant brings an innate capacity to engage and extract responses from the environment. At each period, Mahler observed evidence of the infant's drives, motor capacities, interests, and excitability as evoking reactions from the mother and the mother's reactions prompting the infant's reactions (Mahler & Furer, 1968; Mahler, Pine, & Bergman, 1975).

In the autistic phase, which was thought to take place during the first month or so of life, an infant is primarily focused on satisfying physical needs and achieving a state of biological equilibrium. Mother–infant interactions focus on meeting these needs and creating an appropriate state of physical comfort, wake–sleep cycles, and satisfaction of hunger. The infant's behavior is guided almost entirely by internal drives with little interest in the mother as a separate person.

In the symbiotic phase, which lasts from about 2 to 6 months, the infant takes new pleasure in engaging in rhythmic interactions with the mother. This includes smiling, gazing, some forms of imitation, touching and tickling, and other forms of "dialogue." In this phase, the infant is thought to experience "blissful states of merger" with the mother (Kernberg, 1995, p. 459). The symbiotic phase provides the infant with a sense of confidence and predictability, which also serve as a template for subsequent forms of interpersonal communication. Implied in the term symbiotic is the idea that both the infant and the mother are dependent upon one another and derive satisfactions from their coordinated interactions.

The separation–individuation phase begins at around 4 or 5 months as the infant shows new interest in the world beyond the mother. Mahler viewed this phase as ongoing and open-ended (Mahler, 1972). In the first subphase, *differentiation*, the infant finds new satisfaction in exploration of other things and people, especially the father and siblings, and begins to be able to move away from the mother through creeping and crawling. Although the infant may move out beyond the mother, he or she frequently checks back to locate the mother and is more readily comforted by her. Many of the elements of this period are very similar to the attachment process described in chapter 2. The second step in the separation–individuation phase, called *practicing*, takes place between 11 and 16 months. This period is marked by walking; new excitement in exploration apart from the mother; and some evidence of aggressive behavior toward the mother, including scampering away, resisting her requests, and asserting a new degree of willfulness. In this phase, babies are thought to have a sense of unrealistic omnipotence. Their pleasure in their mother is not fully balanced by an appreciation of their dependence upon her.

The third step in the separation–individuation phase, called *rapprochement*, takes place between 18 months and the end of the 3rd year. Toddlers show clinging, anxious behavior, manipulative demanding behavior, and a desire to control their mother. This phase is thought to be brought on in part by the child's own aggressive impulses and desire for new levels of autonomy coupled with a new realization of how small and vulnerable he or she is among the world of adults. Thus, the child's earlier narcissism and sense of power are diminished in the face of a new level of reality testing. The conflict between needs for autonomy and security are frequent and the child finds himself or herself struggling with angry, resentful feelings and safe, loving feelings toward the mother. The intensity of this period is heightened if the mother has difficulty letting go of her enjoyment of the symbiotic phase, if the child's own aggressive drives result in harsh conflicts with the mother, or if traumatic events such as harsh punishment, object loss, or neglect cause a blow to the child's sense of self-worth.

The last phase of the separation–individuation process, referred to as *toward object constancy,* begins at about 24 months but is never completed. This concept has a lot in common with Piaget's notion of object constancy, which will be discussed in chapter 4. The child is gradually able to integrate the frustrating, angry, and loving memories of his or her mother into a stable representation of self and other. The child achieves a greater tolerance for strains in the relationship with the mother, knowing that the basic bond is pleasurable and positive. Over time, the representation of the integrated, loving, caring mother is internalized through identification, so that the child can use this representation to comfort himself or herself. At the same time, the internalization of the loving mother contributes positively to the child's sense of self-esteem. "I am someone who is safe, loved, and valued." The child experiences the stability of not only giving and receiving love in the interpersonal domain, but integrates a sense of being loveable into a component of the constant self. The process is viewed as ongoing since this representation may be altered through subsequent life events, and the internalized representation of the mother is never a complete substitute for the real mother's love (Tyson & Tyson, 1995).

This view of the development of normal object relations has important implications for caregiving. It acknowledges the lifelong struggle between autonomy and closeness that is inherent in the parent–child relationship. In order to foster a positive separation–individuation process, parents need to create a comforting, secure context for the child to discover both the self and the other. Parental attributes of comforting responsiveness, psychological availability, and calm reassurance are emphasized. Parents are encouraged to enjoy the symbiotic pleasure of the early phase, but to be willing to stand aside and give the child space to experience separateness as the child requires it.

A RESEARCH EXAMPLE: THE REDISCOVERY OF THE UNCONSCIOUS

Let us suppose,...that every mental process...first exists in an unconscious state or phase, and only develops out of this into a conscious phase, much as a photograph is first a negative and then becomes a picture through the printing of the positive. But not every negative is made into a positive, and it is just as little necessary that every unconscious mental process should convert itself into a conscious one. It may be best expressed as follows: Each single process belongs in the first place to the unconscious psychical system; from this system it can under certain conditions proceed further into the conscious system.(Freud, 1924/1960, p. 305)

In the early 20th century, two competing camps argued about mental functioning. The behaviorists discounted mental processes, suggesting that consciousness was irrelevant in the study of behavior. The psychoanalysts argued that unconscious mental processes were the primary source of information for understanding the meaning of behavior. By the 1950s, the strong behavioral and experimental nature of the study of psychology in the United States led to skepticism about the existence of the unconscious (Bruner, 1992). However, over the past 30 years, scholarly interest in cognitive processes has resulted in renewed attention to the notion of the cognitive unconscious, the range of mental structures and processes that operate outside awareness but play a significant role in conscious thought and action (Kihlstrom, 1987). Just as Freud argued, it is becoming evident that conscious thought accounts for only a small proportion of our capacities to identify, analyze, recall, and synthesize information.

One model of the way humans process information suggests that there are a large number of processing units or modules, each devoted to a specific task or category (Rumelhart & McClelland, 1986; Gazzaniga, 1989). This approach is very similar to that proposed by evolutionary psychologists. Figure 3.2. provides a model of how the neural network might work to lead from stimulus to action (Greenwald, 1992). The model suggests that perception, attention, memory, and semantic processing may all be operating at the same time. Activity within the neural system moves from less complex to more complex levels of analysis—from recognition of a feature of a stimulus, to recognition of a complete image, to naming the stimulus and linking it to other related stimuli. Activity also moves vertically across domains so that a stimulus may prompt awareness of shape, color, sound, and texture, all or part of which may lead to recognition of the stimulus and action. Activation of one unit may excite some units and inhibit others.

Information about an object may be found in a number of processing units. The stimulus of an apple, for instance, may be represented in units related to things that are red, fruits, teachers, health (an apple a day keeps the doctor

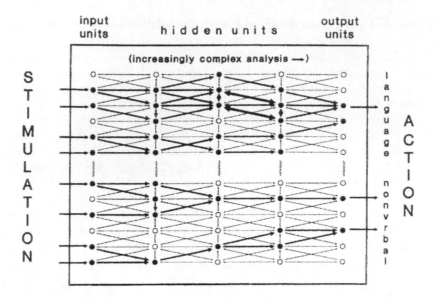

Figure 3.2.   The dynamic organization of neural networks. From: A.G. Greenwald, New Look 3: Unconscious cognition reclaimed. *American Psychologist, 47*, No. 6, 1992, Figure 2, Page 774. Reprinted by permission.

away), and other more idiosyncratic units (such as a fear of bees that swarm around rotting apples, or a pleasant memory of the family picking apples, or the smell of applesauce cooking in Mother's kitchen). Many mental functions, including language, memory, and planning, could be operating in response to the presentation of an apple as a stimulus, although most of them would be occurring unconsciously. Each time the network is used, connections are strengthened as indicated by the darkened arrows and blackened circles. This view of the way the brain is organized gives a major role to unconscious processing, which accompanies all types of conscious activity.

There are three implications of this model for an understanding of unconscious cognition. First, there are many *hidden units* of activity that lead to nonverbal rather than verbal outputs. The implication is that there are processes at work that a person cannot report verbally. Second, in addition to the darkened paths that lead to darkened circles, there are many light paths that lead to the same circles. In other words, there are both conscious and unconscious links between stimuli and action. Some links to output are weak but present and could be strengthened through repeated activation (such as through free association). Third, arrows can move in both directions, toward more complex and less complex levels of analysis as well as across processing modes. Memory can alter perceptions, and perceptions can modify memories.

The nature of the connections that exist in the neural network is very individual. For people with a great depth of expertise in a specific area, such as writing news articles or solving math problems, many of the subnetworks of cognition are well developed and possibly relegated to the less complex area of functioning, leaving more conscious attention for the special problems and unique tasks. Each person's unconscious content will differ depending on the diversity of his or her experiences, the acuity and reliance on specific perceptual systems, and the depth or intensity of his or her special abilities (Bruner, 1992).

A variety of empirical studies provide evidence for the existence of mental processes that occur outside of awareness. Here, we are speaking not only about mental mechanisms such as attention and memory, but about the way information is recognized and interpreted (Greenwald, 1992; Cramer, 2000). Four examples will give a sense of the diversity of evidence. The research on the nature of unconscious cognition is ongoing. Each advance in methodology provides new insight into how unconscious mental activity might operate to protect the ego by allowing it to be more efficient, less likely to be caught off guard, and, in some cases, able to redefine stimuli so that inconsistent or incompatible information does not prevent necessary action.

Perceptual Defense

Among the early research was work by Bruner and Postman (1947; Postman & Bruner, 1948). Using the tachistoscope, an instrument used in studies of perception and memory that can display a stimulus for very brief intervals under a second, one could present a word at a speed that was below the threshold of verbal recognition. Early studies showed that the time it took to recognize a word depended in part on where it stood on a person's hierarchy of values. For example, a person who valued hard work as a means to success would recognize the word *effort* more readily than would a person for whom hard work was not an especially important value. In addition, they found that before participants could fully recognize a word, they would guess that the word was in a similar value domain as the word that had been flashed on the screen. Finally, they found that when they presented a word that was disturbing, reaction times were delayed. They called this *perceptual defense*. This line of research provided early evidence that some level of meaning was processed before a target word was consciously recognized (Bruner, 1992).

Selective Attention

Another line of research has focused on selective attention, particularly dichotic listening, in which a person wears headphones and different information is played into the two ears. Subjects are asked to focus on information coming into one ear while information is also coming into the other ear. Under these conditions, the subject is later tested for information from the secondary source. Results show that there is an ability to recognize features of this unattended auditory stimulus. This is sometimes called *attentionless unconscious cognition*. Although the kind of processing of this unattended information is usually limited to features such as pitch or loudness, if the information in the secondary channel is especially significant, word meaning can be retrieved (Johnston & Dark, 1986; Greenwald, 1992).

Neurological Damage

A third source of evidence about unconscious processing comes from clinical cases. For example, Weiskranz (1986, 1997) described the condition called *blindsight*, in which patients have suffered damage to the cortex of the occipital lobes, thus losing their subjective experience of seeing. However, upon presentation of visual stimuli, these patients can respond correctly to the presence or absence of an object as well as its location and movement, although they cannot provide information about color, form, or identity. In other clinical cases involving amnesia, subjects may have no recall of learning or being exposed to certain words, but they will use information about the word in subsequent learning tasks (Jacoby, Lindsay, & Toth, 1992). In a third example, Galin (1974) reported on the response of a patient in Roger Sperry's split-brain research who had her corpus callosum (the band of fibers that connects the two hemispheres of the brain) severed in an attempt to treat severe epilepsy (as cited in Levin, 1995).

> One film segment [of Sperry's research] shows a female patient being tested with a tachistoscope.... In the series of neutral geometrical figures being presented at random to the right and left [visual] fields, a nude pinup was included and flashed to the right (nonverbal) hemisphere. The girl blushes and giggles. [The experimenter] asks 'What do you see?' She answers, 'Nothing, just a flash of light,' and giggles again, covering her mouth with her hand. 'Why are you laughing then?' [asks the experimenter], and she laughs again and says, 'Oh, doctor Sperry, you have some machine.' (p. 573)

Unconscious Insights

The three examples provided above suggest that there are unconscious processes that recognize stimuli and link stimuli to related neural networks. They do not present evidence of the type of complex, semantic unconscious that is implied in Freud's notion of conflicting unconscious motives, unconscious fantasies, or repressed wishes that might continue to press for expression and, thereby, influence behavior. This final example moves a bit closer to a view of the unconscious as capable of more complex processing that might influence decision making.

In this example, research focuses on the nature of insight. The premise of this research is that in the process of problem solving people may use an unconscious strategy that becomes conscious with repeated activation. The point at which the strategy becomes conscious is typically the moment of insight, but the unconscious is using the strategy as a short cut even before the conscious is aware of its relevance. To illustrate this process, Siegler & Stern (1998) gave second grade children math problems to solve that involved inversion. The problems are of the type A + B - B = A. These problems can be solved mathematically by adding A and B, and then subtracting B. They can also be solved through insight be realizing that the answer is always the first number, A. Children were asked to solve these problems and then to explain how they solved them. The time it took to solve the problems was also measured. When the answer is arrived at through computation, it takes 8 seconds or more to solve these problems. When the answer is arrived at through insight, the solution takes 4 seconds or less.

The children were timed to see how long it took them to solve the problems, and they were interviewed to find out how they solved the problems; 90% of the children discovered the unconscious shortcut before they were able to explain the shortcut verbally. That is, through the speed of their response it was clear that they were using the shortcut even though in their verbal report they said they were using computation to solve the problems. The use of the unconscious shortcut affected the time to solve the problem immediately. In other words, there was an abrupt switch from an average response time of 12 seconds to an average response time of 2.7 seconds. After 3 or 4 trials where they used the unconscious strategy, many children reported using the shortcut as a strategy for solving the problem. However, not all the children who used the shortcut were able to use it as a strategy (Siegler, 2000).

This line of research suggests that the unconscious includes resources for complex analyses and discoveries that can influence behavior even though the person cannot verbally report about them. This research demonstrates the active role of the unconscious in organizing meaningful thoughts. "Having a thought, or even an insight, is not the same as being aware of having that thought or insight" (Siegler 2000, p. 82).

The research summarized provides strong support for an unconscious component to cognition. It is no small challenge to devise experimental evidence of unconscious processes. Obviously, if one can introspect or report about these processes, they are no longer unconscious. At present, most of the experimental evidence suggests an unconscious that functions as a monitor or detector of stimuli rather than as an independent gallery of fantasies, conflicts, and wishes. However, the fact that most people experience the reality of dreams suggests that there is a greater, more complex world of unconscious activity that is likely to be uncovered as our methodological sophistication and ingenuity advance.

AN APPLICATION: PSYCHOSEXUAL THEORY AND PARENTING

Psychosexual theory, focusing as it does on the early experiences of childhood, had a strong influence on the conceptualization of parenting practices. Freud's theory addressed the experiences of young children and the
mental representations of those experiences, not the experiences of parents. Nevertheless, implications from the theory have been used to emphasize the importance of parenting not only for the child's immediate
day-to-day life, but for the impact of the parent–child relationship on subsequent personality development and adult behavior.

Psychosexual theory presented a view of the developing child as experiencing strong sexual and aggressive impulses that shifted in focus from the
oral to the anal to the genital body zone. The child's ability to manage and express these impulses was influenced by the reaction of parents, especially
parents' restrictive or permissive responses, to the child's pleasure-seeking
behaviors. Both overly harsh restriction of the expression of these impulses
and overly permissive indulgence or stimulation of these impulses were
thought to lead to fixations in a primitive mode of sexual gratification. Unconscious conflict about the gratification of these needs, resulting largely
from parental reaction, was viewed as providing a framework for adult personality. In particular, Freud pointed to parenting behaviors related to sucking on the breast, toilet training, and masturbation as highly sensitive
behaviors where conflict over the expression of sexual and aggressive impulses could become a focus for traumatic anxiety. In this context,
psychosexual theory led to two important ideas about parenting:

1. That neuroses were produced by the response of parents or significant
   others to the expression of basic sexual or aggressive drives early in
   childhood.
2. That early traumatic childhood experiences would contribute to the formation of adult personality that would be played out again in one's own
   parenting behaviors.

In addition to the role of parents in frustrating or indulging children's
drives, psychosexual theory also viewed parents as playing a key role in the
formation of the superego. During the phallic stage, a child's conflicting impulses toward his or her parents are resolved through the process of identification. As a result, the child internalizes the parent's values and moral
standards. The child's superego is shaped through interactions with parents
in which impulse expression and misbehaviors are met with acceptance or
rejection, permissiveness or control, consistency or inconsistency. Those
behaviors that parents accept and value or reject and repudiate become integrated into the child's superego. Since the superego is formed while the
child is still young, there is little opportunity for critical reflection and com-

parative assessment about the content of these moral positions. Thus, when the child grows up and enacts the parent role, it is likely that the moral imperatives of childhood, incorporated into the superego, will guide the adult's initial approaches to discipline and child guidance. Many of the early empirical studies in developmental psychology focused on issues that derived from this theory, such as child rearing and discipline practices, moral development, and childhood aggression.

There are several implications for parenting practices that emerged from this theory. First, there was a strong emphasis on the early and long-lasting impact of parenting, especially mothering, on the child's psychosexual development. In this regard, parents were urged to accept the child's sexual and aggressive behaviors as "normal" rather than dirty, sinful, or needing to be "stamped out." Parents were encouraged to avoid either overly harsh or overly permissive reactions to these behaviors. Rather, parents were advised to meet these behaviors with calm acceptance, imposing only those limits that were considered necessary for the child's social integration.

Second, parents were viewed as the primary source of values that formed the content of the superego. Children were thought to incorporate these values through observation and imitation. Thus, parents were encouraged to recognize that their children were observing their actions as well as listening to their words. Parents were advised to model positive behaviors, recognizing that children were often more impressed by the parents' actions than by their words.

Finally, parents were encouraged to support children's ego development through the use of inductions as a form of discipline. Inductions provide explanations for why the misbehavior is wrong, and point out the implications of the misbehavior for others. Inductions may also include suggestions for how the child ought to handle the situation in the future. (I know you want Robby's truck, but you can't just grab it away. Imagine how you would feel if someone grabbed your toy while you were playing with it. You can see how sad Robby feels when you grab his truck. Next time, why don't you ask Robby if you can have a turn with his truck.) The use of inductions supports the ego by giving reasons for controlling an aggressive impulse, and avoids shaming or threatening the ego, strategies which are more likely to result in a defensive reaction.

HOW DOES PSYCHOSEXUAL THEORY ANSWER THE BASIC QUESTIONS THAT A THEORY OF HUMAN DEVELOPMENT IS EXPECTED TO ADDRESS?

What is the direction of change over the life span? How well does the theory account for patterns of change and continuity? Over time, the ego becomes increasingly successful in finding socially acceptable ways to satisfy sexual and aggressive drives. The direction of change is from a primarily libidinal orientation, expressed through primary process thought and guided by the pleasure principle, to a more balanced orientation, expressed through secondary process thought and guided by the reality principle.

The direction of change is largely biologically programmed through five stages of development. However, there are important personal experiences that influence how well a person adapts at each of those stages. Continuity occurs because unconscious drives and conflicts continue to find expression in behavior. Without the benefit of psychotherapy, certain primitive conflicts will continue to require defensive control and certain unfilled wishes will continue to press for expression throughout life.

What are the mechanisms that account for growth? What are some testable hypotheses or predictions that emerge from this analysis? A certain amount of growth is expected as a result of maturation. The focus of the drives shifts from one body zone to the next. These changes occur in the context of socialization pressures to delay gratification or to redirect the aim of gratification to a more socially acceptable target. The conflict between innate drives and social constraints forces the ego to find new avenues for gratification. The ongoing tension between id and superego stimulates new ego development by forcing the ego to resolve this tension in acceptable ways. Growth can be disrupted if the id or the superego are so powerful that the ego cannot find ways of balancing them.

The theory is more explanatory than predictive. However, some predictions can be inferred. First, one would predict that over the first 5 or 6 years of childhood, one would observe a shift in the focus of pleasure seeking from the oral to the anal to the phallic body zone. Second, one would predict that severe punishment for oral, anal, or phallic activities would result in repression of these impulses. Evidence of this repression would be observed in the repetition of symbolically related behaviors in adolescence or adulthood. Third, one would predict that overindulgence of oral, anal, or phallic activities would result in the inappropriate reliance on these forms of gratification in adolescence and adulthood. Specific predictions are difficult because the object of drive satisfaction is closely linked to the environment and developmental time when the drive is seeking expression.

How relevant are early experiences for later development? What evidence does the theory offer to support its view? Early experiences are extremely relevant for later development. In fact, psychosexual theory suggests that basic patterns of personality, defensive style, and need gratification are formed by the age of 6 or 7. Theorists who continued to develop ego psychology and object relations theory suggest that basic patterns of self-organization and interpersonal relationships are established in infancy. These patterns form an orienting structure upon which subsequent experiences are based. Freud used the reports of his adult patients, including childhood memories, dream interpretation, and free association, as evidence of the importance of early childhood experiences.

How do the physical, cognitive, emotional, and social functions interact? How well does the theory explain these interactions? Psychosexual theory suggests that the physical system, particularly the maturation of sexual impulses, provides the impetus for the direction of development. Psychological development is a process of interpreting and expressing those impulses in socially acceptable ways. The theory suggests an integrated mental system in which the biologically based drives, represented by id, cognition, represented by the ego, and society, represented by the superego, seek equilibrium in the face of the need to address the demands of daily life. The emotions, especially anxiety and guilt, are central to the theory. They are adaptive mechanisms that warn the ego of potential threats and provide self-corrective feedback when impulses become too strong. Emotions can also be disruptive, especially when anxiety results in the maintenance of rigid defense mechanisms or maladaptive symptoms.

How do the environmental and social contexts affect individual development? What aspects of the environment does the theory suggest are especially important in shaping the direction of development? Psychosexual theory assumes a basic tension between the individual's desire to satisfy drives, and the society's limited tolerance for individual pleasure seeking. The theory views individuals as motivated by the pleasure principle, which, if left unchecked, would satisfy all of one's desires and disregard the needs of others. The role of the social environment is to establish guidelines in the form of laws, taboos, and moral standards that restrict the expression of drives, limit the object of drives, or restrict the age at which drives can be satisfied. The social environment may also suggest positive directions for channeling drives through valued forms of sublimation.

In psychosexual theory, the most important aspect of the social environment is one's parents. They are the primary love objects. They are also a primary source of fear through their possible retaliation for unacceptable wishes. Children's ideas about the acceptability of various forms of drive satisfaction are thought to originate from the way parents react to their child's pleasure-seeking behaviors. Through identification with parents, children incorporate the social standards and moral principles of their community. Because of the dynamics of the Oedipal or Electra complex, children continue to seek a symbolic representation of their parents as they choose an adult partner.

According to the theory, what factors place individuals at risk at specific periods of the life span? The first 6 or 7 years of life are viewed as the most critical for healthy development, with an additional period of vulnerability emerging during adolescence. A child is born with certain hereditary dispositions for strong or weak libidinal impulses in one drive area or another. The child then experiences appropriate parenting, overly harsh parenting, or overly indulgent parenting. At each stage of development, including the oral, anal, phallic, or genital stages, the combination of the child's biological predisposition, strong wishes for drive gratification, and experiences of parenting will determine whether the emerging adolescent or adult has a vulnerability to neurotic fixations and symptom formation. At some point in adult life an unusual experience, a traumatic event, or an unexpected transition or loss can become symbolically connected with this time of childhood. In some cases, the events of infancy and early childhood produce strong, unacceptable conflicts that appear to lay in waiting in the unconscious until they are brought to life through events of adulthood. In other cases, unmanageable events of adulthood result in regression to a time of childhood when libidinal impulses were more easily gratified.

CRITIQUE OF PSYCHOSEXUAL THEORY

Strengths

Psychosexual theory offers a dynamic approach to understanding mental activity. It offers a model for explaining how a number of variables interact to produce complex behaviors. The drives, the ego, parental expectations, and the superego all interact to produce mental representations and behavior. The theory provides a model of the topography of the human mind and the interaction among structures across conscious and unconscious domains. Through the concept of the unconscious and the notion of primary process thought, the theory provides a way of making sense out of seemingly irrational or maladaptive behaviors. Psychosexual theory recognizes domains of thought that may not appear to be logical to the observer. Many domains of mental activity, including fantasies, dreams, primary process thoughts and symbols, and defense mechanisms, influence the way people derive meaning from their experiences. Through analysis, the analyst develops hypotheses about the meaning of these ideas and interprets them to the patient who, over time, comes to recognize their validity.

The theory emphasizes the importance of early childhood experiences and their influence on adult behavior. While this may seem obvious today, in Freud's time, this was not the accepted view. Children were viewed by some as miniature adults, to be treated as other adults. Another view was that children were blank slates to be shaped by parental teachings. A third view was that children were born in original sin and that their behaviors had to be shaped and punished in order to bring them into a state of acceptance. Freud's theory offered a new insight into the significance of early childhood experiences that were formed by the interaction of biological drives seeking expression in the context of a specific socialization environment.

In addition to emphasizing the importance of childhood experiences, the theory identifies stages of development. This view includes an emphasis on a qualitative shift in the child's needs and the kinds of interpersonal relationships that are necessary to meet those needs. The stage approach led the way to a new scientific study of child development that, when combined with the work of Piaget, provided a more detailed analysis of the patterns of cognitive, social, emotional, and self-concept development that emerged in the early months and years of life.

The theory acknowledges the role of sexual and aggressive motives and the challenges around managing their expression in ways that are socially acceptable. In his writings, Freud emphasized the link between infantile sexual and aggressive drives and drive reduction, and adult pathologies. He provided a way of conceptualizing adult neuroses as maladaptive expressions of normal drives. Whereas the healthy person is able to find socially acceptable sublimations for drive satisfaction, the neurotic person develops symptoms. This approach helped to reduce the psychological distance between mental illness and mental health, encouraging a more normalizing approach to the treatment of mental illness. Psychosexual theory was highly influential in producing a new method of therapeutic intervention. Through techniques of free association, dream interpretation, and the analysis of transference, patients are supported in overcoming the resistance to recognizing these conflicts and identifying the origins of the conflicts. Over time, the patient gains new understanding of the nature of the defense mechanisms that have been used to keep certain conflicts out of awareness, and of the conflicts themselves. By gaining insight into the defensive process, the conflicts, and the role of the symptoms, the patient gains new ego strengths. Energy that had been used to keep conflicts out of consciousness is now available for more flexible, adaptive coping.

Psychosexual theory was influential in stimulating new theories. Theory development grew in a number of directions. Many of those mentioned earlier in this chapter extended Freud's initial work by expanding the ideas of ego development and the importance of early object relations. A second group took issue with some of Freud's original ideas and wrote their own psychodynamic theories. Among the most famous were Alfred Adler, Carl Jung, and Harry Stack Sullivan.

Adler (1964) argued that a will to power was the basic organizing drive rather than sexual and aggressive drives. His theory focused on the initial physical inferiority of children in relation to adults and lifelong efforts to compensate, creating the concept of the *inferiority complex*. Other contributions focused on the nature of sibling relationships and the dynamics of power between first born and later born children. Jung (1960) viewed personality development as a product of goals and aspirations as well as needs.

He saw the direction of development as a striving for unity and integration of the many opposing forces that comprise the self. Jung also introduced the idea that the content of the unconscious included archetypes that were part of the human *collective* unconscious as well as personal experiences.

Sullivan (1953) focused on interpersonal needs and problems in communication. When people become anxious, their communication is likely to be more closely monitored, idiosyncratic, and ineffective. Lack of effective communication increases social isolation and, as a result, increases anxiety.

Each of the theorists mentioned above suggested a new focus for therapeutic intervention. Psychosexual theory emerged out of medicine. However, it quickly expanded into the fields of psychology, education, social work, and nursing. Several of Freud's writings, especially *Moses and Monotheism* (Freud, 1939/1967) and the interpretation of a childhood memory of Leonardo DaVinci (Freud, 1919/1964), suggested expansions of psychosexual theory into psychobiography and psychohistory. Ideas about the role of unconscious sexual and aggressive drives in guiding behavior, the importance of childhood conflicts, and the interpretation of dreams found expression in literature, art, and theater. There is probably not a single textbook about child development, whether in education, psychology, social work, pediatrics, or nursing, that does not refer to Freud's psychosexual theory.

Weaknesses

The approach to motivation offered in psychosexual theory has received wide criticism. Some critics argue that the theory oversimplifies motivation by reducing all behavior to an expression of sexual or aggressive drives. Among these critics are those who suggest a different set of basic, or primary needs that highlight the social-orientation of human beings and strong needs for connection, social affiliation, and power. Others, like Henry Murray, offer a comparatively large list of needs. Still others, like Gordon Allport, suggest that the motivational structure is flexible over the life span so that what might begin as a secondary need can take on greater salience based on experience and goals. Finally, some critics, such as Robert White, take issue with the drive and drive reduction model of human motivation. This criticism suggests that human behavior is more properly understood as competency and mastery-oriented, goal-oriented, and stimulus seeking. Rather than seeking a calm state of equilibrium, human beings often strive to achieve new levels of competence by taking on new and difficult challenges.

Psychosexual theory assumes a universal, biological unfolding of the sensitivity of body zones that results in specific stages of development: the oral, anal, genital, and phallic stages. At each stage, the drive for sexual or aggressive satisfaction is organized around specific avenues for gratification. At the same time, the nature of these modes of gratification are thought to bring the child into conflict with societally imposed sanctions and prohibitions which can produce unconscious conflicts.

Several criticisms have been offered about this view of development. The extent to which these body areas and their related functions become a focus of conflict varies across cultures. The theory, developed during the Victorian era, reflects a cultural context in which such activities as breast feeding, toilet training, and masturbation were treated with great privacy. Children's behaviors in these areas were likely to be targeted with harsh discipline and shaming. However, cultural practices and beliefs about these basic activities range widely from relative openness and permissiveness to strict control. In some cultures, infants are able to nurse at the breast of any one of a number of lactating women; children learn toileting practices from older siblings; and masturbation and sex play are openly accepted as a way for children to learn about reproduction. These cultural practices suggest that the issues Freud identified as organizing developmental stages may not be as universal as he suggested.

A particular criticism about the nature of the stages of development focuses on the Oedipal/Electra model and the process of superego formation. This construction of the origins of morality is viewed as incorrect on several counts: First, it places the formation of the conscience too late in childhood. More recent theorists suggest, as we discussed earlier in the chapter, that superego formation begins in infancy as the child forms an emotional bond with a loving caregiver. Second, it overemphasizes the role of the father as a fearful, threatening figure in the formation of conscience. Much of the research on moral development in childhood suggests that the father plays a modest role, partly because fathers have traditionally not been involved in the daily socialization activities of young children. In contrast, mothers play a major role, especially in the way they combine warmth and limit setting in their disciplinary strategy. Third, the Oedipal/Electra model is especially inadequate for accounting for moral development for girls, particularly the ideas of penis envy and blaming the mother for genital mutilation. Freud concluded that, because girls are less fearful of their mothers than boys are of their fathers, they are less likely to repress their Electra fantasies and would have a less punitive superego. In contrast, most research finds that girls are more conscientious about resisting temptation and obeying rules than boys.

Another criticism is that the developmental stages do not continue into adulthood and later life. From a life span view of development, some argue that psychosexual theory places an overemphasis on the role of childhood experiences in shaping adult behavior, and fails to suggest important new directions for growth in adulthood.

The stages of development and the processes of psychological tension between id, ego, and superego are based on evidence from Freud's clinical cases. As a result, much of what was inferred about normal development was drawn from observations and treatment of adults who had probably experienced childhood trauma. Freud did not develop a theory based on the longitudinal observation of individuals over the course of their lives from infancy through adulthood. Thus, the logic of the theory is retrospective. If an adult experiences a certain symptom, the meaning of that symptom can be traced to a particular phase of childhood when libidinal drives were in conflict or were unusually well gratified.

The theory offers explanations rather than predictions. In most of the cases, the analysis starts with the presenting symptoms and strives to find the explanations for these symptoms. The theory does not predict what the symptom will be. There is too much ambiguity in the path from a given conflict to specific symptoms, so it is not possible to test behavioral outcomes based on a known conflict. In the case of Little Hans, for example, Hans had a fear of horses and because of this he grew afraid to go outside. Freud eventually traced this fear to Hans's fear of his father and the related Oedipal conflict. However, Little Hans might just as well have developed a fear of a machine, or another kind of animal, or a fear of loud noises. The theory does not provide a way to predict which symptom might arise from particular early conflicts.

The theory is difficult to test empirically. Freud and many of his followers even argued that the theory could not be studied outside the context of psychoanalysis. For example, there are no guidelines for assessing restrictiveness or permissiveness in parenting and the conditions under which either of these two approaches will result in fixation. Freud was prolific in providing analytic interpretations for symptoms and for suggesting the possible path of a neuroses from childhood to the present. He did not provide any systematic strategies for assessing the strength of unconscious drives, the disruptive impact of childhood events, or the capacity of a person to benefit from psychotherapy.

KEY TERMS

preconscious

conscious

unconscious

id

ego

superego

primary process thought

secondary process thought

reality testing

stages of development: oral, anal, phallic, genital

Oedipal complex/Electra complex

defense mechanisms

identification

transference

ego psychology

object relations theory

Chapter 4

Cognitive Developmental Theory

CHAPTER OUTLINE

Historical Context

Key Concepts

    Schemes

    Organization

    Adaptation

    Stages of Development

    Egocentrism

    Innovative Research Methods

New Directions

    Moral Reasoning

    Social Cognition

    Theory of Mind

    Cognition in Adulthood

A Research Example: Metacognition

An Application: The Development of Logico-Mathematical Knowledge

How Does Cognitive Developmental Theory Answer the Basic Questions that a Theory of Human Development Is Expected to Address?

Critique of Cognitive Developmental Theory

    Strengths

    Weaknesses

Key Terms

Chapter 4

Cognitive Developmental Theory

Cognition is the process of organizing and making meaning of experience. Interpreting a statement, solving a problem, synthesizing information, critically analyzing a complex task—all are cognitive activities. The modern approach to understanding cognitive development has been stimulated by the work of Jean Piaget. Piaget was trained as a biologist. He thought of the cognitive system as a biological system whose purpose, like other biological systems such as locomotion, respiration, or digestion, was to permit the organism to adapt and survive.

According to Piaget, every organism strives to achieve equilibrium. Equilibrium is a balance of organized structures, including motor, sensory, and cognitive. When these structures are in equilibrium, they provide effective ways of interacting with the environment. Whenever changes in the organism or in the environment require a revision of the basic structures, they are thrown into disequilibrium (Piaget, 1975/1985). Piaget discussed two types of equilibrium: First, equilibrium with the environment, which is achieved through the formation of schemes and operations that form systematic, logical structures for comprehending and analyzing experience; and second, equilibrium within the schemes and operations themselves.

In this theory, *knowing* is an active process of achieving and reachieving equilibrium, not a constant state (Miller, 2002). Knowing is a product of continuous interaction between the person and the environment. We approach new situations with expectations that have developed in the past. Each new experience changes those expectations somewhat. Our ability to understand and interpret experience is constantly changing because we encounter diversity and novelty in the environment that create disequilibrium and put pressure on the mind to return to equilibrium by trying to understand the experience.

HISTORICAL CONTEXT

Jean Piaget was born in Switzerland in 1896. Much like Darwin, he showed talent as a naturalist early in childhood. He observed and studied birds, fossils, and seashells, and at the age of 10 made a contribution about the albino sparrow to a scientific journal. While in high school he began to publish papers describing the characteristics of mollusks. His work in this area was so impressive that he was invited to become the curator of the mollusk collection at the Geneva Museum. He earned his doctorate from the University of Neuchatel in 1918; his dissertation was on the mollusks of Vallais.

The most direct consequence of Piaget's training as a naturalist for the study of cognitive development was his sense that the principles of biology could be used to explain the evolution of knowledge. The observational skills he acquired would serve him well as he developed his theory. Between 1918 and 1921, he worked in the laboratory of Theodore Lipps, whose research focused on the study of empathy and aesthetics. He spent some time working at Eugen Bleuler's psychiatric clinic near Zurich, where he learned the techniques of psychiatric interviewing. He went to the Sorbonne in Paris, where he had the opportunity to work in the laboratory of Alfred Binet. Binet's laboratory was actually an elementary school in which studies on the nature of intelligence were being conducted. Here, Piaget investigated children's responses to reasoning tests. He devised an interview technique to determine how children arrived at their answers to reasoning problems. He became interested in the patterns of thought revealed by incorrect answers. In essence, Piaget focused on how children think rather than on how much they know.

Piaget's observations and interviews provided the basis for his first articles on the characteristics of children's thought processes. One of these articles brought him to the attention of the editor of *Psychological Archives*, who offered him the job of director of studies at the Institut Jean-Jacques Rousseau in Geneva. There, Piaget began to investigate children's moral judgments, theories about everyday events, and language. In the period from 1923 to 1929, Piaget conducted experiments and systematic observations with preverbal infants. In that work, he began to unravel the basic mysteries of the growth of logical thought. This work was significantly enriched by observations of his own children.

While Piaget was working in Europe during the 1920s and '30s, his work was largely unknown in the United States. It was not until the 1960s with John Flavell's publication, *The Developmental Psychology of Jean Piaget*, that Piaget's theory became accessible to the English-speaking academic community in the United States. By that time, learning theory and behaviorism were the dominant forces in American psychology (see ch. 5) and shaped the way psychologists and educators thought about how children learn. This perspective focused on conditions under which stimuli and responses became associated with each other, and the ways that behavioral responses were altered depending on the consequences of those responses. Questions about how children come to know or understand what they know were largely ignored. The notion of intelligence was approached as a construct that could be understood primarily through the administration of standardized tests, based on the response of individuals to questions and tasks requiring verbal and mathematical reasoning. Little attention was paid to how children arrived at the answers to these questions; rather the focus was on comparing individuals' scores to norms that had been established through large-size samples. Against this context, Piaget's work revolutionized the way scholars and eventually educators thought about the development of knowing.

Piaget produced a massive quantity of research and theory about cognitive development, logic, the history of thought, education, and the theory of knowledge (epistemology). In 1969, the American Psychological Association gave Piaget the Distinguished Scientific Contribution Award for the work that had revolutionized our understanding of the nature of human knowledge and the development of intelligence. In 1970, a group of international, interdisciplinary scholars established the Jean Piaget Society (www.piaget.org) to stimulate and advance the study of the developmental construction of human knowledge. Piaget continued his work on the nature of children's cognitive development until his death in 1980, at the age of 83.

KEY CONCEPTS

Piaget assumed that the roots of cognition lie in the person's biological capacities. He hypothesized that logical thought unfolds in a series of biologically guided stages that emerge in a fixed sequence as the person engages and explores the environment. Five concepts form the basis of Piaget's theory: schemes, organization, adaptation, stages of development, and egocentrism.

Schemes

Piaget and Inhelder (1969) defined *scheme* as "the structure or organization of actions as they are transferred or generalized by repetition in similar or analogous circumstances" (p. 4). A scheme is any organized, meaningful grouping of interrelated actions, images, feelings, or ideas that determine how a person interacts with the environment. Piaget preferred the term *scheme* rather than *concept* because it can be used to describe interrelated groups of actions as well as ideas. He used the word to discuss the sensorimotor counterpart of concepts and conceptual networks during the period of infancy before language and other symbolic systems are developed.

Schemes begin to be formed during infancy through the repetition of regular sequences of action. Two kinds of schemes emerge in infancy. The first guides a particular action, such as grasping a rattle or sucking on a bottle. These generalize to patterns of actions for grasping and sucking a wide range of things in the environment. The second type of scheme links sequences of actions, such as climbing into the high chair in order to eat breakfast or crawling to the door to greet Daddy when he comes home (Uzgiris, 1976). Infants are able to distinguish between people who are familiar and those who are unfamiliar. They differentiate between playful sounds, such as cooing and babbling, and sounds that will bring a caregiver, such as crying and screeching. They recognize foods they will eat readily and those they reject. These groupings suggest that schemes are developed by mental coordination processes that evolve over time through repeated actions with specific aspects of the environment. Schemes are created, modified, and organized continuously throughout the life span.

Organization

Piaget argued that all living organisms organize their various structures into a coordinated, integrated system. This is true at the physical and the psychological levels. The capacity for organization is an innate feature of living creatures. At the biological level, the respiratory, circulatory, and digestive systems are organized and integrated in order to sustain survival. At the psychological level, a person organizes visual, auditory, proprioceptive, and motor systems in order to move toward a goal. In early infancy, a child can see an object and grasp an object. They are two separate activities. After some time, the infant organizes these two systems in order to carry out visually guided reaching and grasping. The tendency toward organization operates at the cognitive as well as the behavioral level. The idea of developing a category of objects, such as fruits or animals or family members, is an example of cognitive organization. A person identifies features that a variety of objects have in common, including perceptual features such as shape, smell, color, or functions that the objects can serve such as something to sit on or something to eat. Cognitive organization serves an adaptive function by reducing the amount of information that is needed to respond to individual stimuli.

Adaptation

Piaget (1936/1952) viewed cognition as a continuously evolving process in which the content and diversity of experiences stimulate the formation of new schemes. People are constantly striving to attain equilibrium both with the environment and in the cognitive components of their mental structures. According to Piaget, knowledge is the result of adaptation, or the gradual modification of existing schemes to take into account the novelty or uniqueness of each experience. You can see the similarity between this use of the term adaptation and its use in evolutionary theory. Piaget extended the concept of adaptation, suggesting that it works to produce modifications in the capacity for logical thought. "It is by adapting to things that thought organizes itself," he says, "and it is by organizing itself that it structures things" (1936/1952, pp. 7–8).

Adaptation is a two-part process in which the continuity of existing schemes and the possibility of altering schemes interact. One part of the adaptation process is assimilation—the tendency to interpret new experiences in terms of an existing scheme. Assimilation contributes to the continuity of knowing. For example, Karen thinks that anyone who goes to the private high school in her city is a snob. When she meets Gail, who attends the private school, she expects Gail to be a snob. After talking with Gail for 5 minutes, she concludes that Gail really is a snob. Here we see assimilation: Karen interprets her interactions with Gail in light of an existing scheme about the kinds of students who attend the private school.

The second part of the adaptation process is accommodation—the tendency to modify familiar schemes in order to account for new dimensions of the object or event that are revealed. For example, if Karen and Gail were to spend a little more time together, Karen might discover that Gail is not rich and is attending the private high school on a scholarship. She and Karen actually have a lot of common interests. Gail is quite friendly and wants to see Karen again. Karen decides that not everyone who goes to the private school is a snob. She realizes that she has to postpone judgment about people until she gets to know them a little better. Here we see accommodation: Karen is modifying her scheme about the students who attend the private school in order to integrate the new information she is receiving.

Throughout life we gain knowledge gradually through the related processes of assimilation and accommodation. In order to have a new idea, we must be able to relate a new experience, thought, or event to some already existing scheme. Also, we must be able to modify our schemes in order to differentiate the novel from the familiar. At first, we ask if the element of the environment can be understood by using existing schema to interpret it. We may even distort reality to make it fit existing schema. When current schema are inadequate to account for the new experiences, successful adaptation requires that we adjust them to take into account the demands of reality. According to Piaget, cognitive development proceeds within each stage through this back and forth process—comparing new experiences to what is already known, making modifications in what is known to take into account new information, and then using the revised schema to guide subsequent encounters with the environment. Moderately discrepant experiences can be accommodated, but if discrepancies are too different from one's current level of understanding, cognitive adaptation is not likely to occur.

Stages of Development

Piaget's theory included a description of stages of cognitive development. He was working to describe a fundamental pattern of cognitive maturation, a universal path along which the human capacity for logical reasoning unfolds. Piaget spoke of a stage as a "structure of the whole," that is a structure with a unitary character (Piaget, 1955). The stages he described encompassed abstract processes that could be applied to many content areas and that could be observed at roughly the same chronological age periods across cultures. His theory focused on the epigenesis of logical thought—the development of new structures for thought—not on explanations for individual differences in knowledge and reasoning or on differences that might result from cultural and subcultural experiences. The stages emerge through times of disequilibrium and efforts to achieve new levels of equilibrium through the construction of new mental structures and new strategies for gaining and evaluating information. Development involves periods of preparation or formation followed by periods of completion or equilibrium that bring a qualitatively distinctive organization to thought and problem solving (Piaget, 1955).

Most summaries of Piaget's theory highlight four stages of cognitive development: sensorimotor intelligence, preoperational thought, concrete operational thought, and formal operational thought. At each new stage, the competences of the earlier stages are not lost but are integrated into a qualitatively new approach to thinking and knowing.

Sensorimotor Intelligence

The first stage, sensorimotor intelligence, begins at birth and lasts until approximately 18 months of age. This stage is characterized by the formation of increasingly complex sensory and motor schemes such as reaching and grasping, following an object through its path of movement, and means-end relationships like kicking the cribside in order to get a mobile to wiggle. Sensorimotor schemes allow infants to organize and exercise some control over their environment.

What is Sensorimotor Intelligence?   Think for a moment of a familiar experience, such as tying your shoelaces. The pattern of tying the shoelace unfolds with little, if any, language involved. In fact, the task of explaining to a young child how to tie a shoelace is particularly difficult because very few words or concepts are part of the process. This kind of motor routine is an example of sensorimotor intelligence. When infants begin to adapt their sucking reflex to make it more effective, or when they use different techniques of sucking for the breast and the bottle, they are demonstrating sensorimotor intelligence.

How Do Infants Organize Their Experiences?   According to Piaget's (1970) theory, the chief mechanism governing the growth of intelligence during infancy is sensorimotor adaptation. From the very earliest days of life, infants use their reflexes to explore their world. At the same time, they gradually alter their reflexes to take into account the unique properties of objects around them. Infants do not make use of the conventional symbolic systems of language and mental representation to organize experience. Rather, they form concepts through perception and direct investigation of the environment. Sensorimotor intelligence develops as a result of the elaboration and repetition of patterns of movement and sensory experiences that the child comes to recognize in association with specific environmental events. With each new challenge, a process of adaptation results in the revision of basic schemes to better predict and interpret experience (Gopnick & Meltzoff, 1997). One of the most important components of sensorimotor intelligence is the capacity to anticipate that certain actions will have specific effects on objects in the environment. Infants develop an understanding of causality based largely on sensory and motor experience. Babies discover that if they cry, Mama will come to them; if they kick a chair, it will move; and if they let go of a spoon, it will fall to the floor. These predictable sequences are learned through repetition and experimentation. The predictability of the events depends on the child's initiation of the action and on the consistency with which objects in the world respond. Babies learn to associate specific actions with regularly occurring outcomes. They also experiment with their own actions to determine the variety of events that a single behavior may cause. Eventually they are able to work backward: They can select a desirable outcome and then perform the behavior that will produce it.

The Development of Causal Schemes. The achievement of complex, purposeful causal behavior develops gradually during the first 2 years of life. This achievement requires that infants have an understanding of the properties of objects in their environment and a variety of strategies for manipulating those objects. They must be able to select the most effective strategies for coordinating actions to achieve specific goals.

Piaget and Inhelder (1966/1969) described six stages in the development of causal schemes. Subsequent research and related theoretical revisions confirm these levels of cognitive development (Fischer & Silvern, 1985).

Stage 1: Reflexes. In stage one (approximately birth to 1 month), reflexes, cause and effect are linked through involuntary reflexive responses. The built-in stimulus-response systems of key reflexes are viewed as the genetic origin of intelligence. Babies suck, grasp, and root in response to specific types of stimulation. Piaget viewed the reflexes as adaptive learning systems. In detailed observations of his youngest child, Laurent, he noted daily changes in sucking behavior during the 1st month of life. Laurent became increasingly directed in groping for the breast, forming early associations between those situations in which he would be fed and those in which he would not (Gratch & Schatz, 1987; Piaget, 1936/1952). The reflexes are exercised, both in response to the evoking stimulus and as a part of generalized activity. For example, a newborn begins sucking when the breast is inserted in his or her mouth, but may lose contact and stop sucking. After a few days, the baby finds the nipple more easily, begins sucking more vigorously and can return to the nipple if it slips away. After a few weeks, it is not unusual to see an infant sucking even when there is no bottle or nipple, but purely to exercise this activity pattern.

Stage 2: First Habits. In the second stage, first habits, sometimes called primary circular reactions, the reflexive responses are used to explore a wider range of stimuli (approximately 1 to 4 months). Often by chance, babies find their thumb or fingers near their mouth and begin to suck on them. Over time, they may try to find their hand with their mouth or stuff their whole fist in their mouth. Gradually, they are able to coordinate the movement of their hand or thumb to their mouth and stop or start sucking voluntarily. First habits, or primary circular reactions, typically involve actions restricted to the baby's own body like repeating vocalizations, sucking on fingers or toes, or deliberate kicking. The fact that babies can satisfy their own desires by starting or stopping a motor behavior is a very early form of purposive causal behavior.

Stage 3: Secondary Circular Ractions. The third and fourth stages involve coordination of means and ends, first with familiar situations and then with new ones. In the third stage, secondary circular reactions, babies connect an action with an expected outcome (approximately 4 to 10 months). They shake a rattle and expect to hear a noise; they drop a spoon and expect to hear a noise when it hits the floor; they pull Daddy's beard and expect to hear an "ouch." They do not understand why a specific action leads to the expected outcome, but they show surprise when the expected outcome does not follow (Wentworth & Haith, 1992).

Stage 4: Coordination of Means and Ends. The fourth stage, coordination of means and ends (10 to 12 months), marks the beginning of what we might recognize as true problem solving. Infants use familiar actions or means to achieve new outcomes. They may push away your hand to avoid a spoon of vegetables, shake a rattle to startle Mommy, or reach out their arms to be picked up. Rather than repeating the same action sequence over and over as in the third stage, the action is goal-oriented and the baby has to draw upon some existing scheme to reach the goal. There can be no question about the purposiveness of behavior at this point.

At this stage, coordination of means and ends are closely tied to a specific context. For example, a baby may know how to make certain kicking motions to move a mobile or to get a toy to jiggle in the crib. But, in another room with the same toy, the baby may not make the same connection. This may explain why babies might perform less competently in the laboratory environment than they do at home. Many causal strategies that become part of a baby's daily repertoire are supported by the context of a familiar environment (Rovee-Collier et al., 1992).

Stage 5: Experimentation With New Mcans The fifth stage, experimentation with new means, sometimes called tertiary circular reactions, brings a new inventiveness to intelligence. Around the ages of 12 to 18 months, children begin to experiment with means to achieve new goals. When familiar strategies do not work, children will modify them in light of the situation. At this stage, infants are interested in the features of objects and in discrepancies from the familiar. They may experiment to see which of their toys they can push out through the bars of their crib or which blocks they can fit into their dump truck. One can think of this stage as sensorimotor problem solving.

Stage 6: Invention of New Means Through Insight. The sixth stage, invention of new means through insight, is the last stage in the development of sensorimotor causality, from about 18 months to 2 years. It involves mental manipulation of means-end relationships. Instead of actually going through a variety of physical manipulations, children carry out trial-and-error problem-solving activities and planning in their minds, anticipating outcomes. They can sort out possible solutions and reject some without actually having to try them out. The result is insight. Mental experimentation brings the child to the best solution, which is the only one necessary to enact.

The capacity to perceive one's self as a causal agent and to predict the outcome of one's actions is essential to all subsequent experiences of mastery. This capacity is the cornerstone of the development of a sense of competence. It involves investigation of the environment, directed problem solving, and persistence toward a goal (Yarrow et al., 1983; MacTurk, McCarthy, Vietze, & Yarrow, 1987). Adults' abilities to formulate a plan, execute it, and evaluate its outcome depend on this skill.

Understanding the Nature of Objects.   Babies are active explorers of their environment. From birth they try to make direct sensory contact with objects. They reach for, grasp, and mouth objects. They track objects visually, altering their gaze to maintain contact with them. Although not all manipulative behavior is exploratory, certain combinations of mouthing, looking, and manipulating objects have been categorized as a type of examining behavior that provides infants as young as 5 months of age with a scheme for gathering information about novel objects (Ruff, Saltarelli, Capozzoli, & Dubiner, 1992). As products of this active engagement with the object world, infants gradually develop a scheme for object permanence.

Through looking, manipulating, and examining, infants establish that objects have basic properties. Very young babies recognize the contours of objects and by 4 months they seem to perceive objects just as adults would. That is, babies see objects as separate from each other, defined by boundaries, taking up space, having depth, and having certain attributes of weight, color, malleability, texture, and the capacity to contain something else or not. All of these properties influence the types of actions infants use to explore objects and the ways these actions are eventually woven into other actions (Palmer, 1989; Spelke, von Hofsten, & Kestenbaum, 1989).

Object Permanence.   Piaget (1954a) argued that understanding the properties of objects was one of the foundations of logical thought. One of the most carefully documented of these properties is object permanence, the scheme that objects in the environment are permanent and do not cease to exist when they are out of reach or out of view (Wellman, Cross, & Bartsch, 1986). A permanent object retains its physical properties even when it cannot be seen.

To understand how object permanence develops, one might remove a rattle from a baby's grasp and hide it under a cushion. If the baby makes no effort to pursue the rattle, we can assume that he or she has no sense of its continued existence. However, if the baby pursues the rattle and looks for it under the cushion, we take our experiment one step further. Again, we take the rattle from the baby and place it under the cushion. Then we remove it from beneath that cushion and place it under a second one. This transition from the first cushion to the second cushion takes place in the child's full view. The normal adult would go directly to the second cushion to retrieve the rattle. The child who has developed a sense of object permanence will also do this. Children who are still developing the scheme for the permanent object will look for the rattle beneath the first cushion and, not finding it, cease their search. Slightly older children will trace the movement of the rattle exactly by looking first under the first cushion and then under the second cushion. The last two groups of children have learned some of the steps in pursuing an object but have not yet attained the scheme of object permanence.

Research on the process of developing object permanence finds that babies as young as 9 months can understand that an object has been moved from one location to another. If they are permitted to search for an object immediately after it is hidden, they are effective in finding it. However, if the babies have to wait for 5 or 10 seconds before they can search, or if the object has been moved from one container to another similar container, they may become confused. By the age of about 17 months, infants can solve complex object permanence tasks in which objects are moved from one hiding place to the next in such a way that the infant cannot follow the path of the object (Harris, 1975; Bertenthal & Fischer, 1983; Sophian & Yengo, 1985; Gopnik & Meltzoff, 1997). However, even 2-year-olds can get confused if the object is displaced more than two or three times.

Certain experiences help build the scheme for object permanence. Babies who are adept at crawling or who have mobility through the use of an infant walker seem to be more effective in their search strategies when objects are hidden from view (Benson & Uzgiris, 1985; Kermoian & Campos, 1988). As babies gain greater control over their movement through the environment, they are better able to use landmarks other than their own body to locate objects. They can also experiment with the notion of leaving and retrieving objects, and discovering familiar objects in novel locations.

As the sensorimotor stage comes to a close, infants have the cognitive resources to expect stability and permanence of objects. The next stage of cognitive development adds new flexibility to mental operations as children acquire the capacity to represent objects and actions through symbols and signs.

Preoperational Thought

The second stage of cognitive development, preoperational thought, begins in toddlerhood, when a child begins to represent actions with mental images and ends about age 5 or 6 with the beginning of concrete operational thought. During this stage, children develop the tools for representing schemes symbolically through language, imitation, imagery, symbolic play, and symbolic drawing. Their knowledge is still very much tied to their own perceptions but they are increasingly able to manipulate objects and actions mentally.

The stage of preoperational thought is a transitional period during which the schemes that were developed during infancy are represented internally. The most significant achievement of this new stage of cognitive development is the capacity for semiotic or representational thinking—understanding that one thing can stand for another (Miller, 2002). In semiotic thinking, children learn to recognize and use symbols and signs. Symbols are usually related in some way to the object for which they stand. The cross, for example, is a symbol of Christianity. Signs stand for things in a more abstract, arbitrary way. Words are signs; there is no direct relation between the word *dog* and the animal to which the word refers, yet the word stands for the object. For adults, it seems natural to use match sticks or little squares of cardboard to represent people or buildings, but for children, the idea that a stick may be a car or a horse calls for a dramatic change in thinking that emerges gradually during the preoperational period.

Symbolization brings enormous flexibility to human thought. A symbol embodies an idea of something separate from the thing itself as the cross represents a story of martyrdom, a belief system, and a group of people who share this belief system. Before the period of preoperational thought, children do not really pretend because they cannot let one thing stand for something else. Once the capacity for symbolic thought emerges, children become increasingly flexible in allowing an object to take on a wide variety of pretend identities. With the elaboration of various types of symbols, children can begin to recount events apart from the situation in which they occurred. They can invent worlds that never existed.

In the development of preoperational thought, children acquire five representational skills that support the mental manipulation of objects rather than relying solely on direct behavior: imitation in the absence of the model, mental images, symbolic drawing, symbolic play, and language. Representational skills allow children to share their experiences with others and to create imagined experiences. These skills also free children from communicating only through gestures and open up opportunities to communicate about the past or the future, as well as the present (Nelson, 1999). Children can express relationships they may have observed in the past by imitating them, drawing them, talking about them, or acting them out in fantasy. They can portray events and relationships that they wish would occur or that they wish to alter. They can also experiment with solutions mentally, forming and altering strategies in their thoughts.

Concrete Operational Thought

The third stage, concrete operational thought, begins about age 6 or 7 and ends in early adolescence, around age 11 or 12. During this stage, children begin to appreciate the logical necessity of certain causal relationships. They can manipulate categories, classification systems, and hierarchies in groups. They are more successful at solving problems that are clearly tied to physical reality than at generating hypotheses about purely philosophical or abstract concepts.

The word *operation* refers to an action that is performed on an object or a set of objects. A mental operation is a transformation that is carried out in thought rather than in action. Piaget argued that such transformations are built on some physical relationship that the younger child can perform but cannot articulate. For example, a toddler can arrange a graduated set of circles on a stick so that the largest circle is at the bottom of the stick and the smallest circle is at the top. The child does not have a verbal label for the ordering operation but can perform it. With the emergence of concrete operations, children begin to consider a variety of actions that can be performed on objects and can do so mentally without having to do them physically. Thus, a mental operation is an internal representation of an alteration in the relationships among objects.

Piaget (1972) used the term concrete to contrast this quality of thinking to the more hypothetical reasoning of adolescents and adults. The child reasons about objects and relations among them but has difficulty entertaining hypothetical statements or propositions. Thinking is typically focused on relationships among adjoining or related terms rather than among any two or more terms. For example, children can reason about problems involving grouping trees into different categories and identifying the features of these categories. It would be much more difficult, however, for them to identify variables that relate trees to other life forms such as bacteria, insects, and mammals.

During the stage of concrete operations, the two operational structures that have received the most attention are: (a) conservation and (b) classification. Over the period of middle childhood, children apply these skills to achieve a clearer understanding of the logic, order, and predictability of the physical world. As children take a new approach to problem solving through the use of the logical principles associated with concrete operational thought, they generalize these principles to their thinking about friendships, team play and other games with rules, and their own self-evaluation.

As the order of the physical world becomes more apparent, children begin to seek logic and order in the social and personal domains as well. Sometimes, this search for order is frustrated by the unpredictability of the social world. At other times, children use their enhanced capacities for reasoning to solve interpersonal problems and to arrange their daily life so that it better meets their interests and needs. A hallmark of this period is an increase in logical, focused problem solving. Children are able to consider two competing explanations, look at a problem from another person's point of view as well as their own, and, using this information, plan a strategy to reach a goal.

Conservation. The basic meaning of conservation is that physical matter does not magically appear or disappear despite changes in form or container. The concept of conservation can be applied to a variety of dimensions, including mass, weight, number, length, and volume. A child who conserves is able to resist perceptual cues that alter the form of an object, insisting that the quantity remains the same despite the change in form. One of the most common problems of this type that Piaget investigated involves conservation of mass. The child is presented with two clay balls and asked to tell whether or not they are equal. Once the child is satisfied that the balls are equal, one of them is flattened out into a pancake. The child is then asked, "Which has more—this one [the pancake] or this one [the ball]?" Sometimes, the child is also asked whether the clay pieces are still the same. The child who does not conserve might say the pancake has more clay because it is a lot wider than the ball. This child is still in the preoperational stage of thought. He or she is using personal perceptions to make judgments. In contrast, the child who conserves knows that the two pieces of clay are still identical in mass and can explain why.

Conservation of number is achieved around age 6 or 7 (Halford & Boyle, 1985). Once they have acquired the scheme for conservation of number, children understand that certain physical transformations will not alter the number of units in a set. If 10 poker chips are lined up in a row, the number remains constant whether they are spread out, squeezed tightly together, or stacked. Children can use counting to answer a "how many" question some time between the ages of 3 and 4. For example, they can assign one number to each item in a set of four poker chips and tell you that there are four chips in all. However, young children have more difficulty selecting a set of six chips from a larger pile, or establishing that two sets of chips are equal in number. They also have trouble solving verbal story problems when no concrete objects are present (Jordan, Huttenlocher, & Levine, 1992; Sophian, 1988).

Addition, subtraction, multiplication, and division are all learned at this stage. Children learn to apply the same operations no matter what specific objects or quantities are involved. In a longitudinal study of cognitive development, children who were especially competent in number manipulation tasks during the period of concrete operational thought were more likely to achieve formal operational reasoning as young adolescents (Bradmetz, 1999). Piaget claimed that it is no coincidence that schools begin to instruct children in the basic skills of arithmetic at age 6. It is probably a strength of our schools that they meet an important aspect of intellectual readiness at the appropriate time.

Children eventually use the three concepts illustrated in Figure 4.1 to ascertain that equality in any physical dimension has not been altered. First, the child may explain that the pancake has the same amount of clay as the ball; no clay has been added or taken away. This is an example of the concept of identity: The pancake is still the *same* clay, and nothing has been changed except its shape. Second, the child may point out that the experimenter can turn the pancake back into a ball. This is an example of the concept of reversibility. The child becomes aware that operations can be reversed, so that their effects are nullified. Third, the child may notice that, although the pancake has a larger circumference, the ball is much thicker. When the child can simultaneously manipulate two dimensions, such as circumference and thickness, we observe the concept of reciprocity. In the clay ball example, change in one dimension is compensated for by change in another; the total mass remains the same. With consolidation of the concepts of identity, reversibility, and reciprocity, the child is able to conserve in any physical di-

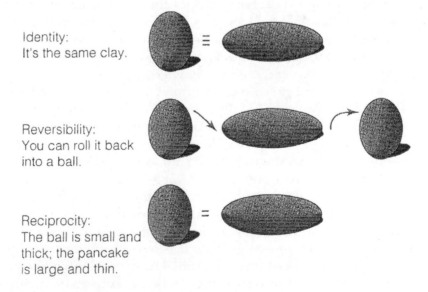

Identity:
It's the same clay.

Reversibility:
You can roll it back
into a ball.

Reciprocity:
The ball is small and
thick; the pancake
is large and thin.

Figure 4.1.   Three concepts that support the scheme for conservation. From *Development Through Life (ISE), A Psychosocial Approach 9th edition* by Newman & Newman, 2006. Reprinted with permission of Wadsworth, a division of Thomson Learning: www.thomsonrights.com

mension. There appears to be a developmental sequence in the capacity to conserve. Children generally conserve mass and number earliest, weight later, and volume last.

Classification Skills. Classification is the ability to identify properties of categories, to relate categories or classes to one another, and to use categorical information to solve problems. An adaptive benefit of categorization is that one can assume that whatever holds true for one member of a category is likely to hold true for other members as well. For example, if water and juice are both liquids, then if you can pour water, you can pour juice. Other substances classified as liquids should also have this property, even substances one has never seen. From the ages 6 to 12, children's knowledge of categories and of the information associated with them expands dramatically. What is more, children have a broad range of categories available into which to incorporate a novel observation. The value of classification skills is not purely to organize objects or experiences into classes, but to take advantage of what is known about these categories to make inferences about the characteristics and dynamics of members of the same categories, members of hierarchically related categories, and objects that are not members of a specific category (Kalish & Gelman, 1992; Lopez, Gelman, Gutheil, & Smith, 1992; Farrar, Raney, & Boyer, 1992).

One component of classification skills is the ability to group objects according to some dimension that they share. The other component is the ability to order subgroups hierarchically so that each new grouping will include all previous subgroups. Vygotsky (1932/1962) suggested a method for studying classification in young children. Children are presented with a variety of wooden blocks that differ in shape, size, and color. Under each block is a nonsense syllable. The children are instructed to select, one at a time, all the blocks that have the same syllable. The youngest children, who would be characterized as preoperational in Piaget's stage theory, tend to select blocks by their color. Their technique for grouping is highly associative. They choose each new block to match some characteristic of the previous selection, but they do not hold in mind a single concept that guides their choices.

Children who have entered the stage of concrete operations tend to focus on one dimension at first, perhaps shape, and continue to select blocks until they discover that they have made an incorrect choice. They use this discovery to change their hypothesis about which characteristics of the blocks are associated with the nonsense syllable. This classification task demonstrates the child's ability to hold a concept in mind and to make a series of decisions based on it. It also demonstrates that during the stage of concrete operations, children can use information from their mistakes to revise their problem-solving strategy.

Piaget studied reasoning about class hierarchies or inclusion by asking questions about whether a group of objects included more members of one subtype than of the group as a whole (Piaget, 1941/1952; Chapman & McBride, 1992). Thus, when a set of pictures shows three ducks, six sparrows, and two robins, one might ask, "Are there more sparrows or more birds in these pictures?" This is an unusual kind of question, one that children are probably rarely asked. By the age of 8 or 9, however, many children can respond correctly because they recognize the distinction between classes and subclasses. In order to handle such problems, children have to inhibit their tendency to reinterpret the question in line with a more common comparison, such as, "Are there more sparrows than ducks?"

In one study of class inclusion reasoning, an intriguing pattern was found. Children aged 3 and 4, who could not repeat the question and who clearly had not learned any rules about classes, were more likely to answer correctly than children of ages 5 and 6. Children aged 7 and 8 performed better than any of the younger children. The 5- and 6-year-olds, who answered quickly and confidently, were consistently incorrect. They seemed unable to inhibit the more obvious comparison in order to consider the actual question (McCabe, Siegel, Spence, & Wilkinson, 1982).

The stage of early school age, about age 5 or 6, marks the beginnings of concrete operational thought. At this age, children's performance on tests of cognitive maturity is inconsistent. For example, children can conserve quantity but may make errors in conservation of weight, volume, or space. They may be able to perform a classification task correctly when they sort by one dimension, such as color, but may make errors when asked to sort objects that have more than one dimension in common. The process of classifying objects and the logic of conservation are not fully integrated until sometime during middle childhood and may not reach peak performance until adolescence or adulthood (Flavell, 1982a).

As concrete operational intelligence develops, the child gains insight into the regularities of the physical world and the principles that govern relationships among objects. Perceptions of reality become less convincing than a logical understanding of how the world is organized. For example, even though it looks as if the sun sinks into the water, we know that what we see is a result of the earth's rotation on its axis.

Formal Operational Thought

At the earliest stage of development, children depend on their senses and motor skills to "know" the world. Each subsequent stage frees them somewhat from their dependence on sensation. Through repeated interactions with the environment, children and adolescents discover logical bases for organizing and interpreting experience. They develop language as a means of communicating and testing their interpretations (Chomsky, 1972; Lorenz,

1935/1981). By adolescence, they are capable of explaining some phenomena through a series of logical hypotheses, whether or not they have observed the phenomena or performed the actions of any of the hypotheses. Their thought processes become increasingly effective at analyzing experience.

As the body undergoes significant changes during puberty, so too does mental activity. Early adolescents begin to think about the world in new ways, as thoughts become more abstract. Young people are able to think about several dimensions at once rather than focusing on just one domain or issue at a time. Thinking becomes more reflective, and adolescents are increasingly aware of their own thoughts as well as the accuracy or inaccuracy of their knowledge. Adolescents are able to generate hypotheses about events that they have never perceived (Keating, 1990). These complex cognitive capacities have been described by Jean Piaget as formal operations (Inhelder & Piaget, 1958; Piaget, 1970, 1972; Chapman, 1988).

Piaget proposed a qualitative shift in thinking during adolescence from concrete to formal operational thought. In the period of concrete operational thought, children use mental operations to explain changes in tangible objects and events. In the period of formal operational thought, young people use operations to manipulate and modify thoughts and other mental operations (Piaget, 1972). A central feature of formal operational reasoning is the ability to separate and distinguish between reality and possibility. For example, in thinking about trying to get a part-time job, adolescents may consider the number of hours they want to work, their access to transportation, the kind of work they want to do, and the kind of work they think they are qualified for before they start filling out applications. They are able to create different scenarios about working, based partly on what they want and partly on what they know, and then modify their plan based on new information they get about available jobs.

An important characteristic of formal operational thought is the ability to raise hypotheses to explain an event, and then to follow the logic that a particular hypothesis implies. One of the classic experiments that Piaget and Inhelder designed to demonstrate the development of hypotheticodeductive reasoning involves the explanation of the swing of a pendulum. The task is to find out what variable, or combination of variables, controls the speed of the swing. Four factors can be varied: the mass of the object, the height from which the pendulum is pushed, the force with which it is pushed, and the length of the string. To investigate this problem, it is necessary to begin by isolating the separate factors and then varying only one factor at a time while keeping the others constant. As it happens, only the length of the string influences the speed of the pendulum. The challenge then is to demonstrate that the length of the string accounts for the speed and that the other factors do not. Children in the stage of concrete operational thought have difficulty coordinating the interaction among four separate variables and may lose track of what is being varied and what is held constant. After trying one or two strategies, they may simply give up. In contrast, being able to use formal operational thought, a child can create a matrix of variables and test each factor separately to evaluate its contribution (Inhelder & Piaget, 1958; Flavell, 1963).

Six Characteristics of Formal Operational Thought.   Six conceptual skills emerge during the stage of formal operations (Neimark, 1982; Demetriou & Efklides, 1985; Gray, 1990). Each one has implications for how adolescents approach interpersonal relationships and the formulation of personal plans and goals as well as for how they analyze scientific and mathematical information.

First, adolescents are able to manipulate mentally more than two categories of variables at the same time; for example, they can consider the relationship of speed, distance, and time in planning a trip (Acredolo, Adams, & Schmid, 1984). They can draw upon many variables to explain their behavior as well as that of others.

Second, they are able to think about things changing in the future. They can realize, for instance, that their current friendships may not remain the same in the years ahead.

Third, adolescents are able to hypothesize about a logical sequence of possible events. For example, they are able to predict college and occupational options that may be open to them, depending on how well they do in certain academic course work in high school.

Fourth, they are able to anticipate consequences of their actions. For instance, they realize that if they drop out of school, certain career possibilities will be closed to them.

Fifth, they have the capacity to detect the logical consistency or inconsistency in a set of statements. They can test the truth of a statement by finding evidence that supports or disproves it. They are troubled, for example, by the apparent contradictions between statements such as "All people are equal before the law" and the reality that people who have more money can afford better legal representation and are likely to have different experiences with the legal system than those who are poor.

Sixth, adolescents are able to think in a relativistic way about themselves, other individuals, and their world. They know that they are expected to act in a particular way because of the norms of their community and culture. Adolescents also know that in other families, communities, and cultures different norms may govern the same behavior. As a result, the decision to behave in a culturally accepted manner becomes a more conscious commitment to the society. At the same time, it is easier for them to accept members of other cultures, because they realize that these people are the products of societies with different sets of rules and norms.

These qualities of thought reflect what is possible for adolescents rather than what is typical. Most adolescents and older adults approach problem solving in a practical, concrete way in their common, daily functioning. However, under the most supportive conditions, more abstract, systematic, and self-reflective qualities of thought can be observed and bring a new perspective to the way adolescents approach the analysis of information and the acquisition of knowledge (Fischer, 1980; Eckstein & Shemesh, 1992; Fischer, Bullock, & Rotenberg, & Raya, 1993).

Egocentrism

The term egocentrism refers to the child's limited perspective at the beginning of each new phase of cognitive development (Piaget, 1926; Inhelder & Piaget, 1958). In the sensorimotor phase, egocentrism appears as an inability to separate one's actions from their effects on specific objects or people. As the scheme for causality is developed, the first process of decentering occurs. Infants recognize that certain actions have predictable consequences and that novel situations call for new, relevant behaviors. For example, one cannot turn the light on by turning the knob on the radio. At each developmental stage, decentering is a process that allows the person to approach situations from a more objective, analytic point of view.

In the phase of preoperational thought, egocentrism is manifested in an inability to separate one's own perspective from that of the listener. When a 4-year-old girl tells you about something that happened to her at the zoo, she may explain events as if you had seen them too. When a 3-year-old boy is explaining something to his grandmother over the phone, he may point to objects in the room, unaware that his grandmother cannot see over the phone lines.

The third phase of heightened egocentrism occurs in the transition from concrete to formal operational thought. As children develop the capacity to formulate hypothetical systems, they begin to generate assumptions about their own and others' behavior that will fit into these systems. For example, an early adolescent boy may insist that cooperation is a more desirable mode of interaction than competition. He argues that cooperation ought to benefit each participant and provide more resources for the group as a whole. This boy may become angry or disillusioned to discover that teachers, parents, and even peers seek competitive experiences and appear to enjoy them. He may think, "If the cooperative system is so superior, why do people persist in their illogical joy in triumphing over an opponent?" This kind of egocentrism reflects an inability to recognize that others may not share one's own hypothetical system.

In early adolescence, decentering requires an ability to realize that one's ideals are not shared by all others. We live in a pluralistic society in which each person is likely to have distinct goals and aspirations. Adolescents gradually discover that their neat, logical life plans must be constantly adapted to the expectations and needs of others. As they develop the flexibility of thought that accompanies formal operational perspective taking, their egocentrism usually declines.

Innovative Research Methods

In addition to describing the characteristics of thought at various stages, Piaget contributed to the methodology of research with children. His theory of intelligence during infancy (sensorimotor intelligence) was based primarily on careful observations and slight manipulations of his own children's behavior (1936/1952). His theory of intelligence during toddlerhood (preoperational thought) was based on children's answers to questions about their dreams and familiar life events, such as what makes things alive and what causes day and night (1924/1952, 1926/1951). He carried out his research on characteristics of the school-age child's thought (concrete operations) and the adolescent's thought (formal operations) by posing a variety of problems, watching children solve them, and questioning them about their solutions (1941/1952, 1954b). The emphasis of these studies was on how the person arrived at the answer rather than on the answer itself. The children became collaborators, providing Piaget with some insight as to the meaning of the problem and the path toward a solution from their own points of view.

NEW DIRECTIONS

The importance of understanding the development of the human capacity for reasoning and knowing has understandably led to an enormous amount of scholarly research. We now have an extensive literature that examines many of Piaget's conclusions and another body of literature that extends his theory in new directions. Evidence in support of qualitatively unique developmental levels of the sort Piaget described is quite impressive. In the following sections we examine four areas where Piaget's theory has stimulated and informed productive lines of research: moral reasoning, social cognition, theory of mind, and postformal reasoning in adulthood.

Moral Reasoning

Moral reasoning is the application of principles of logic to moral issues in order to decide which actions are right or wrong, just and humane. Piaget (1932/1948) described the major transition in moral judgment as a shift from heteronomous to autonomous morality. In heteronomous morality, rules are understood as fixed, unchangeable aspects of social reality. Children's moral judgments reflect a sense of subordination to authority figures.

An act is judged as right or wrong depending on the letter of the law, the amount of damage that was done, and whether or not the act was punished. In autonomous morality, children see rules as products of cooperative agreements. Moral judgments reflect a child's participation in a variety of social roles and in egalitarian relationships with friends. Give and take with peers highlights mutual respect and mutual benefit as rewards for holding to the terms of agreement or abiding by the law. Piaget posed situations like the following to young children in order to help clarify the difference between heteronomous and autonomous morality:

Mark rushes into the kitchen, pushing open the door. Although he did not realize it, his mother had left a set of 10 cups and saucers on a stool behind the door. When he pushed the door open, the cups and saucers fell off the stool and broke.

Matt was climbing up on the kitchen counter to reach some cookies that his mother told him he was not supposed eat. While climbing on the counter, he broke one cup and saucer.

Who committed the more serious moral transgression? Which boy should be more severely punished?

Children operating with a heteronomous morality believe a child who breaks 10 cups by accident has committed a much more serious transgression than the child who broke only one. Children who have achieved an autonomous morality believe that the child who disobeyed and violated his mother's trust committed the more serious transgression. Younger children are likely to judge the moral seriousness of an action based on the magnitude and nature of the consequences. If an action, no matter what the intent, produced harm, it should be punished. Older children are able to consider both the intention and the consequences in making a moral judgment. If an action was intended to harm and produced harm it should definitely be punished (Helwig, Zelazo, & Wilson, 2001).

Expanding on the distinction between heteronomous and autonomous morality, cognitive developmental theorists have described a sequence of stages of moral thought (Kohlberg, 1976; Gibbs, 1979; Damon, 1980). As children become increasingly skillful in evaluating the abstract and logical components of a moral dilemma, their moral judgments change. At the core of this change is the mechanism called equilibration. Stage changes in moral reasoning are associated with efforts to reconcile new perspectives and ideas about basic moral concepts, such as justice, intentionality, and social responsibility, with existing views about what is right and wrong. Children's reasoning may be thrown into disequilibrium by external sources, such as their parents' use of explanations and inductions regarding a moral dilemma or encounters with friends who reason differently about a moral conflict. In addition, children's own cognitive maturation, especially the ability to think abstractly and hypothetically about interrelated variables, determines how their reasoning about moral dilemmas will be structured (Piaget, 1975/1985; Walker, Gustafson, & Hennig, 2001).

Kohlberg (1969, 1976) described three levels of moral thought, each characterized by two stages of moral judgment. At Level I, preconventional morality, Stage 1 judgments of justice are based on whether a behavior is rewarded or punished. Stage 2 judgments are based on an instrumental view of whether the consequences will be good for "me and my family." The first, and to some degree the second, stages of Level I characterize children of early school age. Level II, conventional morality, is concerned with maintaining the approval of authorities at Stage 3 and with upholding the social order at Stage 4. Level III, postconventional morality, brings an acceptance of moral principles that are viewed as part of a person's own ideology, rather than simply being imposed by the social order. At Stage 5, justice and morality are determined by a democratically derived social contract. At Stage 6, a person develops a sense of universal ethical principles that apply across history and cultural contexts.

According to this theory, the stages form a logical hierarchy. At each new stage, individuals reorganize their view of morality, realizing the inadequacy of the stage below. For example, once a person sees morality in terms of a system that upholds and protects the social order (Stage 4), then reasoning that argues for an act as moral because it was rewarded or immoral because it was punished is seen as inadequate. The stages form an invariant sequence, moving from a very idiosyncratic, personal view of morality, to a view in which rules and laws are obeyed because they have been established by an authority or a society, and finally, to an understanding of rules and laws as created to uphold basic principles of fairness, justice, and humanity (Boom, Brugman, & van der Heijden, 2001). Longitudinal studies in a variety of countries observe an evolution of moral thought much like that proposed by Kohlberg in which the reasoning shifts from an idiosyncratic to a more principled approach to evaluating moral conflicts (Gielen & Markoulis, 2001).

Social Cognition

Another area of interest has been social cognition, the development of knowledge about the self and others. Researchers have traced the development of the ability to take the point of view of another person by studying performance on a variety of tasks that challenge the person's own perspective. The terms *empathy* and *perspective taking* are sometimes confused. Empathy typically refers to the ability to identify and experience the emotional state of another person. Perspective taking refers to the cognitive capacity to consider a situation from the point of view of another person. This requires a recognition that someone else's point of view may differ from one's own. It also requires the ability to analyze the factors that may account for these differences

(Flavell, 1974; Piaget, 1932/1948; Selman, 1971). Piaget introduced the importance of perspective taking in his study of moral development and subsequently in his analysis of concrete operational reasoning. He posed problems in which children were asked to place objects on a mat to reflect how the person sitting across from them would see the objects. Young children have difficulty with this type of task; their own view of the situation is more convincing than the idea that someone else sees it differently. With development, children are increasingly able to coordinate multiple perspectives.

Imagine a child who wants to play with another child's toy. If the first child thinks, "If I had that toy, I would be happy, and if I am happy, everyone is happy," then she or he may take the toy without anticipating that the other child will be upset. Recognizing the differences between your own view of a situation and the view of others requires perspective taking. The capacity to take another person's perspective is achieved gradually through parental explanations called inductions, peer interaction, social pretend play, conflict, and role playing.

Robert Selman (1980) studied the process of social perspective taking by analyzing children's responses to a structured interview. Children watched audiovisual filmstrips that depict interpersonal conflicts. They were then asked to describe the motivation of each actor and the relationships among the various performers. Four levels of social perspective taking were described. At Level 1, the youngest children (4–6 years old) recognized different emotions in the various actors, but they assumed that all the actors viewed the situation much as they did. The children at Level 4 (about 10–12 years old) realized that two people were able to take each other's perspective into account before deciding how to act. Furthermore, they realized that each of those people may have viewed the situation differently from the way they did. Many moral dilemmas require that children subordinate their personal needs for someone else's sake. To resolve such situations, children must be able to separate their personal wants from the other person's. Selman's research suggests that children under 10 can rarely approach interpersonal conflicts with this kind of objectivity (Selman, 1994).

As children interact with peers who see the world differently than they do, they begin to understand the limits of their own points of view. Piaget (1932/1948) suggested that peers have an important influence in diminishing one another's self-centered outlook precisely because they interact as equals. Children are not forced to accept one another's ideas in quite the same way as they are with adults. They argue, bargain, and eventually compromise in order to maintain friendships. The opportunity to function in peer groups for problem solving and for play leads children away from the egocentrism of early childhood and closer to the eventual flexibility of adult thought. The benefit of these interactions is most likely to occur when peers have differences in perspective that result in conflicts that must be resolved. The benefits are especially positive for children who interact with slightly more competent peers who can introduce more advanced or flexible approaches to problem solving (Tudge, 1992).

The behavior of well-adjusted, competent children is maintained in part by a number of social-cognitive abilities, including social perspective taking, interpersonal problem solving, and information processing (Dodge, Pettit, McClaskey, & Brown, 1986; Elias, Beier, & Gara, 1989; Downey & Walker, 1989; Carlo, Knight, Eisenberg, & Rotenberg, 1991). These cognitive abilities foster a child's entry into successful peer interactions. At the same time, active participation with peers promotes the development of these social-cognitive abilities.

Theory of Mind

From ages 4 to 6, children become more aware that people have different points of view. Work on theory of mind focuses on the natural way children understand each other's behavior. In day to day functioning, the theory of mind suggests that beliefs, desires, and actions are logically linked. A person engages in some action because he or she believes that this action will satisfy a specific desire. For example, Jakob wants his father to take him to the toy store because he wants a new toy train and he believes that he can get one at the toy store. In trying to understand a person's actions, it is important to consider the interaction of beliefs and desires since they operate together to guide action (Wellman, 1990).

Research on theory of mind typically poses situations to children to see what they understand about someone else's beliefs and desires. For example, in the early research children watched a character named Maxi put a chocolate candy in one location. Then, when Maxi leaves, children watched while another character moved the chocolate to a new place. Children were asked what Maxi thinks or what Maxi will do when he comes back into the room. Where will Maxi think the chocolate is located? Where will Maxi look (action) for the chocolate? Three-year-olds typically said that Maxi will look for the chocolate where they know it is, in the new location. Older children ages 4 and 5 realized that Maxi has an incorrect belief and predict that Maxi will look for the chocolate in its old location (Wimmer & Perner, 1983; Wellman, Cross, & Watson, 2001).

Subsequent research using similar scenarios finds that children as young as 3 are very good at considering what a character wants, even if it is different from what they might want. However, they have trouble thinking about what someone else might believe, especially disconnecting their own knowledge of the situation from the point of view of another. By the time children are 5, however, they are quite facile at detecting the possibility of false or incorrect beliefs. They can separate what they know about a situation from what someone else may know, and they expect that a character's actions will be based on the character's beliefs, even when those beliefs are incorrect (Ziv & Frye, 2003).

The ability to appreciate that what you know or believe to be true is different from what others know and believe to be true is a salient feature of self-awareness. It allows children to begin to speculate about what others may think about them, and how their behavior may be understood or misunderstood.

Cognition in Adulthood

Cognitive theorists are just beginning to document the direction of developmental changes during the stages of adulthood. Research on adult problem solving and reasoning has been inconclusive. Some studies have shown that adults tend to be practical rather than hypothetical in their approach to tasks. Others have emphasized adults' increasing capacity to maintain opposing ideas and to find solutions that are adaptive in a given context (Labouvie-Vief, 1992; Denney, 1982; Denney & Pearce, 1989).

Research based on the standard Piagetian tasks has been criticized for its lack of relevance and familiarity to older adults. The traditional tasks are dominated by the role of pure logic, disconnected from the situation. They emphasize problems that have a scientific rather than a pragmatic focus. Although the solution to most formal operational problems requires the manipulation of multiple variables, there is typically only one correct solution, as in the answer to the pendulum problem. In adult life, most problems involve multiple dimensions with changing or poorly defined variables and more than one solution. (For example, given my limited resources, should I buy more life insurance, put cash in a certificate of deposit, or invest in the stock and/or bond market to best protect my family's financial future?)

As a result of these limitations or criticisms of formal operational reasoning, scholars have begun to formulate a view of postformal thought. Postformal thought has been characterized in the following ways:

A greater reliance on reflection on self, emotions, values and the specific situation in addressing a problem.

A willingness to shift gears or take a different approach depending on the specific problem.

An ability to draw on personal knowledge to find pragmatic solutions.

An awareness of the contradictions in life and a willingness to try to include conflicting or contradictory thoughts, emotions, and experiences in finding a solution.

A flexible integration of cognition and emotion so that solutions are adaptive, reality-oriented, and emotionally satisfying.

An enthusiasm for seeking new questions, finding new frameworks for understanding experience.

People who operate with postformal thought do not do so in every situation. When a problem has clear parameters and needs a single solution, concrete or formal operations will work. However, when a problem is value-laden, ambiguous, or involving many interpersonal implications, postformal thinking comes into play (Sinnott & Cavanaugh, 1991; Labouvie-Vief, 1992).

Within the study of human cognition, many scholars are striving to integrate these conceptual strands around the concept of *self*. This field focuses on understanding how the sense of self emerges and how the mind knows the self. Theorists explore the construct of identity within which adults continue to develop new understandings about the nature of intimate relationships, parenting, work, friendships and other associational relationships. This work examines how constructs such as self, identity, and personhood are situated across cultures and contexts (Lightfoot, Lalonde, & Chandler, 2004).

A RESEARCH EXAMPLE: METACOGNITION

Piaget's description of formal operational reasoning emphasized the capacity for applying principles of logical reasoning to an analysis of one's own thoughts. Rather than operating on objects, as takes place during the stage of concrete operational thought, adolescents and adults can impose propositional logic on hypotheses, carrying out mental operations in order to assess the logic of relationships and propositions. This analysis of the developmental direction of cognition inspired new research on metacognition and executive control. This research suggests that during the second decade of life, the person is increasingly able to manage the focus and direction of his or her thoughts, deciding what to think about and how to evaluate knowledge (Kuhn, 2006). As they approach problem solving and new learning, adolescents are better able than younger children to monitor and manage their learning strategies, and to create effective approaches to gathering and evaluating information.

Metacognition refers to a range of processes and strategies used to assess and monitor knowledge. It includes the "feeling of knowing" that accompanies problem solving, the ability to distinguish ideas about which we are confident from those which we doubt (Butterfield, Nelson, & Peck, 1988; Lagattuta & Wellman, 2001). One element of this "feeling of knowing" is understanding the source of one's beliefs. For example, we can be told about sand, we can see pictures of sand, or we can feel and touch it. All three of these sources of information may coincide to create a single belief, or we may discover that there are inconsistencies between what someone says is true and what we perceive through sight or touch. By the ages of 4 and 5, children are able to understand how all three sources of information have contributed to their understanding of an experience (O'Neill & Gopnik, 1991).

Research on the emotion of *interest* highlights the role of metacognition in the process of knowledge acquisition and learning (Izard & Ackerman, 2000). People are likely to spend more time exploring something if it is interesting. They look longer at paintings that are interesting, spend more time trying to understand written materials that are interesting, and work harder at trying to solve problems that are interesting. The cognitive appraisal perspective suggests that emotions are associated with distinct patterns of appraisal. According to research by Paul Silvia (2005), the emotion we refer to as "interest" is a product of the interaction of two types of appraisals. First, when an event or stimulus occurs, a person makes a *novelty* appraisal. This appraisal assesses whether the event is new, complex, unexpected, mysterious, or in some other way creates disequilibrium in existing schema. Second, the person makes an appraisal of his or her *coping potential* with regard to the stimulus. This refers to an assessment of whether the person has the ability to understand the new stimulus. When a stimulus is appraised as both novel or complex and also understandable, interest is high.

In order to study this, Silvia (2005) asked students to react to an abstract, complex, and unfamiliar poem. For half the group, he provided instructions in which the following information was given:

"The following page has a poem by Scott MacLeod. Please read it, see how you feel about it, and then give your impressions and reactions on the following pages. This poem is entitled *The Whitest Parts of the Body* and it is from his book *The Life of Haifisch.*"

The other half of the group received identical instructions except the following was added:"Haifisch" means "shark" in German. All of the poems in this book, including the poem that you will read, are about killer sharks.

People in the second group who had been given this clue about the poem rated their ability to understand the poem as higher than those who were not given the supplemental clue. Moreover, those in the second group found the poem more interesting than those in the first group. Other experiments support the proposition that the metacogntive process of appraising one's ability to understand something plays a key role in fostering interest or boredom. When complexity is high, as in abstract art or multidimensional problem solving, a person's appraised ability to understand the material will be associated with a greater sense of interest.

In addition to assessing one's ability to understand something, people use metacognition to review various strategies for approaching a problem in order to choose the one that is most likely to result in a solution. People monitor their comprehension of the material they have read and select strategies for increasing their comprehension (Currie, 1999). "I need to reread this section." "I need to underline and take notes to focus my attention on new information." "I need to talk about this with someone in order to understand it better."

Metacognition develops in parallel with other cognitive capacities. As children develop their ability to attend to more variables in their approach to problems, they simultaneously increase their capacity to take an "executive" posture in relation to cognitive tasks. They can detect uncertainty and introduce strategies to reduce it. They can learn study techniques that will enhance their ability to organize and recall information. These capacities continue to develop as the child becomes a more sophisticated learner. They are also quite amenable to training, both at home and at school. Metacognition appears to be a natural component of cognitive development. However, just like first-level cognitive capacities, it is constructed in a social context. Interactions between children and adults or peers may nurture and stimulate metacognition by helping children to identify sources of information, talk about and recognize the differences between feelings of certainty and uncertainty in their knowledge, and devise effective strategies for increasing their "feelings of knowing" (Stright, Neitzel, Sears, & Hoke-Sinex, 2001).

AN APPLICATION: THE DEVELOPMENT OF LOGICO-MATHEMATICAL KNOWLEDGE

Piaget's approach to understanding the development of knowledge led to a new respect for the ways that young children make meaning of their experiences. Children are seen as building or constructing knowledge through active engagement with objects and exploration of physical relationships among objects. According to Piaget (1967/1971), there are three types of knowledge: physical knowledge, which refers to what one knows about the properties of the physical world (a ball is round, it rolls downhill); social conventional knowledge, which refers to the conventions people in a community use to refer to ideas (we use words like one, two, and three in English; in French those same concepts are un, deu, trois); and logico-mathematical knowledge, the internal schemes that are formed in a child's mind. Constance Kamii (2000a), one of the most influential scholars to apply Piaget's theory to educational settings, explains logico-mathematical knowledge with the following example. Imagine that a child is playing with pick-up sticks. Are two sticks similar or different? If the child focuses on the color of two sticks, one red and one green, then the child will view the sticks as different. If the child focuses on the shape and size of the two sticks, then the sticks are similar. The ideas of similar and different are examples of logico-mathematical knowledge, constructed on the basis of mental operations imposed on physical knowledge. While color, shape, and size are observable properties and the names we give to various colors and shapes are social conventional knowledge, the understanding of objects as similar or different are not directly observable, but are a product of mental operations (Kamii, Rummelsburg, & Kari, 2005).

One of the essential aspects of logico-mathematical knowledge is an understanding of number. Kamii has explored a variety of educational interventions in order to foster the logico-mathematical knowledge that underlies arithmetic competence in young children. Her premise is that children need to have ample time to gain physical knowledge in order to construct the underlying relationships that are essential for solving arithmetic problems. Simply giving children manipulatives, asking them to fill out workbook pages, or supplying them with counters are not sufficient for solving arithmetic problems when children do not bring logico-mathematical knowledge of number as a quantity, part–whole relationships, and sequential relationships to the tasks (Kamii, Lewis, & Kirkland, 2001).

In one study, a group of 26 low-performing, low-SES first graders were involved in physical-knowledge activities during their regular math class rather than typical math instruction. This group was compared to a similar group in another school who experienced traditional arithmetic instruction. The experimental group spent the first half of the year engaged in physical-knowledge activities. Examples of some of these activities included pick-up sticks, bowling, and balancing small construction pieces on a paper plate that was placed on the neck of a bottle. When they were ready for solving arithmetic problems, these children were shifted to an approach that emphasized arithmetic games and word problems in which children worked together and exchanged views on how to solve problems. The curriculum was built upon Piagetian principles, including the focus on direct involvement with physical objects, opportunities to solve problems in the context of play, and the opportunity to work with other age mates to invent strategies. This latter feature of the learning environment is thought to help reduce overly personal or egocentric understanding and fosters an appreciation for multiple views of a problem and its solution (DeLisi, 2002).

At the end of the school year, children in the two groups were compared on two types of math abilities: mental arithmetic problems (17 addition problems of the type 5 + 4, with 3 seconds for each answer); and four story problems. An example of a story problem was: There were three children. There are six cookies for them to share. How many cookies will each child get? Children in the experimental group did better on all but one of the mental arithmetic problems; their performance was significantly better on 8 of 17 problems. More children in the experimental group solved the story problems than children in the traditional classrooms, and the differences were significant in two of the problems. In the example of the cookies problem, half the children in the experimental group solved it correctly; none of the children in the traditional group solved the problem.

In general, Kamii argues, when children are challenged in play-based contexts to think hard about solving problems requiring physical knowledge they build a strong logico-mathematical foundation that makes solving arithmetic problems easier. Understanding that parts make up a whole, for example, means that when faced with a problem such as 4+3, a child can move quickly, counting on 3 more from 4, rather than starting to count from 1. They can devise mental strategies to solve story problems, remembering the numerical facts of the problem and inventing ways to coordinate information to arrive at a solution. According to Piagetian theory, asking children to memorize strategies such as *carrying* or *borrowing* to solve arithmetic problems relies on a type of social conventional knowledge that comes from outside the child. In order to foster mathematical problem solving, it is better to let children arrive at an understanding of ideas of quantity through constructivist abstraction (Kamii, Lewis, & Kirkland, 2001). Kamii and others have applied Piagetian cognitive developmental theory to the creation of many strategies for the use of manipulatives and games that foster children's thinking about quantity, number, spatial, and sequential relationships (Kamii & Joseph, 1988; Kamii & DeVries, 1993/1978; Kamii, 2000b).

HOW DOES COGNITIVE DEVELOPMENTAL THEORY ANSWER THE BASIC QUESTIONS THAT A THEORY OF HUMAN DEVELOPMENT IS EXPECTED TO ADDRESS?

What is the direction of change over the life span? How well does the theory account for patterns of change and continuity? Cognitive developmental theory proposes four stages of development. In infancy, knowledge is based primarily on action and direct investigation of objects in the environment. Actions become coordinated, and schemes or mental representations are formed that link actions into coordinated operations. In toddlerhood, new capacities emerge that allow the child to represent experience symbolically. This is a critical transformation, leading to an increased freedom from direct experience. In early and middle childhood logico-mathematical knowledge emerges. Children begin to understand that certain principles underly the relationships among objects, and they can use these operations to solve problems. With development, cognition becomes increasingly abstract and multidimensional. Logical thought can be imposed on hypothetical propositions, rather than on concrete objects and relationships. Knowledge is always based on action. Thus, the direction of change over the life span is from direct sensorimotor actions on objects to mental actions on mental operations. At each more advanced stage, ways of knowing of earlier stages are integrated into new, more abstract and flexible approaches.

What are the mechanisms that account for growth? What are some testable hypotheses or predictions that emerge from this analysis?   C o g n i tion is an adaptive capacity that has its basis in evolution. The concept of cognitive adaptation includes a dialectical tension between two basic developmental processes—assimilation and accommodation—the former a conservative tendency and the latter a progressive tendency. Assimilation operates to preserve existing structures by incorporating new information and confirming that what is already known is useful in making sense of experience. Accommodation operates to alter existing structures in the direction of new environmental demands, thereby creating a new basis for future assimilations (van Geert, 1998).

According to cognitive developmental theory, cognition emerges in a predictable pattern as infants and young children encounter discrepancies between existing schemes and contemporary experiences. There is an assumption of a fundamental striving toward cognitive equilibrium, where one's schemes match experience. Logico-mathematical knowledge emerges when children have to concentrate on tasks that challenge their physical and social-conventional knowledge. Encounters with all types of novelty, especially experiences that are moderately distinct rather than widely different from what is already known, are important for advancing new ideas and new ways of organizing thought. Encounters with different opinions and ways of solving problems, especially through peer interactions, discussion, and problem solving, help reduce egocentrism and stimulate reflection on new ways of understanding the world.

The theory predicts that there is a level of developmental readiness for movement from one stage to the next. According to this view, children should not be able to solve certain types of problems until they have attained a level of mental operations that supports the underlying concepts associated with the problem. For example, until children understand the concept of quantity, they will not be able to be successful in solving arithmetic problems. The theory also predicts that this level of understanding is best achieved through active engagement with objects rather than being taught rules and strategies for solving problems. Children who have constructed foundational principles through active engagement in the physical world will have a stronger, more immediate grasp of the logic underlying the organization of the mathematical, physical and social worlds.

How relevant are early experiences for later development? What evidence does the theory offer to support its view?   As the previous discussion suggests, cognition is an active, gradually changing process. New knowledge is based partly on the schemes that were formed earlier, and partly on encounters with new information. New information requires the reframing and reorganization of earlier schemes. At the same time, one's approach to problem solving becomes increasingly flexible and abstract. Once the child has reached the stage of concrete operational thought, knowledge about the physical world becomes more compelling than perceptions. In the conservation task, for example, the tall thin glass may "appear" to have more juice than the wide, short glass because the liquid level is higher, but children at the stage of concrete operational thought know that height and weight compensate for one another. Thus, their logico-mathematical knowledge overrides their sensory knowledge. Some of Piaget's studies of memory illustrate this principle, showing that as children move from the preoperational to the concrete operational stage, they remember problems differently based on what they now "know" to be true.

How do the physical, cognitive, emotional, and social functions interact? How well does the theory explain these interactions? The theory rests heavily on the physical origins of knowing, linking advanced forms of reasoning to the very earliest reflexes. Affect is also critical for cognition. Cognitive disequilibrium is assumed to be distressing, and resolving this disequilibrium is assumed to be associated with positive affect. The emotion of interest is critical for sustained problem solving. The constraints that are thought to come with unequal power between children and parents or teachers are considered potential impediments to learning, whereas the freedom that is associated with egalitarian peer relationships is considered a positive context for cognitive growth. Piaget's emphasis on the role of peer interaction suggests that children and adolescents benefit when they can engage in social exchange as part of the problem-solving process. Social interactions with peers are expected to help reduce egocentrism, and allow children and adolescents to consider multidimensional problems from alternative points of view.

How do the environmental and social contexts affect development? What aspects of the environment does the theory suggest are especially important in shaping the direction of development? Cognitive theory views development as a product of a biologically guided plan for growth and change. The elements that make cognitive growth possible are all present in the genetic information that governs the growth of the brain and nervous system. However, the process of intellectual growth requires interaction with a diverse and responsive environment. Cognitive development is fostered by recognition of discrepancies between existing schemes and new experiences. Through the reciprocal processes of assimilation and accommodation, schemes are modified and integrated to form the basis for organizing and explaining experience.

According to this view knowledge emerges through active engagement with the environment. Children as well as adults select, explore, and experiment with objects and later with ideas. They create the basis of logical reasoning through encounters with novelty. The way the environment is structured, especially opportunities for exploration and investigation guided by a child's natural curiosity, will promote cognitive reasoning. At subsequent stages, especially during the period of formal operational reasoning, environments differ in the extent to which they encourage and evoke abstract, hypothetical reasoning. For example, in some cultures formal operational reasoning is observed only in a few of the leaders, not in all adults. Within the school environment, settings that place a greater emphasis on rote memorization will be less likely to support formal operational reasoning than settings that encourage active problem solving and project-based inquiry. Methods of instruction, beginning in preschool and continuing through college, can foster or inhibit the formulation of abstract conceptualization and executive functioning that Piaget suggests are possible.

According to the theory, what factors place individuals at risk at specific periods of the life span? The theory assumes a biological unfolding of cognitive capacities in the context of a supportive environment. Any of a number of neurological challenges could place a person at risk for failure to develop the more advanced cognitive capacities. Because cognition unfolds in a sequential process, sensory and motor delays in infancy may interfere with later capacities for logical reasoning. The absence of physical stimulation and restrictions on exploration place infants at risk for development. In the toddlerhood period, when representational skills are emerging, a lack of a communication partner and limited opportunities for verbal interaction as well as lack of encouragement or punishment for pretend play would place children at risk. In the period of concrete operational reasoning, undue emphasis on rote memorization and repetition as well as instruction in which children are given rules and strategies rather than having opportunities to invent or discover them weaken the foundation for logico-mathematical reasoning. This type of environment continues to impede cognitive growth in adolescence. At later stages, a learning environment that is overly authoritarian and lacking in active, peer-based learning opportunities is likely to result in a rigid approach to rules rather than the desired deep level of understanding about the application of principles of logic to complex problems. Any environment that gives children answers or solutions in order to speed learning along rather than waiting for children to discover them takes away the positive emotions that accompany understanding. The learning environment should present problems at levels that are appropriately challenging, just discrepant enough from what is already known to engage interest but not overly complex that discourage the promise of successful solutions.

CRITIQUE OF COGNITIVE DEVELOPMENTAL THEORY

Strengths

Piaget's theory emphasized the importance of cognition in the study of development. In contrast to other developmental psychologists who focused on mechanisms of learning or individual differences in intelligence, motor development, or temperament, Piaget brought new attention to how children, including very young infants, acquire knowledge and approach problem solving. This focus on cognition had a dramatic and permanent impact on the field of developmental science leading to vast amounts of research on the way children make meaning.

Within this theoretical framework, Piaget took a new look at children's reasoning, highlighting distinctions in the way children of different ages approach problems and noting differences in the quality of children's thinking from that of adults. His work led to a new appreciation of the infant as actively constructing knowledge about objects and people in the environment, and a new respect for infant intelligence that went beyond the child's ability to imitate adult actions or respond to adult instructions.

Piaget's approach to the study of cognition, including the invention of a variety of unique tasks and the use of the interview technique to inquire about a child's reasoning, resulted in a rich body of descriptive data about how children behave and what they understand. This approach influenced inquiry into other fields, including moral development, social development, and metacognition.

From the point of view of characteristics of a "good theory," Piaget's work has had an enormous impact on subsequent research (Flavell, 1996). In the 1970s and '80s, cognition dominated the field of developmental psychology, and most studies were designed to replicate, test, or extend Piaget's theories. Since that time, research and theory have emerged to address identified weaknesses in Piaget's theory, considering new ways to integrate research on information processing, the social contexts of cognition, and the neurological bases of cognitive functioning. Recent neurological studies of brain development have provided evidence to support the stage-like shifts in cognitive capacity that were first characterized by Piaget, although the nature of these new capacities is not identical to those he predicted (Giedd et al., 1999).

Weaknesses

Perhaps the greatest weakness or criticism of Piaget's theory focuses on his view of stages of development. Although qualitative changes in problem solving are observed, cognition is much more variable than a strict stage approach implies. Children and adolescents solve problems in different ways depending on the domain, and children within an age group are much more variable in their cognitive capacities than one might expect given Piaget's description of stages. Research on cognition suggests that Piaget may have underestimated the cognitive capacities of infants and young children, and overestimated the capacities of adolescents.

Piaget's view of development suggests that there is a period of maturational readiness for the application of logical operations to physical objects. Left to their own process of exploration and experimentation, Piaget argued that children would discover the regularities and operations that underlie conservation. Showing a child a conservation problem and then explaining and reinforcing the correct answer should not be very effective if the child is not ready to assimilate this information. However, research has shown that it is possible to train young children of preschool age to conserve (Brainerd, 1977). These training studies suggest that it is possible to introduce such concepts as identity and reversibility so that children as young as 4 can achieve conservation. Children also transfer conservation from the tasks involved in training to other materials and dimensions (Field, 1981; May & Norton, 1981). Preschool and kindergarten age children can integrate and apply more abstract concepts than Piaget's theory predicted. For example, children as young as 3 and 4 have shown that they understand the idea that materials are made of tiny particles that retain their properties even when they are invisible. They can use this notion of particles to explain how a substance, such as sugar continues to exist in a solution and retain its sweetness even when it is invisible (Au, Sidle, & Rollins, 1993; Rosen & Rozin, 1993). These examples illustrate the criticism that Piaget's theory underestimates the abstract reasoning abilities of the preoperational age child.

At the other end of the developmental continuum, the stage of formal operations may overestimate the way that most adolescents and adults approach problems. Although most researchers agree that formal operational thinking exists and does characterize mature, scientific reasoning, many studies show that adolescents and adults typically do not function at the formal operational level, and that their use of formal reasoning is inconsistent across problem areas (Bradmetz, 1999). For example, Neimark (1975) followed changes in the problem-solving strategies of adolescents over a 3½-year period. Even the oldest participants in her study who were 15 did not apply formal operational strategies across all problems.

Another criticism of Piaget's theory is that his descriptions of concrete and formal operational thought are too narrow and do not encompass the many dimensions along which cognitive functioning matures. Increases in speed, efficiency, and capacity of information storage and retrieval have been documented during the period from ages 11 to 16 (Kwon & Lawson, 2000; Kuhn, 2006). Improvements in logical reasoning are in part a result of being able to handle greater quantities of information more quickly and efficiently. In addition to development in basic processes, there are gains in knowledge both as a result of schooling and experience. Knowledge in each specialized subject such as mathematics, language, or science expands, bringing not only increases in logic but increases in understanding the procedures or strategies that are most likely to work for a given problem. Complementing changes in specialized knowledge, adolescents demonstrate increases in self-monitoring, conscious control and guidance of mental activity, such as the ability to hold conclusions in abeyance while they examine alternative solutions or gather new information. These capacities for executive cognitive functioning and greater flexibility contribute to the potential for more mature solutions (Donald, 2001).

Finally, some critics focus on the nature of Piaget's techniques and specific experiments as limiting the way he characterized young children's cognitive capacities. For example, in studying object permanence, Piaget relied on an infant's motor ability to pursue a hidden object as evidence that the child understood that the object continued to exist. Baillargeon (2004) has shown that by altering the experimental methods, one can demonstrate that young infants who do not yet crawl can anticipate an object's trajectory and can follow an object through different ways of hiding it. Others have pointed to similar problems in conservation tasks. If you ask a child to judge whether two balls of clay are the same, and then flatten one of the balls into a pancake and ask the question again, a child may assume that since you are asking the question again, something has changed. In one study, children ages 5 to 7 were asked how certain materials looked and how they really were. Giving the children this verbal distinction between appearance and reality led to increases in the number of children who gave the correct answer (Bijstra, van Geert, & Jackson, 1989). These examples illustrate that the limitations Piaget pointed out in children's cognitive functioning could be in part a result of the constraints imposed by his methods.

KEY TERMS

accommodation

adaptation

assimilation

autonomous morality

causal schemes

classification

combinatorial skills

concrete operational thought

conservation

conventional morality

decentering

disequilibrium

egocentrism

equilibrium

formal operational thought

heteronomous morality

identity

insight

logico-mathematical knowledge

metacognition

object permanence

operations

preconventional morality

preoperational thought

postconventional morality

postformal thought

reciprocity

reversibility

schema

sensorimotor intelligence

signs

social cognition

symbols

Part II

Theories That Emphasize Environmental Factors

Over the course of the 20th century, one of the persistent controversies in the study of human development was whether nature or nurture was more important in shaping the direction of development. The theories we reviewed in the preceding section fell more on the side of nature, emphasizing the role of a biologically based plan for development that guides the direction of maturation and growth. The theories we will review in this section fall more on the side of nurture. There were strong forces within the field of psychology and human development that took the position that development was essentially a product of the events that the person experienced. If we return to the analogy of a plant, one might say that given the general direction of development, which may be guided by the genetic information within a seed, all the environmental factors such as nutrients, sun, water, soil, and air temperature are exactly what will determine whether the plant flourishes.

Environmental factors are a source of enormous variation, including exposure to nutrition, health care, cognitive stimulation, interpersonal interactions, educational opportunities, financial resources, stressors, community resources, work settings, cultural artifacts and rituals, climate, and geographical conditions. These environmental factors produce differences in individual thought and behavior; they shape expectations, which, in turn, shape individual goals and actions.

The three theories that are presented in this section, learning theories, social role theory, and life course theory, each operate at a different level of analysis: Learning theories examine links between stimuli and responses and day to day experiences; social role theory focuses on the impact of the integrated environmental framework of social roles; and life course theory addresses the broad scope of historical/social eras with their diverse opportunities and constraints. Each theory provides a distinct perspective on how to conceptualize the environment and the specific mechanisms that account for how environmental events alter or influence behavior.

Learning theories assume that the person will change his or her behavior in response to systematic changes in the environment. To the extent that environments remain the same, habits that are formed will continue to be expressed across settings. The reason that people of a certain age behave in a similar way is due to the fact that they have encountered similar reinforcement schedules and have been rewarded for behaving in similar ways.

Social role theory emphasizes age-graded roles that guide the direction of development throughout life. These roles vary from one society to another. Continuity is explained by the enactment of roles that endure over long periods, such as child or parent. Continuity is also explained by participation in reciprocal roles; one learns about the expectations of one's own role and the adjoining roles. Change is explained by the process of role gain, role loss, and entry into an increasing number of roles that produce new levels of societal engagement.

Life course theory suggests that lives become increasingly diverse with age and that as individuals set goals and make decisions, their capacity to do this improves. As such, the theory assumes that there will be change, and that this change is a result of age-graded social expectations, roles and the sequencing of roles, the linking of lives, the impact of human agency or choice, and the influence of historical events that open up or close certain opportunities that can alter one or more trajectories.

The three theories have a common focus on the role of environments for shaping the direction of growth. As such, they highlight important sources of individual variability based on the effects of experience. They differ in the aspect of the environment that is emphasized. The learning theories draw attention to the micro level of moment to moment consequences of action. Social role theory considers the impact of social organization on guiding patterns of social interaction and self definition. Life course theory takes the broadest view of the environment, bringing into focus intergenerational and cultural dimensions of the environment within which individuals interpret their experiences and project their future.

Chapter 5

Learning Theories

CHAPTER OUTLINE

Historical Context

Key Concepts of Four Theories of Learning

Classical Conditioning

Operant Conditioning

Social Learning

Cognitive Behaviorism

New Directions

Information Processing

Experiential Learning Theory

A Research Example: Learned Helplessness and Learned Resourcefulness

An Application: Cognitive Behavioral Therapy

How Do Learning Theories Answer the Basic Questions that a Theory of Human Development Is Expected to Address?

Critique of the Learning Theories

Strengths

Weaknesses

Key Terms

Chapter 5

Learning Theories

Learning theories have proposed mechanisms to account for the relatively permanent changes in behavior that occur as a result of experience. This definition does not limit learning to the types of experiences we encounter in school. The outcomes of learning can include such varied behaviors as stopping at a red light, feeling hungry at 6 o'clock in the evening, figuring out how to use the online research data base, and riding a bicycle. The changing and changeable nature of human behavior is largely due to human beings' extensive capacity for learning. Four theories of learning have made significant contributions to the study of human development: (a) classical conditioning, (b) operant conditioning, (c) social learning, and (d) cognitive behaviorism. As you read about these theories, you will begin to appreciate that the term *learning* encompasses a wide variety of processes.

HISTORICAL CONTEXT

The learning theories emerged in the later part of the 19th century and the first part of the 20th century, as scholars began to apply the Newtonian principles of science to an analysis of human behavior. Psychologists were looking for principles to explain human behavior that could be verified through systematic observation, objective measurement, and statistical probability, as opposed to reflection, intuition, introspection, and logic. They found ways to apply the experimental method to the study of learning and memory, isolating specific cause–effect links between stimuli and responses (Slee & Shute, 2003). In most of the learning theories, the person is viewed as largely malleable, able to adapt flexibly to the demands and rewards of the environment. Research and theory went hand in hand as psychologists invented new experimental contexts in which to identify the mechanisms through which experiences in the environment would alter and sustain changes in behavior.

Learning theories emerged from the work of many scholars including Ivan Pavlov, E. L. Thorndike, John Watson, B.F. Skinner, Clark Hull, Albert Bandura, Edward Tolman, and Walter Michel. For the most part, they did not begin their work specifically to study human development. However, many of the ideas that are included as part of the broad field of learning theories have been applied to work with children and adolescents, including parenting and the socialization process, teaching and management of the classroom environment, and the creation of therapeutic environments.

KEY CONCEPTS OF FOUR THEORIES OF LEARNING

Classical Conditioning

Ivan Pavlov was a Russian physiologist whose early research focused on the digestive system. He was studying the reflexive responses of digestion when food was placed in an animal's mouth. While he was working on this research, Pavlov noticed that events at a distance, such as the sight of food, the sight of a person delivering the food, or noises that occurred regularly in the room, produced digestive responses. Pavlov realized that the animals had learned to associate a reaction with a stimulus that one would not think would produce that reaction. He called these associations *conditioned reflexes*. The type of learning that Pavlov studied was called *classical conditioning* (Pavlov, 1927).

In classical conditioning, a bond already exists between some stimulus in the environment and some physiological response of the learner. These naturally occurring stimulus-response bonds are called reflexes. Because of his interest in digestion, the reflexive response Pavlov was most interested in was the salivation response to food. In classical conditioning the stimulus that naturally produces a reflexive response is called the *unconditioned stimulus* (US). The natural reflexive response is called the *unconditioned response* (UR). This bond between US and UR occurs without need for prior learning. Examples of other US–UR bonds besides that of the food-salivation reaction include the reaction of the eye to threat (the eyeblink reflex), the reaction of the eye to different intensities of light (the pupillary reflex), and the reaction to a loud, sudden noise (the startle reflex).

Pavlov discovered that events happening regularly just before the events that trigger a reflexive response will also produce a version of the reflexive response. For example, sounds that occur regularly just before an animal is fed will eventually cause an animal's digestive system to secrete chemicals in the same way it does to food. These sounds are, in themselves, neutral. If they occur at other times of day and in other contexts they do not normally result in evoking the dog's salivation response. However, when they are linked in time over several days, they become "meaningful" signals that food is coming. As a result, these formerly neutral sounds begin to be associated with food and, as such, they evoke a conditioned salivation response.

The model for classical conditioning is seen in Figure 5.1. Before conditioning, the bell is a *neutral stimulus* (NS). It elicits a response of interest or attention, but nothing more. The sight and smell of food are *unconditioned stimuli* (US) that elicit salivation, the *unconditioned response* (UR). During conditioning trials, the bell is rung shortly before the food appears. The dog is said to have been conditioned when it salivates to the sound of the bell, before the food is presented. The bell, therefore, comes to control the salivation response. It is now the *conditioned stimulus* (CS). Salivation that occurs in response to the bell alone is called the conditioned response (CR). The CR is usually not exactly identical to the UR.

A loud noise will produce a startle response, including tightening of muscles, rapid respiration, and heightened arousal. Let's imagine that whenever an infant is taken to the pediatrician for a checkup, she is startled by the sudden loud cries of other infants in the examination rooms. After two or three visits, she begins to make a partial startle reaction as she enters the doctor's office. The doctor's waiting room becomes a CS for the startle response, CR. As she gets older, her mother tries to prepare her for visits to the doctor's office. The visits are very infrequent, but the child continues to show an anxiety reaction to the mere discussion of the doctor and the coming visit. The words and imagery associated with the doctor combine to maintain the CS–CR bond. The transfer of the CR from the waiting room to the discussion of the doctor's visit is called *higher order conditioning*.

Subsequent research on Pavlovian conditioning demonstrated that conditioning is a means by which the learner identifies structure in the environment (Davey, 1987; Rescorla, 1988). The pairing of two events, such as the sound of a bell and the presentation of food, becomes significant because one stimulus becomes a signal for the other. Conditioning does not take place randomly between any two events linked in time. If there is no systematic relationship between the two, conditioning will not take place. The light

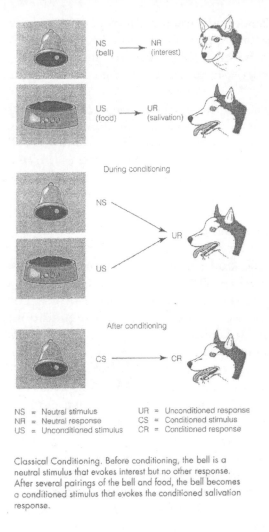

NS = Neutral stimulus   UR = Unconditioned response
NR = Neutral response   CS = Conditioned stimulus
US = Unconditioned stimulus CR = Conditioned response

Classical Conditioning. Before conditioning, the bell is a
neutral stimulus that evokes interest but no other response.
After several pairings of the bell and food, the bell becomes
a conditioned stimulus that evokes the conditioned salivation
response.

Figure 5.1.   Classical conditioning. From *Development Through Life (ISE), A Psychosocial Approach 9th edition* by Newman & Newman, 2006. Reprinted with permission of Wadsworth, a division of Thomson Learning: www.thomsonrights.com.

may be on in the kitchen whenever the telephone rings, for example, but since there is no predictable relationship between the light and the telephone, the light does not become a signal that the telephone is going to ring. Conditioning is not an artificial paradigm; it is an actual process by which one stimulus provides information about another.

Furthermore, the CS itself is not totally neutral. A visual stimulus such as a colored light will prompt visual orienting, for instance, whereas an auditory stimulus may simply increase attention or arousal. In a conditioning experiment, the learner builds many associations simultaneously. Although the focus of a particular experiment may be on establishing a link between one CS and one US, the learner will build links among many elements of the environment—its visual, auditory, and olfactory components, including the US. Pavlovian conditioning provides a model for understanding how multiple associations can be established and triggered in the process of concept formation, memory, and problem solving (Lavond & Steinmetz, 2003).

Extinction and Spontaneous Recovery. The formation of the CS–CR bond needs support in order to be maintained. When the CS is presented by itself for a number of trials without the US, the CR will be weakened and eventually eliminated. This process is called *extinction*. When a bell that used to signal food is no longer followed by food the salivation response will eventually fade. When CS–CR are meaningfully linked and the CS is no longer a signal for the US, then the response pattern is no longer maintained. In the laboratory, a CR may be extinguished on one day by repeatedly presenting the CS without the US. However, if you bring the animal back to the laboratory the next day and present the CS, the CR will occur. This is called *spontaneous recovery*. The response strength is not quite as great at the point of spontaneous recovery as it was at the peak of conditioning. After extinction, the response can either be readily reconditioned or extinction trials can eventually fully inhibit the response.

The phenomenon of spontaneous recovery demonstrates that extinction is different from forgetting. Once a CS–CR bond has been established, an inhibitory force must be developed to interfere with the learning. In extinction, we see another example of the adaptive nature of learning. A new response is maintained as long as it is an accurate reflection of environmental conditions. When conditions change, the learner is capable of revising its responses to reflect those changes. The phenomenon of spontaneous recovery shows that the learner will test the environment to confirm that conditions have permanently changed. If the conditions that were present during learning are reestablished, the learned response can be readily restored. However, if after several tests the conditions no longer support the original learning, the response is inhibited.

Over the course of development, a person confronts a variety of different environments. The meaningful connections between stimuli and responses may not be the same from one environment to the next. The process of extinction helps explain how responses that are not adaptive in a specific setting drop away, while new, meaningful response are acquired.

Generalization. Another characteristic of learning is *generalization*. When a CS–CR bond is established, stimuli that are similar to but not exactly the same as the CS will also produce some measurable CR. The new response generalizes to stimuli that are similar to the original CS. The size or strength of the CR will depend upon the degree of similarity between the new stimulus and the conditioned stimulus. The more similar the CS and the new stimulus, the stronger the CR.

Generalization means that the same associations are not relearned in each new situation. When the stimuli in different situations are fairly similar, the learned associations or behaviors will be applied. We know that a red traffic light means stop, regardless of the exact shade of red that is used in the light. Generalization aids in managing the large amount of information we encounter in the environment by allowing the person to respond in the same way to stimuli that are approximately the same.

Discrimination.   The opposite of generalization is *discrimination*. In discrimination, the learner makes a response to a specific CS, but inhibits responding to stimuli that are similar to the CS. For example, the CS could be a red light, and other similar stimuli could be orange, pink, or reddish-orange lights. When the CS (red light) is presented it is always followed by food, the US. When a stimulus similar to the CS, for example, an orange light, is presented, it is never followed by food. Gradually, the animal learns to make the conditioned response to red, the stimulus that was followed by food, and not to make the conditioned response to orange, the stimulus that was not followed by food. You discriminate red from green at every stop light.

Pavlov explored the limits of discrimination learning. He conditioned a dog to distinguish between a circle and an ellipse. Once the dog could reliably differentiate the two, Pavlov began to alter the shape of the ellipse so it became more and more circular. After a number of modifications, the dog could not distinguish between the two stimuli even though one was followed by food (US) and the other was not. The dog's ability to discriminate grew worse. In addition, the dog's behavior in the experimental situation became disorganized. The dog barked and squealed; it tore at the apparatus and resisted being taken into the experimental room. After 3 weeks, when it was tested with the original circle and ellipse, the dog could no longer differentiate between them. Pavlov described this sequence of behaviors as a case of experimentally induced neurosis. He speculated that disorganization of behavior would be produced when the tendency to make a response and to inhibit that response are both present because the situation produces anxiety.

Classical conditioning can account for a great deal of the associational learning that occurs throughout life. When a specific symbol is paired with an image, emotional reaction, or object, that symbol takes on new meaning. The associations that are made through classical conditioning may involve labels and concepts, but they do not necessarily require language skills. During infancy and toddlerhood, a variety of positive and negative emotional reactions are conditioned to people, objects, and environments as the child develops attachments. Our reactions to the taste of a certain type of food or the feel of a particular material may be the result of conditioned learning that has persisted until adulthood. Similarly, fears can be the results of classical conditioning. Fear can be conditioned to a specific cue, such as a sound, light, or smell, which signals the onset of a painful experience. It can also be conditioned to the context in which the painful event occurred (Godsil, Quinn, & Faqnselow, 2000). Many people recall at least one frightening experience, such as nearly drowning or falling from the top of a slide. The association of fear or pain with a specific target may lead to systematic avoidance of that object for the rest of one's life.

Operant Conditioning

E. L. Thorndike (1898), an American psychologist, studied a different type of learning called *operant conditioning* at about the same time that Pavlov was working on classical conditioning. He observed cats as they figured out how to escape from a cage. Thorndike described a process of trial-and-error learning in which the cats made fewer and fewer random movements and increasingly directed their behavior to the correct solution (pulling a string to release a latch). Thorndike argued that the improvement in problem solving was not the result of learning an idea or an insight but the gradual association between a stimulus and a response. A *stimulus* is any event or energy source in the environment. It can also be an internal event like a pain or a thought. A *response* is any behavior that occurs in reaction to the stimulus. Thorndike (1911) proposed the *law of effect* to explain how specific stimuli are linked to specific responses. According to the law of effect, a bond is established between the situation and the reaction depending on the feeling state accompanying the reaction. Other things being equal, when a response is followed by a positive feeling state, it strengthens the bond between the stimulus and the response. When faced with a similar situation, the response is likely to recur. When a response is followed by a negative feeling state, it weakens the bond between the stimulus and the response. When faced with a similar situation, the response is less likely to recur. Thorndike also proposed the *law of exercise*. In trial-and-error learning, the pattern of connections between the stimulus and responses is established by the consequences that follow the responses. Patterns are strengthened through repetition. The law of exercise states that the more frequently a stimulus response connection is repeated, the stronger it becomes. The pattern is called a *habit* when it appears to be automatic.

Through the combination of the laws of effect and exercise, a specific response to a stimulus occurs immediately. Other possible responses do not occur. Complex behaviors can be established as the response from one stimulus becomes a stimulus for the next response. For example, think about your sequence of activities when you get up in the morning. You go to the bathroom, you wash your hands, brush your teeth, take a shower, get dressed, have breakfast, assemble your papers to get ready for your day, and leave the house. This sequence occurs every day in the same order with little planning or thought. It is a complex pattern of habits. Each step in the sequence can be thought of as a response and as a stimulus for the next step. Once a bond is formed between a stimulus and a response, learned behaviors can be very efficient and lead the way to complex habit sequences freeing the person to use their conscious thought for other tasks.

American psychologist B. F. Skinner had the benefit of reviewing Pavlov's work on classical conditioning and Thorndike's work on *trial-and-error learning*. In an early paper, Skinner (1935) summarized the essential differences between the two kinds of learning:

1. In classical conditioning, the conditioned reflex can begin at zero level; that is, it is not present at all. In trial-and-error learning, the response must be made if it is to be reinforced or strengthened.
2. In classical conditioning, the response is controlled by what precedes it. In trial-and-error learning, the response is controlled by what follows it.
3. Classical conditioning is most suitable for internal responses (emotional and glandular reactions). Trial-and-error learning is most suitable for external responses (muscle movements, verbal responses).

Skinner's (1935) work followed along the lines of Thorndike's. His focus was on the modification of voluntary behaviors as a result of the consequences of those behaviors. In the traditional operant conditioning experiment, the researcher selects a response in advance and then waits until the desired response (or at least a partial response) occurs. Then the experimenter presents a reinforcement. *Reinforcement* is operationally defined as any stimulus that makes a repetition of the response more likely. There are two kinds of reinforcers. *Positive reinforcers*, such as food and smiles, increase the rate of response when they are present. *Negative reinforcers*, such as electric shock, increase the rate of response when they are removed.

In one experiment, a researcher places a rat in a cage. An electric grid in the floor of the cage is activated. As soon as the rat presses a bar, the electric shock is turned off. Soon the rat learns to press the bar quickly in order to turn off the shock. The shock is a negative reinforcer because its removal strengthens the response of bar pressing. Suppose a mother gets upset whenever she hears her baby cry. She may try a number of responses to stop the crying—rocking, feeding, talking, changing the baby's diapers. If one of these behaviors leads to an end to the noise, it is reinforced. The mother is more likely to try that behavior the next time. The baby's cry is a negative reinforcer because when it stops, the specific caregiving response is strengthened.

Shaping.   One means of developing a new complex response is *shaping*. Here the response is broken down into its major components. At first a response that is only an approximation of one element of the behavior is reinforced. Gradually new elements of the behavior are added, and a reinforcer is given only when two or three components of the response are linked together. Once the person makes a complete response, earlier approximations are no longer reinforced.

Parents often use the shaping process to teach their young children such complicated behaviors as using the toilet and caring for their belongings. Parents may begin toilet training, for example, by reinforcing children when they behave partially in the desired way, such as by telling the parents that they have to go to the bathroom. Eventually the children receive reinforcers only when they have completed the entire behavior sequence (including wiping, flushing, adjusting clothing, and washing hands).

Schedules of Reinforcement.   Within the field of operant conditioning, research has been devoted to identifying which conditions of learning result in the strongest, longest-lasting habits. *Schedules of reinforcement* refer to the frequency and regularity with which reinforcements are given (Ferster & Skinner, 1957). A new response is conditioned rapidly if reinforcement is given on every learning trial. This schedule is called *continuous reinforcement*. Responses that are established under conditions of continuous reinforcement are very vulnerable to *extinction*—that is, if the reinforcement is removed for several trials, performance deteriorates rapidly. Some schedules vary the amount of time or the number of trials between reinforcements. This procedure is called *intermittent reinforcement.* The learner responds on many occasions when no reinforcement is provided but does receive reinforcement every once in a while. Such schedules result in the most durable learning. Intermittent reinforcement lengthens the time an operant behavior remains in the learner's repertoire after reinforcement has been permanently discontinued (Ferster & Culbertson, 1982; Shull & Grimes, 2003). Some form of intermittent reinforcement schedule is probably truer to real life. It would be very difficult for anyone to learn a behavior if every instance of it had to be reinforced. A person often exhibits a new response when no observers are present, when teachers are attending to other matters, or in the context of other behaviors that are followed by a negative consequence. Research on operant conditioning demonstrates that conditions of intermittent reinforcement are precisely those under which the longest-lasting habits are formed.

Extinction and Punishment.   Positive and negative reinforcement are associated with trying to build up or increase the likelihood of a behavior. Operant conditioning also has concepts associated with damping out or reducing the likelihood of a behavior. Extinction is a process in which an expected reinforcer no longer occurs following the response. When parents or teachers are advised to ignore a child's undesirable behavior, they are using extinction as a means of eliminating the behavior. Theoretically, if the tendency to make a specific response can be strengthened through reinforcement, it can be weakened though extinction. *Punishment* refers to a noxious consequence that follows an undesirable behavior. In an experiment with animals, a behavior might be punished by administering an electric shock after the animal presses a bar. After a few trials, the animal will no longer press the bar. However, Skinner argued that punishment did not work any more quickly than extinction and often was accompanied by undesirable side effects. Some students find the concepts of negative reinforcement and punishment confusing. In our two examples with rats described previously, in Example 1, bar pressing is learned when it stops electric shock (negative reinforcer); in Example 2, bar pressing stops when it is followed by the electric shock (punishment).

The principles of operant conditioning apply whenever the environment sets up priorities for behavior and conditional rewards or punishments for approximating a desired behavior. Operant conditioning refers to the development of behavior patterns that are under the learner's voluntary control (Davey & Cullen, 1988). The person can choose to make a response or not, depending on the consequences associated with the behavior. People change whenever their operant behaviors adapt to changes in environmental contingencies. The environment controls the process of adaptation through the role it plays in establishing and modifying contingencies (Skinner, 1987). Behavior can be modified in the desired direction as long as the person who is guiding the conditioning has control over the distribution of valued reinforcers. We believe that these principles are especially applicable to the learning that takes place during toddlerhood (2 to 4 years) and early school age (4 to 6). Children of these ages are unlikely to be able to conceptualize about the existing framework of reinforcement. Once individuals can interpret a reinforcement schedule, they may choose to adapt to it, resist it, or redefine the environment in order to discover new sources of reinforcement. There is no doubt that operant conditioning occurs at all ages. Reinforcement schedules set by work, spouse, and self operate on much of an adult's behavior. Reinforcement conditions determine the behaviors that will be performed. Conditions of learning influence how long a given behavior will persist once the reinforcement for it is removed.

Social Learning

All learning cannot be explained by the principles of classical and operant conditioning. The concept of *observational learning* or *vicarious learning* evolved from an awareness that much learning takes place not because of the deliberate manipulation of the association of stimulus and response or reinforcements but because of the person's tendency to observe and imitate other people's behavior (Bandura & Walters, 1963). Albert Bandura described it this way: "Fortunately, most human behavior is learned observationally though modeling: from observing others, one forms an idea of how new behaviors are performed, and on later occasions this coded information serves as a guide for action" (Bandura, 1977, p. 22).

In reflecting on his views about conditioning, Bandura states: "Much of the early psychological theorizing was founded on behavioristic principles that embraced an input–output model linked by an internal conduit that makes behavior possible but exerts no influence on its own behavior " (Bandura, 2001, p. 2).

Bandura points out the distinction between learning and performance. He argues that the behaviorist concepts represent a theory of performance rather than a theory of learning. A boy may learn a great deal about how to play football by watching other children. He may also learn a great deal about how to play the game by watching adults on television. No one would realize that the child knows about football until there is an opportunity to play. The boy's learning would be cognitive, occurring without reinforcement of any overt behavior.

The people who are being observed are called *models* and the process of learning is called *modeling*. In one of the early modeling studies, nursery school children watched two adult models interact with a large inflated doll called Bobo. One group of children watched a model who ignored the doll and played with Tinker Toys. The other group of children watched a model who attacked the doll. The experimenter designed the attack so that it was unlike anything the children had done themselves or seen others do. A third group of children did not see a model. After observing, the children were placed in a situation with the Bobo doll. The children who had seen the model attack the doll showed much more aggressive behavior than children in either of the other two groups. Often the attacks were almost exact duplications of the attacks they had witnessed. They threw the doll into the air, pounded it with a mallet, kicked it, and shouted at it in the same way the model did (Bandura, Ross, & Ross, 1961).

In a subsequent study, children saw a film of an adult attacking a Bobo doll. One group of children saw the model rewarded after the attack, a second group saw the model punished, and a third group did not observe any consequences to the model after attacking the doll. A fourth group (the control group) saw no model and no attack. In the play period following the film, the children who had seen the model rewarded demonstrated the greatest amount of aggressive behavior. The group that observed the attack and no consequences demonstrated the second highest amount of aggressive behavior. The group who saw the attack and saw the model punished showed considerably less aggressive behavior than either of the first two groups. The least amount of aggression was displayed by the control group. Thus, it was shown that the consequences that follow the model's behavior influence whether it will be imitated and the degree of imitation (Bandura, 1965).

A great deal of research has been devoted to identifying conditions that determine whether or not a child will imitate a model (Bandura, 1971, 1977, 1986). A number of studies have shown that when children observe a model who is acting in a helpful or generous way, the children's generosity and sharing increase. In one study, children between ages of 7 and 11 saw a model play a game and give away his winnings. Months later, the children played the same game with a different experimenter. Those children who had observed a generous model gave away more of their winnings than a control group who had not observed a generous model (Rushton, 1976). Under the right conditions, children will imitate aggressive, altruistic, helping, and stingy models. They are most likely to imitate models who are prestigious, who control resources, or who themselves are rewarded. The concept of social learning highlights the relevance of models' behavior and the observed consequences of the behavior in guiding the behavior of others. These models may be parents, older siblings, entertainment stars, or sports heroes.

The principles of social learning are assumed to operate in the same way throughout life. Observational learning may take place at any age. Insofar as exposure to new influential, powerful models who control resources may occur at any life stage, new learning through the modeling process is always possible. Exposure to a certain array of models and a certain pattern of rewards results in the encouragement to imitate some behaviors rather than others. The similarity in behavior among people of the same ages reflects their exposure to a common history of models and rewards.

Cognitive Behaviorism

One objection that is frequently raised to classical and operant conditioning as theories of learning is that they have no language or concepts to describe events that occur in the learner's mind. In these approaches, learning is described as a relationship between environmental stimuli and individual responses. Edward Tolman (1932/1967, 1948) discussed the notion of *intervening variables*. He suggested that cognitions intervened between stimulus and response. He said that the learner develops a *cognitive map*, which is an internal mental representation of the learning environment. Individuals who perform a specific task in a certain environment attend primarily to that task, but they also form a representation of the rest of the setting. This internal representation forms the cognitive map. The map includes expectations about the reward system in operation, the existing spatial relationships within the setting, and the behaviors accorded highest priority. An individual's performance in a situation represents only part of the learning that has occurred. The fact that people respond to changes in the environment indicates that a complex mental map actually develops in the situation. He emphasized the purposive aspects of behavior. This involves how people use information from the environment to direct their responses and how they use information following their responses to correct or modify their behavior in developing new responses.

Cognitive behaviorists study the many internal mental activities that influence behavior. These theories of learning are included in this part of the book where environmental influences are emphasized because much of the focus is on what the learner comes to know and expect about the environment. Nonetheless, the cognitive behaviorists bring to light the internal representation of the environment, which emerges as a result of experience, but is also influenced by the learner's level of cognitive complexity, attention, and motivation, all of which might be biologically based. Thus, the cognitive behavioral theories of learning are less mechanistic and less reliant upon environmental factors as the primary cause of behavior than is operant conditioning.

According to Walter Mischel (1973, 1979), at least six cognitive factors must be taken into account if a person's behavior is to be understood: cognitive competencies, self-encoding, expectancies, values, goals and plans, and self-control strategies. *Cognitive competencies* consist of knowledge, skills, and abilities. *Self-encoding* is the evaluation and conceptualization of information about the self. An interesting finding in this area is that depressed people tend to evaluate themselves more realistically than those who are not depressed. Mischel (1979) argued that "to feel good about ourselves we may have to judge ourselves more kindly than we are judged" (p. 752). In other words, most people who are not chronically depressed may bias their evaluations of themselves in a self-enhancing way.

Expectancies refer to expectations about one's ability to perform, the consequences of one's behavior, and the meaning of events in one's environment. *Values* consist of the relative importance one places on the outcomes of situations. One person may value high levels of task performance, while another may value success in social situations. One's behavior in a situation is influenced by how one values its possible outcomes. *Goals and plans* are personal standards of performance and the strategies one develops for achieving them. Obviously individuals differ in their goals and plans; these differences will lead to considerable variation in behavior. *Self-control strategies* are the techniques an individual develops for regulating his or her own behavior. Self-control helps us to understand how we may leave the realm of stimulus control in order to gain control over our behavior. The more aware we are of the effects of stimuli on our behavior, the more effectively we may overcome, channel, or eliminate their influences.

Of these six areas, one that has received considerable attention among those interested in learning and performance is the area of expectancies. People's judgments about how well they expect to perform, or whether or not they expect to improve their skill level through training, have a clear impact on their performance. Albert Bandura (1982, 1989) has identified *self-efficacy* as a key element in the cognitive basis of behavior. Self-efficacy is defined as the sense of confidence that one can perform the behaviors demanded by a situation. According to Bandura, the decision to engage in a situation, as well as the intensity of effort expended in the situation, are dependent upon a person's confidence about success.

Bandura theorized that four sources of information contribute to judgments of self efficacy. The first source is *enactive attainment,* or prior experiences of mastery in the kinds of tasks that are being confronted. Children's general assessment of their ability in any area (e.g., mathematics, writing, or gymnastics) is based on their past accomplishments in that area (Skaalvik & Hagtvet, 1990). Successful experiences increase their perceived self-efficacy whereas repeated failures diminish it. Failure experiences are especially detrimental when they occur early in the process of trying to master a task. Many children are diverted from mastering such sports as tennis and baseball because they have made mistakes early in their participation. They develop doubts about their abilities which then prevent them from persisting in the task.

The second source of information is *vicarious information*. Seeing a person similar to oneself perform a task successfully may raise one's sense of self efficacy; seeing a person similar to oneself fail at a task may lower it. *Verbal persuasion* is the third source. Children can be encouraged to believe in themselves to try a new task. Persuasion is likely to be most effective with children who already have confidence in their abilities and it helps boost their performance level. The fourth source of information that contributes to judgments of self-efficacy is *physical state*. People monitor their bodily states in making judgments about whether they can do well or not. When children feel too anxious or frightened they are likely to anticipate failure. In contrast, children who are excited and interested but not overly tense are more likely to perceive themselves as capable of succeeding.

Those who have a high sense of efficacy visualize success scenarios that provide positive guides for performance and they cognitively rehearse good solutions to potential problems. Those who judge themselves as *inefficacious* are more inclined to visualize failure scenarios and to dwell on how things will go wrong. Such inefficacious thinking weakens motivation and undermines performance (Bandura, 1989). Bandura points out that adjustment depends on one's judgment about the outcome of the situation. If a woman with a strong sense of self-efficacy is in an environment that is responsive and rewards good performance, she is likely to behave in a self-assured, competent way. If this same woman is in an environment that is unresponsive and does not reward accomplishment, she is likely to increase her effort and even try to change the environment. People who judge their efficacy to be low tend to give up and become apathetic in unresponsive environments. In responsive environments they may become more depressed and self-critical as they see others who appear to be similar to themselves succeeding. The concept of self-efficacy clarifies how people adapt when they enter new roles or new situations. The successes and failures we observe in others and the encouragement we receive from others influence our expectations.

Cognitive behaviorism suggests that through the processes of classical conditioning, operant conditioning, and observational learning, the learner acquires cognitive structures that influence subsequent learning and performance. We might say that the learner acquires an outlook on the learning situation. This outlook may influence the learner's feeling of familiarity with the task, motivation to undertake the task, optimism about performing the task successfully, and strategies for approaching the task. In addition to everything a parent, teacher, or supervisor might do to structure a learning environment, one must always take into account the outlook the learner brings to the task. Differences in judgments of self-efficacy, self-control strategies, values, and goals all influence the way people approach a learning situation.

NEW DIRECTIONS

Learning theories have led to several new directions in the study of development. These include: information processing, experiential learning, learned helplessness and learned resourcefulness, and the use of classical and operant conditioning paradigms in the study of neurological development and preverbal development. In addition, learning theory has been applied to the treatment of psychological problems and the teaching of skills for adjustment to individuals with limitations. Both employ learning models in order to systematize the environmental input to populations that tend to become overwhelmed by complexity or who are in other ways unable to deal with more random environmental input.

Information Processing

Information processing focuses on how individuals make sense of the great amount of information that is present in their environment, how they analyze tasks in order to perform them effectively, how they translate their analyses into plans for action, and how they implement their plans. In comparison to the learning theories that use the language of stimulus and response, information-processing strategies focus on the relationship between input and output. The computer is the primary metaphor for this approach. Within a developmental perspective, studies have focused on six areas where aspects of information processing improve from childhood to adolescence: attention, working memory, long-term memory, processing speed, organizational strategies, and self-modification (Keating & Bobbitt, 1978; Demetriou, Christou, Spanoudis, & Platsidou, 2002).

The first step in information processing is *attention*. In order for something to be processed, the person has to attend to it. Every sensory system has a sensory register or a capacity to process a particular kind of sensory information. A person's attention can be directed to a stimulus through one or more of these sensory systems. Something comes to your attention because you hear it or smell it. Things can also come to one's attention through several systems at once—you smell and hear the stimulus. Information is held in the sensory register for a brief time, and then processed further in short-term memory. There is evidence that as a person gets older development involves improvements in *selective attention*, where a person focuses on one kind of information and ignores others, and improvements in divided attention, where a person can stay focused on two different sources of information (Higgins & Turnure, 1984; Schiff & Knopf, 1985; Casteel, 1993). Reading and listening to music at the same time is an example of *divided attention*. Problems in the development of attention, such as Attention Deficit and Hyperactivity Disorder (ADHD), have become extremely prevalent in our society as we increase demands for information processing.

Short-term memory is also called *working memory*. Once information has made an impact on the sensory register it is held for a brief time in the working memory. Adults can generally keep five to nine units of information in working memory for about 30 seconds. After that time, the information is either transferred to long-term memory by linking it to other knowledge and information, repeated in order to hold it in short-term memory, or lost from memory. When you meet a new person and ask their name, you can recall the name easily for 30 seconds. However, unless you take some steps to transfer the name into long-term storage, it is likely that you will forget the name once the next event catches your attention and makes an impression on the sensory register. Strategies for transferring the information from working memory to long-term memory can include repeating the information several times, putting the information in a familiar context, or connecting the information with a unique word or image that will help you retrieve it. The short-term memory can be used as a scratch pad for combining new information with information from long-term memory to perform calculations or other manipulations, such as planning. You can also call up information from the long-term memory to review it, build thoughts and concepts, and evaluate outcomes.

Long-term memory is a complex network of information, concepts, and schemes related by associations, knowledge, and use. It is the storehouse of a lifetime of information. Studies of memory focus on different kinds of tasks, each with their own trajectory of growth and decline. Semantic memory focuses on basic knowledge such as recalling the meaning of words such as vegetable, democracy, or insect. Once learned, information in the semantic memory is very resistant to loss. *Episodic memory* focuses on specific situation and data. Studies of episodic memory may ask people to recall words from a list or to recall what they had for breakfast three days ago. Unless the events have some particular importance, they may not be encoded or they may be difficult to retrieve. *Prospective memory* is memory about events or actions that will take place in the future. An example would be remembering to take your medicine at 4 o'clock in the afternoon or remembering to go to class at 10 a.m. This type of memory requires that something needs to happen at a future time or under some future condition and also remembering what needs to be done.

Memory capacity appears to improve from infancy through adolescence due to several factors (Keating, 2004). With age, neurological development results in increased processing speed. This means that it takes less time to encode and retrieve information. There is also a process of neural pruning, resulting in stronger associations among neural networks. As children acquire more information, this permits more rapid storage of new information in connection with existing knowledge and results in a greater chance for retrieval. In studies of memory capacity in adulthood, short-term memory does not differ much between younger and older adults. However, older adults appear to have greater difficulty transferring new information from short-term to long-term storage, and then retrieving it upon demand. They also rely more on context and meaning for information storage and retrieval, and are not as effective as younger adults in recalling random numbers or nonsense syllables, especially when this type of information is presented rapidly (Zelinski & Lewis, 2003).

There are different types of memory for different kinds of activities. The more a child reads, the easier it is to recognize new words. Memory for words does not necessarily result in better memory for solving puzzles or computing arithmetic problems. Exposure to each area of knowledge is associated with a growing capacity to store information and retrieve it. In adulthood, effective coping requires that one directs attention on storing and retrieving the details of information that are most salient for success in work and family life.

Over time, children also become more proactive in imposing *organizational strategies* that will help preserve and retrieve information, manage more information by chunking or grouping bits of information together, and by linking new information with information that has already been stored (Siegler & Crowley, 1991). For example, young children learn to whisper instructions to themselves, repeat information, give numbers or letters to a list of items, or make up rhymes to help them remember things. With practice, certain tasks become more routine or habitual, thus requiring less use of memory. With experience, children and adolescents recognize the similarities between new tasks or problems and problems they have solved in the past. They can approach the new tasks more quickly because they remember the basic strategy they used to solve a similar problem in the past. Beginning in adolescence and continuing throughout adulthood, long-term memory and prospective memory are supported by a variety of strategies such as having date books, address books, palm pilots, and daily planners. Some people have secretaries or executive assistants who support their long-term memory and help to keep the flow of information manageable. With education and experience, people expand the capacity of their long-term memory by learning where information can be found. Rather than relying on their own ability to store and retrieve all the information they need, they store information about the sources of information.

Other aspects of information processing that are currently being studied include planning, decision making, goal setting, coping, and the relationship of motivation to these activities. Cognitive neuroscience is an emerging field that links these cognitive aspects of information processing to neurological processes, providing evidence for changes in neural networks as a result of experience, and the involvement of various aspects of the brain in different types of cognitive tasks.

Experiential Learning Theory

Proponents of experiential learning theory (ELT) claim that the theory describes a model of the learning process as well as a model of adult development. Like other learning theories, ELT emphasizes the central role that experience plays in the learning process. However, the theory combines aspects of behavioral and cognitive learning theory by linking experience to both reflection and action (Kolb, 1984). The ELT model portrays two distinctly different ways of grasping experience—concrete experience (CE) and abstract conceptualization (AC). The first is knowledge you have because of your experiences; the second is knowledge you have because you read about it or were taught about it, but you did not necessarily experience it directly. There are also two opposing modes of making use of knowledge: *reflective observation* (RO) and *active experimentation* (AE). Knowledge gained either through concrete experience or through abstract conceptualization can result in reflective observation, that is, thinking more about the topic, asking new questions, or generating hypotheses about this knowledge. Similarly, knowledge gained either through concrete experience or through abstract conceptualization can result in active experimentation, trying out new behaviors that are based on the knowledge to see what benefit may result. According to the four-stage learning cycle shown in Figure 5.2, ELT proposes a cycle of learning from CE through each of the subsequent stages to AE. Immediate or concrete experiences are the basis for observations and reflections. These reflections are assimilated and distilled into abstract concepts from which new implications for action can be drawn. These implications are actively tested and serve as guides in creating new experiences.

Although ELT suggests that all four processes are involved in learning, the theory also suggests that individuals have their preferred ways of gaining and using knowledge called *learning styles* (Kolb, Boyatzis, & Mainemelis, 2000). The learning styles shown in Figure 5.2 are likely combinations of one approach to knowing and one approach to transforming or using information. They are described as diverging, assimilating, converging, and accommodating. The following descriptions are adapted from Kolb et al. (2000).

Diverging.   The dominant learning abilities are concrete experience (CE) and reflective observation (RO). Best at viewing concrete situations from many different points of view. Perform better in situations that call for generation of ideas, such as a "brainstorming." Have broad cultural interests, like to gather information, interested in people, tend to be imaginative and emotional, tend to specialize in the arts. Prefer to work in groups, listening with an open mind and receiving personalized feedback.

Assimilating.   The dominant learning abilities are abstract conceptualization (AC) and reflective observation (RO). Best at understanding a wide range of information and putting into concise, logical form. Less focused on people and more interested in ideas and abstract concepts. Value the logical

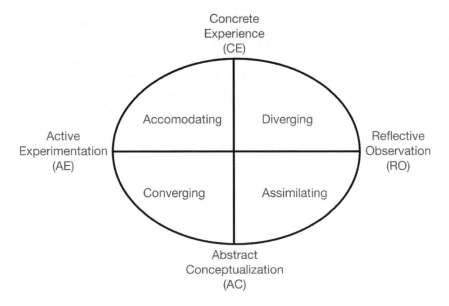

Figure 5.2.   Experiential learning theory and four learning styles. From Kolb, Boyatzis, and Mainemelis (2000). Reprinted by permission of Lawrence Erlbaum Associates, Publishers.

soundness of a theory over its practical value. Important for effectiveness in information and science careers. Prefer readings, lectures, exploring analytical models, and having time to think things through.

Converging.   The dominant learning abilities are abstract conceptualization (AC) and active experimentation (AE). Best at finding practical uses for ideas and theories. The ability to solve problems and make decisions based on finding solutions to questions or problems. Prefer to deal with technical tasks and problems rather than with social issues and interpersonal issues. Important for effectiveness in specialist and technology careers. Prefer to experiment with new ideas, simulations, laboratory assignments, and practical applications.

Accommodating.   The dominant learning abilities are concrete experience (CE) and active experimentation (AE). The ability to learn from primarily "hands-on" experience. They enjoy carrying out plans and involving themselves in new and challenging experiences. Tendency to act on "gut" feelings rather than on logical analysis. In solving problems, rely more heavily on people for information than on their own technical analysis. Important for effectiveness in action-oriented careers, such as marketing or sales. Prefer to work with others to get assignments done, to set goals, to do field work, and to test out different approaches to completing a project.

Although it has its critics, ELT has been very influential in the field of adult education, guiding the way professional development courses are structured, and energizing the wide spread emphasis on experiential learning as a component of academic coursework at the undergraduate and graduate levels.

Information processing theory and experiential learning theory are two different ways to conceive of the cycle of learning from stimulus or input/experience to response or output/action. Information processing theory focuses on the micro level, providing a model of how the mind manages to encode, organize, and use information to guide action. The theory has led to detailed analyses of cognitive tasks, and simulations of mental activity that help explain how children and adults approach decision making, problem solving, and mastery of complex tasks. The theory has been applied in educational settings to help children develop new strategies for managing their own learning. It has also been useful to guide intervention by recognizing the demand properties of a task and observing which components of the task are especially difficult for a child.

Experiential learning theory focuses on the macro level, considering the bigger picture of how people might change and grow as they reflect on their experiences, develop some general principles, and experiment to see if what they learned holds up in the next concrete situation. The theory has led to the description and measurement of learning styles, which has had a major impact on how teachers conceptualize the learning process in order to promote deeper levels of understanding across a greater diversity of learners.

A RESEARCH EXAMPLE: LEARNED HELPLESSNESS AND LEARNED RESOURCEFULNESS

Drawing upon the principles of classical conditioning and operant conditioning, Martin Seligman devised an experimental procedure to explore the pattern of learned responses when negative events are unavoidable. *Learned helplessness* is a term applied to the effects of uncontrollable negative events on later learning. In his early research, Seligman (1975) described the behavior of dogs who received shock that they could not escape from. One group of dogs (Group 1) was confined in a harness and trained to turn off a shock with their nose by pressing a panel. A second group of dogs (Group 2) experienced the same number of shocks in the same pattern and duration. However, nothing the dogs could do would end the shock. A third group of dogs (Group 3) were confined in the harness but no shocks were delivered.

Twenty four hours after the dogs had been in the harness treatment, they were placed in an escape avoidance shuttle box. This box has two compartments with a barrier between. When the barrier is lifted, there is still a hurdle in the middle of the box. The dog has to jump the hurdle to move from one compartment to another. The floor of the box can be electrified. At first, a signal such as a sound or light is followed by an electric shock. The dog can escape the shock by leaping over the hurdle. In later trials, the dog can leap the hurdle in response to the signal and escape the shock completely. In the shuttle box, Group 1 that could control the shock when in the harness and Group 3 that was never shocked when in the harness quickly learned to jump over the barrier to avoid the shock. However, 6 of the 8 dogs that could not control the shock when they were in the harness never learned the escape response in the shuttle box.

Seligman proposed a theory of learned helplessness in humans that was based on the reactions of both animals and humans to uncontrollable stress. *Helplessness* is defined as an expectation that an outcome will not be influenced by any response that a learner makes. Once this expectation is formed, it interferes with learning to respond effectively in situations where the outcomes are controllable. Learned helplessness interferes with new learning in three ways: (a) it reduces the motivation to control the outcome of events; (b) it interferes with learning that some responses do control events; and (c) under extreme stress, it produces fear for as long as the person is uncertain about the uncontrollability of the outcome. This prolonged fear leads to depression.

In the typical experimental situation designed to study learned helplessness, a person is faced with a set of conditions where there is no effective or successful solution. Responses that would normally be effective in the situation do not work. In these conditions, one often observes efforts at self-regulation. For example, a person will strive to remain goal directed, use some new planning or problem-solving approach, remain calm, or use reassuring verbalizations in order to stay focused. These are all efforts to continue to address the task effectively, even when nothing seems to work. This combination of self-regulatory or self-control strategies is called *learned resourcefulness.* People differ in the extent to which they have acquired this repertoire of learned resourcefulness behaviors (Rosenbaum & Ben-Ari, 1985).

In our stressful world, where people are often confronted by an uncontrollable influx of demands and stimuli, people who are high in learned resourcefulness are better able to cope. They are more capable of adopting health-related behaviors that require the kind of self-control that is directed at breaking habits in order to adopt new and more effective behaviors (Rosenbaum, 1989). Rather than emphasizing risk and vulnerability, research about learned resourcefulness has guided thinking about positive adaptations to stressful life events. Following along this line of research, Seligman and his colleagues have fostered a focus on *positive psychology* (Seligman, Steen, Park, & Peterson, 2005). Positive psychology emphasizes the pleasant emotions of happiness and joy, the cognitive outlooks of optimism and hopefulness, and the adaptive, creative behaviors that result in mastery and efficacy.

AN APPLICATION: COGNITIVE BEHAVIORAL THERAPY

Cognitive behavioral therapy (CBT) is a form of psychotherapy that integrates many of the principles of classical conditioning, operant conditioning, and cognitive learning theory (National Association of Cognitive-Behavioral Therapists, 2005). CBT is based on the scientifically supported assumption that most emotional and behavioral reactions are learned. Therefore, the goal of therapy is to help clients *unlearn* their problematic reactions and to learn a new way of reacting. CBT is a form of psychotherapy that emphasizes the important role of thinking in how we feel and what we do. If we are experiencing unwanted feelings and behaviors, it is important to identify the thinking that is causing the feelings or behaviors and learn to replace this thinking with thoughts that lead to more desirable reactions. Although there are several different forms of CBT, most have the following characteristics, as outlined on the website of the National Association for Cognitive-Behavioral Therapists (http://macbt.org):

1. CBT is based on the cognitive model of emotional response. Cognitive behavioral therapy is based on the premise that thoughts cause feelings and behaviors. The benefit of this assumption is that thoughts can be changed to help a person feel better or behave more effectively, even if the situation does not change. With a revised way of thinking, the person may, in fact, be able to behave in the situation in order to change it for the better. However, even if the situation cannot be changed, the person can feel less distressed by having a new outlook.

2. CBT is brief and time-limited. Cognitive behavioral therapy is considered among the "fastest" in terms of results obtained. The average number of sessions clients receive (across all types of problems) is only 16. Other forms of therapy, like psychoanalysis, can take years. What enables CBT to be briefer is its highly instructional nature and the fact that it makes use of homework assignments. Because CBT is comparatively brief, it is also less expensive, thus bringing an effective form of psychotherapy within reach of a much larger number of people.

3. Learning to think differently is the focus of therapy. Some forms of therapy assume that the main reason people get better is because of the positive relationship between the therapist and client. Cognitive behavioral therapists believe it is important to have a trusting relationship with clients, but that is not enough. CBT therapists believe that the clients change when they learn to think differently; therefore, CBT therapists focus on teaching new rational thinking skills that the person can use when he or she is no longer in counseling.

4. CBT is a collaborative effort between the therapist and the client. Cognitive behavioral therapists seek to learn what their clients want out of life (their goals) and then help their clients achieve those goals. The therapist's role is to listen, teach, and encourage, while the client's roles is to express concerns, learn, and implement that learning.

5. CBT is based on teaching how to minimize negative and upsetting emotions. Cognitive behavioral therapy does not tell people how they should feel. However, most people seeking therapy want to change the way they feel. CBT teaches the benefits of feeling calm when confronted with undesirable situations. It also emphasizes the fact that people have undesirable situations. If people are upset about their problems, they have two problems—the problem, and their emotional state about it.

6. CBT therapists ask questions and teach clients to ask questions. Cognitive behavioral therapists want to gain a very good understanding of their clients' concerns. That's why they often ask questions. They also encourage their clients to ask questions of themselves, such as, "How do I really know that those people are laughing at me?" "Could they be laughing about something else?"

7. CBT is structured and directive. Cognitive behavioral therapists have a specific agenda for each session. Specific techniques and concepts are taught during each session. CBT focuses on helping clients achieve the goals they have set. The assumption is that if clients knew what the therapist had to teach them, clients would not have the emotional and behavioral problems they are experiencing. When people understand how and why they are doing well, they can continue to practice what they have learned and apply it to new situations when the therapy has ended.

8. CBT theory and techniques rely on evaluating thoughts. Often, people upset themselves about things when, in fact, the situation isn't like they think it is. Therefore, CBT encourages clients to treat their thoughts as hypotheses that can be questioned and tested. If they find that their hypotheses are incorrect, perhaps because they have new information, then they can change their thinking to be in line with how the situation really is. Often this results in a change in emotions that were a product of prior incorrect analysis of the situation.

9. Homework is a central feature of CBT. Goal achievement, if obtained, could take a very long time if all a person were only to think about the techniques and topics taught for 1 hour per week. CBT therapists assign homework exercises, and reading each week to encourage their clients to engage in the new learning frequently between therapy sessions, just as one would be encouraged to practice the piano between lessons. Through repetition, new techniques are acquired more quickly and supported by weekly reinforcement from the therapist.

CBT is a product of several of the different types of theories we have discussed. It draws upon principles of classical conditioning to understand the association between thoughts and feelings. It also draws on the principles of operant conditioning, especially the focus on the way that habits are built based on the positive or negative consequences of one's behaviors. Finally, it takes into account the complex forms of thinking that intervene between stimulus and response as outlined in cognitive learning theory, especially expectations, values, and goals. The technique has grown rapidly over the past 30 years and has been applied to a wide array of mental health problems including depression, various forms of anxiety disorders, and social skill deficits. One meta-analysis of the effectiveness of CBT in treating generalized anxiety disorders reported that in comparison to waiting list or placebo control groups, CBT was more effective. Several studies also showed CBT to be more effective than pharmacotherapy, with the notable feature that individuals remained in therapy longer when in CBT than when being treated with drugs (Mitte, 2005). Techniques of CBT have also been applied to populations of children, for example socially rejected children, to teach them positive relationship skills and to overcome negative attribution biases that occur because they expect others to react negatively to them.

HOW DO THE LEARNING THEORIES ANSWER THE BASIC QUESTIONS THAT A THEORY OF HUMAN DEVELOPMENT IS EXPECTED TO ADDRESS?

What is the direction of change over the life span? How well does the theory account for patterns of change and continuity?   Theories of learning do not suggest a direction for development over the life span. In contrast to the psychosexual or cognitive developmental theories, which offer a predictable sequence of stages, the learning theories assume that the adaptive learner will change his or her behavior in response to systematic changes in the environment. To the extent that environments remain the same, habits that are formed will continue to be expressed across settings. Ideas such as self-efficacy and expectations, which emerge from social learning theory and cognitive behaviorism, suggest that a person's beliefs about the self and the environment will contribute to continuity in behavior over time. According to the learning theories, the reason that people of a certain age behave in a similar way is due to the fact that they have encountered similar reinforcement schedules and have been rewarded for behaving in similar ways.

What are the mechanisms that account for growth? What are some testable hypotheses or predictions that emerge from this analysis?   The learning theories offer a number of mechanisms that account for relatively permanent changes in behavior. These mechanisms are described in Table 5.1. More than many other theories discussed in this book, the learning theories offer a number of testable hypotheses about the conditions under which change takes place. Testable hypotheses have focused on the timing and sequencing of associations; the effects of reinforcement and schedules of reinforcement on learning; generalizability of responses; the role of expectations and goals on learning; the conditions under which models will be imitated; and the components of a task that influence speed and effectiveness of processing.

How relevant are early experiences for later development? What evidence does the theory offer to support its view?   Classical conditioning has the most to offer about how early experiences of infancy contribute to patterns of expectations. The meaningful links between sights, sounds, smells, and tactile stimulation that occur as part of an infant's daily care provide early structures that are connected to reflexive responses such as nursing, grasping, smiling, or clinging. Classical conditioning also suggests a mechanism through which signs and symbols come to have meaning through repeated association with the objects they represent. Operant conditioning offers a way

TABLE 5.1
Mechanisms That Account For Change

Learning Theory	Mechanism That Accounts for Change
Classical Conditioning	Associational learning: The pairing of two events, such as the sound of a bell and the presentation of food, becomes significant because one stimulus becomes a signal for the other.
Operant conditioning	The Law of Effect: When a response is followed by a positive feeling state it strengthens the bond between the stimulus and the response. When faced with a similar situation, the response is likely to occur. When a response is followed by a negative feeling state, it weakens the bond between the stimulus and the response. When faced with a similar situation, the response is less likely to occur.
	The Law of Exercise: Patterns are strengthened through repetition; the more frequently a stimulus response connection is repeated, the stronger it becomes.
	People change whenever their operant behaviors adapt to changes in the environmental contingencies.
Social Learning	Modeling: New learning occurs through the observation and imitation of models. Those models who are perceived as powerful and who control resources are most likely to be imitated.
Cognitive Behaviorism	Cognitions or mental representations are formed that intervene between the stimulus and the response. The learner acquires cognitive structures that influence subsequent learning and performance. Some of the most significant of these include a cognitive map of the environment, expectancies about the reward structure of the environment, a sense of self-efficacy, and goals.

of understanding the formation of early habits that are acquired in the context of systematic reinforcements such as food, social reinforcement, smiles, hugs, and kisses. As early habits are formed, certain behaviors become automatic and can be linked together to form more complex behaviors.

Social learning theory introduces the notion that learning can happen rapidly; not as a chain of simple responses, but as a result of observing and then imitating entire behavior sequences. Most likely, many of the expressions, activities, and strategies children use are acquired in this way, and then used to achieve a child's own idiosyncratic goals. The role of imitation in child development has been widely studied, pointing to the conditions that make it most likely that a model will be imitated. This research has led to a widely held belief in the importance of models, and their potential impact on children who observe and emulate their behaviors.

As information processing theory suggests, the trajectory from novice to expert provides a way of conceptualizing the gradual transformation of early experiences, which may be isolated, discrete behaviors, into complex strategies for solving problems. The educational system is designed to encourage increasingly complex, efficient approaches to problem solving. At each age, society is organized to introduce the person to more information, to expect individuals to make use of new problem solving strategies, and to build on these strategies in order to achieve new levels of expertise.

How do the physical, cognitive, emotional, and social functions interact? How well does the theory explain these interactions? The different learning theories highlight some of these capacities more than others. In classical conditioning, learning begins through association with innate, physical reflexes. Just as Piaget viewed cognition as having its origins in the biological nature of the learner, so classical conditioning starts from these physical, automatic responses. Classical conditioning also includes features such as attention and arousal, thus including the affective or emotional aspects of learning. Operant conditioning began by selecting a behavior that the learner was able to do, such as pushing a button or pressing a bar. The focus of this type of learning is to build complex behaviors from smaller, simple elements. In addition, the reinforcement often had a physical basis, such as food or shock. As the learning theory experiments were extended to children, treats such as candy were used. After a while, these physical rewards were replaced by symbolic rewards such as stickers or tokens, and social rewards such as smiles and hugs. However, social learning theory was the one to bring the social aspect of learning into the forefront by recognizing that learning occurs in a social environment, and that the salient behaviors that children want to imitate are those that are being enacted by the important figures in their social world. Finally, cognitive behaviorism introduced the more complex cognitive capacities into the learning process by integrating concepts such as self-encodings, expectancies, values, plans, and goals into the mix.

How do the environmental and social contexts affect development? What aspects of the environment does the theory suggest are especially important in shaping the direction of development? As one might expect, this is a strength of the learning theories, in that these theories have done much to highlight salient aspects of the environment that influence behavior. The early theories emphasized the association of stimuli that occur close together in time. Learning was tied almost exclusively to stimuli in the environment and to the consequences of behavior. With social learning theory, the lens was widened to include more elaborate behavioral sequences that could be observed and imitated. The early learning theories were described as ignoring the mind entirely or referring to the mind as a "black box" that was unknowable. Subsequent theories, especially cognitive behaviorism, information processing, and experiential learning theory, focus more on cognitive capacities that allow the learner to make senses of the environment, but they still assume that behavior is intimately shaped by the learner's transactions with the physical and social environments.

According to the theory, what factors place individuals at risk at specific periods of the life span? Several factors are known to interfere with learning. First, any neurological damage occurring prenatally as a result of exposure to teratogens or as a result of genetic anomalies, neurological damage due to accident or illness, drug use, or deterioration associated with the illnesses of aging can interfere with learning and memory. Second, anxiety such as that created through inconsistent or noncontingent reward and punishment, trauma, or harsh punishment can interfere with the ability to learn. Finally, fear of failure can produce undue cautiousness and an over reliance on established habits which may not be adaptive to changing environmental contingencies. According to social learning theory, a low sense of self-efficacy in a particular area can interfere with new learning. Those with low self-efficacy are more likely to assume that they will not be successful, and give up in the face of difficult challenges thereby missing the opportunity to reach new levels of competence.

CRITIQUE OF THE LEARNING THEORIES

The learning theories include several different views about how systematic changes in the environment produce relatively permanent changes in behavior. Classical conditioning and operant conditioning focus on relatively simple forms of learning which, when chained or linked together, can account for some complex behaviors. Social learning theory and cognitive behaviorism examine the processes involved in relatively more complex types of learning, including learning of social behavior, the reward structure of situations, and the development of problem-solving strategies. Cognitive behaviorism and information processing theories also offer ways to think about self-correcting systems where information gathered from the consequences of action can be used to modify understanding of the situation and alter subsequent behavior.

Strengths

The learning theories draw attention to the way that even some minute, incidental events influence learning and produce change. The focus on reinforcement and its association with behavior have led to new ways of thinking about how to structure the environment in order to promote new learning, to alter unacceptable behaviors, and to encourage more desirable behaviors. The learning theories have provided ways of analyzing systematic features of environments and have highlighted the capacity of humans to detect and respond to those features. As a result, the learning theories have had widespread application in the design of educational, industrial, and therapeutic environments.

The emphasis on the environment leads to ideas about how a person might respond differently depending on the nature of the setting or situation and its reinforcing properties. In contrast to some of the theories discussed in Part I, which suggest that people at a certain stage of development are likely to behave similarly across settings, the learning theories predict that behavior is shaped by environmental contingencies, and that these contingencies are likely to vary from setting to setting. This approach to understanding behavior has led to a greater appreciation of contexts for learning and development.

More than many other theories discussed in this book, the learning theories evolved as a result of tightly controlled experiments. Because the theories, especially classical conditioning, operant conditioning, and social learning, focused on conditions associated with changes in behavior, the constructs offered in these theories were systematically translated into observable behaviors such as salivation to the sound of a bell, bar pressing, or imitation of a model. These theories emerged through a step by step deductive process as experiments were carried out, results were examined, and general principles were formulated. More than many other theories of change, the learning theories have produced testable hypotheses about causal relationships between antecedents and consequences. Some of the basic laws of behavior, such as the notion that a behavior is likely to be repeated when it is followed by a positive consequence, have emerged through the experimental science associated with learning theories. As the learning theories took into account more cognitive processes such as expectancies, values, goals, and plans, some of this advantage of testability was lost in the interest of addressing more complex features of learning.

All theories of development are expected to offer ideas about the direction of change and the processes that may account for change. The learning theories have contributed greatly to our understanding of the mechanisms of change, especially as they apply to the acquisition of new behaviors and the alteration of old habits. Basic concepts about mechanisms of change emerging from the learning theories include: the association of events in time, the effects of repetition, the effects of reinforcement, the speed of learning and resistance to extinction under various conditions of reinforcement, the salience of role models for learning new behaviors, the development of expectancies and the internal representation of environments as guides for behavior, and the feedback loop for modification of behavior. These theories suggest that there is an incremental nature to change in which habits or responses become consolidated and strengthened through repetition. These theories also offer ideas about how change is maintained across situations, through the concept of generalization and the notion that schedules of reinforcement produce resistance to extinction. Bandura's concept of self-efficacy suggests a mechanism through which the learner comes to have confidence in the possibility of change and is willing to persist over the course of some failures in order to achieve a goal.

Weaknesses

The principles of learning theories emerged from very carefully controlled experimental situations that were designed to be able to test causal relationships. As a result, many of these experiments lacked ecological validity. Animals were placed in environments such as the T–maze, the Skinner box, or the Pavlovian harness. In fact, animal and human behavior takes place in complex settings where the learner has access to additional environmental cues that may contribute to learning. Studies of animal behavior in the natural environment have demonstrated that animals are capable of much more flexible and complex responses than were observed in the laboratory. The reliance on animal studies and the use of artificial learning conditions that are quite unlike the learner's natural environment raise questions and suggest limitations regarding the applicability of the learning principles to explain processes of learning for humans.

Both classical conditioning and operant conditioning experiments typically used deprivation to manipulate motivation. Animals were placed on a very restrictive feeding schedule in order to ensure that food would be a valued reinforcement. These theories do not address the orientation of organisms to learn about their environment because of exploratory motives such as curiosity or the desire to exercise mastery in the face of challenge. Cognitive behaviorism addressed this deficit by including concepts such as goals and values, suggesting that the learner has the capacity to impose an agenda on the direction of behavior change. As an example, in the process of career management, a person may decide to learn new skills in order to be successful in competing for a particular type of job, or to achieve a salary raise or promotion. The goal itself becomes a long-term reward that motivates behavior change.

The application of learning theory to behavioral control in environments such as prisons, or with people who have difficulty regulating their impulses, often exploit the use of tokens to reward specific behaviors. These "token economies" keep people relatively deprived by establishing a strict regimen with few choices or privileges. The tokens become valuable in such an environment because they can purchase items that the person is deprived of or has no other way of obtaining. The application of these ideas with more typically developing children and adolescents may fail to consider the power of competence, curiosity, and mastery as motivations for learning. For example, you do not need to reward a child with a sticker for solving a problem or getting a good score on a test. You want children to enjoy the internal experience of mastery and the related feelings of competence, which are independent of an external reward. These internal reinforcements transcend environments and are important for guiding an individual's behavior over the life span.

Learning theories typically do not take into account the developmental level of the learner. The developmental level of the person is a product of physical maturation, cognitive level, social relationships, previous learning, and the synthesis of complex habits. For example, a 2-year-old child may be motorically coordinated, demonstrate effective language skills, and enjoy play and social interaction. However, even with much social reinforcement, and the opportunity to observe and imitate his older brother, he cannot pedal a tricycle. His legs are not quite long enough and strong enough to make the needed pedal strokes. He does not quite understand the idea of steering with the handle bars, and he is likely to tip over when he tries to turn the tricycle around. By age 3, the child will most likely be able to accomplish this new task. Similar examples can be seen with 4- and 5-year-old children who are not developmentally ready to read, and seventh graders who do not have the formal operational reasoning and abstract conceptualization necessary to understand algebra.

Learning theories place a great deal of emphasis on the structure of the environment and the ability of the learner to alter behavior in order to adapt to environmental regularities. They do not have a systematic way of taking into account the developmental level of the learner. There is an assumption that the principles or mechanisms of learning account for behavior change universally. There is no consideration of the need to identify developmentally appropriate reinforcements, to take into account the physical or cognitive maturation of the learner, or to consider the changing values or goals of the learner at different stages of life. The learning theories suggest that the person is completely malleable; however, the theories fail to account for differences in capacity or motivation that are a product of maturation.

KEY TERMS

classical conditioning

unconditioned stimulus (UCS)

unconditioned response (UCR)

neutral stimulus (NS)

conditioned response (CR)

conditioned stimulus (CS)

higher order conditioning

extinction

spontaneous recovery

generalization

discrimination

operant conditioning

stimulus

response

law of effect

law of exercise

habit

trial-and-error learning

reinforcement

positive reinforcer

negative reinforcer

shaping

schedules of reinforcement

continuous reinforcement

intermittent reinforcement

punishment

social learning

observational learning

vicarious learning

models

modeling

cognitive behaviorism

intervening variable

cognitive map

cognitive competencies

self-encoding

expectancies

values

goals

plans

self-control strategies

self-efficacy

enactive attainment

vicarious information

verbal persuasion
physical state
information processing
attention
selective attention
divided attention
short-term memory
working memory
long-term memory
semantic memory
episodic memory
prospective memory
organizational strategies
experiential learning
learned helplessness
learned resourcefulness

Chapter 6

Social Role Theory

CHAPTER OUTLINE

Historical Context

Key Concepts

   A Definition of Social Roles

   Dimensions of Social Roles

   Reciprocal Roles

   Role Expectations and Norms

   Influence of Multiple Roles on Development

   The Contribution of Changing Social Roles on Development

      Movement through Age Roles

      Abrupt Entry into New Roles

      Attainment of Desired Roles

      Role Loss

New Directions: Gender Roles and Gender Identity Development

A Research Example: Balancing Work and Family Roles

An Application: Supporting Refugee Families and Youth

How Does Social Role Theory Answer the Basic Questions that a Theory of Human Development Is Expected to Address?

Critique of Social Role Theory

   Strengths

   Weaknesses

Key Terms

Chapter 6

Social Role Theory

A major question in the study of human development is how the immature child is transformed into a mature, well-integrated member of society. The learning theories point to moment-by-moment features of the environment that shape behaviors and form enduring habits. In contrast, social role theory focuses on how children, adolescents, and adults are able to locate their positions and status within the society, and how they learn the behaviors, feelings, and expectations that are associated with their roles. Social role theory traces the process of socialization and personality development as a person moves through life, occupying and enacting increasingly diverse and complex social roles.

HISTORICAL CONTEXT

The idea of describing patterns of human behavior as social roles emerged in several fields in the late 1920s and 1930s. Early scholars differed in the way they conceptualized roles and their functions in shaping social behavior

(Biddle, 1979). Anthropologist Ralph Linton, for example, saw roles as units of culture and assumed that roles were consistent throughout a society (Linton, 1936, 1945). The sociologist Talcott Parsons (1951) suggested that roles belonged to the social system. The fact that they resulted in common patterns of behavior across individuals was explained by the shared role expectations held by members of the social group. Parsons argued that common role behaviors were supported by shared sanctions. George Herbert Mead (1934) saw role taking as an essential socialization process through which the self-concept is formulated as the person identifies with and internalizes the goals and values of society.

Roles are thought to be a form of self-other systems. As a person learns how to enact a role, he or she also learns what others expect. Thus, social role learning includes acquiring a patterned set of behaviors and an internalized understanding of how others will react to those behaviors. Building on these ideas, J.L. Moreno (1934/1953), the creator of *psychodrama*, applied the activity of role playing to education and psychotherapy. Because of the compelling premise that social roles shape key interactions that individuals have with others, the concept of social roles and associated processes gained momentum in the study of socialization, identity theory, interpersonal relationships, and the function of social organizations (Brim, 1966).

This perspective brought new insights to the field of development, which, in the early 1900s, had been dominated by a greater emphasis on maturation than socialization and more focused on descriptions of physical and cognitive maturation than social and interpersonal behavior (Brim, 1966). In the 1950s and 1960s a number of research directions emerged in the field of human development that grew out of assumptions closely tied to social role theory. Albert Bandura's social learning theory highlighted the concept of role models, suggesting that children observe and imitate individuals who play key roles in their lives, especially authority figures, peer leaders, and television or film heroes and heroines (Bandura & Walters, 1963). Eleanor Maccoby (1961) wrote about the importance of role taking, pointing out that children learn much about the complementary roles that are enacted by their parents as they coordinate their behaviors with those of their caregivers. As a result, internalization of societal expectations occurs in part through participation in complementary role relationships.

Scholars who were interested in adult development drew upon social role theory as a way of thinking about mechanisms of change. Bernice Neugarten (1963; Neugarten, Moore, & Lowe, 1965) introduced the idea of age norms and age constraints, suggesting that society has age-graded expectations for the timing of entry into or exit from key roles. Orville Brim, Jr. (1968) focused on the new expectations associated with continuing roles and entry into new roles requiring new learning as two mechanisms that accounted for development in adulthood. Thus, the study of development expanded to include analysis of adulthood largely through a conceptualization of the timing and nature of adult roles.

KEY CONCEPTS

A Definition of Social Roles

A *role* is any set of behaviors that has a socially agreed upon function and an accepted code of norms (Biddle, 1979; Biddle & Thomas, 1966; Brown, 1965). We are children, parents, teachers, friends, students, workers, citizens, competitors, and lovers. These and other roles refer to particular positions. Aspiring to enact certain roles, and feeling pressure from others for adequate role performance make an impact on the consolidation of personality. Especially roles that endure across many life stages, including the roles of child, parent, and worker, carry certain norms for behavior that will be integrated into a personal conception of self. What is more, the acquisition of new roles is generally accompanied by internalized expectations, or values about how particular roles ought to be enacted. We come to define ourselves in terms of the primary roles we hold. Moreover, through the process of role enactment we internalize expectations for our own behavior and the behavior of others that shape subsequent interactions.

The term *role* was taken from the theater. In a play, actors' behaviors are distinct and predictable because each actor has a part to play and follows a script. Role theory uses the theatrical metaphor to explain the structure of society and the integration of the individual in social life (Biddle, 1986). Social roles serve as a bridge between the individual and the society. Every society has a range of roles, and individuals learn about the expectations associated with them. As people enter new roles, they modify their behavior to conform to these role expectations.

However, the theatrical metaphor should not be misunderstood to suggest that roles are a form of pretense. People experience their roles as meaningful, demanding, and compelling aspects of their identity. People may experience conflicts among their roles, or conflicts among role groups within societies that result in intense emotional stress

An infant has few roles that have socially agreed upon functions. In our own culture, the roles of an infant may include that of child, sibling, and grandchild. At successive life stages, the person acquires a variety of roles within the family, as well as within the context of other social institutions, such as school, business, and community.

The concept of role highlights the importance of the social context in the developmental process. Individuals bring their own unique temperaments, skills, and values to bear on the interpretation and enactment of their roles.

Nonetheless, most roles exist independently of the people who enact them. For example, our expectations about the role of a teacher guide our evaluation of each new teacher we meet. Those same expectations influence the way people who perform the role of teacher actually behave in this role. Knowledge of the functions and norms associated with any given role will influence both the performance of the person who assumes it and the responses of a whole network of people associated with the performer (Goffman, 1959; Biddle, 1979).

Dimensions of Social Roles

Social roles can be seen as having four dimensions. First, one must ask about the number of roles in which a person is involved. As that number increases, the person's appreciation of the social system as a whole increases. Cognitive complexity, social perspective taking, and interpersonal problem-solving ability can be expected to increase with the number and diversity of social roles. In fact, Parsons (Parsons & Bales, 1955) has argued that the process of socialization can best be understood as an outcome of participation in a growing number of increasingly diverse and complex social roles. People who resist involvement in new roles can be viewed as forestalling their development by closing off access to new responsibilities as well as new demands.

A second dimension along which roles vary is the intensity of involvement that they demand or that a person brings to them. Sarbin and Allen (1968) proposed an 8-point scale of role involvement, from zero, or noninvolvement, to 7, at which the self is indistinguishable from the role. At the low end, they give the example of a person whose membership in a club has lapsed for a number of years. Such a position holds no immediate expectations for behavior, although the person could resume involvement at any time. At the high end, they give the example of a person who believes he or she is the object of witchcraft. The total being is so involved in the role that death can result.

The more intense a person's role involvement is, the greater their investment of attention and energy in the role. The greater their emotional commitment to the role, the greater their anxiety about failure to meet role expectations. As a person becomes fused with a role, his or her personality comes increasingly to be influenced by the socialization pressures that are tied to it.

A third dimension of the social role is the amount of time the role demands. This dimension is important because a time-consuming role sets up the basic structure for many daily interactions. The role of gas station attendant, for example, may not involve high intensity, but it may require so many hours per day that the person has few opportunities to enact other roles. In fact, a low-intensity role may be a source of constant personal frustration if it continues to demand a large number of waking hours.

The fourth dimension of a role that influences its impact on personality is the degree of structure specified for it. Social roles vary in the extent to which expectations are specified and in the degree of consensus about how they should be performed. Some social roles, such as member of Congress, police officer, and college president, have written criteria for their enactment. Such public figures are generally held accountable for their performance of the services they were elected, hired, or appointed to provide. The role performer and the audience agree upon certain behaviors as being appropriate to the role. Even less public roles, such as secretary, bookkeeper, and salesperson, have written criteria stating a specified degree of structure. Like public figures, these workers are expected to perform the services for which they were hired.

Other roles are much less clearly articulated. They may be defined by cultural myths (for example, the role of explorer) or by community norms (such as the role of neighbor). Enactment of some roles is quite private—viewed only by members of the immediate family or a few close friends. In these instances, one is free to define and to enact the role as it suits the few people who are involved. Lovers, siblings, close friends, and marriage partners can develop relationships along a variety of paths without coming under the scrutiny of elaborate socialization pressures for specific role performances. This does not mean that no expectations accompany these roles; rather, they provide room for individual agreements and improvisation.

When roles are highly structured, the issue of person–role fit comes into question. Under conditions of lack of fit, a role occupant experiences continual frustration at the demands for behavior that are not compatible with his or her temperament, talents, or motives. In contrast, when the fit is comfortable, a highly structured role may provide the reassurance and support that come from knowing the expectations for behavior. Under conditions of person–role compatibility, a highly structured role may offer opportunities for the development of new competences that will contribute to a person's maturation and growth.

When there is less consensus about a role, the occupant generally has more opportunities to shape it to reflect personal predispositions. However, privately defined roles can generate considerable conflict if the people in reciprocal role positions cannot agree about how a role should be played. For example, although the roles of husband and wife offer considerable latitude for expressing personal preferences and values, if the partners cannot agree about the expectations that accompany these roles, the marriage will suffer from continual conflict and uncertainty.

Reciprocal Roles

Each role is usually linked to one or more related or *reciprocal* roles. The student and the teacher, the parent and the child, and the salesperson and the customer are in reciprocal roles. Each role is partly defined by the other roles that support it. The function of the role is determined in relation to the surrounding role groups to which it is allied. When you enact a role, you also learn about how the person in the reciprocal role is likely to behave. As in ballroom dancing, in order to perform the role well, it is necessary to anticipate and coordinate your actions with those in the complementary role.

Role Expectations and Norms

Social roles are characterized by certain expectations for behavior including obligations the person is expected to carry out and privileges that are permitted to the person in the role (Gold & Douvan, 1997). These expectations are typically understood by the person in the role, by people in complementary or reciprocal roles, and by any audience of observers to the role enactment. Norms are the shared beliefs held by others, not just those involved in the role, about role expectations. For example, a man and woman may have role expectations about how mothers and fathers ought to handle the discipline of their children. The woman may expect that fathers are responsible for carrying out discipline for serious misbehavior and she may communicate this expectation to her husband and her children. If most people in the community share this expectation, including both men and women, then the expectation could be considered a norm of the father role. However, some men may have different expectations about who handles discipline, perhaps expecting that mothers do most of the discipline and fathers support their wives by insisting that the children respect their mothers. This illustrates a situation in which the expectations for the father role differ between the husband and wife, and perhaps these differences are reflected more widely in the community. Thus, in this instance there are no norms for the father's role regarding discipline.

In modern society, with changing gender roles such that there is greater equality between husbands and wives, and new expectations for both husbands and wives to be involved in both work and parent roles, there are fewer norms regarding the mother and father roles. These roles are still defined by expectations but the expectations emerge in the context of interpersonal relationships between partners more than through the pressure of norms that are widely held in the community.

Influence of Multiple Roles on Development

In general, the pattern of increased participation in a greater number of complex roles is viewed as a normal and positive experience. Social-role theorists argue that the underlying mechanism of development is the opportunity to expand one's repertoire of role enactments (Brim, 1966; Nye, 1976; Parsons & Bales, 1955). With the increase in the number of simultaneous roles that a person plays comes a demand to learn new skills of role playing, role differentiation, and role integration. With each new role, the person's self-definition changes, and his or her ability to influence the environment increases (Brim, 1976a). Allport (1955, 1961) argued that the first criterion for a healthy personality is that the person demonstrate an extension of the self. This means that the person derives satisfaction and pleasure from diverse activities, participates in a variety of roles and activities, and shows involvement in meaningful relationships with others. This suggests that it is not only normal but growth-producing to participate in many roles simultaneously.

This is not to say that the experience of simultaneously occupying several roles is easy or free from stress. Quite the opposite may be true. There is often competition or conflict between the demands of two or more roles. Many college students experience difficulty managing the role expectations of their work and student roles. Young adults who are in an early phase of their occupational role find that they have trouble meeting the role expectations from work, family, friends, and intimate relationships. Particularly among dual-career couples, the intensity of role involvement at work may interfere with meeting role expectations of one's spouse or intimate partner. While part of role learning involves a widening of competences and relationships, another part involves balancing the conflicting responsibilities of simultaneous role expectations.

A case study of 4 Mexican American boys illustrates the complexity of role enactments and how multiple roles provide knowledge, influence, and marginality all at the same time (Smith & Whitmore, 2006). These boys are sons and parents, living with family members who care about them. They are active members of the CRIP gang, which provided a peer group role and expectations for role enactment. As one consequence of their illegal gang activity, they are considered to be delinquents by the juvenile court with the associated definition, status, and expectations of this deviant role. Finally, they are tied to a school community as students and dropouts, viewed as "at risk" students in this context. These boys enact roles that are central to some social systems and marginal to others; they have insights about how to traverse multiple communities; and they illustrate how inadequate it is to categorize an individual on the basis of only one of the many roles a person plays.

Although the stresses from role conflict can be great, they may also be a force toward growth. When role demands conflict, the person must begin to set priorities about how much energy can be devoted to each role. In the process of bringing many diverse roles into balance, the person imposes his or her own value system on life's demands. There may be ways to bring diverse roles into harmony or to eliminate roles that are no longer meaningful. In adulthood, the challenges posed by role conflict may foster a reevaluation of personal goals, as well as an integration of role behaviors. In striving to resolve role strain, the person can achieve, in each of the roles, competences that can enhance the performance of other roles. Having achieved a workable balance of role commitments, one has the opportunity to function at new levels of effectiveness. We might even hypothesize that the ability to resolve role strain effectively may, in itself, generate energy that will allow the person to take on additional roles or to perform existing roles with increased vigor.

Ineffective efforts to resolve role conflict, however, may detract from role performance in several roles. Failure to resolve role conflict drains energy from the total system. The person who is unable to bring work and family expectations into balance may experience chronic tension, physical symptoms, and disruption in the performance of both the work and family roles. What is more, this cycle of role failure is self-perpetuating. Drained of energy, a person is likely to falter as an effective worker, which may lead to ostracism by other workers, lack of promotion, or being fired. Inability to perform the role of spouse effectively may lead to estrangement, dissolution of the marriage, or social rejection by the extended family or the community. Because many roles are so essential to the maintenance of social organizations, failure at role enactment generally has serious consequences.

The Contribution of Changing Social Roles to Development

Entry into new roles across the life span has the potential for stimulating development. Three kinds of role changes are especially important to the process of reorganization of personality.

Movement Through Age Roles. Successive age roles are part of every culture's organization. For example, in traditional Chinese culture (Ch'ing dynasty, 1644 A.D.–1911 A.D.) development was differentiated into five periods: infancy (birth to age 3 or 4), childhood (4 to 15), adolescence (16 to marriage), fertile adulthood (marriage to about 55), and later adulthood (55 to death) (Levy, 1949). The notion of life stages reflects sequential changes in personal competences as well as changes in cultural expectations and demands. At each new stage, the person is able to function more effectively, to master new tasks, and to focus attention on new areas of concern. At the same time, the culture offers new opportunities, new areas of responsibility, and new restrictions (Newman & Newman, 2006).

Development at each new life stage can be understood as adaptation to both the opportunities and the restrictions of the new age role. Each age role brings a change in the person's status as well as a change in the range of behaviors that are expected. In order to meet these expectations, the person normally has to acquire new skills. Growth is promoted as the person tries to live up to the expectations for a new age role. The person is also usually expected to give up some of the earlier modes of behavior. The adolescent who threatens to tell his mother about a peer's misbehavior may be told to stop acting like a baby. The adult who is very moody, impulsive, and self-centered is described as acting like an adolescent. The older adult who decided to have a hair transplant and a facelift and to try out singles bars is criticized for refusing to "grow old gracefully." Consensus about the appropriate age for certain life attainments or activities seems to work as a prod to keep people moving along in their socialization as adults (Neugarten, Moore, & Lowe, 1965). Especially in middle and later adulthood, people tend to perceive age-related norms as motivating guidelines for behavior. Age norms about marriage, parenting, financial independence from parents, emotional independence from parents, and involvement with one's children force many people to give up old, familiar patterns in order to live up to the cultural expectations of a new age role.

Abrupt Entry Into New Roles.   The second kind of change in roles that prompts development is the relatively abrupt entry into new roles. There are some life experiences for which training or preparation is minimal. Some examples are starting school, dating, marriage, parenting, and retirement. Each of these experiences requires new learning on many levels at once. The role requires the development of many new skills, it generally involves increased uncertainty and anxiety, and there is considerable pressure from others in reciprocal roles to achieve effective enactment of the role. Because of the lack of training, one must draw on inner resources to cope with the uncertainty and social pressures tied to these new role positions. Effective coping will lead to the acquisition of new information, new strategies for responding to emerging demands, and the use of existing skills in new, more appropriate ways. What may begin as an anxiety-producing new role can stimulate an important expansion of competence. The satisfactions of the new role eventually bring about greater identification with the functions and norms of the role until the new role becomes integrated into the self-concept. In many instances, the opportunities of a new role bring to the surface latent competences and predispositions of which the person was not aware. The new parent may for the first time identify his or her potential for nurturance or playfulness. The new retiree may discover a latent capacity for intellectual development or for mastery of a manual skill that had never been given the opportunity to flourish.

With each new role, the person changes in two ways. First, the person attempts to meet new demands by making use of existing skills, making the role an extension of what he or she already does well. Second, the person modifies existing skills or acquires new skills in order to function more effectively in the new role. Over time, the person understands the role more fully, plays the role more effectively, and views the role as a less alien part of his or her life pattern.

Attainment of Desired Roles.   The third important source of role change is the attainment of desired roles. Whereas age roles are attained as a function of chronological age, some roles are achieved through effort and skill. Examples of achieved roles to which a person might aspire are: leader of a student organization, leader of a gang, mentor, or elected official. Often, one's ideals are stated in terms of roles. A person may hope to improve the conditions for people in his or her neighborhood by running for city council or by becoming a social worker and establishing a social service agency. People may become deeply involved in attaining desired roles because many motives are being satisfied at the same time.

As a person strives to attain desired goals, a process of reality-oriented reevaluation takes place. If a desired goal is achieved, the person is encouraged about the attainment of goals and the possibility of success in subsequent effort. One also has an opportunity to evaluate whether these ideals are really satisfying. One might try to become a school leader and then discover that the role is less glamorous or less satisfying than one had expected. There is also a reality-oriented reevaluation that comes from failing to achieve desired roles. When goals are missed, the person begins to redefine personal aspirations so that they more adequately reflect existing competences. Or the person may be highly motivated to strengthen existing competences and try, once again, to attain the goal that is being sought.

Some of the most important life roles persist through several stages. For example, we are someone's child from infancy until death, and we may be a partner in an intimate sexual relationship from adolescence through later adulthood. In each of these roles there is both continuity and change (Feldman & Feldman, 1975). The expectations for the role performance remain the same in some respects but change in others. We can begin to see how social roles provide a thread of consistency to life experience and how they prompt new learning.

Role Loss.   Over the life span we also lose roles. The most dramatic instance comes with the death of a reciprocal role partner. When a parent, child, or spouse dies, we lose an important role. Graduation from school, divorce, loss of employment, and retirement are other transitions that result in role loss. Social role theory helps us to understand the stressful nature of these changes by taking into account the time, emotional intensity, structure, and culturally shared meaning that are bound up in a single life role and the subsequent disorientation that is likely to follow its loss.

NEW DIRECTIONS: GENDER ROLE AND GENDER IDENTITY DEVELOPMENT

Gender is a critical element of one's identity. All cultures construct gender-differentiated roles, and these roles are associated with expectations to perform distinct tasks, have access to certain resources, and display certain powers and attributes. People expect one another to behave in certain ways because they are male or female. Perhaps more important, they form expectations of how men and women ought to act when they are together so that the distinctions between the genders are demarcated (Freud, 1994). How these expectations are taught and learned beginning in early childhood and throughout life has been a focus of extensive research in the field of gender role socialization.

The specific nature of gender role expectations differs from one culture to the next. Early in socialization, children are encouraged to conform to the norms of their gender. The gendered nature of the family is an especially important factor in shaping gender identity. Family experiences from the past provide the gender script with which children and adolescents are most familiar. The family life they envision for themselves in the future creates many of the priorities that shape young adults' current commitments and goals (Valsiner, 2000).

In the United States, gender role standards have been changing over the past 20 years, and the standards are also quite varied across ethnic cultural groups. Nonetheless, young children continue to identify certain toys, activities, and occupations as appropriate for girls and others as appropriate for boys. For example, in the Sex Role Learning Index, children are shown drawings of 20 objects traditionally associated with gender roles, 10 for the male gender role (such as hammer, shovel, and a fire helmet) and 10 for the female gender role (such as a stove and dishes). Children are asked to identify whether certain activities, occupations, or traits are more frequently associated with males, females, or both. By age 7, most children make a perfect score on this type of test (Beere, 1990; Serbin et al., 1993; Levy, 1998). Knowledge of gender-typed personality traits, such as gentle and affectionate or adventurous and self-confident, emerge at a slightly older age. In a study of 550 sixth graders, 90% answered questions of this type correctly (Serbin et al., 1993). This knowledge about gender role standards shapes a child's preferences and behavior. For example, once children identify certain toys or activities as more appropriate for girls and others for boys, their own preferences for toys, activities, and play companions are guided by this knowledge (Martin, Eisenbud, & Rose, 1995; Levy, Barth, & Zimmerman, 1998; Martin & Ruble, 2004).

One outcome of the formation of gender identity in childhood is that children's friendship groups are likely to be sex-segregated. When boys and girls are free to choose their play companions, they tend to choose others of their own sex. This pattern of same-sex social grouping among children is found not only in the United States, but in many other cultures (Edwards & Whiting, 1988). Sex segregation is promoted by both cognitive and behavioral factors (Barbu, Le Maner-Idrissi, & Jouanjean, 2000). Children expect others of the same sex to like similar activities, toys, and forms of play. Children form internal representations of what boys and girls are like as friends and playmates. These internal models guide the inferences they make as they engage in peer interactions. Thus, children are likely to seek others of the same sex because they believe these other children will have the same play preferences they have (Markovits, Benenson, & Dolenszky, 2001). At the same time, boys and girls appear to play differently, with young boys enjoying more rough and tumble play and girls enjoying fantasy-based, relational play. Thus, a preference for same-sex playmates may be fostered by feelings of comfort or discomfort within same sex or mixed sex play groups. Some cultures discourage boys and girls from playing together. For example, when children in a Brazilian tribal culture play family, the boys ("husbands") go off to pretend to be hunting and fishing, returning with leaves that are then given to the girls ("wives") to cook them and pass them out to the boys to eat (Gregor, 1977).

There is some evidence that pressures to behave in gender-stereotyped ways intensifies in early adolescence. Many of the stereotypical differences between boys and girls are accentuated in adolescence. This process may be tied to the new role of dating partner, rather than to changes associated with puberty itself. As teens begin to date, early popularity may be increased for those boys and girls who conform to current gender-role stereotypes. Girls who do not act feminine enough, often translated as gentle, sociable, sweet, or kind, and boys who do not act masculine enough, often translated as assertive, ambitious, confident, and self-sufficient, may be less popular with both same sex and opposite sex peers (Crouter, Manke, & McHale, 1995; Alfieri, Ruble, & Higgins, 1996).

In general, adolescent males who do not conform to the traditional norms for masculinity are viewed as more deviant by their peers than are girls who do not conform to the traditional norms for femininity. In fact, girls who have certain masculine characteristics, such as assertiveness and independence, have higher self-esteem and fewer mental health problems than the extremely feminine girls. Girls may feel pressured to act in feminine ways in order to be popular, but they are not punished if they continue to express their individual interests in areas such as athletics or science. Boys, on the other hand, are both pressured to act in stereotypically masculine ways, and punished if they give evidence of behaviors associated with the female gender role (Egan & Perry, 2001).

In later adolescence, young men and women begin to develop an analysis of what it takes to "get ahead" in their social world, whether success is defined as finding a mate, getting a good job, being a good parent, or being popular. They may learn to be more flexible in their interpersonal behavior, modifying their strategy to suit their goals. They discover that such traits as assertiveness, goal-directed behavior, competitiveness, being a good communication partner, personal disclosure, and negotiation are all required in social situations, and they learn to develop and apply theses skills as required. In previous generations, some of these traits were considered "masculine" and some "feminine". Today, however, they are perceived as helpful to both men and women to be able to succeed in their work and family roles.

A RESEARCH EXAMPLE: BALANCING WORK AND FAMILY ROLES

Almost everyone manages a career while juggling commitments to spouse, children, parents, other household members, and friends. A decision to assume more authority, work longer hours, accept an offer with another company, quit a job, accept a transfer to a new location or start up one's own business will touch the lives of other household and family members.

In thinking about balancing work and family roles, it is useful to consider three interrelated concepts: *role overload*, *role conflict*, and *spillover* (Nickols, 1994). Role overload occurs as a result of too many demands and expectations to handle in the time allowed. For example, a parent with three children ages 8, 11, and 15 may find that the demands of getting the children ready for school, attending functions at three different schools, picking children up and dropping them off at various places and trying to be emotionally available for the "problem of the day" is exhausting. Role overload can be experienced in one or more adult roles.

Role conflict refers to ways that the demands and expectations of various roles conflict with each other. For example, role conflict occurs when a worker is expected to stay late at the job to finish a project, but that same night is a spouse's birthday or a child's performance.

Spillover occurs when the demands or preoccupations about one role interfere with the ability to carry out another role. For example, a person may be disrupted at work by worries about an ill parent or distracted at home by a work assignment that is due the next day.

The combination of role overload, role conflict, and spillover can lead to reduced satisfaction at work and in family roles, and in a decline in the person's sense of well-being (Beale, 1997). On the other hand, multiple role involvement has been shown to contribute to well-being. Spousal support for the partner's involvement in work can increase work satisfaction, and feelings of success and pride in one's accomplishments at work can contribute to marital satisfaction (Dreman, 1997).

The domains of work and family, both central to adult lives across cultures, are likely to conflict under certain circumstances. In order to understand the nature of this conflict, researchers have identified the elements of work and the elements of family roles that appear to be most central to this conflict. The basic assumption is that there are role pressures from work and family that are mutually incompatible, so that meeting the expectations in one domain makes it very difficult to meet expectations in the other. Moreover, there may be interactions such that conflicts from work make it difficult to meet role expectations in the family, but then the disruptions in the family make it difficult to meet role expectations at work (Frone, 2003). Despite these tensions between work and family obligations, people strive to find ways for the two roles to work together (work–family fit), which leads to greater job satisfaction. Job flexibility is viewed as a factor that can contribute to this successful adaptation. This model is presented in Figure 6.1.

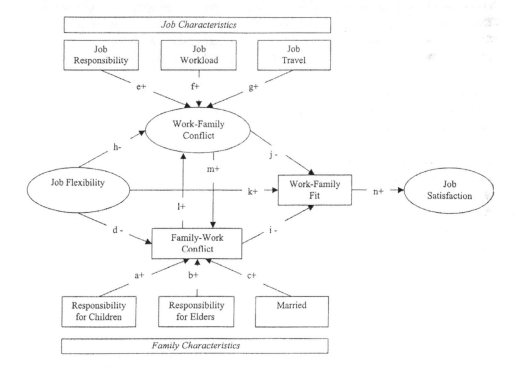

Figure 6.1. A model of work–family role fit. Paths marked with a *plus* (+) indicate a positive relationship; paths marked with a *minus* (-) indicate a negative relationship. Source: E. J. Hill, C. Yang, A. J. Hawkins, & M. Ferris, A cross-cultural test of the work–family interface in 48 countries. *Journal of Marriage and the Family*, 66, No. 5, Figure 1, p. 1302. Reprinted by permission of Blackwell Publishing.

In a study of the interface between work and family roles, the model just described was tested in 48 countries (Hill, Yang, Hawkins, & Ferris, 2004). The characteristics of a job that were identified as producing work–family conflict were: *job responsibility*, *job workload*, *and job travel*. The characteristics of the family that were identified as producing family–work conflict were: *responsibility for children, responsibility for elders,* and *being married*. The model was tested by analyzing survey responses of more than 25,000 IBM workers, whose average age was 39. The countries were divided into 1 group of Eastern countries with a collectivist orientation, and 3 groups of countries with a more individualist orientation: Western developing countries, Western affluent countries, and the United States.

The results of this study showed that the model was a good fit for all four groups of countries. The three job characteristics were significantly related to work–family conflict across all 48 countries, although the strength of the relationship was greater in the 3 individualist groups of countries. Responsibility for children and elders were related to family–work conflict across all the countries, but this relationship was stronger for women than for men. Contrary to expectations, marriage was related to less family–work conflict across all the countries. Job flexibility was associated with work–family conflict in the Eastern countries and the Western developing countries but not in the Western affluent countries or the United States. Across all the countries, work was much more likely to create conflict in family life than family life was to be disruptive for work. The general model was a good predictor of job satisfaction across very different work environments. One might ask whether the global corporate environment of IBM might have smoothed out some of the cultural variations that might have been observed had workers been drawn from a greater diversity of businesses. However, this research is an exciting beginning to understanding the dynamics of work–family role interactions at a global level.

The cross-national study adds to a growing literature documenting that women are more distressed by family–work conflict, possibly because responsibilities for household and child care continue to rest more on the shoulders of employed women than on those of employed men (Voydanoff, 2000). Nonetheless, trends in the United States are moving toward a more egalitarian model. Men and women increasingly agree about the value of having women in the labor market and the importance of family-friendly workplace policies. Employed men are spending an increasing amount of time on household and childcare tasks, both on workdays and nonworkdays. Between 1977 and 2002, the gap between the amount of time women and men spent on household tasks decreased from 3 hours to 1 hour on nonworkdays, and from 2.5 hours to 1 hour on workdays. As men spend more time on childcare tasks, the result is that children actually have more time with a parent than they did in 1977 (Barnett, 2004).

Women use a variety of strategies to cope with the strains of balancing work and family life (Denmark, Novick, & Pinto, 1996). Some women resolve the conflict between career aspirations and family commitment by limiting their competitive, achievement-oriented strivings. For them, the dual-earner relationship is a matter of negotiation with their spouse, who is regarded as giving them permission to go to work and who sets the limits on their involvement in work. In contrast, other women find that their workplace sets limits on their achievement through gender-stereotyped assumptions about the woman's commitment to her family role (Ridgeway & Correll, 2004). In these settings, women do not tend to be promoted to high-level administrative or managerial positions in which work demands would begin to invade family commitments. As an example, some companies are reluctant to put women in positions in which they may have to be transferred for fear that their husbands will refuse to make the move. Sometimes women who request flexible or part-time work schedules are labeled as not serious enough about their career. Finally, other women create a salient professional identity and look for a partner who will support their ambitions.

What is the impact of the dual-career arrangement on men? The emphasis in the literature on the difficulties women face in combining work and family life has created a perception that men are singly devoted to the world of work and are indifferent to or uninvested in home and family life. This is clearly not the case. Studies consistently find that men's happiness in their family roles is a stronger predictor of psychological well-being than adjustment at work (Pleck, 1985). Most men find personal meaning and emotional support in their roles as husband and father. For many men, the positive quality of their marital and parental roles helps them cope more effectively with the stresses of work (Barnett, Marshall, & Pleck, 1992). In many instances, specific lessons from home, including the patience and communication necessary to be an effective parent, the willingness to plan and work out alternative strategies for managing daily tasks with his wife, and the admiration he has for his wife in her paid labor force activities, actually help a man function more effectively at work.

Perhaps because of the centrality of the quality of home life to men's well-being, many men are sensitive to the possibility that their wife's involvement in the labor force may interfere with the emotional comfort and stability they seek at home. A wife's success in the world of work may reduce a husband's sense of power or importance in the marital relationship. Many men are especially uncomfortable if their wives earn more money than they do. In addition, some men find themselves ill-prepared to assume the more direct responsibilities of childrearing in order to support their wives' involvement in the labor market. However, among dual-career couples, marital harmony is sustained when husbands support their wives' involvement in the world of work and do not feel competitive with them (Wright, Nelson, & Georgen, 1994).

Adaptations to balancing work and family life are not simple. We are looking at the interface of multiple, interacting systems—each partner's work environment, each partner's role, demands within the family, and the partners' relationships with one another and with their children. An interesting example of this dynamic interaction was highlighted in research about the link between work-related stress and its impact on children's adjustment. When mothers worked long hours and felt overloaded, they were less warm and accepting toward their adolescent children. When fathers worked long hours and felt overloaded, they experienced more conflict with their adolescent children. In addition, husbands' negative work-related stressors also increased their wives sense of overload, beyond what the wives were experiencing because of their own work situation (Crouter & Bumpus, 2001). Thus, for wives, balancing work and family life required coping with their husband's experiences of work-related strain as well as their own.

The ability to bring positive energy from work to family is a product of individual and workplace characteristics. Voydandoff (2004) referred to this as *work–family facilitation*. Although people experience many types of work–family conflict, they may also find that experiences in the workplace increase their sense of self-worth, competence, and fulfillment, resulting in a more positive outlook on their interpersonal relationships at home. Voydanoff (2004) suggested that work–family facilitation is supported when the workplace revises its expectations for the worker role to include a greater consideration of the fact that most workers are also striving to meet pressing family role expectations within the scope of their daily lives. For example, policies that allow workers to take family-related leaves without risking their job security, or to take time off during the day to take a child to the doctor or meet with a teacher, reduce work–family conflict. A supportive work climate in which supervisors help workers feel comfortable about using these family-flexible policies and accommodating significant family obligations contributes to work–family facilitation. The implication of this research is that responsibility for success in achieving an effective balance between work and family roles should fall not only on the coping strategies of individuals but on the policies and climate of the work setting that support efforts to integrate the demands of multiple roles.

There are many dual-career arrangements, each involving the negotiation of roles and responsibilities to meet the convergence of work and family needs. A major issue in coping with the dual-career pattern seems to be each partner's capacity to revise basic expectations for his or her own behavior and his or her spouse's behavior. This is not easy. It touches on deep emotional commitments to one's view of one's self as a man or a woman, a husband or a wife, and a mother or a father. It also affects the enactment of one's values about being a breadwinner, and making significant work-related accomplishments.

AN APPLICATION: SUPPORTING REFUGEE FAMILIES AND YOUTH

Concepts from role theory are especially helpful in thinking about how best to support refugee families and youth as they cope with the many aspects of cultural and social change. Refugee families, especially those who are forced to migrate due to political persecution or wartime violence, experience the collision of multiple roles: life before the violence or war; life during the violence, sometimes accompanied by imprisonment or life in refugee camps; and life as a new U.S. immigrant. Once in the United States, refugees try to enact adult roles as parents, spouses, extended family members, members of a religious community, and workers, trying to forge some kind of meaningful accommodation to the different role expectations and cultural norms of their new home. Typically, they experience varying degrees of role conflict as they try to preserve essential cultural beliefs and values associated with the key life roles from the past while striving to ensure safety, economic and educational opportunities, and a hopeful future for their children in the new social environment.

In a qualitative study of Bosnian refugees in the Chicago community, researchers noted that Bosnian families expressed intense concern about problems experienced by their adolescent children. These problems included school-related difficulties, such as underachievement, school failure, and dropping out of school; family conflict; and association with delinquent youth (Weine, et al., 2006). This research team wanted to learn more about how the trauma associated with war and genocide, forced migration, and life in exile in a major U.S. urban center might be contributing to these problems. Twenty one families, including fathers, mothers, and adolescent children, participated in a guided 7-week discussion program facilitated by Bosnian refugees trained and supervised by university researchers. Themes from the discussion groups were coded to reveal basic family beliefs, homeland factors, and refugee factors that were influencing the families' adaptation and youth behavior. Through this work, four ideas associated with role theory emerged:

1. Parents held role expectations for themselves and their children that reflected their Bosnian traditions before the war. These included the view that families should be together and spend time together; children should respect their elders; and the family should stay connected to the extended family. They believed that the enactment of certain traditions, such as drinking coffee together, practicing the Muslim religion, and speaking the Bosnian language, were important.

2. Parents had clear role expectations for the worker role; they believed in working hard and striving to achieve economic stability. They believed that their children should apply this same work ethic to their school work and to earning money when they were old enough to work.

3. Parents saw their refugee status in the United States as a way of ensuring a better life for their children. Many believed that their own adult future was lost; their work roles were menial and their status within Bosnian society was lost. This meant that they were more deeply invested in the parent role than they might have been had they remained in Bosnia. Their hope was for a life of peace, happiness, and possibilities for their children that could not be attained for them in their home country.

4. Parents had grave concerns over the negative influence of American culture on their children. They believed that their children were being drawn into the youth culture too quickly. They saw pressures toward individualism, materialism, lack of discipline, exposure to crime, sex, and drugs, and delinquent peer associations. Parents recalled a time in Bosnia before the war, when they did not have to worry as much about their children and their children were free to be independent. Now, they found themselves redefining their parent role in order to limit their children's exposure to the undesirable influences of American life. The idea that the United States is a culture that could provide new roles and related opportunities and unwanted loss of one's cultural identity is not uncommon among refugee populations.

Each of these sets of role expectations posed some challenges for youth. The first set of expectations regarding family togetherness and family traditions was difficult for many Bosnian adolescents to satisfy given that they were trying to enact new role expectations conveyed by parents, peers, and teachers in their school and neighborhood. They wanted to have time to explore their community and to take advantage of new opportunities, such as after school activities and community programs. They found their parents to be judgmental and critical of the way they spent their time. With parents working long hours, and often multiple shifts, and many youth also working, they were not able to spend as much time with their parents as they might have liked.

Youth and parents expressed concerns about the school environment. Adolescents reported being bored; some said they did not get the kind of counseling or advice they had hoped for from teachers about how to adjust to U.S. social and cultural life. Parents believed that the schools were not challenging their children. There was some disappointment in the way U.S. teachers enacted the teacher role, with parents saying they believed the teachers should use a more strict form of discipline and insist on greater respect from students. Unfamiliar with the U.S. school system, the parents did not know how to communicate their expectations. Often, their disapproval was directed to their children who became increasingly disengaged from the student role.

Youth tended to have two different ways of coping with the intense investment that their parents were making in their future. Some believed that they could find a promising future in the United States by attending school, planning for college, working, and spending time with their parents and their relatives. They explored their new environment but tried not to worry their parents.

Others felt that they had been victimized by the Serbs and the war; displaced from their home; and misunderstood by their family, teachers, and peers. They experienced an irreconcilable role conflict between their parents' expectations for them to succeed in school and to prosper in the American community, and their parents' mistrust of American values and disappointment in American schools. They saw their parents as trying to guard them against a culture they had brought them to. As a result, they experienced the role loss of the trusting, harmonious parent–child relationship of their past, and hopelessness about the possibilities for meaningful role enactment as a student, child, or friend in their new culture.

HOW DOES SOCIAL ROLE THEORY ANSWER THE QUESTIONS THAT A THEORY OF HUMAN DEVELOPMENT IS EXPECTED TO ADDRESS?

What is the direction of change over the life span? How well does the theory account for patterns of change and continuity? Most societies have a series of age-graded roles that guide the direction of development throughout life. The roles vary from one society to another. In societies where there is cultural continuity, roles may remain quite constant from age to age, with new levels of mastery expected at each age. In societies where there is cultural discontinuity, childhood roles are very distinct from adult roles, and one must go through certain rites of passage or training to enter the adult roles. Continuity is explained by the enactment of roles that endure over long periods, such as child or parent. Continuity is also explained by participation in reciprocal roles; one learns about the expectations of one's own role and the adjoining roles. Change is explained by the process of role gain, role loss, and entry into an increasing number of roles that produce new levels of societal engagement.

What are the mechanisms that account for growth? What are some testable hypotheses or predictions that emerge from this analysis? Role norms and expectations, as well as the norms for reciprocal roles, are mechanisms that guide development. Individuals learn the norms of the roles they enact and the norms for the roles they expect to enact in the future. The idea of a role model suggests that individuals can observe, emulate, and internalize the behaviors of others so that they are able to enact these roles effectively at the appropriate time.

One testable hypothesis is that people who occupy the same role will demonstrate common behaviors, which reflect the norms and shared expectations for people in that role.

A second testable hypothesis is that the way a person enacts a role, such as teacher, is influenced by the expectations of those in reciprocal roles, such as students. In other words, a teacher's behaviors are shaped in part by his or her students' expectations and the students' behaviors are influenced by teachers' expectations.

A third testable hypothesis is that role enactment is guided by salient role models. For example, as one enacts the parent role, one is guided by the observations of one's own parents, and other adults one has observed in the parenting role.

How relevant are early experiences for later development? What evidence does the theory offer to support its view?   Early experiences are relevant for later development in several ways. First, children have opportunities to enact a variety of roles that provide insight into the point of view of others, especially through role taking, as in fantasy play or team sports. Second, family roles, roles in school, religious settings, and communities provide avenues for social participation that can provide a positive foundation for later social integration. Third, through the enactment of certain roles, children gain insight into the reciprocal roles that complement their own. This gives them ideas about what will be expected of them in adulthood. In the role of student, the child learns about teachers. If he or she becomes a teacher, the person has ideas about how teachers behave based on how he or she experienced teachers while in the student role. A parent who is interacting with a child's teacher has ideas about what teachers should be like based on his or her own experience with teachers in childhood.

In contrast to these ways that early experience can influence adult development, role theory also offers many ideas about new learning and new paths for development in adulthood. Many new roles open up in adulthood that require new learning. Experiences of role loss and role gain require flexible adaptations. Expectations about the timing and sequencing of adult roles, and the need to balance competing roles, are challenges that are associated with new growth in adulthood. As society changes, new roles may emerge that were not available during one's childhood. This is especially true in the world of work. New technologies may introduce new roles, such as online dating partner, sperm donating father, surrogate mother, or blogger. Role theory offers a way to think about new opportunities and demands for adaptation, and a supportive structure for personal development.

How do the physical, cognitive, emotional, and social functions interact? How well does the theory explain these interactions?   Roles are social; they are defined by social systems and link individuals to social structures. Roles require different levels of emotionality. For example, one might think of an accountant as a role in which one is supposed to keep emotions in check in order to stay focused on the task and not let emotions interfere with attention to detail. In contrast, a psychotherapist is expected to have high levels of empathy, and to be attuned to the emotional climate of interactions. The more salient a role is for a person, the more likely it is that the person will care about role performance. This may involve positive emotions if the role is recognized or valued, and negative emotions if the role is devalued or lost.

The cognitive aspects of role enactment have to do with knowing what is expected of the role and learning the skills required of the role. Most roles have implied ethical or moral guidelines for behavior, and some roles, such as being a lawyer, minister, or policeman, are substantially influenced by moral/ethical principles. Thus, one cognitive component of many roles includes knowing the moral standards for the role, and guiding one's behavior by these standards.

The physical demands of roles also vary widely. Certain roles include physical requirements and physical training. In some roles, such as soldier, athlete, or fireman, the physical demands also require a great deal of cognitive understanding, emotional commitment and regulation under highly stressful situations, and appropriate interpersonal cooperation and competition.

How do the environmental and social contexts affect development? What aspects of the environment does the theory suggest are especially important in shaping the direction of development? Social roles are a key component of the environment. The direction of development is shaped largely by the roles that are available at each period of life, the demands and expectations for those roles, and the sanctions associated with role enactment. People are influenced by the roles they play, the reciprocal roles linked to these roles, and the roles they aspire to in the future.

According to the theory, what factors place individuals at risk at specific periods of the life span? Role theory offers several ideas about factors that may place individuals at risk. First, individuals may be unable to meet role expectations due to physical, cognitive, or emotional limitations. For example, role expectations for students in the elementary grades may include sitting quietly, taking turns, focusing attention, listening attentively to others, and completing tasks. Children who have been diagnosed with Attention Deficit and Hyperactivity Disorder have six or more symptoms of inattention or impulsivity that make these role expectations very difficulty to achieve.

A second factor that may place individuals at risk is the possibility of role conflict, role overload, or role strain. Especially in adulthood, individuals experience many highly demanding roles. When these roles are particularly salient, as with parenting and work roles, a person may find that he or she simply cannot meet all the expectations of each role adequately. Role strain is a form of stress that can result in physical and mental health problems.

A third factor that may result in risk is uncontrolled or unwanted role loss, like unemployment, widowhood, or nonvoluntary retirement. To the extent that a social role provides a structure for personal identity and social integration, role loss can bring serious problems of alienation and social isolation.

CRITIQUE OF SOCIAL ROLE THEORY

Strengths

Social role theory offers a way of linking the individual and the social world. The concepts of social roles and the process of role enactment suggest a mechanism for socialization, a framework for relationships, and a structure for adult life. In societies where individualism is prized, the construct of social roles offers a way of understanding how people may experience a sense of autonomy and self-directed goal attainment by choosing to enter certain roles, and still behave in ways that are similar to others who occupy similar roles.

As societies change, new institutions emerge offering new roles. These new roles are mechanisms that recruit people for the operation of the new institutions and at the same time provide new scripts for how people interact and work together effectively in the new or changing institution. For example, with the emergence of public education in the late 19th century came the professionalization of the teacher role; roles for faculty in colleges specifically designed to prepare teachers; a hierarchy of administrative roles related to the organization of school districts and schools; roles for state and federal officials who established funding and credentialing of teachers; new expectations for children in the student role; and new expectations for parents to support their children's education by encouraging school attendance and engagement rather than by educating their children themselves.

Social role theory helps explain how identity becomes focused in adulthood and how it continues to change through role gain, role loss, and the integration of multiple roles. In contrast to many other developmental theories that do not deal with adult development, social role theory has provided a rich and fruitful framework for conceptualizing continuity and change in adulthood. Much of the research on managing work and family life, career development, transition to parenthood, retirement, widowhood, and grandparenthood uses concepts from social role theory as an organizing framework.

The theory is specific enough to offer testable hypotheses. Many studies have demonstrated that constructs from the theory such as role strain, role conflict, and role loss can be measured and that they are salient sources of stress that can interfere with mental and physical health. The research on gender roles illustrates the premise that a role can shape one's attitudes and behaviors as well as one's interactions with others.

Weaknesses

One assumption of social role theory is that individuals are attuned to the expectations of others in order to guide their role enactment. The theory does not elaborate the mechanisms through which individuals learn and internalize role expectations. We do not know how people at different stages of life read or interpret the expectations of others. Young children may be less aware than adolescents or adults of others' expectations. Expectations are difficult to measure. Role expectations may vary in how strongly held they are and how clearly they are communicated. The theory does not provide guidance about how these variations will influence role commitment or role enactment.

Another assumption of social role theory is that societies are structured by roles that have agreed upon norms, expectations, and sanctions for violating these expectations. In modern, postindustrialized society, there appears to be less consensus around role norms and expectations. There is increasing variability in whether individuals choose to enact significant roles, such as marriage partner or parent. If a person does choose one of these roles, there are also fewer agreed on norms for associated expectations. Accompanying these changes in shared expectations, there is also a decline in associated sanctions for violating role expectations. The legal system may continue to operate to enforce specific types of role enactment, but the informal community mechanisms of social control appear to have weakened. As a result, one might say that the theory is less applicable to development in contemporary postindustrial life where individual expression is more highly prized than preservation or protection of the social group.

The theory does not provide much guidance about how role loss, role gain, or role conflict operate to alter development. One needs additional constructs tied to identity, self-directed goal attainment, and self-actualization in order to understand how role acquisition or loss impacts the person. Roles may be salient or relatively unimportant. Role loss may be voluntary or involuntary. The meaning of the role and its place in the person's worldview will influence how changes in the role will impact subsequent adjustment. The theory is limited by the lack of an integrated developmental perspective that links role acquisition and enactment to other aspects of the self theory.

KEY TERMS

role

gender role

role models

gender identity

role taking

role overload

age norms

role conflict

age constraints

spillover

expectations

role strain

role gain

role loss

person-role fit

reciprocal roles

Chapter 7

Life Course Theory

CHAPTER OUTLINE

Historical Context

Key Concepts

   Trajectories and Transitions

   Four Basic Principles

   Mechanisms that Link Changing Times and Individual Lives

New Directions

A Research Example: Work and Family Trade-offs in Three Cohorts

An Application: Life Course Theory and Trajectories of Criminal Behavior

How Does Life Course Theory Answer the Basic Questions that a Theory of Human Development Is Expected to Address?

Critique of Life Course Theory

   Strengths

   Weaknesses

Key Terms

Chapter 7

Life Course Theory

The life course perspective offers a framework for understanding and explaining how changing societal conditions and social forces influence development through life. The term *life course* refers to the integration and sequencing of phases of work and family life over time. Glen H. Elder, Jr. (1985, 1995), a leader in the elaboration of the life course perspective, has created a way of thinking about individual lives embedded in developmental and historical time as well as the linking of interdependent lives over time.

HISTORICAL CONTEXT

In the late 1920s and early '30s, Harold and Mary Jones, Jean MacFarlane, and Nancy Bayley launched their pioneering longitudinal studies of children from the Berkeley Institute of Child Welfare (now called the Institute for the Study of Human Development). There were few other projects engaged in studying children over time. Harold and Mary Jones established the Oakland Growth Study with a group of children born in 1920–22. The Berkeley Guidance sample included children born in 1928–29. Initially these studies were not intended to examine development beyond childhood. However, opportunities arose to allow investigators to continue to study these participants through the Depression, World War II, and the post-war period. Data gathered through these studies offered a window into the transformation of children of the depression into adolescents, adults, parents, and workers (Elder, 1974; Elder & Caspi, 1988).

In the 1960s, Glenn Elder turned to these longitudinal studies to examine the impact of periods of marked historical change including the Great Depression and the Second World War on patterns of coping and adaptation in adolescence and adulthood. He also explored how relative economic deprivation during the Depression altered marital and parent–child relations. He asked how the economic depression of the 1930s affected the subsequent development of children who had grown up in middle and working class families before the economic collapse. Elder described the impact of these data on his own thinking about development.

> The archival data from year to year broadened my vision of lives and revealed the dramatic instability of families under changing economic conditions, the Great Depression. A good many study members could say that they were once "well off" and then "quite poor." Institute records noted frequent changes of residence and jobs. A child in an economically deprived family who seemed "old beyond his time" recovered his youthful spirit when family income improved. (Elder, 1997)

These observations focused Elder's attention on new ways of thinking about social change, life pathways, and individual development. In his view, these pathways refer to the social trajectories of education, work, and family that are followed by individuals and groups through society. He hypothesized that the multiple pathways of individuals and their developmental implications are basic elements of the "life course," which could be conceptualized in research and theory. At the time, the field of life span development was newly emerging. Few theories offered ways of thinking about change over time that recognized the impact of historical context on development, the interconnections of multiple roles, and the processes through which events that impacted adults might alter the developmental experiences of children and adolescents.

Elder's conceptualization of life course theory was influenced by a number of theoretical traditions (Elder, 1996). First, Charlotte Buhler's (1935) study of individual lives through biographies provided close-up and detailed analysis of the development of individuals and an appreciation for mechanisms of personal change in response to key life events. The second tradition is exemplified by the work of Thomas and Znaniecki (1918–1920) who did life history studies of Polish peasants in Europe and the United States. Typically, childhood socialization prepares children to enter adult roles. The experiences of immigration illustrate the disruptions in the life course that can occur when the lessons of childhood are no longer appropriate preparation for the roles available in adult life. Thomas (as cited in Volkart, 1951, p. 593) emphasized that priority should be given to the longitudinal approach to life history: "Studies should explore many types of individuals with regard to their experiences in various past periods of life in different situations and follow groups of individuals into the future getting a continuous record of experiences as they occur."

The third tradition examined the meanings of age in accounts of birth cohorts (Elder, 1974; Ryder, 1965; Riley, Johnson, & Foner, 1972). Ryder's essay about the importance of the cohort in the study of social change pointed out that people who grow through time together in a society experience historical events at specific age-stages and these experiences may influence the development of people in a certain stage in specific ways. Ryder's idea of a cohort provides a way of linking historical time and individual time. It also points out a problem with cross-sectional research designs. Studies that compare people of different ages typically overlook the historical contexts of each age group. Behaviors, attitudes, or coping strategies that appear to characterize people of different ages could be a result of the different historical events to which each cohort was exposed as well as a result of developmental maturation.

The fourth tradition that influenced Elder was the study of culture and intergenerational models (Kertzer & Keith, 1984). Generations of a family are interdependent. Children are influenced by the changing realities of their family environments. Families are changed by the changing capacities and resources of individual family members. As children mature and form families of their own, they bring some of the experiences they have had as young children into their relationships as marital partners and parents. For example, children who have problems with impulse control, emotional regulation, and aggressiveness may find that their adult intimate relationships are unstable and characterized by negativity. Children raised in such families are more likely to experience emotional problems of their own, thus transmitting the parents' problem behaviors to the next generation of children.

This kind of model of intergenerational transmission is especially relevant for thinking about the process through which cultural values, beliefs, and practices influence the life course. Early childhood socialization includes cultural socialization into a worldview about age, gender roles, family and occupational goals and ambitions, and moral values. Historical factors may frustrate or facilitate these cultural aspirations and commitments. For example, in the United States, a common cultural view is that people who work hard and are competent will be able to earn money and support their families. In the Great Depression, many adults lost their jobs, were unable to find work, and experienced depression, irritability, and interpersonal strain. Young boys whose families lost their economic base developed a sense of low self-worth, low social competence, and impaired goal orientation.

These psychosocial disadvantages persisted into their adulthood with evidence of heavy drinking, low energy, and discouraged attitudes about work (Elder, 1979). Thus, in many families, an historical event disrupted the intergenerational transmission of cultural values.

Finally, the fifth influential tradition was the broad area of personality development and life-span psychology (Baltes, 1987; Funder, Parke, Tomlinson-Keasey, & Widaman, 1993). This perspective emphasizes the importance of viewing development across the full life span from infancy through very old age (Newman & Newman, 2006). Although considerable attention is given to how events of early childhood and adolescence impact the transitions into adulthood, it has become increasingly evident that decisions of adult life influence the resources and adaptive capacities of later adulthood and aging. Role transitions, disruptions in pathways, and interrelationships across multiple roles can occur at many points in the life span, and can have an impact on subsequent adaptation. What is more, childhood socialization is carried out in the context of a view of the life span, in an effort to prepare children to be successful in the cultural contexts they will encounter in early and middle adulthood. The changing person is adapting to changing cultural and historical contexts over the full life span, accumulating resources, encountering risks, and exercising personal agency within a framework of personal and social ambitions and expectations.

KEY CONCEPTS

Trajectories and Transitions

Two central themes in life course theory are *trajectories* and *transitions*. A trajectory is the long-term path of one's life experiences in a specific domain, particularly work and family life. The family trajectory might include the following sequence: marriage, parenthood, grandparenthood, and widowhood. A transition is a component within the trajectory marked by the beginning or close of an event or role relationship. In a person's work trajectory, for example, transitions might be getting one's first job, being laid off, and going back to school for an advanced degree. Transitions are the events that make up a lifelong trajectory. Life course theory analyzes the impact of social change on individual lives by observing evidence of changes in trajectories and transitions that are associated with specific periods of historical change.

Four Basic Principles

Four major principles are central to life course theory (Elder, 1996):

Human development takes place in historical time and place. M o s t theories of development focus on the individual as if he or she was living in an historical vacuum. In contrast, life course theory emphasizes that periods of significant historical change will differentiate the developmental trajectories of specific cohorts.

Development takes place during an historical time. You cannot separate the story of development from the historical context during which the life unfolds. The life course of a person who was born in 1900 and died in 1975, including the ages of entry into marriage, completion of educational attainment, work, and retirement, would look quite different from that of a person born in 1925 and reaching age 75 in 2000. The two people would have gone through the same chronological ages and stages of life, but during different periods of history with different opportunities, expectations, and challenges. Cultural expectations for the timing of the transitions as well as the pattern of the family and work trajectories have changed dramatically over the century.

As a specific example, Stewart and Ostrove (1998) described two groups of women who were in their mid 20s; a sample of Radcliffe college graduates from 1964 and one from 1975. At comparable ages, about two-thirds of the older cohort were married and 16% had children; 13% of the younger cohort were married and none had children. The majority of the younger cohort of women was in the labor force or enrolled in graduate school. Thus, even though the women may have many sociological characteristics in common, the landscape of their early adulthood roles looked remarkably different.

Differences in medical advances, occupational opportunities, educational resources, and the number of people in the cohort are four factors that may affect the pattern of life events. In addition, major crises, such as war, famine, and political unrest, may alter a trajectory by introducing unanticipated transitions—for example, closing off certain activities, as when young men interrupt their education to go to war, and opening up new opportunities, as when women enter the labor market because many of the men are in the military (Elder, Caspi, & Downey, 1986; Elder, 1987; Elder, Shanahan, & Clipp, 1994).

For the baby boom generation of women, reaching later adolescence and early adulthood during the women's movement and the civil rights movement, the political and social transitions of the time had a significant impact. Participation in these movements had consequences for their political participation and also for their role enactment at later points in life. Stewart, Settles, and Winter (1998) reported the way these experiences were woven into women's public and private lives:

the women's movement led (me) to feel 'freer to leave my husband for a more fulfilling sex life' and another who said that the movements generally 'made the whole free-thinking, autonomous style of my life possible, both then and now' (as cited in Stewart & Ostrove, 1998, p. 1192)

People operate as agents in their own behalf choosing among the opportunities that are available in their time and society. People make choices that become building blocks of their life course, such as choosing to be married or to leave a marriage, deciding to become a parent and at what age one decides to become a parent, and choosing career directions from among the options available. Within a cohort, the choices people make contribute to individual differences.

In reflecting back on her early adulthood, one woman who was in college in the 1960s expressed regret about decisions she made then: "When I was in college I considered a career in medicine. Due to lack of support from family members and future husband, I didn't pursue it. I would have at least tried it if I were 20 today" (Stewart & Ostrove, 1998, p. 1188).

Another woman, interviewed when she was 50, described a more proactive stance: "For me, 35 was the big waking up—looking around and saying, 'Is this it? Is this all there is? Is this what life has dealt me?' If so, I'm getting up and doing something about it" (Stewart & Ostrove, 1998, p. 1188).

The timing of lives, particularly social time and the social meaning of age, gives structure to the life course. Social time focuses on the entry and exit from age-graded social roles, the sequencing of these roles, and the social and cultural meaning or expectations associated with these roles. One form of cultural expectation is what Bernice Neugarten and her colleagues (Neugarten et al., 1965) termed the *social clock*. This term refers to "age norms and age expectations [that] operate as prods and brakes upon behavior, in some instances hastening behavior and in some instances delaying it" (p. 710). Neugarten and her associates suggested that social class groups tend to agree on the appropriate age for significant life events, such as marriage, childrearing, and retirement.

This consensus exerts social pressure on individuals, pushing them to assume a particular role at an expected age. Age norms may also suppress behaviors that are considered inappropriate for one's age. Adults are aware of existing norms regarding the timing of certain behaviors and evaluate their own behaviors as being "on time" or "too soon" or "too late." The social clock is constantly being reset as people confront the challenges, demands, and new structures of modern society. In contemporary society, with the lengthening of the life expectancy and the increasing vitality of older adults, there are fewer and fewer domains in which a person is considered "too old" to participate (Neugarten, 1990).

Implied in the notion of the social clock are expectations about the sequencing of entry into new roles. For example, European American adults in the United States tend to view an ideal sequence as work, marriage, and parenting in that order. Research indicates that for women, following this sequence is associated with better mental health, including less depression and greater happiness in adulthood. Among African Americans, however, the sequence of work, parenting, and then marriage is associated with less depression and greater happiness (Jackson, 2004). This suggests that different social norms for role sequencing may be operating in the respective ethnic communities.

(a)Lives are linked through social relationships and influenced by the social regulation, social support, and patterning that occur through these relationships. This principle is very important for explaining how the events happening for parents impact their children. For example, when parents experience economic strain, they may become more irritable and depressed. This can disrupt their marital relationship and result in harsh parenting or withdrawal from parenting. Both of these are known to have negative effects on children. Two other examples include the sense of filial obligation of adult children to their aging parents and the disruption of friendship networks as a result of divorce.

(b)Within an individual life course, the trajectories and transitions within trajectories are linked and influence one another. For example, life course theory focuses on the age-linked changes in occupational and family careers. You can map the convergence of transitions across the occupational and family trajectories over time, highlighting periods of potential harmony and conflict between the demands in the two trajectories. The interlocking of occupational and family careers would look quite different for the following: a woman who extends her educational preparation to include a professional degree, works before marriage, and delays childbearing into her middle to late 30s; a woman who remains single and dedicates her energy to excellence in a career; and a woman who marries right after high school, begins having children at age 18, works during her childbearing years out of economic necessity, and then retires at 55 to enjoy her grandchildren and her personal freedom. These three women experience distinct work and family trajectories, entering and leaving roles at different ages and making commitments to certain roles over others.

The four principles described above bring a new perspective to the study of lives. Other historical and sociological studies have considered how cohorts differ, without examining the pathways through which historical change results in different individual trajectories. Developmental research often considers how individuals change over time without considering the unique impact of the historical context on development. Life course theory suggests that major historical events result in transforming environments that influence an individual's basic patterns of behavior.

Mechanisms that Link Changing Times and Individual Lives

The following five mechanisms are proposed as ways to understand the links between the sociological or historical level of change and the individual level (Elder, 1996):

The life stage principle.   The influence of an historical event depends upon the stage of life at which a person experiences the event. Rather than assuming that an historical event has the same impact on everyone who is alive at the time, this principle suggests that the transforming nature of the event depends on the person's developmental stage. Developmental life stages can be viewed as socially defined positions, such as child, adolescent, or adult. These age statuses may be linked to specific expectations for behavior, rights, and responsibilities. Developmental life stages may also be viewed theoretically, as in Piaget's stage of concrete operational thought or Freud's genital stage. Within a life course perspective, it is important to consider a person's developmental stage in trying to speculate about how social events might make an impact on individual lives. The transforming nature of historical events will vary depending upon the way individuals make meaning, their degree of dependence or interdependence on others, their commitment to certain social relationships, their personal and financial resources, and their aspirations and goals, all of which change at various stages of the life span.

Stewart and Healy (1989) offered a model of how to think about the differential impact of historical events depending upon a person's stage of development. In their model, events that occur during childhood are most likely to shape a person's "assumptions about life and the world," thus guiding core values. Events that occur during late adolescence are most likely to shape a person's "conscious identity," guiding decisions about life roles and lifestyle choices. Events that occur during the phases of early, middle, and later adulthood are likely to influence "opportunities that are open to them" rather than their values or identities.

This model is finding support in the field of political psychology. Political generations are forged as individuals in late adolescence and early adulthood encounter salient events, such as war, depression, and social unrest. According to Donald Kinder (2006) " people command more vivid memories and deeper knowledge for events that take place during their late adolescence and early adulthood" (p. 1906). Those young people who are working on identity issues at the time of major historical transitions, such as the Great Depression, World War II, the civil rights movement, and the Vietnam War, know more about these events and tend to apply the lessons they learned about government, policies, and politics during that time to their contemporary political outlook. These views, once established, are stable but not unchanging. According to Kinder, key role transitions, including entry into marriage, parenthood, the military, homeowner, and neighbor, are times when people may change their views.

The principle of interdependent lives. As stated above, the life course perspective emphasizes the interlocking of lives. Psychosocial development depends heavily on being embedded in a supportive, effective network of relationships where individuals, whether they are children, adolescents, or adults, experience a sense of being valued. Historical events that disrupt social relationship networks rob individuals of social capital and produce feelings of isolation or alienation.

Finley and Schwartz (2006) surveyed a sample of ethnically diverse university students about expressive and instrumental dimensions of their fathers' involvement with them. They compared perceptions of students from intact families and students whose parents were divorced. The students in divorced families reported significantly lower levels of father involvement on the most traditional father functions—providing income, protection, discipline, moral/ethical development, and encouraging responsibility. With regard to many of the expressive functions, students in divorced families described their fathers as *rarely involved*. This research, which was designed to explore possible historical changes in the enactment of the father role, was significant in illustrating the potential process through which parental divorce may disrupt social role development and life course trajectories for children.

The principle of the control cycle. When a person loses control, or when personal freedoms are threatened, there is generally an attempt to preserve or regain control. Historical events can influence individual behavior by eliminating or threatening the elimination of freedoms and resources. In reaction to this loss or threat of loss, the person takes steps to preserve control through a wide range of possible coping strategies.

The principle of the situational imperative. Every situation has certain demand properties or requirements. If the situation changes, new behaviors are required. For example, the behaviors that are necessary to be successful in college are different from those necessary to be successful in manual labor. During the Cultural Revolution in China, colleges were all closed and college-age youth were sent into the rural areas to assist with the farming. Survival and success depended on the ability to refocus energy from scholarly to the physical activities.

The accentuation principle. Under conditions of crisis or critical transition, the person's most prominent personality characteristics and coping strategies will be accentuated. People who have a tendency toward anxiety will become more anxious; those who are temperamentally withdrawn will become more withdrawn. Those who have had experience taking action or providing leadership are likely to exercise leadership in times of crisis. In a study of Navajo women, Schulz (1998) described the strength that could be gained from successfully coping with life's adversities: To be Navajo is "to be able to handle any problem—even if we get to a place where we can't go forward, we always find a way." (p. 347)

Given the notion of a situational imperative, people will cope with a changing situation by trying to regain control through the exercise of their most enduring, well-learned habits. This principle suggests a modulating dynamic such that people try to cope with change by remaining as consistent as possible with their prior sense of self.

In summary, the life course perspective invites us to think about the intersection of three different views of time: the time of life of an individual, often referred to as a person's developmental stage; the timing of events, often referred to as social time; and the period when the person is experiencing certain life events, referred to as historical time. Life course theory links individual, social, and historical time. Each person's life course can be thought of as a pattern of adaptations to the configuration of cultural expectations, resources, and barriers experienced during a particular historical period.

NEW DIRECTIONS

Life course theory has opened up many new directions in the study of development. In contrast to the study of typical or modal patterns, life course theory leads to an examination of differences among cohorts, differences within cohorts across locations, and differences within cohorts depending on social capital and human agency. Over the past 15 years, the theory has been useful in guiding international investigations and cross-national comparisons, especially where social change has impacted military service, work, and family roles, and the timing of marriage and childbearing. The life course perspective has also challenged investigators to take a long-term perspective, thinking about how events of childhood or adolescence may influence the life course of adults and the elderly; and how life transitions for children and grandchildren may influence the parent and grandparent generations through the concept of linked lives.

The idea of transitions and trajectories introduced a new way of conceptualizing life by linking discrete events, such as entry into parenthood, into a larger framework with implications of timing and sequencing for personal well-being and subsequent opportunities. This perspective has led to new ways of thinking about the accumulation of advantages and disadvantages over the life course (O'Rand, 1996). It has also led to consideration of the notion of *turning points*, or unique life events that may result in significant reorganization or reframing on one's life trajectory (Laub & Sampson, 1993). Examples might include immigration, severe economic loss, or death of a close family member or friend.

The life course perspective has increased our attention to the impact of social policies on development for certain cohorts. This is illustrated by studies of the impact of changes in U.S. social welfare policies on individuals and families, particularly single mothers and their children. It has led to a more contextualized analysis of basic developmental processes, such as friendship formation, academic achievement, and parent–child relationships, by exploring how changes in family, school, and community resources may impact the formation and survival of essential social networks (Mitchell, 2003).

A RESEARCH EXAMPLE: WORK AND FAMILY TRADE-OFFS IN THREE COHORTS

In chapter 6, social role theory, we described the results of cross-national research that examined the nature of work and family roles, and the dimensions of these roles that are most likely to contribute to work–family conflict or work–family facilitation (Hill et al., 2004). The research was carried out in 48 countries with IBM workers whose average age was 39. The current research example, to highlight the life course theory perspective, also focuses on the general theme of balancing work and family life, but places this inquiry in the context of the historical period. Since World War II, there have been dramatic social changes that have altered social norms about married women in the workplace and men involved in family and household obligations. Over this time, there have also been marked changes in the nature of the labor market, with fewer manufacturing jobs and more jobs in the service, information, health care, and computer-technology sectors. Norms have changed from expectations of gender-role specialization, with women focusing on family tasks and men focusing on labor-market tasks, to a less differentiated view of men's and women's work and family roles. The current research was undertaken to explore two basic questions: First, when men and women decide to pull back from or step out of the labor market in order to meet the demands of their family roles (work–family trade-offs), does this effect their sense of their occupational opportunities and their self-acceptance? Second, if there are work–family trade-off effects, do they differ by birth cohort, life stage, and/or gender?

Data were taken from the Midlife Development in the United States (MIDUS) survey of 3,000 adults who were ages 25 through 74 in 1995 (Carr, 2002). With this broad age span, the study was able to focus on three historical cohorts: those born between 1931 and 1943 (during the Depression);

those born between 1944 and 1959 (Baby Boom generation); and those born between 1960 and 1970 (Baby Bust generation). The investigator argued that over the three historical periods, role expectations shifted from a norm for a clear gender-specialized division of labor to a view that men and women will engage equally in the employee and parent roles. The first wave of this shift, from the oldest to the middle cohort, emphasized the increasing participation of women in the labor market. The second wave of this shift, from the middle to the youngest cohort emphasized the increasing participation of men in childrearing and household management. Thus, the impact of social change could be thought to have a greater impact on women in the middle cohort where the shift was toward greater expectations for labor force participation; and for men in the youngest cohort where the shift was toward greater expectations for family participation.

Work–family trade-offs were assessed based on whether people adjusted their work life in order to meet family responsibilities, especially responsibilities for childrearing. These adjustments were defined by asking about three possible modifications: (a) you stopped working at a job to stay home and care for the children; (b) you cut back on the number of hours worked at a job to care for the children; and (c) you switched to a different job that was less demanding or more flexible to be available to the children. Each person was assessed for whether they had made any of these three adjustments and for the specific adjustments they made.

In order to assess the impact of work–family trade-offs, Carr chose to measure two variables: perceptions of work opportunities and self-acceptance. The first relates to whether people who made work–family trade-offs believe that they have had the same opportunities for employment and good quality jobs as others who did not make these trade-offs. The second relates to whether people who made work–family trade-offs have the same level of self-acceptance as those who did not make these trade-offs.

The data on reported trade-offs provided three notable patterns. First, looking at the entire sample, women were much more likely to report some type of work–family trade-off than were men (53% versus 14%). Second, over the three cohorts men showed a steady increase in the percentage who said they had made some type of work–family trade-off. More men in the youngest cohort (25%) than in the middle cohort (20%) and the oldest cohort (10%) made decisions to work less or change their job in order to spend more time with their families. Third, for women the change across cohorts was noted in the percentage who said they left the work force altogether in order to meet family responsibilities. Roughly two-thirds of all women said they made some type of work–family trade-off in each cohort, but the percentage who said they left the labor market declined from 58% in the oldest cohort to 47% in the middle cohort, and 38% in the youngest cohort. The youngest cohort shows the highest degree of gender similarity in seeking coping strategies that support work–family integration.

There is an assumption that when people are conforming to the social norms of their time, they will experience social approval and other types of reinforcement, which should contribute to their own self-acceptance. Thus, one would expect to see a change in the relationship between making work–family trade-offs and self-acceptance depending on the social norms of the period. For example, among the oldest cohort, women who continued to work while raising a family and men who modified their labor force participation in order to meet childrearing responsibilities could be expected to have lower self-acceptance because these behaviors were contrary to the social norms of their time. Figures 7.1 and 7.2 show the relationship of self-acceptance to making work–family trade-offs for the three cohorts of women and men.

Among the women, three groups were compared: those who stopped working, those who cut back, and those who continued working with no trade-offs. The clearest pattern is for the oldest cohort. Those who stopped working had significantly higher self-acceptance than those who cut back or continued working without any trade-offs. In comparison, for the middle and youngest cohorts, those who continued working had slightly higher levels of self-acceptance than those who stopped working or cut back. Among men, the comparison was made between those who made some type of trade-off and those who made no trade-off. The contrast is sharpest between the oldest and the youngest cohorts. For the oldest men, self-acceptance was lower among those who made trade-offs than among those who made no trade-offs. Among the youngest cohort

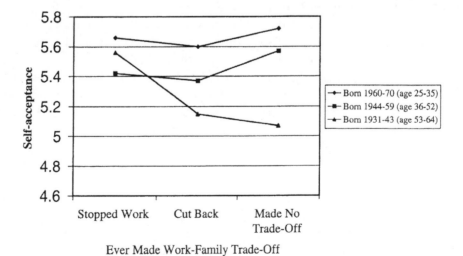

Figure 7.1. Self acceptance: Women of MIDUS, 1995. From The psychological consequences of work–family trade-offs for three cohorts of men and women. *Social Psychology Quarterly*, 2002, *65* (2), p. 117. Reprinted with permission from the American Sociological Association and D. Carr.

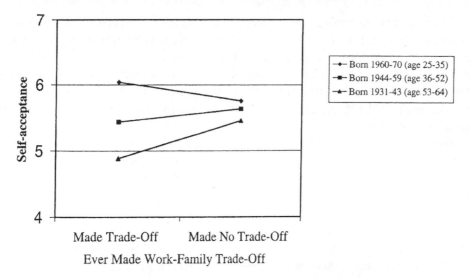

Figure 7.2.   Self acceptance. Men of MIDUS, 1995. From The psychological consequences of work–family trade-offs for three cohorts of men and women. *Social Psychology Quarterly*, 2002, 65 (2), p. 117. Reprinted with permission from the American Sociological Association and D. Carr.

the pattern was reversed; self-acceptance was lower among those who made no trade-offs.

The results of this study illustrate several of the key concepts of life course theory: (a) human development takes place in historical time and place; (b) people operate as agents in their own behalf choosing among the opportunities that are available in their time and society; and (c) within an individual life course, the trajectories and transitions within trajectories are linked and influence one another. The study supports the idea that the impact of certain life decisions on personal development depends on the interaction of the decision and the social meaning of that decision within a specific historical context.

AN APPLICATION: LIFE COURSE THEORY AND TRAJECTORIES OF CRIMINAL BEHAVIOR

In the field of criminology, considerable emphasis is given to trying to understand the developmental course of criminal behavior. When and why do adolescents begin to perform criminal acts? Do patterns of criminal activity persist from adolescence into young and middle adulthood? Are there differences between those who commit violent crimes as compared to crimes against property or "white collar" crimes? One can image at least four different trajectories with respect to criminal behavior: (a) those who are never involved in crime; (b) those who are involved in crime as children or adolescents but not as adults; (c) those who are involved in crime as adults, but not as children or adolescents; and (d) those who are persistently involved in crime from childhood and adolescence well into their adulthood. Are there different explanatory factors that account for these life trajectories? The concepts of life course theory have begun to be applied to an understanding of criminal trajectories.

Sampson and Laub (2004) developed their application of life course theory to criminal behavior on data gathered in an historic study of 500 delinquent and 500 nondelinquent boys studied over three time periods when their average ages were 14, 25, and 32. These boys were initially studied by Sheldon and Eleanor Glueck and included a vast amount of quantitative and qualitative data, including interviews with teachers, neighbors, and employers, psychiatric assessments, and agency records (Glueck & Glueck, 1950, 1968). After a long period of data reconstruction and analysis, Sampson and Laub (1993; Laub & Sampson, 2003) were able to analyze the continuities and changes in the lives of these boys into their adulthood. Eventually, they added new sources of data, which allowed them to examine a 50-year window on the persistence and desistance of crime from childhood into later life (Laub & Sampson, 2003)

The basic idea in this work is that the same principles can help to explain both the persistence or continuation of criminal behavior and the desistance or discontinuation of criminal behavior over the life course. Three basic causal mechanisms were identified: social controls, routine activities, and human agency (Sampson & Laub, 2004).

Family, school, and peer relationships provide the contexts through which social controls impact young children. Exposure to low levels of parental supervision, inconsistent and harsh punishment, and weak or insecure parental attachment are three aspects of family life that are consistently associated with delinquent behavior. In addition, a lack of a sense of school belonging or school engagement are associated with delinquent behavior. And attachment to delinquent friends is also independently associated with delinquent behavior. Taken together, these three sources of social control appear to be the processes through which structural factors such as poverty or neighborhood make their impact on children and adolescents.

However, when one takes a longer-term view of the life course trajectory of criminal behavior, patterns diverge. Some adults who had little or weak social control in childhood and adolescence find new sources of social control and stabilizing social structures in adulthood. Three of the most important of these are marriage, job stability, and military service. Social bonds that are formed in these three contexts are linked to disengagement from criminal activity. On the other hand, job instability and marital conflict, weak marital attachment, or absence of a marriage partner are associated with an increased likelihood of criminal involvement. Thus, the life course view offers a picture of the possibility of both continuity and change in the criminal life trajectory depending on positive involvement with key social institutions and the formal and informal social controls, social ties, and daily routines they provide.

Sampson and Laub (2004) were able to identify important turning points in the lives of adult men leading away from criminal behavior. These new situations, which often included marriage, the military, reform school, work, or neighborhood change, operated to split or "knife off" the past from the present. These new situations provided supervision and monitoring, new routines, new opportunities for social support, and new opportunities to revise their identities.

Within the context of these new situations, however, those who turned away from crime made active efforts to do so. In comparison, those who persisted in criminal activity also acknowledged responsibility for their actions. The principle of human agency figured heavily into this analysis, making predictions about individuals and their trajectories very difficult. The men did not seem to passively fall into or out of criminal behavior. Based on the interview data, it appears that the men made deliberate decisions to give up crime in order to be a hard worker, a family man, or a good provider. Others deliberately persisted in criminal activity, often for the perceived rewards of crime, to defy authority, or to stand in opposition to a system that they viewed as corrupt and unfair.

In order to understand the life trajectory of criminal behavior, one needs to understand the timing and opportunities for social connections, but this is not sufficient. One must also consider the importance of human agency and the extent to which a person is willing to make a commitment to a life of crime or to resist this life. Especially for those who have had an earlier life marked by weak or absent social bonds and social controls, the prolonged periods of unemployment, institutionalization, and social rejection may make the formation of social bonds in adulthood more difficult to envision or establish.

HOW DOES LIFE COURSE THEORY ANSWER THE QUESTIONS THAT A THEORY OF HUMAN DEVELOPMENT IS EXPECTED TO ADDRESS?

What is the direction of change over the life span? How well does the theory account for patterns of change and continuity? The life course is defined as "a sequence of socially defined events and roles that the individual enacts over time" (Giele & Elder, 1998, p. 22). The sequence is comprised of trajectories and transitions within these trajectories. There may also be turning points—critical experiences that lead to a new direction, such as a decision to become more invested in religion, or that terminate a trajectory, such as deciding to give up criminal behavior. Lives become increasingly diverse with age. As individuals set goals and make decisions, their capacity to do so improves.

What are the mechanisms that account for growth? What are some testable hypotheses or predictions that emerge from this analysis?   The theory assumes that there will be change a result of age-graded social expectations, roles and the sequencing of roles, the linking of lives, the impact of human agency or choice, and the influence of historical events that open up or close certain opportunities that can alter one or more trajectories. Every situation has certain demand properties or requirements. If the situation changes, new demand properties emerge and new behaviors are required.

Stability can be expected when the demand properties of the situation remain unchanged. Stability is also a product of the constraints placed on the person through his or her embeddedness in a network of interdependent relationships.

The following four testable hypotheses emerge from this theory:

1. The influence of an historical event depends upon the stage of life at which a person experiences the event. For example, an important technical innovation such as the internet, which began to be widely available on a commercial basis in the 1990s, might be predicted to have a different impact on individuals who first had access to the internet as young children as compared to those who first had access to the internet in middle adulthood.
2. Lives are interdependent. Positive psychosocial development is predicted to occur for those who are embedded in a supportive, effective network of relationships where they are able to experience positive social bonds. Negative psychosocial development is predicted for those who are unable to participate in a supportive network of relationships.
3. When a person loses control, or when personal freedoms are threatened, there is generally an attempt to preserve or regain control.
4. Under conditions of crisis or critical transition, the person's most prominent personality characteristics and coping strategies will be accentuated. This hypothesis addresses stability of behavior, suggesting that when the person confronts sudden and dramatic environmental change, the initial response is to rely on behaviors that were well-established from the past.

How relevant are early experiences for later development? What evidence does the theory offer to support its view?   The theory suggests that early life decisions, opportunities, and conditions affect later outcomes, but that subsequent events and the response to these events can alter these trajectories. For example, dropping out of school can initiate a chain of events that have negative economic, occupational, and interpersonal consequences as well as consequences for one's health and mental health. However, the cumulative disadvantage may be disrupted if a person encounters a new opportunity, for example, through military service or a community action initiative, to complete his or her GED and gain valued technical training.

How do the physical, cognitive, emotional, and social functions interact? How well does the theory explain these interactions? The theory does not focus on intraindividual psychodynamics. The assumption of human agency and personal choice implies a high degree of emotional and cognitive competence as individuals face and adapt to rapidly changing social conditions. However, the theory does not explain the origins of these capacities or how they might be altered as a result of specific life events.

How do the environmental and social contexts affect development? What aspects of the environment does the theory suggest are especially important in shaping the direction of development?

The theory has highlighted features of the social context that had been largely ignored in other theories. First, the theory emphasizes social change and the impact of the historical period in shaping the trajectories and transitions of the life course. Second, the theory points to social expectations or norms and the degree to which these shape entry, exit, and sequencing of social roles. Third, the theory highlights the interconnections among lives and the ways that people are effected by the quality of these linkages as well as the changes in the lives of those close to them. Fourth, the theory recognizes the importance of social institutions and social structures, such as schools, families, the military, and business organizations, in so far as these provide opportunities for the formation of social bonds and support for effective behavior in key roles. Institutions can create a framework for the life course, for example, where businesses offer professional development training, a promotional ladder, and a pension or other retirement benefit. These same institutions can disrupt the life course trajectory with large layoffs, downsizing the workforce, relocating workers to new communities, or recalculating or reducing retirement benefits.

According to the theory, what factors place individuals at risk at specific periods of the life span? A central premise of life course theory is that the impact of critical events depends upon the stage of life when the events occur. A crisis or dramatic social change places individuals at risk when a person loses control, or when personal freedoms are threatened. The theory would then guide us to consider how a critical event might threaten the sense of control or personal freedom for individuals at various points in development. For example, in his work on the Great Depression, Elder found that the younger children experienced a greater disruption in their development than did the adolescents when their parents lost their jobs or faced dramatic financial losses (Elder, Caspi, & Downey, 1986). The younger children relied more on their parents to provide stability and security in their lives than did the adolescents. Parents who became psychologically distant, irritable, and inconsistent or harsh in their discipline transmitted their own sense of loss of control or threat to their children. Adolescents, on the other hand, were able to preserve some sense of control and even reduce their parents' distress by helping out at home, finding some ways to earn a bit of money, and take care of themselves.

A second source of risk is the absence or disruption of social bonds. The theory emphasizes the importance of linked lives. Over the life course, individuals who care about each other provide social capital. At any point in the life course, the absence or loss of social bonds can increase a person's vulnerability. Examples include the relationship of a lack of parent–child attachment and the absence of parental monitoring and supervision to the emergence of delinquent behavior in the early phase of life, and the relationship of social isolation and the absence of kinship support to poor physical and mental health in later adulthood.

A third source of risk is being "off-time" or "off-sequence" in entry or exit from social roles. The assumption of life course theory is that there is an ideal or optimal sequence of transitions in a work, educational, or family trajectory, which is shaped by the norms of the community during a particular historical period. Conformity to the timing norms of the community provides social reassurance and should result in positive self-appraisal. Those who are off-time or out of sequence may experience social rejection, ridicule, or find themselves closed out of important opportunities. One of the most widely studied of these off-time events is early entry into parenthood (under age 18) which, for certain groups, is associated with reduced educational attainment, low income, larger family size, and mental health problems.

CRITIQUE OF LIFE COURSE THEORY

Strengths

Life course theory has provided a unique lens for exploring the impact of the larger social environment on development, especially changes in social and economic conditions. In this respect it has increased awareness of the relevance of the historical context for interpreting patterns of behavior and behavior change.

The life course perspective encourages a long-term outlook on development. As a result, it has encouraged research on the relationship of earlier periods of childhood and adolescence to adulthood and aging. It has also stimulated the study of intergenerational influences, both downward from older to younger generations, and upward from younger generations to older. For example, the life course perspective has led to studies of how grandchildren influence the outlook of their grandparents and how divorce among adult children influences the caregiving received by aging parents. It has offered a way of thinking about the transmission of patterns of behavior and family practices from one generation to the next. This long-term perspective has also provided theoretical justification for investing in long-term longitudinal research, and for reanalysis of existing longitudinal data from a life course perspective.

Life course theory has provided a rich set of concepts for studying adulthood. It recognizes the central focus of adult life on a few trajectories, especially work and family life, and examines the interconnections among roles. It highlights the significance of the social bonds and social network that surround and support life trajectories, and the potential negative consequences when these bonds are disrupted. The theory also integrates the idea of agency and personal decision making, which results in a view of adulthood as shaped but not wholly determined by social forces. Thus, it helps us understand how individual lives are both patterned and increasingly unique over time. Because of its focus on linking historical change with individual development, life course theory has become increasingly useful in guiding research on cross-national comparisons when people of similar age groups are faced with distinct social conditions and historical events.

Weaknesses

Life course theory has been viewed by some as more of a perspective than a theory. While it is useful in pointing out the importance of social factors in shaping development, it does not offer specific causal hypotheses. There is no agreed on set of predictions about which types of social change at particular life stage periods will result in specific consequences. The theory does not specify what historical changes are most likely to impact a cohort. This process appears to be empirically derived, based on knowledge of history and social change. The theory is just beginning to develop ideas about the mechanisms through which social change influences development, and many of these ideas have not been empirically tested.

Similarly, the theory predicts that the effects of historical change will differ depending on the stage of life at which a person experiences it. However, the theory has a limited framework for predicting which aspects of development are most likely to be vulnerable to social change at particular stages. Without this type of developmental component the impact of social change would be studied differently, depending on each researcher's decision about what outcomes are considered important.

Although the theory acknowledges the increasing diversity of individuals over the life course, it does not offer many ideas about the source of these differences. For example, in thinking about the interconnections among roles and trajectories, the theory does not address the reality that people differ in the salience of particular roles and their motivation for sustaining or abandoning these roles. As another example, the theory emphasizes the importance of human agency, especially at key turning points, but does not offer explanations for individual differences in agency. What accounts for the fact that some people are more passive and others more assertive in the face of change? What accounts for the fact that some people have a greater tolerance for change and are more flexible while others are more stressed by change? The theory can be most useful when combined with a theory of intrapsychic development that would help focus attention on the correlates of agency, and the domains of likely vulnerability and growth in the context of social change.

KEY TERMS

accentuation principle

birth cohort

control cycle

historical time

human agency

interdependent lives

intergenerational transmission

life course

life history

life span

life stage

linked lives

linked trajectories

longitudinal research

situational imperative

social bonds

social clock

social regulation

social support

social time

trajectories

transforming environments

transitions

turning points

work–family trade-offs

Part III

Theories That Emphasize the Interaction Between the Person and the Environment

The theories presented in the first section of the book highlighted biologically based patterns or directions of development that unfold in the context of adaptation to varied environments. The theories presented in the second section of the book highlighted the impact of varied environments in shaping thought and action. The theories covered in this final section view development as a product of ongoing interaction between the person and the environment. The distinction between person and environment is less clear in these theories. A few examples might help to illustrate this perspective.

When a baby emits babbling and cooing noises, these noises become part of the baby's auditory environment. Thus, the infant is producing his or her environment. At later phases of development, individuals make choices about toys to play with, friends, books to read, places to live, activities and so on that reflect the person's temperament, skills, interests, and needs. In this sense, a person's environment is, in part, an expression of the person.

On the other hand, the environment is integrated into the person and guides action. For example, an infant will use a different mode of locomotion on a flat surface, an incline or on steps. The kind of motor pattern you observe includes the infant's adaptation to the environment. Action is context-specific. The behaviors you may observe when a person meets you for the first time are not the same behaviors you would observe if the person knows you well. The person modifies his or her behavior to adapt to the context. Knowledge of the environment and past experiences in similar situations influence a person's expectations and subsequent actions.

These examples illustrate the bidirectional influences of person and environment, and suggest the need for new ways of thinking about the interpenetration of person and environment as they contribute to development.

The three theories that illustrate this perspective are Psychosocial theory, Cognitive Social Historical theory, and Dynamic Systems theory. Each of these theories offers a way of thinking about the ongoing interaction of individuals and their environments over time. Psychosocial theory focuses on the development of personality, self-understanding, and a world view that guides a person's orientation toward self and others over the life course. Cognitive Social Historical theory focuses on the development of thought and language, meaning, and the interconnections between learning and development. Dynamic Systems theory offers a framework for exploring the mechanisms of continuity and change in any type of living system. The theory has been applied to human development in a variety of domains including motor development, skill development, parent–child relationships, and cognition.

Psychosocial theory grew from roots in psychosexual theory, cultural anthropology, and psychosocial evolution. The theory defines human development as a product of the ongoing interaction of an individual's biological and psychological needs and abilities on the one hand, and societal expectations on the other. Psychosocial theory predicts an orderly sequence of change in ego development and social relationships from infancy through late life. At each stage, new abilities and coping strategies emerge for engaging in social relationships and for meeting the demands of an ever-changing, increasingly complex social world.

Cognitive Social Historical theory was developed in the time shortly after the Russian Revolution and argued that development began in a social relationship between mother and child. The components of this relationship were internalized by the child and guided his or her behavior. Over the course of development, cognition advances from sources external to the child (intermental) to internalized thinking (intramental). The child learns best when a responsive adult or more skilled peer poses problems and guides solutions that are slightly beyond a child's current level of functioning. The child learns to guide his or her own behavior by developing an inner voice or inner speech that is a product of this social support and guidance.

Dynamic Systems theory has its roots in the fields of mathematics, physics, chemistry, and biology. It was initially applied to the study of human development through the analysis of motor behavior. Development is understood as the result of multiple, mutual and continuous interactions among all levels of a developing system from the molecular to the cultural. The premise is that development is not guided by an executive, hierarchical plan either at the biological or the environmental level. Rather, new organizational patterns emerge as a result of the coordination and integration of recurring actions on many levels at once. The theory offers a way of linking the substantial variability of individual behaviors with the emergence of patterns and qualitative shifts in behavior over time.

Chapter 8

Psychosocial Theory

CHAPTER OUTLINE

Historical Context

Key Concepts

    Stages of Development

    Psychosocial Crisis

    Radius of Significant Relationships

    Prime Adaptive Ego Qualities

    Core Pathologies

New Directions

    Additional Psychosocial Stages

    Integration of Developmental Tasks

    The Central Process for Resolving the Psychosocial Crisis

A Research Example: Individual Identity

An Application: The Role of Hope in Coping and Problem Solving

How Does Psychosocial Theory Answer the Basic Questions that a Theory of Human

Development Is Expected to Address?

Critique of Psychosocial Theory

    Strengths

    Weaknesses

Key Terms

Chapter 8

Psychosocial Theory

Psychosocial theory seeks to explain changes in self-understanding, social relationships, and one's relationship to society as a product of interactions among biological, psychological, and societal processes. Changes in one of the three systems (biological, psychological, or societal) generally bring about changes in the others. From the psychosocial perspective, development results from the continuous interaction of the individual and the social environment. At each period of life, people spend much of their time mastering a unique group of psychological tasks that are essential for social adaptation within their society. Each life stage brings a normative crisis, which can be viewed as a tension between one's competencies and the new demands of society. People strive to reduce this tension by using a variety of familiar coping strategies and by learning new ones. A positive resolution of each crisis provides a new set of social abilities that enhances a person's capacity to adapt successfully in the succeeding stages. A negative resolution of a crisis typically results in defensiveness, rigidity, or withdrawal, which decreases a person's ability to adapt successfully in succeeding stages.

HISTORICAL CONTEXT

Erik Erikson was born in Frankfurt, Germany, in 1902. His mother was unmarried, and he never knew the identity of his biological father. Erikson's Danish mother, Karla Abrahamsen, married a Jewish stockbroker before Erikson's birth, but the marriage did not last. Before his 3rd birthday, Karla married a German-Jewish pediatrician, Theodor Homburger, who gave Erik his surname. In his detailed biography of Erikson, Lawrence Friedman (1999) describes Erikson's continuing efforts to unravel the mysteries of his origin, and the convergence of this personal dilemma with Erikson's emphasis on identity and the identity crisis.

Erikson was not a very good student and had trouble settling on a vocation. At age 18, after completing gymnasium (German secondary school that prepares students to study at a university) Erikson traveled around Europe for a year, spending several months on the shores of Lake Constance, reading, writing, and enjoying the beauty of the setting. When he returned home, he enrolled in art school and pursued this study for the next few years. After traveling to Florence, Italy, where he concluded that he was not going to succeed as an artist, he and some of his friends, including Peter Blos, wandered around for a time searching for a sense of themselves and their personal resources (Coles, 1970).

Erikson and Blos accepted an invitation to teach at a private school that had been founded by Anna Freud for the children of students at the Vienna Psychoanalytic Society. Erikson proved to be so talented in working with children that he was selected to be a full member of the society, where he studied the techniques of psychoanalysis and underwent a training analysis with Anna Freud. His decision to become an analyst was encouraged by the supportive, influential analysts of the Vienna Psychoanalytic Society who were eager to help promising people enter the field they had created. Erikson's admission to training was unusual in that he had neither a university nor a medical degree.

In 1933, after analytic training and marriage to Joan, whom he met in Vienna, he set off to the United States. He became one of the first child analysts in Boston, and began collaborating with Henry Murray at Harvard. By 1935, he went to Yale, and 2 years after that he went off to study the Sioux Indians in South Dakota. He benefited from the support and encouragement of a number of cultural anthropologists and sociologists who encouraged his interest in the integration of psychoanalysis and sociocultural processes.

After completing his research about the Sioux, he opened a clinical practice in San Francisco. During this time, he also became a faculty member at the University of California at Berkeley. In 1950, Erikson left Berkeley and became an analyst on the staff of the Austin Riggs Center in Stockbridge MA.

In the late 1950s he became a professor of human development at Harvard, and retained this position until his retirement. Erikson's major theoretical work, *Childhood and Society*, was synthesized while he was at Berkeley and published in 1950 when he was 48. In this work, Erikson presented his psychosocial theory of development. A revised edition was published in 1963, and he expanded and revised his theory in many other books and papers.

His thinking was influenced by a variety of sources. His training as an analyst was very influential in his view of an epigenetic, stage view of development. He viewed development as a progression in which the orientation or outlook acquired in earlier stages influenced one's approach to subsequent stages. In comparison to the psychoanalytic tradition, which is focused on psychosexual development, Erikson became increasingly interested in the emergence of the skills necessary to participate in social life and to be meaningfully integrated into one's society. He focused on the emergence of ego strengths and competences rather than on the vulnerabilities and defenses that crystallize when needs are not gratified. Nonetheless, by casting his view of development as a dialectic tension between positive and negative forces, his theory offers a way of conceptualizing vulnerabilities as well as strengths.

Erikson's observations of American Indian tribes were guided by current research in cultural anthropology, and awakened his understanding of the way cultural norms and values are transmitted through childrearing and the socialization of children. He was a careful observer of daily behaviors such as nursing, toilet training, play, discipline, and other forms of adult–child interaction. In contrast to Freud's theory which relied on reports from adult patients' about recollections of their childhood, Erikson's ideas were based more on the direct observations of children.

The fact that he was not trained in a specific intellectual field at the university level meant that Erikson was open to a variety of intellectual traditions. He was able to conceptualize aspects of social life that he observed but that were not yet part of traditional disciplines, such as psychology or psychoanalysis. For example, he corresponded with Julian Huxley, who was an evolutionary theorist. Huxley used the term *psychosocial evolution* to refer to those human abilities that have allowed people to gather knowledge from their ancestors and transmit it to their descendants. Childrearing practices, education, and modes of communication transmit information and ways of thinking from one generation to the next. At the same time, people learn how to acquire new information, ways of thinking, and ways of teaching their discoveries to others. In Huxley's thinking, psychosocial evolution proceeded at a rapid pace, bringing with it changes in technology and ideology that have allowed people to create and modify the physical and social environments in which they live (Huxley, 1941, 1942).

In one of his letters to Erikson, Huxely asked how we could account for certain higher level social concepts, such as intimacy, identity, generativity, and wisdom. His point was that these are some of the finest aspects of human capacity, but they were not really addressed in the existing psychological theories. Much of Erikson's theoretical focus was on trying to account for the emergence of these higher order capacities in adolescence and adulthood.

During this time, other theorists also were focusing on the development of mature competences that help support advanced functioning over the life course. Scholars such as Bernice Neugarten (1968), Robert Havighurst (1953), and Robert White (1960) were building a framework for the study personality development, competence, and mastery in adulthood. In the 1970s, theorists, including Daniel Levinson (1977; Levinson, Darrow, Klein, Levinson, & McKee, 1978), and Roger Gould (1972), developed related ideas about stages or phases of adult life, with a particular emphasis on the search for meaning that accompanies shifts in work, family, parenting, and self-understanding. The focus of this chapter is on Erikson's construction of psychosocial theory, with a recognition that his ideas converged with others working at about the same time.

KEY CONCEPTS

As proposed by Erik Erikson, psychosocial theory accounts for systematic change over the life span through five basic concepts: (a) stages of development, (b) psychosocial crises, (c) a radius of significant relationships, (d) prime adaptive ego qualities, and (e) core pathologies.

Stages of Development

A developmental stage is a period of life that is characterized by a specific underlying organization. At every stage, some characteristics differentiate it from the preceding and succeeding stages. Stage theories propose a specific direction for development. At each stage, the accomplishments from the previous stages provide resources for mastering the new challenges. Each stage is unique and leads to the acquisition of new skills related to new capabilities (Davison, King, Kitchener, & Parker, 1980; Flavell, 1982b; Fischer & Silvern, 1985; Levin, 1986).

Erikson (1950/1963) proposed that the stages of development follow the *epigenetic principle*, a biological plan for growth that allows each function to emerge systematically until the fully functioning organism has developed. An assumption of this and other stage theories is that the stages form a sequence. Although one can anticipate challenges that will occur at a later stage, one passes through the stages in an orderly pattern of growth. In the logic of psychosocial theory, the entire life span is required for all the functions of psychosocial development to appear and become integrated. There is no going back to an earlier stage because experience makes retreat impossible. In contrast to other stage theories, however, Erikson suggested that one can review and reinterpret previous stages in the light of new insight and/or new experiences. In addition, the themes of earlier stages may reemerge at any point, bringing a new meaning or a new resolution to an earlier conflict. Joan Erikson reflects on the fluidity and hopefulness in this perspective:

> This sequential growth…is now known to be more influenced by the social milieu than was in previous years considered possible…. Where a strength is not adequately developed according to the given sequence for its scheduled period of critical resolution, the supports of the environment may bring it into appropriate balance at a later period. Hope remains constant throughout life that more sturdy resolutions of the basic confrontation may be realized. (Erikson, 1988, p. 74-B75)

Erikson (1950/1963) proposed eight stages of psychosocial development. The conception of these stages can be traced in part to the stages of psychosexual development proposed by Freud and in part to Erikson's own observations and rich mode of thinking.

Figure 8.1 is the chart Erikson produced in *Childhood and Society* to describe the stages of psychosocial development. The diagonal boxes identify the main psychosocial ego conflicts of each stage. These ego conflicts produce new ego skills. In Erikson's original model, you will note that the periods of life are given names, such as *oral sensory* or *puberty* and *adolescence*, but no ages. This approach reflected Erikson's emphasis on an individual timetable for development, guided by both biological maturation and cultural expectations. (See Fig. 8.1.)

The concept of life stages permits us to consider the various aspects of development such as physical growth, social relationships, and cognitive capacities at a given period of life and to speculate about their interrelation. It also encourages a focus on the experiences that are unique to each life period—experiences that deserve to be understood both in their own right and for their contribution to subsequent development.

Despite the usefulness of a stage approach, one must avoid thinking of stages as pigeonholes. Just because a person is described as being at a given stage does not mean that he or she cannot function at other levels. It is not unusual for people to anticipate later challenges before they become dominant. Many children of toddler and preschool age, for example, play house, envisioning having a husband or a wife and children. You might say that, in this play, they are anticipating the issues of intimacy and generativity that lie ahead. The experience of having a child, whether this occurs at age 18, 25, or 35, is likely to raise issues of generativity, even if the theory suggests that this theme is not in its peak ascendancy until middle adulthood (McAdams & de

Oral Sensory	Trust vs. Mistrust							
Muscular-Anal		Autonomy vs. Shame, Doubt						
Locomotor-Senital			Initiative vs. Guilt					
Latency				Industry vs. Inferiority				
Puberty and Adolescence					Identity vs. Role Diffusion			
Young Adulthood						Intimacy vs. Isolation		
Adulthood							Generativity vs. Stagnation	
Maturity								Integrity vs. Disgust, Despair

Figure 8.1.   Erikson's model of the psychosocial stages of development. From *Childhood and Society* by Erik H. Erikson. Copyright © 1950, © 1963 by W. W. Norton & Company., renewed ©1978, 1991,by Erik H. Erikson. Used by permission of W. W. Norton & Company, Inc.

St. Aubin, 1998). While some elements of each psychosocial theme can be observed at all ages, the intensity with which they are expressed at certain times marks their importance in the definition of a developmental stage. Erikson et al. (1986) put it this way:

> The epigenetic chart also rightly suggests that the individual is never struggling only with the tension that is focal at the time. Rather, at every successive developmental stage, the individual is also increasingly engaged in the anticipation of tensions that have yet to become focal and in reexperiencing those tensions that were inadequately integrated when they were focal; similarly engaged are those whose age-appropriate integration was then, but is no longer, adequate. (p. 39)

As one leaves a stage, the achievements of that period are neither lost nor irrelevant to later stages. Although the theory suggests that important ego strengths emerge from the successful resolution of conflicts at every stage, one should not assume that these strengths, once established, are never challenged or shaken. Events may take place later in life that call into question the essential beliefs established in an earlier period.

For example, the psychosocial conflict during early school age is initiative versus guilt. Its positive outcome, a sense of initiative, is a joy in innovation and experimentation and a willingness to take risks in order to learn more about the world. Once achieved, the sense of initiative provides a positive platform for the formation of social relationships as well as for further creative intellectual inquiry and discovery. However, experiences in a highly authoritarian school environment or in a very judgmental, shaming personal relationship may cause one to inhibit this sense of initiative or to mask it with a facade of indifference.

The idea of life stages highlights the changing orientations toward one's self and others that dominate periods of the life span. Movement from one stage to the next is the result of changes in several major systems at approximately the same time. The new mixture of needs, capabilities, and expectations is what produces the new orientation toward experience at each stage.

Psychosocial Crisis

A *psychosocial crisis* arises because one must make psychological efforts to adjust to the demands of the social environment at each stage of development (Erikson, 1950/1963). The word *crisis* in this context refers to a normal set of stresses and strains rather than to an extraordinary set of events. Societal demands vary from stage to stage. People experience these demands as mild but persistent guidelines for and expectations of behavior. They may be demands for greater self-control, further development of skills, or a stronger commitment to goals. Before the end of each stage of development, the individual tries to achieve a resolution, to adjust to society's demands, and at the same time to translate those demands into personal terms. This process produces a state of tension that the individual must reduce in order to proceed to the next stage. It is this tension state that produces the psychosocial crisis.

Psychosocial Crises of the Life Stages.   Figure 8.1 lists the psychosocial crisis at each stage of development from infancy through old age. This scheme, derived from Erikson's model, expresses the crises as polarities—for example, trust versus mistrust, and autonomy versus shame and doubt. These contrasting conditions suggest the underlying dimensions along which each psychosocial crisis is resolved. According to psychosocial theory, most people experience both ends of the continuum. The inevitable discrepancy between one's level of development at the beginning of a stage and society's push for a new level of functioning by the end of it creates at least a mild degree of the negative condition. Even within a loving, caring family environment that promotes trust, an infant will experience some moments of frustration or disappointment that result in mistrust. The outcome of the crisis at each stage is a balance or integration of the two opposing forces. For each person, the relative frequency and significance of positive and negative experiences will contribute to a resolution of the crisis that lies along a continuum from extremely positive to extremely negative.

The likelihood of a completely positive or a completely negative resolution is small. Most individuals resolve the crises in a generally positive direction, supported by a combination of positive experiences combined with natural maturational tendencies. At each successive stage, however, the likelihood of a negative resolution mounts as societal demands become more complex and the chances of encountering societal barriers to development increase. A positive resolution of each crisis provides new ego strengths that help the person meet the demands of the next stage.

To understand the process of growth at each life stage, we have to consider the negative as well as the positive pole of each crisis. The dynamic tension between the positive and negative forces respects and reflects the struggles we all encounter to restrain unbridled impulses, to overcome fears and doubts, and to look past our own needs to consider the needs of others. The negative poles offer insight into basic areas of human vulnerability. Experienced in moderation, the negative forces result in a clarification of ego positions, individuation, and moral integrity. While a steady diet of mistrust is undesirable, for example, it is important that a trusting person be able to evaluate situations and people for their trustworthiness and to discern cues about safety or danger in any encounter. In every psychosocial crisis, experiences at both the positive and the negative poles contribute to the total range of a person's adaptive capacities.

The term *crisis* implies that normal development does not proceed smoothly. The theory hypothesizes that tension and conflict are necessary to the developmental process; crisis and its resolution are basic, biologically based components of life experience at every stage. In fact, they are what drive the ego system to develop new capacities.

The term *psychosocial* draws attention to the fact that the psychosocial crises are, in part, the result of cultural pressures and expectations. As part of normal development, individuals will experience tension because of the culture's need to socialize and integrate its members. The concept acknowledges the dynamic conflicts between individuality and group membership at each period of life. The concept of crisis implies that at any stage something can interfere with growth and reduce one's opportunities to experience personal fulfillment.

The exact nature of the conflict is not the same at each stage. For example, few cultural limits are placed on infants. The outcome of the infancy stage depends greatly on the skill of the caregiver. At early school age, the culture stands in fairly direct opposition to the child's initiative in some matters by discouraging curiosity or questioning about certain topics, and offers abun-

dant encouragement to initiative in others. In young adulthood, the dominant cultural push is toward the establishment of intimate relationships; yet
an individual may be unable to attain intimacy because of the lack of time to
cultivate intimate relationships, competing pressures from the workplace,
cultural norms against certain expressions of intimacy, or restrictions
against certain types of unions.

As reflected in the epigenetic principle, the succession of crises occurs in a
predictable sequence over the life course. Although Erikson did not specify
the exact ages for each crisis, the theory hypothesizes an age-related progression in which each crisis has its time of special ascendancy. The combination
of biological, psychological, and societal forces that operate to bring about
change has a degree of regularity within society that places each
psychosocial crisis at a particular period of life.

Radius of Significant Relationships

The third organizing principle of psychosocial theory is the *radius of significant relationships* (Erikson, 1982, p. 31). These relationships are thought to
be the vehicle or channel through which age-related cultural and community expectations are communicated. A person's ego includes a social processing system that is sensitive to social expectations. Initially, a person
focuses on a small number of relationships, beginning with the primary
caregivers, siblings, and other close family members. During childhood, adolescence, and early adulthood, the number of relationships expands and
the quality of these relationships takes on greater variety in depth and in intensity. In later adulthood, the person often returns to a smaller number of
extremely important relationships that provide opportunities for great
depth and intimacy.

At each stage of life, this network of relationships determines the demands that will be made on the person, the way he or she will be taken care
of, and the meaning that the person will derive from the relationships. The
relationship network varies from person to person, but each person has a
network of significant relationships and an increasing readiness to enter
into more complex social life (Vanzetti & Duck, 1996). The quality of these
relationships and the norms for interaction influence the way the
psychosocial crisis of the stage is experienced, and the interpersonal context
in which it is resolved.

Prime Adaptive Ego Qualities

According to psychosocial theory, at each stage of life, consistent efforts to
face and cope with the psychosocial crisis of the period results in the forma-

tion of basic adaptive capacities referred to as the *prime adaptive ego qualities*. When coping is unsuccessful and the challenges of the period are not adequately mastered, individuals are likely to form maladaptive orientations, referred to as the *core pathologies*.

Erikson (1978) postulated prime adaptive ego qualities that develop from the positive resolution of the psychosocial crisis of a given stage and provide resources for coping with the next. Drawing upon his concept of an epigenetic principle, Erikson viewed the prime adaptive ego qualities as guided by evolution and embedded into the developmental blueprint for human maturation. "Without them, and their re-emergence from generation to generation, all other and more changeable systems of human values lose their spirit and their relevance" (Erikson, 1950/1963, p. 274).

When the psychosocial crisis is resolved with a favorable balance between the positive and the negative poles, an enduring strength emerges. Erikson described these qualities as mental states that form a basic orientation toward the interpretation of life experiences. A sense of competence, for example, permits a person to feel free to exercise his or her wits to solve problems without being weighed down by a sense of inferiority.

The prime adaptive ego qualities and their definitions are: (a) infancy–hope, which is an enduring belief that one can attain one's deep and essential wishes; (b) toddlerhood–will, which is a determination to exercise free choice and self control; (c) early school age–purpose, which is the courage to imagine and pursue valued goals; (d) middle childhood–competence, which is the free exercise of skill and intelligence in the completion of tasks; (e) early adolescence–fidelity to others, which is the ability freely to pledge and sustain loyalty to others; (f) later adolescence–fidelity to values, which is the ability freely to pledge and sustain loyalty to values and ideologies; (g) early adulthood–love, which is a capacity for mutuality that transcends childhood dependency; (h) middle adulthood–care, which is a commitment to concern about what has been generated; and (i) later adulthood–wisdom, which is a detached yet active concern with life itself in the face of death.

These ego qualities contribute to the person's dominant worldview, which is continuously reformulated to accommodate new ego qualities. The importance of many of the prime adaptive ego qualities has been verified by research. For example, hope has been identified as a significant factor in allowing people to cope with adversity as well as to organize their actions to achieve difficult goals (Snyder, 1994). People with a hopeful attitude have a better chance of maintaining their spirits and strength in the face of crisis than people who are pessimistic. In interviews with people in very old age, Erikson and his colleagues found that those who were hopeful about their own future as well as that of their children were more intellectually vigorous and psychologically resilient than those not characterized by this orientation (Erikson et al., 1986).

Core Pathologies

Although most people develop the prime adaptive ego qualities, a potential core pathology or destructive force may also develop as a result of ineffective, negatively balanced crisis resolution at each stage (Erikson, 1982) The core pathologies and their definitions are: (a) infancy–withdrawal, social and emotional detachment; (b) toddlerhood–compulsion, repetitive behaviors motivated by impulse or by restrictions against the expression of impulse; (c) early school age–inhibition, a psychological restraint that prevents freedom of thought, expression, and activity; (d) middle childhood–inertia, a paralysis of action and thought that prevents productive work; (e) early adolescence–dissociation, an inability to connect with others; (f) later adolescence–repudiation, rejection of most roles and values because they are viewed as alien to oneself; (g) early adulthood–exclusivity, an elitist shutting out of others; (h) middle adulthood–rejectivity, unwillingness to include certain others or groups of others in one's generative concern; and (i) later adulthood–disdain, a feeling of scorn for the weakness and frailty of oneself and others.

The core pathologies also serve as guiding orientations for behavior. These pathologies move people away from others, tend to prevent further exploration of interpersonal relations, and obstruct the resolution of subsequent psychosocial crises. The energy that would normally be directed toward mastering the developmental tasks of a stage is directed instead toward resisting or avoiding change. The core pathologies are not simply passive limitations or barriers to growth. They are energized worldviews leading to strategies that protect people from further unwanted association with the social system and its persistent, tension-producing demands.

NEW DIRECTIONS

Psychosocial theory has been expanded and elaborated upon as a framework for studying development across the life span (Newman & Newman, 1975). This perspective integrates two additional constructs, especially developmental tasks and a central process for resolving the psychosocial crisis. It also expands the number of life stages and the related psychosocial crises. The three additional stages are prenatal development, early adolescence, and very old age.

Additional Psychosocial Stages

The addition of these three new stages provides a good demonstration of the process of theory construction. Theories of human development emerge and change within a cultural and historical context. Patterns of biological and psychosocial evolution occur within a cultural frame of reference. The prenatal stage is added to the stages of psychosocial development in the context of a growing body of research that illuminates the dynamic interaction of the genetically guided plan for fetal development and the fetal environment. This fetal environment is further influenced by features of the social and cultural contexts within which pregnancy occurs. Thus, the status of the fetus at birth is already a product of a psychosocial dynamic.

The division of the adolescent period into two psychosocial stages is a product of changes in the timing of onset of puberty in modern society, the expanding need for education and training before entry into the world of work, related changes in the structure of the educational system, and the variety of the available life choices in work, marriage, parenting, and ideology. The period of later adolescence, which is described in many of Erikson's writings as characterized by its focus on individual identity, is an effort to find a meaningful integration of one's roles that is acceptable and valued by society. Recent research has linked this capacity for self-reflection and the capacity to integrate diverse information into a complex, abstract sense of oneself with the continuing maturation of the prefrontal cortex tied to decision making, planning, and goal setting (Steinberg, 2005). The idea of later adolescence as a distinct stage of development has been supported by a growing body of research summarized by Jeffrey Arnett (1998, 2000, 2004). Arnett refers to this stage of life as *emerging adulthood*.

The period of early adolescence is characterized by its focus on social or group identity and its ties to the psychosocial transitions associated with pubertal change. The psychosocial crisis of this stage is group identity versus alienation. This crisis captures the tension between feeling that one is meaningfully connected to a valued social group and a sense of social estrangement. The prime adaptive ego quality is *fidelity to others,* a willingness to pledge one's loyalties to others and to sustain one's commitments to them. The core pathology is *dissociation*, a sense of separateness, withdrawal, and a reluctance to make the types of enduring commitments to others that foster long term friendships (Newman and Newman, 1976, 2006).

The addition of a period of very old age was stimulated by interest in the adaptive strategies that characterize people who have exceeded the life expectancy of their birth cohort. In the United States, those 85 and older are the fastest growing age group, expected to reach 7.2 million by 2020. Erikson hinted at this final stage in his book, *Vital Involvements in Old Age* (Erikson et al., 1986). We expanded on these ideas, taking into consideration the courage, vitality, and innovative coping strategies that are observed in this group, as well as the impact of advanced age on one's self-concept and one's outlook on mortality. The psychosocial crisis of very old age is immortality versus extinction (Newman & Newman, 2006). This crisis reflects a tension between a view of life as transcending mortality through a symbolic, societal, or spiritual continuity, and the sense that death brings a final and permanent end to one's existence and one's impact. The prime adaptive ego quality is *confidence*, a trust in one's self and the meaningfulness of life. The core pathology is *diffidence*, an inability to act because of overwhelming self-doubt.

The need to differentiate the period of very old age from later adulthood was confirmed in the writings of Joan Erikson who has proposed a ninth stage of the life cycle (Erikson & Erikson, 1997). Joan Erikson wrote about this stage of life in the years after Erik died, while she was in her 90s. As a result of physical decline, social isolation, the loss of loved ones, and cultural neglect or disregard, Erikson suggested that the dystonic or negative poles of the eight psychosocial stages become newly salient. In addition, she distinguished the sense of despair in the eighth stage of the theory, which was despair over past opportunities and regret over past decisions, from a new kind of despair over the mounting disintegration and loss of capacities resulting from the physical declines of very old age. She wrote of the failure of society to find an appropriate strategy or program to embrace the realities of advanced aging that permits older adults to remain engaged, in touch, and integrated into social life.

The counter force to this process of decline and despair is what Joan Erikson described as *gerotranscendence.*

> To reach for gerotranscendence is to rise above, exceed, outdo, go beyond, independent of the universe and time. It involves surpassing all human knowledge and experience. How, for heaven's sake, is this to be accomplished? I am persuaded that only by doing and making do we become. Transcendence need not be limited solely to experiences of withdrawal. In touching, we make contact with one another and with our planet. Transcendence may be a regaining of lost skills, including play, activity, joy, and song, and, above all, a major leap above and beyond the fear of death. It provides an opening forward into the unknown with a trusting leap. Oddly enough, this all demands of us an honest and steadfast humility. These are wonderful words, words that wind us up into involvement. Transcendence—that's it, of course! And it moves. It's one of the arts, it's alive, sings, and makes music, and I hug myself because of the truth it whispers to my soul. No wonder writing has been so difficult. Transcendence calls forth the languages of the arts; nothing else speaks so deeply and meaningfully to our hearts and souls. The great dance of life can transport us into all realms of making and doing with every item of body, mind, and spirit involved. I am profoundly moved, for I am growing old and feel shabby, and suddenly great riches present themselves and enlighten every part of my body and reach out to beauty everywhere. (Erikson & Erikson, 1997, p. 127)

Integration of Developmental Tasks

At each stage of development, one faces a new set of *developmental tasks* consisting of a set of skills and competencies that contribute to increased mastery over one's environment. These tasks reflect areas of accomplishment in physical, cognitive, social, and emotional development, as well as development of the self-concept. The tasks define what is healthy, normal development at each age in a particular society. Success in learning the tasks of one stage leads to development and a greater chance of success in learning the tasks of later stages. Failure at the tasks of one stage leads to greater difficulty with later tasks or may even make later tasks impossible to master.

Robert J. Havighurst (1948/1972), who used the concept of developmental tasks in thinking and teaching about human development and education, believed that human development is a process in which people attempt to learn the tasks required of them by the society to which they are adapting. These tasks change with age because each society has age-graded expectations for behavior. "Living in a modern society is a long series of tasks to learn" (Havighurst, 1948/1972, p. 2). The person who learns well receives satisfaction and reward; the person who does not suffers unhappiness and social disapproval.

Havighurst credits Erik Erikson's psychosocial theory as playing a major role in his use of the concept of developmental tasks. It is a concept that bridges the individual and the society, assuming an active learner who is interacting with an active social environment. Although Havighurst's view of development emphasizes the guiding role of society in determining which skills need to be acquired at a certain age, he believed that there are sensitive periods for learning developmental tasks—that is, times when the person is most ready and most likely to expend effort to acquire a new ability. Havighurst called these periods *teachable moments*. Most people learn developmental tasks at the time and in the sequence appropriate in their society. If a particular task is not learned during the sensitive period, learning may be much more difficult later on.

A relatively small number of major developmental tasks dominate a person's problem-solving efforts and learning during a given stage. Keep in mind that one is changing on several major levels during each period of life. Tasks involving physical, emotional, intellectual, and social growth, as well as growth in the self-concept, all contribute to one's resources for coping with the challenges of life. As these tasks are mastered, new competencies enhance the person's ability to engage in more complex planning, decision making, and relationship building. Successful cultures provide opportunities for their members to learn what they need to know at each age, for both their own survival and that of the group.

Mastery of the developmental tasks is influenced by the resolution of the psychosocial crisis of the previous stage, and it is this resolution that leads to the development of new social capabilities. These capabilities orient the person toward new experiences, a new aptitude for relationships, and new feelings of personal worth as he or she confronts the challenges of the developmental tasks of the next stage. In turn, the skills learned during a particular stage as a result of work on its developmental tasks provide the tools for the resolution of the psychosocial crisis of that stage. Task accomplishment and crisis resolution interact to produce individual life stories.

The Central Process for Resolving the Psychosocial Crisis

Every psychosocial crisis reflects some discrepancy between the person's developmental competencies at the beginning of the stage and new societal pressures for more effective, integrated functioning. How is the discrepancy resolved? What experiences or processes permit the person to interpret the expectations and demands of society and internalize them in order to support change? The *central process* suggests a way that the person takes in or makes sense of cultural expectations and undergoes adaptive modifications of the self (Newman and Newman, 1975/2006). The term *process* suggests a means by which the person recognizes new social pressures and expectations, gives these expectations personal meaning, and gradually changes. The process, unfolding over time, results in a new relationship between self and society. The central process might be compared to the physical phenomenon of absorption and evaporation through which moisture enters the body, is used and transformed, and leaves the body. At each life stage, specific modes of psychological work and social interaction must occur if a person is to continue to grow.

For example, in toddlerhood, the psychosocial crisis raises the question of how children increase their sense of autonomy without risking too many experiences that provoke a sense of shame and doubt. Imitation is the central process for psychosocial growth during toddlerhood (ages 2 and 3). Children expand their range of skills by imitating adults, siblings, television models, playmates, and even animals. Imitation provides toddlers with enormous satisfaction. As they increase the similarity between themselves and admired members of their social groups through imitation, they begin to experience the world as other people and animals experience it. They exercise some control over potentially frightening or confusing events by imitating elements of those occurrences in their play.

The movement toward a sense of autonomy in toddlerhood is facilitated by the child's readiness to imitate and by the variety of models available for observation. Imitation expands children's range of behavior, and through persistent imitative activity, children expand their sense of self-initiated behavior and control over their actions. Repetitive experiences of this kind lead to the development of a sense of personal autonomy.

The central process for coping with the challenges of each life stage provides both personal and societal mechanisms for taking in new information and reorganizing existing information. It also suggests the means that are most likely to lead to a revision of the psychological system so that the crisis of a particular stage may be resolved. Each central process results in an intensive reworking of the psychological system, including a reorganization of boundaries, values, and images of one's self and others. The central processes that lead to the acquisition of new skills, the resolution of the psychosocial crisis, and successful coping at each life stage are: (a) infancy–mutuality with a caregiver; (b) toddlerhood–imitation; (c) early school age–identification; (d) middle childhood–education; (e) early adolescence–peer pressure; (f) later adolescence–role experimentation; (g) early adulthood–mutuality among peers; (h) middle adulthood–person/environment fit and creativity; (i) later adulthood–introspection; and (j) very old age–social support.

A RESEARCH EXAMPLE: INDIVIDUAL IDENTITY

Erik Erikson provided a comprehensive treatment of the meaning and functions of individual identity, from his inclusion of this concept in the theory of psychosocial development in 1950 to his analysis of American identity in 1974. His notion of identity involves the merging of past identifications, future aspirations, and contemporary cultural issues. The major works in which he discussed identity are the article "The Problem of Ego Identity" (1959) and the book *Identity: Youth and Crisis* (1968). Later adolescents are preoccupied with questions about their essential character in much the same way that early school-age children are preoccupied with questions about their origins. In their efforts to define themselves, later adolescents must take into account the bonds that have been built between them and others in the past as well as the direction they hope to take in the future. Identity serves as an anchor point, providing the person an essential experience of continuity in social relationships. Identity achievement is associated with an internal sense of individual uniqueness and direction accompanied by a social or community validation about the direction one has chosen.

One of the most widely used conceptual frameworks for assessing identity status was devised by James Marcia (1980; Waterman, 1982). Using Erikson's concepts, Marcia assessed identity status on the basis of two criteria: *crisis* and *commitment*. Crisis consists of a period of role experimentation and active decision making among alternative choices. Commitment consists of a demonstration of personal involvement in activities and relationships that reflect one's beliefs and values in the areas of occupational choice, religion, political ideology, and interpersonal bonds. On the basis of Marcia's interview, the status of one's identity development is assessed as either identity achieved, foreclosed, moratorium, or diffused (See Table 8.1.).

People who are classified as *identity-achieved* have already experienced a crisis time and have made occupational and ideological commitments. People who are classified as *foreclosed* have not experienced a crisis but demonstrate strong occupational and ideological commitments. Their occupational and ideological beliefs appear to be close to those of their parents. The foreclosed identity is deceptive. A young person of 18 or 19 who can say exactly what he or she wants in life and who has selected an occupational goal may appear to be mature. This kind of clarity of vision may impress peers and adults as evidence of a high level of self-insight. However, if this solution has been formulated through the wholesale adoption of a script that was devised by the young person's family, it may not actually reflect much depth of self-understanding.

People who are classified as being in a state of *psychosocial moratorium* are involved in an ongoing crisis. They are in a period of exploration and experimentation; they have not yet made commitments. Finally, people who are classified as *identity-diffused* may or may not have experienced a crisis, according to Marcia, and they demonstrate a complete lack of commitment. He described several types of identify diffusion including people who have a rather cavalier, "party" attitude to others who are more acutely confused and might be experiencing more serious psychopathology.

A significant body of research has shown patterns of personal characteristics associated with the four identity statuses that are consistent with Erikson's theory. Those who are classified as identity achieved show greater ego strength. They have higher levels of achievement motivation, moral reasoning, intimacy with peers, and career maturity. Those in the moratorium status are more anxious and have conflict over issues of authority. They are more flexible and less authoritarian than the other groups. Those in the foreclosed status are the most authoritarian; they are the least autonomous and have the greatest need for social approval (Berzonsky & Adams, 1999; Waterman, 1999a, 1999b; Zimmermann & Becker-Stoll, 2002).

TABLE 8.1
The Relationship of Crisis and Commitment to Identity Status

Identity Status	Crisis	Commitment
Achievement	+	+
Foreclosure	-	+
Moratorium	+	-
Diffusion	+/-	-

The most maladaptive resolution of the crisis is identity diffusion. Individuals in this status have been shown to have low self-esteem, they are more likely than those in the other statuses to be influenced by peer pressures toward conformity, and they approach problem solving with tendencies toward procrastination and avoidance which contribute to difficulties in adjusting to the college environment (Berzonsky & Kuk, 2000; Kroger, 2003). In comparison to the moratorium group, young people in the diffused status are less conscientious, more likely to experience negative emotions, and more disagreeable (Clancy & Dollinger, 1993). They are generally not outgoing; rather, they describe themselves as self-conscious and likely to feel depressed. Their relationship with their parents is described as distant or rejecting. Several studies have found that young people who are characterized as identity-diffused have had a history of early and frequent involvement with drug use and abuse (Jones, 1992). Difficulties in resolving earlier psychosocial crises, especially conflicts related to autonomy versus shame and doubt and initiative versus guilt, leave some young people with deficits in ego formation that interfere with the kind of energy and playful self-assertiveness that are necessary in the process of identity achievement.

The theoretical construct of identity status assumes a developmental progression from diffusion to foreclosure, moratorium, and finally achievement. Identity diffusion reflects the least defined status. Movement from any other status to diffusion suggests regression. A person who has achieved identity at one period may conceivably return to a period of moratorium. However, those who are in a moratorium or achieved status can never be accurately described as foreclosed, since by definition they have already experienced some degree of crisis (Waterman, 1982; Meeus, 1996). A number of studies, both cross-sectional and longitudinal, show that over time more young people are characterized as having the identity statuses of moratorium and achievement, and fewer are in foreclosure or identity diffusion. However, many of these studies also find that as many as half the participants studied retain their foreclosed or identity-diffused status from the beginning to the end of college; and some studies find regression from the achieved to the foreclosed status (Meeus, Iedema, Helsen, & Vollenbergh, 1999). One implication is that both the diffused and foreclosed identity may be more stable during later adolescence than has been theoretically conceptualized. Another implication is that the statuses are better thought of as self-theories or ways of linking information about the self and the world rather than formal stages that evolve in a strict sequence from one level to the next (Berzonsky, 2003).

AN APPLICATION: THE ROLE OF HOPE IN COPING AND PROBLEM SOLVING

Erikson (1982) argued that the positive resolution of the psychosocial crisis of trust versus mistrust leads to the adaptive ego quality of hope. The prime adaptive ego qualities shape a person's outlook on life in the direction of greater openness to experience and information, greater capacity to identify a variety of pathways to achieve one's goals, more willingness to assert the self and to express one's wishes and views, and a positive approach to the formation of close relationships. Even in the face of difficulties and stressful life events, these qualities contribute to higher levels of functioning and well-being (Peterson & Seligman, 2003).

As the first of the prime adaptive ego qualities, hope pervades the entire life story. It is a global, cognitive orientation that one's goals and dreams can be attained and that events will turn out for the best. As Erikson described it:

> Hope bestows on the anticipated future a sense of leeway inviting expectant leaps, either in preparatory imagination or in small initiating actions. And such daring must count on basic trust in the sense of a trustfulness that must be, literally and figuratively, nourished by maternal care and—when in endangered by all-too-desperate discomfort—must be restored by competent consolidation. (1982, p. 60)

Hopefulness combines the ability to think of one or more paths to achieve a goal with a belief in one's ability to move along that pathway toward the goal (Snyder, Cheavens, & Sympson, 1997). The roots of hopefulness lie in the infant's understanding of the self as a causal agent. Each time a baby takes an action to achieve an outcome, the sense of hope grows. When babies encounter obstacles or barriers to their goals, sensitive caregivers find ways to remove the obstacles or lead them along a new path toward the goal. The infant's sense of self as a causal agent combined with the caregiver's sensitivity create the context for the emergence of hope.

Research with adults shows that people who have a hopeful, optimistic outlook about the future have different achievement beliefs and emotional reactions in response to actual achievement than do people who have a pessimistic outlook (Dweck, 1982; Norem & Cantor, 1988). People who have higher levels of hopefulness undertake a larger number of goals across life areas and select tasks that are more difficult. Hopefulness is generally associated with higher goals, higher levels of confidence that the goals will be reached, and greater persistence in the face of barriers to goal attainment, thus leading to higher overall levels performance (Snyder, 2002).

Feelings of hope have been shown to help people deal with their most difficult challenges, including serious illness, injury, bereavement, and facing the end of life (Sullivan, 2003). In the face of many difficulties as a result of separation from their mothers, poverty, and disruptive home environments, children who have higher levels of hope have been found to have fewer emotional and behavioral problems. These children are more likely to have ideas about how to overcome challenges in their lives rather than to be overwhelmed by the problems they face (Hagen, Myers, & Mackintosh, 2005).

In studies of college students, hope has been found to be closely linked with academic success (Snyder et al., 2002). In a 6-year longitudinal study, students who were more hopeful had better grades and were more likely to graduate from college. Students' hopefulness was associated with having more clearly identified goals based on internal standards. Their goals served to energize their behavior and increase efforts to perform well. Hopeful students were more focused on their goals and less likely to be distracted by self-deprecating thoughts or negative emotions that undermined their efforts. Finally, students who were hopeful were able to identify several different paths toward their goals. If one path was blocked, they would use the information to find another alternative. In contrast, students low in hopefulness tended to stick with one strategy even when it was not working and, as a result, became more passive and disengaged.

Hope plays a key role in the therapeutic process (Snyder & Taylor, 2000). An assumption of counseling is that the client and the therapist can imagine a better future and that together they will explore pathways toward that future (Egan, 2002). Counselors nurture hope by helping clients to identify new possibilities for their future, clarify their goals, devise strategies or paths to achieve these goals, and increase their sense of agency about being able to enact these strategies. By modeling confidence and reassurance, the counselor creates an environment in which the client can begin to experience hopefulness about the future (Snyder & McDermott, 1999).

HOW DOES PSYCHOSOCIAL THEORY ANSWER THE BASIC QUESTIONS THAT A THEORY OF HUMAN DEVELOPMENT IS EXPECTED TO ADDRESS?

What is the direction of change over the life span? How well does the theory account for patterns of change and continuity?

Psychosocial theory attempts to explain human development across the life span—especially patterned changes in ego development, which is reflected in self-understanding, identity formation, social relationships, and worldview. The theory defines human development as a product of the ongoing interaction of an individual's biological and psychological needs and abilities on the one hand, and societal expectations on the other hand. Psychosocial theory predicts an orderly sequence of change in ego development and social relationships from infancy through late life. At each stage, new abilities and coping strategies emerge for engaging in social relationships and for meeting the demands of an ever-changing, increasingly complex social world.

Meaning is created out of efforts to interpret and integrate the experiences of the biological, psychological, and societal systems. A primary focus of this meaning making is the search for identity. Humans struggle to define themselves—to achieve an identity—through a sense of connectedness with certain other people and groups and through feelings of distinctiveness from others. We establish categories that define whom we are connected to, whom we care about, and which of our own qualities we admire. We also establish categories that define those to whom we are not connected, those whom we do not care about, and those qualities of our own that we reject or deny. These categories provide us with an orientation toward certain kinds of people and away from others, toward certain life choices and away from others. The psychosocial perspective brings to light the dynamic interplay of the roles of the self and the other, the I and the We, as they contribute to the emergence of identity over the life course.

Psychosocial theory addresses issues of both continuity and change over the life course. At each stage of life, the resolution of the psychosocial crisis of the stage results in the attainment of certain prime adapative ego strengths or core pathologies. At each stage of life, one is embedded in a radius of significant relationships. These two factors, carried forward into the next stage, as well as the tendency to anticipate the issues of the stages ahead, contribute to continuity in development. At the same time, the epigenetic principle assumes an unfolding of new capacities in the context of changing social expectations. As a result, one can expect new ways of understanding the relationship of self and other, and new facets of one's identity to emerge over the life span. Although there is no going back to earlier stages of life, there is a capacity for reflection and revisitation through which the resolution of earlier crises may be reevaluated.

What are the mechanisms that account for growth? What are some testable hypotheses or predictions that emerge from this analysis? The basic mechanism that accounts for growth is the psychosocial crisis. The crises arise as a result of the epigenetic principle through which tension is created due to the discrepancy between one's competencies at each stage and the new demands of society. People strive to reduce this tension by using a variety of familiar coping strategies and by learning new ones. The following testable hypotheses emerge from the theory:

1. A normal crisis arises at each stage of development, and a central process operates to resolve this crisis. The resolution of the crisis at each stage determines one's coping resources, with a positive resolution contributing to ego strengths and a negative resolution contributing to core pathologies.

2. Each stage of development is accompanied by a specific psychosocial crisis. Issues of later stages can be previewed at an earlier time, but each issue has its period of ascendance. It takes the entire life course, from the prenatal period through very old age, for all aspects of the ego's potential to be realized.

3. Each person is part of an expanding network of significant relationships that convey society's expectations and demands. These relationships also provide encouragement in the face of challenges.

4. Development will be optimal if a person can create new behaviors and relationships as a result of skill acquisition and successful crisis resolution during each stage of growth. Lack of development and core pathologies result from tendencies that restrict behavior (especially social behavior) in general and new behavior in particular.

How relevant are early experiences for later development? What evidence does the theory offer to support its view?   Early experiences are highly relevant for subsequent development. The strengths and skills acquired through the resolution of earlier crises are important for resolving later crises. The prime adaptive ego qualities of early life stages prepare a person to approach subsequent crises with an outlook of hope, determination, and empowerment. Similarly, crises that are resolved toward the negative pole contribute to a more cautious, inhibited, or withdrawn outlook. What is more, psychosocial theory suggests that each life crisis is foreshadowed in earlier stages, and that each crisis is played out in a more complex way at later stages. Thus, all of life is a tapestry in which the issues of the past are expressed in new forms at later stages, and issues of later stages are anticipated in less mature forms in earlier stages.

How do the physical, cognitive, emotional, and social functions interact? How well does the theory explain these interactions?   According to psychosocial theory, human development is a product of the continuous interaction of the biological, the psychological, and the societal systems. The person's emerging sense of self is guided by the complex interaction of biological and psychological competencies that are shaped by culture and social relationships, and internalized into a worldview. At each stage of life, culture and society give meaning to newly emerging biological, cognitive, emotional, and social capacities. At the same time, these capacities alter the way a person engages the social environment and imposes the self into the social world.

The biological system includes all those processes necessary for the physical functioning of the organism. Biological processes develop and change as a consequence of genetically guided maturation; environmental resources, such as nutrition and sunlight; exposure to environmental toxins; encounters with accidents and diseases; and lifestyle patterns of behavior, including daily exercise, eating, sleeping, and the use of drugs. The biological system changes over time, in part as a result of a genetically guided maturational process and in part as a result of interactions with the physical and social environment. Cultures differ in their support of physical growth and health, depending on such factors as the availability of adequate nutritional resources, the treatment of illness, and exposure to environmental toxins and hazardous conditions.

The psychological system includes those mental processes central to a person's ability to make meaning of experiences and take action. Emotion, memory, and perception; problem solving, language, and symbolic abilities;

and our orientation to the future all require the use of psychological processes. Psychological processes develop and change over one's life span. Change is guided in part by genetic information. The capacity for intellectual functioning and the direction of cognitive maturation are genetically guided. A number of genetically transmitted diseases may result in intellectual impairment and a reduced capacity for learning. Change also results from the accumulation of experiences and from encounters with various educational settings. The psychological processes are enhanced by numerous life experiences, such as playing sports, camping, traveling, reading, and talking with people. Finally, change can be self-directed. A person can decide to pursue a new interest, learn another language, or adopt a new set of ideas. Through self-insight, one can begin to think about oneself and others in a new light.

The societal system includes those processes through which a person becomes integrated into society. Societal influences include social roles; social support; culture, including rituals, myths, and social expectations; leadership styles; communication patterns; family organization; ethnic and subcultural influences; political and religious ideologies; patterns of economic prosperity or poverty and war or peace; and exposure to racism, sexism, and other forms of discrimination, intolerance, or intergroup hostility. The impact of the societal system on psychosocial development results largely from interpersonal relationships, often relationships with significant others. Through laws and public policies, political and economic structures, and educational opportunities, societies influence the psychosocial development of individuals and alter the life course for future generations.

How do the environmental and social contexts affect development? What aspects of the environment does the theory suggest are especially important in shaping the direction of development? As its name implies, psychosocial theory emphasizes the ongoing interaction of the individual and society. An assumption of this theory is that the development of the person and the continued adaptive functioning of society are interdependent. Societies shape development through the messages that are conveyed to individuals through the radius of significant relationships, beginning with the first nurturing caregivers and expanding outward to siblings, grandparents, other family members, friends, coworkers, admired role models, intimate partners, children, grandchildren and so on. As the radius of significant relationships expands, people engage in an increasingly complex set of roles with more diverse individuals. With advanced age, the number of relationships may decline, but the ego development that was stimulated through this complex set of relationships continues to be expressed through characteristics of integrity and wisdom. Individuals shape societies through the ways they establish and preserve relationships, make commitments to work, family, and ideologies, and nurture future generations through their generative actions.

According to the theory, what factors place individuals at risk at specific periods of the life span? The theory offers a stage-based guide to experiences that place individuals at risk. At each stage, the negative pole of the psychosocial crisis suggests a potentially high risk outcome for that period of life—mistrust, shame and doubt, guilt, inferiority, etc. When the psychosocial crisis is resolved with a balance in the direction of the negative pole, the result is likely to be the emergence of a related core pathology. These core pathologies interfere with the formation of new relationships, produce defensiveness, interfere with the creation of new, flexible coping strategies, and leave the ego vulnerable to sentiments of resentment and despair.

From a societal perspective, the early ego development of the child and the likelihood of a positive resolution of the psychosocial crises of infancy, toddlerhood, early and middle childhood is heavily dependent on the ego maturity and well-being of the caregiver. In that regard, societal conditions that undermine the financial or emotional well-being of caregivers, or that disrupt the social support for caregivers, can be considered risk factors for children. Poverty is a major obstacle to optimal development. Under conditions of poverty, individuals have fewer options and less opportunity to escape or avoid other forms of societal oppression such as racism, sexism, or homophobia. It is well documented that poverty increases the risks that individuals face, including risks associated with malnutrition, poor quality health care, living in a hazardous or dangerous neighborhood, and attending ineffective schools. Poverty and prolonged economic strain tend to erode the self-esteem of caregivers, resulting in more harsh parenting, parent conflict, and emotional withdrawal. Beyond childhood, poverty is linked with reduced access to the basic resources associated with survival. To the extent that poverty is stigmatized and associated with demeaning social treatment it has potentially powerful and pervasive effects on psychosocial development across the life span.

CRITIQUE OF PSYCHOSOCIAL THEORY

Strengths

Psychosocial theory provides a broad, integrative context within which to study life-span development (Hopkins, 1995; Kiston, 1994). The theory links the process of child development to the stages of adult life, individual development to the nature of culture and society, and the personal and historical past to the personal and societal future. Although many scholars agree that such a broad perspective is necessary, few other theories attempt to address the dynamic interplay between individual development and society (Miller, 2002).

The emphasis of psychosocial theory on ego development and ego processes provides insight into the directions of healthy development throughout life. The theory provides a framework for tracing the process through which self-concept, self-esteem, and ego boundaries become integrated into a positive, adaptive, socially engaged person (Hamachek, 1985, 1994). Emphasizing the normal, hopeful, and creative aspects of coping and adaptation, the theory has taken the study of development beyond the deterministic position of psychosexual theory or the mechanistic view of behaviorism, providing an essential conceptual framework for the emergence of positive psychology.

At one time, some argued that a weakness of psychosocial theory was that its basic concepts were presented in language that is abstract and difficult to examine empirically (Crain, 2000; Miller, 2002). However, over the past 20 years, such terms as hope, inhibition, autonomy, personal identity, intimacy, generativity, and integrity—to name a few—have been operationalized (Bohlin, Bengtsgard, & Andersson, 2000; Christiansen & Palkovitz, 1998; Kroger, 2000; Lopez & Snyder, 2003; Marcia, 2002; McAdams & de St. Aubin, 1998; Snyder, 2002). Concepts central to the theory—such as trust, autonomy, identity achievement, coping, well-being, social support, and intergenerational interdependence—have become thoroughly integrated into contemporary human development scholarship. Researchers have developed instruments to trace the emergence of psychosocial crises and their resolution in samples varying in age from adolescence to later adulthood (Constantinople, 1969; Darling-Fisher & Leidy, 1988; Domino & Affonso, 1990; Hawley, 1988; Waterman & Whitbourne, 1981; Whitbourne, Zuschlog, Elliot, & Waterman, 1992).

Unlike some other stage theories, psychosocial theory identifies tensions that may disrupt development at each life stage, providing a useful framework for considering individual differences in development. The positive and negative poles of each psychosocial crisis offer a way of thinking about differences in ego development at each stage of life as well as a model for considering cumulative differences across the life span. This matrix of crises and stages also provides a useful tool for approaching psychotherapy and counseling.

The concept of normative psychosocial crises is a creative contribution that identifies predictable tensions between socialization and maturation throughout life. Societies, with their structures, laws, roles, rituals, and sanctions, are organized to guide individual growth toward a particular ideal of mature adulthood. However, every society faces problems when it attempts to balance the needs of the individual with the needs of the group. All individuals face some strains as they attempt to experience their individuality while maintaining the support of their groups and attempting to fit into their society. Psychosocial theory gives us concepts for exploring these natural tensions.

Longitudinal research using psychosocial theory as a framework for studying patterns of personality change and ego development has found support for many of its basic concepts. Changes in psychological outlook that reflect the major themes of the theory—such as industry, identity, intimacy, and generativity—appear to emerge and become consolidated over time (Whitbourne et al., 1992). There is also evidence of a preview of themes prior to their period of maximum ascendancy (Peterson & Stewart, 1993) and evidence for the notion of revisitation through which adults are stimulated to rework and reorganize the resolutions of earlier issues (Shibley, 2000).

Weaknesses

One weakness of psychosocial theory is that the explanations about the mechanisms for resolving crises and moving from one stage to the next are not well developed (Miller, 2002). The theory does not offer a universal mechanism for crisis resolution, nor a detailed picture of the kinds of experiences that are necessary at each stage if one is to cope successfully with the crisis of that stage.

The specific number of stages and their link to a biologically based plan for development have been criticized. The nature and number of stages of life is arguably highly culturally specific. For example, in some societies, the transition from childhood to adulthood is swift, leaving little time or expectation for identity exploration. In many traditional societies, parents choose one's marital partner, there are few occupational choices, and one is guided toward one's vocation from an early age. Thus, although there is always a biological period of pubescence, there may be little experience of the psychosocial processes of adolescence (Thomas, 1999). In contrast, in our highly technological society, adolescence appears to be extended for some, especially as the age at first marriage is delayed and the complexity of preparing for and entering the labor market increases.

Along this same line of criticism, other human development scholars have taken a more differentiated view of the stages of adulthood and later life. In later life, health status, life circumstances, and culture interact to produce increasing variation in life stories. In a growing line of research, distinctions are being made between the "young-old" and the "old-old." These distinctions are sometimes based on health status and the person's capacity to manage tasks of daily life (Deeg, Kardaun, & Fozard, 1996).

In other research, distinctions are made on the basis of chronological age. For example, Leonard Poon has written extensively about the differences between centenarians (people who are 100 or more), octogenarians (people in their 80s), and sexagenarians (people in their 60s) (Martin, Poon, Kim, & Johnson, 1996). Each cohort of older adults has been exposed to different historical crises, educational, health and occupational opportunities, and shifting societal values. Therefore, it is likely that the normative patterns used to describe development in adulthood and later life will become dated and need reexamination (Siegler, Poon, Madden, & Welsh, 1996). The increasing life expectancy, accompanied by a longer period of healthy later life and the elaboration of lifestyles, makes it difficult to chart a normative life course from early adulthood into very old age.

Finally, the psychosocial theory and related research have been criticized as being dominated by a male, Eurocentric, individualistic perspective that emphasizes agency—the ability to originate plans and take action—over connection and communion—the commitment to and consideration for the well-being of others (Bar-Yam Hassan & Bar-Yam, 1987; Gilligan, 1982/1993). The themes of autonomy, initiative, industry, and personal identity all emphasize the process of individuation. Critics have argued that ego development, separateness from family, autonomy, and self-directed goal attainment have been equated with psychological maturity, and that relatively little attention has been given to the development of interpersonal connection and social relatedness. These latter themes have been identified as central for an understanding of the psychosocial maturity of girls and young women. They also emerge in the study of collectively oriented ethnic groups—cultures in which maturity is equated with one's ability to support and sustain the success of the family or the extended family group rather than with one's own achievement of status, wealth, or recognition (Boykin, 1994; Josselson, 1987).

In our view, this last criticism is possibly overstated given the orientation of psychosocial theory toward the ongoing dynamic interaction of the individual and society. Within the framework of psychosocial theory, the theme of connection is addressed directly through the first psychosocial crisis of trust versus mistrust in infancy, and in subsequent psychosocial stages of early adolescence, early and middle adulthood, when group identity, intimacy, and generativity highlight the critical links that individuals build with others. The concept of the radius of significant relationships helps to maintain the perspective of the person interwoven in a tapestry of relationships, focusing especially on family and friends in childhood; the family, peer group, love relationships, and close friends in early and later adolescence; and intimate partners, family, friends, and coworkers in adult life. A basic premise of psychosocial theory is that the ego is taking shape in constant interaction with the community (Schlein, 1987).

KEY TERMS

agency

biological system

central process

communion

core pathologies

developmental stage

developmental tasks

ego development

epigenetic principle

prime adaptive ego qualities

psychological system

psychosocial crisis

psychosocial evolution

radius of significant relationships

societal system

Chapter 9

Cognitive Social–Historical Theory

CHAPTER OUTLINE

Historical Context

Key Concepts

   Culture as a Mediator of Cognitive Structuring

   From Intermental to Intramental

   Inner Speech

   The Zone of Proximal Development

New Directions

A Research Example: Cultural Management of Attention

An Application: Implications of Vygotsky's Theory for Instruction

   Mediated Learning

   Theoretical Learning

How Does Cognitive Social-Historical Theory Answer the Basic Questions
that a Theory of Human Development Is Expected to Address?

Critique of Cognitive Social-Historical Theory

   Strengths

   Weaknesses

Key Terms

Chapter 9

Cognitive Social–Historical Theory

Piaget's focus on cognitive development emphasized a process in which children investigate, explore, discover, and rediscover meaning in their world. Although Piaget acknowledged the significance of social factors, especially parents and peers, in the cognitive process, his theory focused on what he believed to be universal processes and stages in the maturation of cognition from infancy through adolescence. In contrast, Vygotsky, often referred to as an interactionist, argued that development can only be understood within a social-historical framework. At the heart of his work is a focus on thinking, especially in childhood, which he links to the development of language and speech.

> The development of the child's thinking depends on his mastery of the social means of thinking, that is, on mastery of speech.... This thesis stems from our *comparison* of the development of inner speech and verbal thinking in man with the development of speech and intellect as it occurs in the animal world and the earliest stages of childhood. This comparison demonstrates that the

former does not represent a simple continuation of the latter. The very type of development changes. It changes from a biological form of development to a socio-historical form of development. (Vygotsky, 1987a, p. 120)

Vygotsky, like many other theorists and philosophers of his time, was trying to account for the development of higher mental processes from their simpler forms. He saw development as following a continuous path from other animals to humans, and also a discontinuous path. This was captured in his view of *natural* or *lower mental processes,* which could be observed in animal behavior and the problem solving behaviors of infants and very young children, and *higher mental processes,* which arise as children encounter and master the cultural tools of their society. He viewed human beings across cultures as both similar to the extent that they shared basic physical characteristics and natural psychological processes, and substantially different depending upon the cultural symbol systems to which they are exposed, and how those systems shape thinking and behavior.

Higher mental processes, particularly language and meaning, emerge from the child's ongoing interactions within social, historical, and cultural contexts, as well as from the child's biological maturation. The child and the culture are intricately interwoven through the process of social interaction. New levels of understanding begin at an interpersonal level as two individuals, initially an infant and an adult, coordinate their interactions. Eventually interpersonal collaboration becomes internalized to make up the child's internal mental framework. Through continuous interaction with others, especially adults and older children, a child revises and advances his or her levels of understanding. Over time, it is the mastery of these cultural tools or symbol systems that permit individuals to alter their environments and guide, regulate and redefine themselves.

HISTORICAL CONTEXT

Lev Semyonovich Vygotsky lived a brief but extremely productive life. Born in 1896 (the same year as Jean Piaget) to a professional family, his father was a banking executive and his mother was a teacher. In a family of eight children, family life was interesting with many evenings spent in lively conversation and debate. As a teenager, Vygotsky became known as the "little professor" because he liked to organize debates and mock trials where friends took the roles of historical figures such as Aristotle and Napoleon (Wertsch, 1985). He loved to read history, literature, and poetry. In 1917 he graduated from Moscow University with a specialization in literature. Later, he wrote a dissertation on Shakespeare's *Hamlet*. From 1917 to 1923, he taught literature and psychology at a teacher's college in Gomel, where he had attended school as an adolescent.

In 1924 Vygotsky gave an inspiring talk on the link between conditioned reflexes and conscious behavior. He deeply impressed Alexander Luria, a researcher at the Moscow Institute of Psychology, who later became a founder of the field of neuropsychology. Luria recommended Vygotsky for a position at the Institute. This began Vygotsky's intensive career as a researcher, educator, and clinical practitioner. Along with Luria and Alexei Nikolaivitch Leontiev, he dedicated his efforts to the formulation of an integrated theory of psychology that would be compatible with the broad principles of Marx's and Engels's political philosophy.

Vygotsky contracted tuberculosis sometime during his return to Gomel, and died in 1934. Some of his works were published shortly after his death, but from 1936 to 1956 his works were banned by the Communist Party. As a result, many of his theoretical ideas were slow in reaching a broader western audience. His first book, *Thought and Language* (later retranslated as *Thinking and Speech*, 1987) was published in Russia in 1934, but was not translated into English until 1962.

Vygotsky entered the field of psychology at a time when there was a divide between those who were studying the physiology of the brain, reflexes, and sensory systems (psychology as a "natural science") and those in the Gestalt school who were studying higher order mental processes, especially the integrative capacities of meaning making and interpretation (psychology as a "mental science") (Cole & Scribner, 1978). He was an avid reader, and actively formed international connections with scholars whose work informed his own thinking. He knew of the works of Darwin, Piaget, and Freud and often compared his own concepts to theirs. In the formulation of his work, he built on the research of zoologists, who studied the relationship of instincts and intellect; ethnographers, who studied the thoughts and practices of people in traditional societies; and comparative psychologists, who created experimental demonstrations of animal problem-solving behaviors (van der Veer & Valsiner, 1991).

He was also deeply influenced by the writings of Marx and Engels. Marx's theory of historical materialism argued that changes in human consciousness and behavior are a result of changes in society and material life (Marx, 1844/1988). He was especially interested in the human capacity for tool use and production. He claimed that production was an inherently social process wherein people collaborate in order to grow things, build things, or sustain and protect their territory. He thought that people's values and ideas, their higher order cognitive processes, were a product of their material life, that is the way they live, work, produce, and exchange goods. Marx's theory suggested that history reflects a dialectical process—the conditions of production change over time. New tools and technologies come into conflict with existing patterns of production. As a result, new social and economic systems emerge that lead to new beliefs and values. He maintained that all phenomena should be considered as being in a process of change, influenced by historical changes in society and material or technological life. In order to understand contemporary behavior, one must reconstruct the origins of that behavior and the course of development from its simplest to its more complex expressions. Thus, Marx's contributions to Vygotsky's thinking included a commitment to a developmental analysis embedded in social and historical contexts.

Extending Marx's focus on the importance of tools as a means of production, Engels (1925/1940) wrote about the relationship of tools and evolution. He suggested that tool use led to the expansion of human consciousness. With the earliest invention of tools, human beings were prompted to new ways of examining the objects in their environment in order to assess their compatibility with existing tools or the ways that their tools could alter these objects. Tools led to new needs for communication and social interaction. And, tools brought about a new view of the environment as something that could be altered to meet human needs. The capacity to clear land, plant crops, and harvest them brought new cognitive capacities for planning and anticipating future needs. According to Engels, new tools led to new cognitive capacities. "The tool specifically symbolizes human activity, man's transformation of nature: production" (Marx & Engels, 1953, p. 63). From this critical insight, Vygotsky pursued the idea of "cultural tools," such as language, writing, and number systems which, once acquired, also alter and advance complex cognitive capacities. Symbolic tools are initially external to the person and a product of human culture. However, these tools gradually become internalized, changing the person and his or her way of thinking. "But tools affect their users: language, used first as a communicative tool, finally shapes the minds of those who adapt to its use" (Bruner, 1987, p.3).

Vygotsky worked to create an integrated psychology of cognitive behavior that recognized the interaction of neurological mechanisms, a developmental history of cognition from its simple to its more complex forms, and the role of the society in influencing the ways higher order cognitive capacities emerge (Vygotsky, 1978a). His work placed an especially strong emphasis on language as a cultural tool that allows the person to modify the stimulus situation as part of the process of responding to it. He devoted a substantial part of his professional life to the conceptualization of educational strategies to reduce illiteracy and to support language functioning among children and adults who suffered from mental and physical disabilities.

KEY CONCEPTS

Four concepts in Vygotsky's theory are introduced here: culture as a mediator of cognitive structuring, movement from the intermental to the intramental, inner speech, and the zone of proximal development.

Culture as a Mediator of Cognitive Structuring

Culture consists of physical settings; tools and technologies; and a patterned system of customs, beliefs, information, and social relationships. Within broad cultural groups, subcultures also exist with unique but shared patterns of behavior, values, and goals. When Vygotsky argues that cognitive development can only be understood in the context of culture, he is bringing our attention to this pervasive sense of culture. Think for a moment about the many ways that culture shapes the content of thought and the processes through which ideas are developed. A simple conversation between a mother and a child or a situation in which an older sibling is trying to instruct a younger sibling include layers of cultural beliefs and strategies—beliefs about what children think about; the skills they are encouraged to attain; the sources of information that are available to them; the ways that information is shared; the kinds of activities that children, adolescents, and adults are permitted to engage in; and the limits that are placed on participation in certain settings or certain forms of interaction. Bakhurst (1996) provides a helpful summary of Vygotsky's model:

> The human child enters the world endowed by nature with only elementary mental capacities. The higher mental functions constitutive of human consciousness are, however, embodied in the social practices of the child's community. Just as the child's physical functions are at first maintained only through connection with an autonomous system beyond the child, so his or her psychological life is created only through inauguration into a set of external practices. Only as the child internalizes or masters those practices is he or she transformed into a conscious subject of thought and experience. (p.202)

Of the many elements of culture that shape cognition, one that was of special interest to Vygotsky was the idea of tools and signs as human inventions that shape thought. Technical *tools*, such as plows, cars, and weapons, and *signs*, sometimes referred to as *psychological tools*, such as symbolic systems, counting systems, and strategies for remembering, modify the child's relationship to the environment. Through the use of tools, humans change the way they organize and think about the world. Vygotsky viewed tools as a means through which the human mind is shaped and modified over the course of history.

Based on a variety of experimental demonstrations in the areas of memory, categorization, and attention, Vygotsky was able to show that children follow a common path in the development of higher order thinking. First, in the early years, they do not make any systematic use of cultural tools such as words, pictures, or other symbols to help in their problem solving. In the second phase, they are able to make use of cultural tools—for example, the use of a picture that has been given to them to recall a word—but they are not able to impose or actively create a symbolic aid if it has not already been provided. In the third phase, children can create their own links between pictures and words to be remembered, or find new strategies to help them remember words or categorize objects. In the final stage, the child internalizes these prompts or clues, no longer relying on the physical device to aid in their work. The cultural tools eventually mediate the task, supporting new levels of behavior that appear more integrated and automatic (Vygotsky, 1928, as referenced in van der Veer & Valsiner, 1991).

In particular, Vygotsky emphasized language as a sign system that dramatically altered human cognition. Language, which begins as a primarily social process linking individuals, becomes a tool that guides mental activity. Through language, children can recall the past, create problem-solving strategies, organize and categorize experiences, and talk and plan for the future. Vygostky argued: "The most significant moment in the course of intellectual development, which gives birth to the purely human forms of practical and abstract intelligence, occurs when speech and practical activity, two previously completely independent lines of development, converge" (Vygotsky, 1978a, p. 24).

Vygotsky eventually came to the conclusion that word meaning was the single unit of analysis that could link speech and thought. It is both speech and thinking. A word without meaning is not a word, just a sound. At the same time, any meaningful word is a concept. Thus, word meaning is both speech and cognition; it is an irreducible reflection of reality.

> The consciousness of sensation and thinking are characterized by different modes of reflecting reality. They are different types of consciousness. Therefore, *thinking and speech are the key to understanding the nature of human consciousness.* If language is as ancient as consciousness itself, if language is consciousness that exists in practice for other people and therefore for myself, then it is not only the development of thought but the development of consciousness as a whole that is connected with the development of the word.... The word is the most direct manifestation of the historical nature of human consciousness. (Vygotsky, 1987c, p. 285)

This idea of words as units that integrate speech and thought and that reflect human consciousness illustrates the interactionist perspective of Vygostsky's theory. The word unites the inner world and the interpersonal world; it unites the historical past and the present. The word has a developmental history as it emerges from actions that become socially meaningful and can be named.

From Intermental to Intramental

Perhaps contrary to common sense, Vygotsky argued that high level mental functions begin in external activity that is gradually reconstructed and internalized. He gives the example of pointing. Vygotsky claims that initially an infant will reach toward an object that is out of reach stretching the hand in the direction of the object and making grasping motions with the fingers. This is a movement directed to the object. But as soon as the mother recognizes that the child wants the object and is able to satisfy the child's request, the child begins to modify the reaching and grasping motion into a socially meaningful gesture—pointing. The mother's understanding of the gesture and intermental coordination between mother and infant result in an intramental process for the infant, an understanding of the special relationship in this case between the desired goal, the mother as mediator, and the pointing as a meaningful sign. According to Vygotsky:

> Every function in the child's cultural development appears twice: first on the social level, and later, on the individual level; first, between people (interpsychological), and then inside the child (intrapsychological). This applies equally to voluntary attention, to logical memory, and to the formation of concepts. All the higher functions originate as actual relations between human individuals. (Vygotsky, 1978b, p.57)

Vygotsky's view is that society and its psychological tools precede individual development. Development begins at the intermental or interpersonal system level. Interpersonal interactions are the context within which subsequent advanced cognitions emerge.

Infants and young children are part of a structured social unit in which individuals participate in coordinated interactions facilitated by a shared symbol system of language and other psychological tools. Once the infant's behavior is recognized and interpreted by others, the meaning of the behavior can gradually be internalized. The child's subsequent behavior is a product of the meaning that has been given in previous interactions. With the advantage of the tool of language, children can describe and analyze a given situation, draw upon their accumulation of past experiences, and decide how to act. All higher mental functioning including planning, decision making, evaluation of information, and reflection or metacognition, begins in the intermental or interpersonal domain and is gradually integrated into the person's cognition.

Vygotsky emphasized the role of speech for influencing social interactions. As a first step, the adult uses speech to guide, inform, or redirect a child's behavior. Mother says, "No, don't touch that, it might break!" Subsequently, the child begins to use the word *no* to control the actions of his mother, a sibling, or a friend. "No, don't touch, Mine!" Eventually, the command "No, don't touch" becomes internalized and is used in the form of inner speech to guide the child's own behavior.

The more complicated the cognitive demands of a task, the more a child is likely to use spoken language to guide problem solving. The child uses the tool of language, which is normally thought of as functioning in the social system, to help focus and structure their intramental functioning. Thus, Vygotsky became especially interested in the mediating role of egocentric or inner speech as it contributed to the emergence of new concepts (cognition) and ideas about the self (metacognition).

> The specifically human capacity for language enables children to provide for auxiliary tools in the solution of difficult tasks, to overcome impulsive action, to plan a solution to a problem prior to its execution, and to master their own behavior. (Vygotsky, 1978a, p. 28)

Inner Speech

Vygotsky (1978a) argued that speech plays a central role in self-regulation, self-directed goal attainment, and practical problem solving. He described the problem-solving behaviors of toddlers as involving both speech and action. Toddlers use what was described by Piaget (1952) as egocentric speech to accompany their behavior. They talk out loud, but do not seem to be concerned about whether anyone can hear them or understand them. He described the talk as egocentric because it did not seem to have any social intension. Piaget suggested that the development of communication began with inner thinking of a very private, nonsocialized nature. In toddlerhood, he viewed egocentric speech as evidence of the relative absence of social life and the great extent of nonsocialized thoughts that the child is unable to express.

Vygotsky (1987a) proposed a completely different developmental pathway to account for egocentric speech and its function. He represented the scheme as: Social speech—egocentric speech—inner speech.

As discussed above, Vygotsky viewed speech as beginning in the social interactions between children and adults or other children. The first and foremost function of speech is social. Egocentric speech is a transformation of this social speech inward. The child uses speech that was initially acquired through interactions with others to guide his or her own behaviors. It does not have a social intention; rather, it is a tool that helps to guide problem solving. Vygotsky viewed egocentric speech and actions as part of the same problem-solving function. The more difficult the problem, the more speech is necessary for the child to find a solution. "Children solve practical tasks with the help of their speech, as well as their eyes and hands" (Vygotsky, 1978a, p. 26). Eventually, the egocentric speech of an audible nature dwindles (but does not disappear entirely) and becomes inner speech.

Inner speech gives children a new degree of freedom, flexibility, and control in approaching tasks and working toward a goal. They can use words to call to mind tools that are not visible. They can plan steps toward a goal and repeat them to guide their actions. They can use words such as *slowly, be careful,* or *hold tight* to control their behavior as they work on a task. Language skills and self-control operate together to help children inhibit negative emotions and disruptive behavior during times of frustration (Lynam & Henry, 2001).

The kind of speech that guides problem solving emerges from the social speech that characterizes children's interactions with adults and eventually becomes inner speech. Often, when young children try to figure out how to work something or how to get something that is out of reach, they turn to adults for help. Vygotsky suggested that the kind of talk that adults use as they guide young children is then used by the children themselves to support and guide their own behavior. (That is the idea of movement from intermental to intramental.) He referred to this process as the "internalization of social speech." In a sense, a child's capacity for self-directed goal attainment depends on what he or she has taken in of the spoken, practical advice and guidance given by adults and older peers who have tried to help the child solve problems in the past. In adulthood, these speech-like cognitions are not typically audible; they are experienced as inner talk or self-talk, that help organize complex tasks (e.g., first make an outline), encourage persistence (e.g., concentrate, stay focused), or review and revise (e.g., doesn't fit, try the bigger one*).*

The Zone of Proximal Development

Taking the idea of internalization a step further, Vygotsky proposed the concept of the *zone of proximal development* to help explain the relationship of learning and development. Each child can be described as functioning at a certain mental age and as having the potential to function at a more advanced mental age. The zone of proximal development is "the distance between the actual developmental level as determined by independent problem solving and the level of potential development as determined through problem solving under adult guidance or in collaboration with more capable peers" (Vygotsky, 1978c, p.86).

We have all experienced a situation in which we were unable to solve a task by ourselves, but with the assistance and advice of someone else we were able to be successful. The typical efforts of parents to help a child put together a jigsaw puzzle by suggesting strategies, such as selecting all the straight edged pieces first to make the border, or sorting the many pieces into those with a similar color, is an example of how learning takes place within the zone. Children watch older children perform a task and they copy the strategy; children ask their parents or teachers for help when they get stuck in a task; teachers give children suggestions about how to organize a task or how to use resources that will help them complete an assignment. In these and many other instances, we recognize the variety of ways that children expand the level of their independent problem solving capacities by drawing upon the expertise of others.

Vygotsky suggested that the level of functioning a child can reach when taking advantage of the guidance of others reflects the functions that are in the process of maturation, as compared to those that have already matured. What is more, recognizing and validating this social context in which learning takes place illustrates that cognitive development grows in the direction of the intellectual characteristics of those who populate the child's world. "Human learning presupposes a specific social nature and a process by which children grow into the intellectual life of those around them" (Vygotsky, 1978c, p. 88). Contrary to the thinking of the time, Vygotsky argued that development lags behind learning. When children are exposed to new ideas beyond what they already know or understand, the child is stimulated to engage these new ideas and, as a result, development moves forward. In a very immediate and direct way, as children function in their zone, culture and the social context guide the direction in which learning promotes development. Learning within the zone of proximal development sets into motion the reorganization and internalization of existing developmental competences which then become synthesized at a new and higher intramental level.

Vygotsky used the term zone of proximal development to refer to a range of potential performance. When trying to assess a child's developmental level, it is important to understand not only what the child already knows and can already perform, but also the domains that are "in progress," so to speak, the areas that are emerging as new fields of mastery. Normally adults, especially parents and teachers, and more advanced peers promote development by engaging children in activities and problem-solving tasks that draw children into the new directions along which their capacities are maturing. This idea has been very influential in guiding educational instructional strategies. Effective instructional strategies not only move children from their current developmental level to their potential level, but, as the concepts are acquired, the zone itself expands upward (VanGeert, 1998).

A unique contribution of Vygotsky's concept of the zone of proximal development is the notion of the interplay between two concurrent developmental levels, one that could be considered the child's actual or base line level of cognitive functioning, and the other that is the child's potential level of functioning given appropriate instruction, support, and encouragement. According to Vygotsky, both of these levels exist within the zone for each domain of knowledge. If properly structured, educational settings create a zone of proximal development for specific school subjects.

A creative insight offered by Vygotsky is that movement within the zone can be prompted not only by instruction but in the child's own play. In play, Vygotsky saw a cognitive process that in and of itself captures a preshadowing of the child's next higher level of functioning. Vygotsky (1978d) captured a unique feature of fantasy play:

> Play creates a zone of proximal development of the child. In play a child always behaves beyond his average age, above his daily behavior; in play it is as though he were a head taller than himself. As in the focus of a magnifying glass, play contains all developmental tendencies in a condensed form and is itself a major source of development. (p. 102)

In pretend play, children address areas where they do not yet feel competent in their lives and try to act as if they were competent. They set rules for their performance, and commit themselves to function according to them. So if a child is pretending to be a good mother, she brings forward all the ideas she has about how to be a good mother and applies them to the pretend situation. Similarly, if a child is pretending to be a superhero, she imposes all the rules of power, goodness, and helpfulness that she knows of and tries to limit her actions to those rules. Vygotsky regarded fantasy play as a window into the areas of competence that the child is striving to master but are still out of reach.

NEW DIRECTIONS

Vygotsky's theory has had enormous influence on the cross-cultural study of development. Before Vygotsky's theory became well known, cross-cultural psychology of the 1960s and '70s focused largely on exploring how children in different cultures would approach tasks and problems that had been developed in Europe or the United States. Many scholars were interested in determining, for example, whether the Piagetian stages of concrete operational and formal operational thought would be observed at about the same age, and in the same sequence among children in traditional societies as they were in industrial societies (Rogoff & Chavajay, 1995). Tasks involving conservation, manipulation of multiple variables, logic, classification, and memory were modified for presentation to children in different cultures.

As the results of these studies were summarized and compared, several themes became clear. First, the tasks were not as readily generalizable across cultures as researchers had expected. Children who performed poorly in some of these tasks were observed to function in quite complex ways when engaging in activities natural to their every day lives (Cole & Scribner, 1977). Second, the extent to which children were exposed to a Western type of schooling influenced their approach to these tasks. Variations in schooling across cultural groups substantially altered the ways that children approached specific tasks, including their understanding of the testing situation, as well as their ability and willingness to engage in the abstract tasks presented by the researchers (Cole, 1990).

Influenced by Vygotsky's theory, scholars began to move away from treating culture as a static variable within which individuals develop. In many of his writings, Vygotsky implied that cognition is culturally situated. However he did not have time to explore specific dimensions of cultural variation in detail. He pointed to language, instructional strategies, the nature of social interaction and the social expectations adults had about children, as factors that might influence cognitive development. In the new, sociocultural approach, researchers began to find new and varied ways of conceptualizing a process through which a child's cognitive development is intricately intertwined with the activities in which a child participates, the other people who engage in the activities with the child, and the cultural practices and institutional structures that provide the context for the activities. Rather than thinking of the individual and the society as distinct, the sociocultural approach attempts to contextualize development at every step.

One of the primary strategies for achieving this integration of person and society is to focus on activities or events as the unit of analysis. "The activity or event is a unit of analysis that focuses on people engaged in sociocultural endeavors with other people; working with and extending cultural tools and practices inherited from previous generations" (Rogoff & Chavajay, 1995, p. 871).

As an example, one can think of "doing mathematics" as an activity. Studies have found that Japanese children perform better on mathematics problems than do children in the U.S. (Trends in International Mathematics and Science Study, 2004). This is true even though there do not appear to be differences in intelligence between children in these cultures. A sociocultural approach to understanding this difference highlights the following features of Japanese culture. First, Japanese parents believe that mathematics competence is a result of hard work and persistence whereas U.S. parents tend to view mathematics competence as largely a result of ability. When children have difficulties in math, a belief in trying harder is more likely to lead to improvement than a belief in ability. Secondly, U.S. parents tend to overestimate their child's mathematical abilities, perhaps as part of their desire to see their child as unique or special. U.S. parents are basically satisfied with the level of mathematics ability their children have achieved. In contrast, Japanese mothers tend to keep encouraging their children to improve, focusing on wanting their children to fit in with their group. Children whose parents and teachers set high standards are more likely to continue to strive than children whose parents and teachers have lower expectations for their performance (Stevenson, Chen, & Lee, 1993). Third, the Japanese language places special emphasis on the quantitative aspect of the environment with different words for counting different types of objects such as people, birds, broad thin objects such as paper, and long thin objects such as sticks. Japanese parents frequently play counting and number games with their children as a way of encouraging young children's attention to quantity (Hatano, as cited in Siegler, 1998).

Finally, mathematics instruction in Japanese classrooms is very different from instruction in U.S. classrooms. In Japan, teachers spend more time introducing new concepts and less time reviewing previous concepts. They focus more on complex problems that require four or more steps to reach a solution and spend more time on problems that are mathematically related but not simply a repetition of previous problems. There are usually two teachers in the classroom, one who can assist students who are having difficulty so that the class can move along together to the next level of work. Within this context, Japanese students also spend substantially more time on homework out of class than U.S. students. As a result, their mathematics understanding matures at a faster rate, they are able to become involved in more interesting problems, and they have greater confidence about their ability to master mathematics, a confidence that is supported by parental expectations, well-designed classroom experiences, and prior successes (National Center for Education Statistics, 2004).

In contrast to considering the impact of culture on individual development, researchers using the sociocultural approach view the individual, the interpersonal, and the cultural levels as operating together in an integrated fashion (Rogoff, 1995). One can focus on one level of analysis as the figure, and the others as ground, but one cannot fully understand development without an analysis of all three of these levels.

For example, among the Zinacantecos of Southeastern Mexico, newborn infants are draped in a long skirt held in place by a belt or wrap. Zinacanteco babies are rarely on the floor. Rather, they are held in the mother's lap, in her arms or carried on her back. In contrast to U.S. parents, Zinacanteco mothers rarely urge their babies to perform new motor behaviors and show no special recognition or excitement when a new behavior is accomplished. Zinacanteco babies are quieter and less demanding that typical U.S. babies. They lag behind U.S. babies by about 1 month in motor development, but they show about the same pattern of motor skill over the 1st year of life.

Cognition is nurtured through observation and imitation rather than through direct exploration and manipulation, as is the case among U.S. babies. The childrearing practices of the Zinacanateco instill two culturally valued characteristics: restrained movement and a tendency to observe and respond rather than to initiate behavior. These qualities, transmitted from one generation to the next through consistent childrearing practices, provide a source of continuity in cognition and behavior from infancy into adulthood, and across generations (Greenfield & Childs, 1991; Brazelton, Robey, & Collier, 1969). The example illustrates the integration of individual, interpersonal, and cultural processes in even the earliest development of motor skills.

In the sociohistorical study of cognition, variation is assumed rather than similarity or generality (Rogoff & Chavajay, 1995). Since development is thought to occur in specific contexts at particular periods of time, one focuses on how people in a particular cultural community engage with one another to achieve a specific goal. The learning that takes place or the growth in understanding that occurs cannot be generalized across individuals within a community, across communities, or across activities in various settings. As a result, the findings from any empirical study cannot be widely generalized. Rather, the field grows slowly through multiple, contextualized observations. Over time, one hopes to gain insight into how individuals integrate existing cultural understanding and produce new understanding, how participation in activities or events alters cognitive processes, and how shared cognitions across individuals and generations alter the practices of a culture.

Finally, the sociohistorical perspective has led to a greater awareness of the way in which the tools and methods of scientific inquiry are themselves culturally situated. As an example, in research on logical thinking, Luria (1976) asked schooled and nonschooled adults to solve a problem of logic: "In the Far North, where there is snow, all bears are white. Novaya Zemlya is in the Far North and there is always snow there. What color are the bears there?" Nonschooled peasants would not answer this kind of question, arguing that they have never been to Novaya Zemlya, so they could not speak about the color of the bears who lived there. "We always speak only of what we see; we don't talk about what we haven't seen" (as cited in Rogoff & Chavajay, 1995, p.861). Other researchers have observed this similar reluctance on the part of certain cultural groups to accept information based on inference and to trust only what they have experienced or what someone who is greatly respected may have experienced. This does not mean that people from these cultural groups cannot reason logically; they are perfectly able to evaluate someone else's reasoning and conclusions as logical or inconsistent, but they are unwilling to reach a conclusion about a premise that they cannot verify (Scribner, 1977; Rogoff & Chavajay, 1995).

Vygotsky's insights about the cultural nature of symbolic tools extends to the tools of measurement and experimentation. Scholars in this field have become more attuned to the sociocultural and historical assumptions that underlie their research questions and their methods. They are increasingly striving to design approaches to inquiry that are appropriate to the world view of the community being studied.

A RESEARCH EXAMPLE: CULTURAL MANAGEMENT OF ATTENTION

The principle that individual development is integrated with culture is illustrated in research on the management of attention described here. Attention is a basic process that has been investigated starting in the early study of sensation, perception, and cognition. Beginning with the early experiments in psychophysics, scientists asked questions about the level of stimulation required to cause a change in attention. In the study of infant perception, the process of habituation was used to explore sensory thresholds. Measures of attention, including gazing time, were used as operational definitions of preference. In the field of information processing, research was carried out to examine the limits of the capacity for attending to competing sources of information. Studies have found that with maturation from childhood to adolescence, there is improvement in both selective attention, the ability to screen out interfering information in order to focus on the primary task, and divided attention, the ability to attend to two tasks at the same time (Higgins & Turnure, 1984; Schiff & Knopf, 1985). In general, there has been an assumption in the field that the ability to attend to several stimuli or events at once is limited by some type of neural "bottle neck." As a result, the ability to function at an optimal level is impaired or delayed when the situation requires attention to competing demands (Pashler, 1992). The research led to the conclusion that attention was a basic, universal process that functions in the same way across cultures.

Vygotsky contributed to this body of knowledge by pointing to the school-age child's development of voluntary memory and voluntary attention (Vygotsky, 1987b). The component elements of conscious awareness, sensation, perception, memory, and attention, become increasingly differentiated in toddlerhood and early childhood. By school age, memory and attention are sufficiently developed that the child can begin to be aware of them, permitting the child to direct attention purposefully.

The dissemination of Lev Vygotsky's ideas led Rogoff and her colleagues to suspect that the emphasis on sequential, focused attention might be a result of the researchers' cultural preference. Ethnographic and anecdotal reports suggested that there were people from cultural groups who were especially skilled at managing attention to multiple tasks while sustaining a high level of functioning. For example, Ochs (1988) found that Samoan transcribers were able to listen to audio tapes and follow the conversations of three or four different people who were talking at once.

In order to pursue the idea that some cultural communities value and nurture the coordination of attention to multiple events, systematic studies were conducted that compared Guatemalan Mayan mothers and their toddlers from San Pedro with mothers and toddlers from Salt Lake City, Utah (Rogoff, Mistry, Göncü, & Mosier, 1993; Chavajay & Rogoff, 1999). Sixteen mothers and their toddlers (mean age = 17 months) from each community were interviewed at home. All the toddlers had older siblings who were 3 to

5 years old and who were home during the interview. At one point, mothers were given a number of novel objects and asked to involve their toddler with the objects one at a time. This segment was videotaped for 10 minutes; when the interview resumed, 10 more minutes of adult-focused interview time was videotaped. Both segments were coded, looking at how adults and toddlers managed instances of competing events. Thus, the study considered how mothers and toddlers in two communities managed instances of competing attention during a child-focused interaction (mother helping child play with a new object) and during an adult-focused interaction (mother responding to interviewer's questions).

The San Pedro mothers and their toddlers were more likely to attend to competing events simultaneously than the Salt Lake City mothers and their toddlers. The Salt Lake City mothers and their toddlers were more likely to shift their attention from one event to the next than the San Pedro mothers and their toddlers. The San Pedro toddlers were more likely to attend to events simultaneously than the Salt Lake City mothers, suggesting an early and pervasive preference for simultaneous attention in the Mayan community. The Mayan preference for simultaneous attention was shown across toddler-focused and adult-focused interactions, and was unrelated to the number of years of schooling experienced by the Mayan mothers.

The results of this research suggest that there are patterns of managing attention that differ in the two communities under study. One implication is that focused, selective attention is not the preferred or optimal cognitive strategy across communities. Rather, as hypothesized by Vygotsky, cognitive processes are varied and develop in cultural context. A second implication is that very young children can become skilled at managing their attention to competing events if the social community encourages this kind of coordinated attention. This illustrates the operation of the zone of proximal development.

A third implication is that cultural preferences about attention may be linked to patterns and expectations for social interaction. For example, the European idea of *dyadic intimacy*, in which we encourage mother and child to set aside all other tasks in order to interact with each other, is not necessarily the only way to achieve intimacy. In some communities, closeness is achieved when a group of people, including children and adults, interact around a variety of tasks in each other's presence. The comparison of attention strategies across cultural communities can highlight the tie between cognition and human interaction. This validates Vygotsky's ideas about the bond between the individual and society. Finally, in the modern world, the demand to attend to multiple sources of information appears to be increasing. The strong cultural pressure in the European or western communities toward focused attention on one event at a time may be in conflict with the growing technological pressure toward "multitasking". This may be an unrecognized source of cultural stress in Western societies.

AN APPLICATION: IMPLICATIONS OF VYGOTSKY'S THEORY FOR INSTRUCTION

Vygotsky's theory has influenced educational practices in the United States and in Russia. As you might expect given the sociocultural perspective introduced above, the application of the theory has taken somewhat different forms in these two countries. In the United States, the theory has contributed to strategies for promoting metacognition, that is interventions that are intended to increase children's responsibility for planning, directing, monitoring, checking, and evaluating their learning. The approach is referred to as *mediated learning*, or *reciprocal learning* (Haywood, 1996; Palincsar, Brown, & Campione, 1993). In Russia, the theory has contributed to approaches to promote the understanding of scientific knowledge by linking knowledge about concepts with knowledge about procedures. The approach is referred to as *theoretical learning* (Davydov, 1972; Karpov & Haywood, 1998).

Mediated Learning

According to Vygotsky's theory, complex cognitive capacities emerge first in social interaction and are gradually internalized through their use in guiding the behaviors of self and others. This idea has been translated into the educational domain by creating instructional experiences where students and teachers share responsibility for teaching. The mediated learning environment is structured as a community of learners where teachers model certain strategies for planning, summarizing, clarifying, and questioning the problem solving process, and gradually turn these responsibilities over to the students. Students cooperate and share in the mutual regulation and control of the learning process, taking turns in observing, helping, and evaluating each other's work. This method of involving students in each other's learning and achievements creates an environment of social support for complex learning as well as creating opportunities for children to learn from both the teacher and the other students. Over time, the metacognitive skills of monitoring, planning, and evaluating are transferred to other academic domains, especially in learning environments where teachers invite students to engage in active discourse and critical analysis in order to think and make meaning of course content (Miller, 2006; Forman & Cazden, 1995).

Theoretical Learning

Vygotsky distinguished between two types of concepts: *spontaneous concepts* and *scientific concepts*. Spontaneous concepts are similar to the kinds of schemes that Piaget described as emerging during the sensorimotor and preoperational stages; they are generalizations drawn from daily, personal, direct experiences. Spontaneous concepts form the basis of knowledge that has not been guided by systematic instruction or explanation from more experienced adults.

Scientific concepts are the ideas, laws, and information that have been accumulated over generations as a result of systematic research, philosophy, and shared, historical experience. According to Vygotsky, scientific concepts cannot be expected to be discovered or reinvented in the course of a single child's education, and therefore require knowledge transfer through a process of instruction. Once these ideas are internalized, they can be used to mediate new experiences and to create new applications or discover new scientific concepts.

However, the Russians found that the simple didactic presentation of scientific knowledge was not effective in helping students to achieve mastery of these concepts. They recognized that students needed to understand the procedures that are used to gain this knowledge as well as the concepts themselves in order to use the ideas for further problem solving. Theoretical learning is the approach they created in order to integrate knowledge of the signs and symbols of scientific concepts with the procedures that are used to generate these concepts. Theoretical learning involves teaching children a method or model for organizing and analyzing information appropriate to the subject matter, and then helping children use that method to solve new problems.

For example, when working with children to put together a jigsaw puzzle, the adult might suggest starting with the "edge" pieces to create the outline of the puzzle. When a 5-year-old first faces the challenge of putting together a 25 or 30 piece puzzle, he or she is often baffled at how to begin. Initial efforts are likely to fail; and with this failure comes frustration and the likelihood of giving up. The child knows that the pieces are supposed to come together to make the picture, but exactly how this can be done is not clear. The edge pieces have a common feature, the flat edge. The child is now able to identify a subset of the pieces, and to focus attention on them rather than being overwhelmed by all the pieces at once. As the child experiences success by putting together some of the edge parts, the child begins to feel hopeful about finding the solution to the whole puzzle. Having internalized this strategy, it can be applied to all two dimensional puzzles. Experiencing success in problem solving through the application of a particular strategy gives children the idea that many complicated problems may have a method or approach that will help them find the solution. Once children have had the opportunity to experience success by applying a procedure to solve a problem, they are likely to anticipate that there are other procedures that would be helpful in solving other types of problems (Davydov, Pushkin, & Pushkina, 1972; Chi, Feltovich, & Glaser, 1981).

In their analysis of the application of Vygotsky's theory to education, Karpov and Haywood (1998) suggest that the integration of theoretical learning and mediated learning might be optimally effective. Theoretical learning does not exploit the power of the learning community. Both the verbal knowledge and the procedural knowledge first come from the teacher, and then are expected to be internalized by students without the benefit of social exchange or mutual instruction. Mediated learning focuses on the metacognitive processes of observing, planning, checking, and evaluating that should increase motivation and self-directed learning. However, it does not include a process for engaging students in mastery of the signs and symbols or procedures that create scientific knowledge. By integrating the two approaches, students could be asked to master the scientific concepts and procedures of a field, and then work together in order to solve problems using these strategies. Some students would attempt to solve a problem, while others would check and evaluate the work; then they would switch roles so that the metacognitive capacities and scientific knowledge would advance together.

HOW DOES COGNITIVE SOCIAL-HISTORICAL THEORY ANSWER THE BASIC QUESTIONS THAT A THEORY OF HUMAN DEVELOPMENT IS EXPECTED TO ADDRESS?

What is the direction of change over the life span? How well does the theory account for patterns of change and continuity?   The direction of change is from intermental to intramental—from social speech, to egocentric speech, to inner speech. The theory suggests that major transitions in cognitive complexity are observed twice, first at the interpersonal or social level and then as internalized concepts. The direction of change is toward increasing cognitive complexity guided by the scientific knowledge and cultural values about intelligence that shape the sociohistorical context. A particular focus of the theory is on increasing capacities for metacognition and self-regulation which occur as the child internalizes guiding strategies for monitoring, analyzing, and evaluating problem solving efforts that were initially provided by more skilled adults.

What are the mechanisms that account for growth? What are some testable hypotheses or predictions that emerge from this analysis?   Vygotsky asked how the developing child incorporates the tools and scientific concepts of his or her culture in order to function as a contributing member of the culture and possibly to contribute to what is known through his or her own innovative problem solving. He was interested in conceptualizing how the intrinsic, biologically guided forces interact with cultural forces to produce new levels of cognitive functioning. One mechanism that Vygotsky offered to account for this growth is participation in collaborative problem solving with adults and more skilled peers. Children learn new strategies, use those strategies to regulate their own behavior and those of others, and eventually internalize those strategies for application in subsequent problem solving situations.

A related mechanism is the concept of the zone of proximal development. The theory proposes a distinction between typical and optimal functioning. Children bring a spontaneous capacity for understanding and problem solving to each new situation. However, they also have the potential for a higher or more cognitively complex level of functioning that can be prompted through guidance by more skilled participants. Teachers and peers can foster new levels of cognitive functioning by introducing signs, symbols, and procedures that the child can learn to apply in new situations.

Drawing on the concept of a zone of proximal development, one can predict that with a small amount of help or guidance, children should be able to solve more difficult problems than they can solve independently. The challenge is to identify problems that are "within the zone" and the level of help that preserves the child's continued interest and motivation to engage the problem. Presumably, when a child is given a clue or strategy for solving a problem that is within the zone, the solution should come rather easily and the child should exhibit enthusiasm and interest in working on the task. If the problem is beyond the zone, the same clue or strategy will not result in a successful solution, and the child may experience a sense of confusion or disinterest. Thus, the ability to locate where a child is in his or her zone of proximal development depends upon the developmental level of the child, the nature of the activity or problem, and the nature of the guidance or support that the child is receiving. All of these factors interact to influence the child's success.

How relevant are early experiences for later development? What evidence does the theory offer to support its view? According to Vygotsky's social-historical perspective, cognition emerges from social interactions and the use of cultural tools which are gradually internalized. As a result, the early experiences of communication with caregivers, exposure to the social community and the cultural environment, and experiences of nurturing and care are all critical in the way early cognitions are formed. Early in development, children hear and use words that have been used in adult speech. Although the child may understand the word in a more concrete form, and the adult understands it in a more abstract form, the child is able to coordinate his or her word use in a way that corresponds with the adult's understanding; by recognizing the child's use of a word, the adult supports the child's language use. This early coordination of language use is central to subsequent concept development.

As illustrated earlier in the chapter, early experiences shape the way children attend to events around them. Exposure to verbal and nonverbal cues provide additional tools for conceptualizing events. Patterns of teaching and evaluating knowledge that are characteristic of a culture become internalized and mediate the way children come to interpret new information. Thus, early experiences are critical for shaping the direction of subsequent development.

At the same time, at each new phase of life, individuals may participate in new social contexts that may introduce new ways of thinking. Schooling, for example, will introduce children to new procedures and tools, such as experimentation, which may lead to new kinds of scientific knowledge. As individuals mature, they may find ways to enter new zones of proximal development, by seeking out more challenging apprenticeships, educational settings, or training so that their earlier learning is transformed, and possibly replaced by new knowledge.

How do the physical, cognitive, emotional, and social functions interact? How well does the theory explain these interactions? The theory focuses largely on the interactions of the cognitive and social domains. A particular emphasis is placed on language, which is both social and cognitive. Language is social insofar as it sustains interpersonal relationships that produce the intermental cognitive space. It is cognitive insofar as language guides private, inner speech that eventually becomes thought. Over time, language and other symbolic tools of the culture that have permeated the child's social experience, become internalized. Eventually, these thoughts mediate new experiences, allowing the child to reflect upon and analyze them. According to this theory, one should be able to see a similarity in the ways people in the culture talk to and explain things to children, and the ways children approach new information, and ask for help in solving problems.

The sociocultural perspective emphasizes the child's experiences. This level of analysis captures and integrates physical, cognitive, emotional, and social functions at once. The biologically developing child is capable of engaging in different kinds of activities depending on his or her level of physical and cognitive development. Through action, the physical and cognitive capacities of the child have an impact on the social group; at the same time the cultural tools and social opportunities provided by the activity have an impact on the child and his or her experiences of meaning.

In the concluding chapter of *Thinking and Speech*, Vygotsky (1987c) brings the cognitive and affective domains together as he struggles to show the difficulty in following the path from thoughts which are large, integrated, and multidimensional, to speech which must unfold in a partitioned, sequential fashion, word by word. "The path from thought to word lies through meaning," and this meaning is built upon impulses, intentions, interests, needs, and emotions.

> Understanding the words of others also requires understanding their thoughts.... And even this is incomplete without understanding their motives

or why they expressed their thoughts. In precisely this sense we complete the psychological analysis of any expression only when we reveal the most secret internal plane of verbal thinking—its motivation. (p. 283)

How do the environmental and social contexts affect development? What aspects of the environment does the theory suggest are especially important in shaping the direction of development? In this theory, cognition is not located in the individual or in the society but in the specific meaning of a child's actions in context. Activities are socially constructed and have cultural meaning and value. Vygotsky argued against the idea of conceptualizing the environment as separate from the child. He placed greater attention on a child's *experiences* which are a product of a functional relationship between the individual and the environment. "Experience is a unit of personality and environment as they exist in development. Experience must be understood as the internal relationship of the child as an individual to an given aspect of realty" (1984, p 382). For example, in U.S. culture, there is a great value attached to an infant's transition from crawling to walking. Parents and other adults attribute considerable importance to walking, and view a child's age at walking as an indication of maturation. Cultural tools such as the "walker" have been invented to support or facilitate early walking. Thus, in the United States, walking is an activity that symbolizes maturity and readiness for the child to achieve a new level of autonomy and distance from the caregivers.

However, walking may be viewed differently in different subcultures, and may be regarded differently for boys and girls. In some families, walking at an early age may be a sign of athletic promise—a future football player, a soccer player, or a runner. In other families, early walking may be viewed as a sign that the child is on a path toward getting into difficulty—"We really need to keep our eye on this one; he's going to be a trouble maker." In other families, walking may be a worry because now the baby needs shoes and shoes are expensive. In still other families, as the baby begins to walk, the parents begin to "baby proof" the house, locking cabinets, moving items to new, higher locations, and installing covers on electrical outlets. All of these different reactions to walking illustrate how the biologically based capacity for walking interacts with the social and cultural context to give the activity specific meaning. Walking provides a basis for qualitatively different kinds of activities in the setting, and the meaning of those activities will differ depending on the sociocultural context.

According to the theory, what factors place individuals at risk at specific periods of the life span? A primary source of risk would be the relative absence of interaction with caregivers and other caring adults. Because of the importance given to the role of social interaction, conditions that restrict a child's participation in social interaction would result in impoverished language and cognition. Given the importance placed on the role of skilled adults and peers who introduce the child to problem solving strategies, new information, and new procedures for gaining scientific knowledge, the lack of access to schooling or alienation from the world of schooling would also place a child at risk with respect to achieving more advanced cognitive functioning. Each culture has its own tools and mechanisms for transmitting knowledge from one generation to the next. Children who, for whatever reason, lose their access to these resources will be at risk. This might result from poverty, war, natural disasters, homelessness, childhood servitude or slavery, or other crises that disconnect a child from family, friends, school, and community.

According to this theory, learning and development scaffold each other. As children mature, they are able to learn new and more complex information, and to explore new procedures. This new learning stimulates new levels of cognitive awareness, provides alternative approaches to problem solving, and helps the child conceptualize problems from new perspectives. The child's new insights may lead to a desire for more information, which once again propels the child toward increasingly complex levels of cognitive functioning. At any point in this process, the child's further development can be inhibited if new opportunities for learning are restricted.

CRITIQUE OF COGNITIVE SOCIAL-HISTORICAL THEORY

Strengths

Vygotsky did more than bring our attention to the social, cultural and historical contexts of development. Rather, he introduced an entirely new perspective on cognition, locating it at the interface of the person and the culture. The idea that the higher mental functions begin outside the person in the social environment and become internalized offered a unique perspective about the boundary of the self and the society and the direction of development. With this insight, one is able to appreciate that people in different cultures have different ways of representing their experiences and different preferences for higher order problem solving. Emerging from these ideas is a new excitement about ways of looking at development as a product of continuous and fluid exchanges between maturation, environmental opportunities and resources, and cultural tools.

Vygotsky took on big ideas including the nature of consciousness, the basic unit of psychological analysis, the interrelationships of mental functions to create integrated experiences of thought, and the integration of thought and behavior. He resisted tendencies toward reductionism and was constantly reminding us to look at the big picture.

Vygotsky provided a new way of understanding the relationship of learning and development by introducing the concept of the zone of proximal development. The child has both a current mental age and a mental age potential. Through the process of instruction, the child's insights about a subject advance, thus promoting new levels of cognitive development. Vygotsky's view about the role of instruction in development is gaining popularity within educational circles. A child has strong internal motivation to experiment and explore. However, according to Vygotsky, the child's intrinsic interest and curiosity will not be adequate for learning the scope of knowledge that is required to function in adult life. What is more, in order for children to acquire scientific knowledge, they need to be taught about the systematic tools and procedures of their culture. Vygotsky's concept of the zone of proximal development gives a specific role to teachers to guide children to new, more complex levels of functioning by giving them just the right amount of help at just the right time.

Vygotsky was devoted to an analysis of development. His many experimental demonstrations were designed to simulate the emergence of a new mental capacity, from its early origins to its more advanced, culturally informed level. He designed experiments that he thought would provide an opportunity for learning and development for those children who participated. His work with traditional cultures, with children who were developmentally delayed, and his interest in primate research all preserved the focus on describing and explaining the transformation of capacities from lower to higher forms.

In many developmental theories, the focus has been on identifying general principles or patterns of growth. By focusing on the child's capacity to adapt to specific settings, and the culturally situated nature of thought and language, Vygotsky emphasized diversity in development, an idea which has become increasingly integrated into the study of development and its application to education. Consideration of varieties of learning styles, rates of development, types of intelligence, and temperament have become increasingly prominent in studies of cognition. Similarly appreciation for varieties of instructional strategies, tasks, and cultural values and contexts for learning has become a priority in understanding the educative process. Finally, the meaning of behavior is expected to vary depending on the setting in which the behavior takes place. This emphasis on specific context gives credit to the child who detects the expectations of others within a setting, and to the culture, which operates to encourage certain types of behaviors in certain settings.

Weaknesses

Vygotsky, who was remarkably productive for such a short time, explored many ideas that he and his students and colleagues did not have time to develop. This was due in part to his untimely death, and in part due to the suppression of his work. As a result, many of his ideas reemerged in the later part of the 20th century in partial translation, and without adequate experimental or empirical evidence to support them

The concept of the zone of proximal development, which has probably been the most widely accepted concept from his theory, has been criticized on several fronts. The concept provides a framework for conceptualizing how learning and development are interconnected, and for how instruction can advance development. The construct suggests a physical space or distance that could be measured. One might think of development as movement across the zone, from the entry point where the child is able to solve problems of a certain difficulty alone. In the zone, the child becomes able to solve more difficult problems with the help of someone else. The upper boundary of the zone is the level of difficulty of problems that the child is able to solve only with the help of others. At some point, the child moves into a new zone where problems that were once solved with the help of others can now be solved independently, and the process begins again.

There are multiple definitions of the zone resulting in a lack of agreement about ways to operationalize this idea. A major question is how the social aspect of the zone should be construed. Some interpretations focus on the difference between what a child can do alone and with some help. Some interpretations focus on the difference between the child's everyday knowledge and the scientific or mature knowledge that exists in the culture. Some interpretations focus on the ability of an individual and the socially constructed knowledge of the larger community (Lave & Wenger, 1996).

The width of the zone, that is how far a child can progress with help, differs for different kinds of problems, and for different children. The concept does not provide guidance for how much help a person should give or what type of help a person should give to foster movement in the zone. It is unclear if movement in the zone is long-lasting once the help is removed, or if one should expect improvement in the zone for one domain of learning to generalize to other domains. Finally, children enter the zone at different levels of expertise. There may be more room for growth for children who are at the beginning or novice level than for children who are more advanced in their competence. Researchers in the field have not arrived at an agreed on method for establishing a zone of proximal development or for measuring movement in the zone.

Vygotsky placed a major emphasis on the cultural tool of speech as shaping mental processes. Some cognitive scientists might view this argument as an overstatement of the way speech and thought interact. As the work on the cognitive unconscious suggests, there are integrative aspects of higher mental functioning that are not consciously regulated by language.

The theory was developed in the context of a powerful social/political philosophy of Marxism. As such, it emphasized that the mind is born from participation in the community:

> Vygotsky and his colleagues wanted to change citizens' thinking from a feudal (landlords and serfs) mentality of helplessness and alienation to a socialistic mentality of self-directed activity and commitment to a larger social unit based on sharing, cooperation, and support. In the new Soviet view, each person was responsible for the progress of the whole society. (Miller, 2002, p. 370)

The theory is based on the premise that the conditions of economic production influence the nature of working conditions and interpersonal interactions, and that these interactions influence cognition. The value of shared goods was translated into the notion of shared knowledge, with the idea that it was the responsibility of those who were trained and educated to transmit this information to others in order to advance the society. As such, the theory is much more of a collectivist than an individualist view of cognition. To some extent, this balances the individualist emphasis of many of the other theories. However, the social and historical events of the past 20 years suggest that the marriage of these two traditions, Marxist philosophy and cognitive science, may be flawed.

After the fall of the Soviet Union, it turned out that many deeply held ethnic and subcultural traditions and values that had been suppressed for several generations resurfaced. The training, instruction, and socialization of the Soviet regime did not succeed in becoming fully internalized as one might have expected. Vygotsky may have placed too much faith on the willingness of teachers and parents to encourage movement through the zone through gentle encouragement and hints rather than by insistence on a specific approach to problem solving. The theory is naïve in assuming that the powerful members of society will willingly share the full extent of their knowledge in order to promote the advancement of all its children. The theory underestimates the willingness of communities to communicate multiple value systems that remain part of the intuitive knowledge base and are not displaced by the more formal, scientific knowledge base of those in power. The theory underestimates the contribution of the individual mind that may achieve a greater degree of independence from societal values and teachings once the tools of language and other symbolic resources have been mastered.

KEY TERMS

cultural tools

inner speech

internalization

intermental

intramental

metacognition

mediated learning

theoretical learning

sign

sociohistorical

sociocultural analysis

scientific concepts

spontaneous concepts

symbol

word

zone of proximal development

Chapter 10

Dynamic Systems Theory

CHAPTER OUTLINE

Historical Context

Key Concepts

    Systems

        Open Systems

        Properties of Open Systems

        System Hierarchy

    Emergence

        Principles of Change

    Self Organization

New Directions

    The Constructive Web

    Dynamic Skill

    Scale of Behavioral Complexity

A Research Example: Newborn Stepping

An Application: A Dynamic Systems Model of Antisocial Development

How Does Dynamic Systems Theory Answer the Basic Questions that a Theory of Human Development Is Expected to Address

Critique of Dynamic Systems Theory

    Strengths

    Weaknesses

Key Terms

Chapter 10

Dynamic Systems Theory

Over the course of development, there is both continuous and qualitative change. Continuous change can be seen, for example, as the number of words in a child's vocabulary increases or as the child grows in height in inches. Qualitative change can be seen as an infant's locomotive abilities change from slithering or crawling to walking; gestures, babbling, and one-word utterances are integrated into grammatically correct sentences; and visual and motor information are integrated in order to perform effective reaching and grasping. Dynamic systems theory attempts to explain how new, complex patterns or properties of behavior come into existence as a result of simpler components or processes that are already part of the system. It also seeks to address the reality of both variability and pattern in development. The theory can be applied to all systems from the microscopic level of cells to the macroscopic level of societies. Development is understood as the result of multiple, mutual, and continuous interactions among all levels of a developing system from the molecular to the cultural. A unique feature of the dynamic systems perspective is the premise that development is not guided by an executive, hierarchical plan either at the biological or the environmental level, but emerges as a result of moment by moment actions on many levels at once.

Whereas most students who have studied development come to understand that you need to take many variables into account in order to explain behavior, dynamic systems theory goes beyond this notion. It claims that the processes that may account for behavior, such as a child's genetic potential and physical characteristics, parenting strategies, family structure, and personal goals and motives, are inseparable; they are not independent causal factors in development. For example, the theory suggests that you cannot separate a child's characteristics and his or her parents' parenting strategies as distinct causal factors in the development of behaviors. We will discuss this idea further in the review of research about antisocial behavior. This notion of the ongoing interplay among related factors is why the approach is nonreductionistic and nonlinear. As such it challenges many deeply held views about the processes that account for change. The idea of interdependence across many levels and domains, and the probabilistic nature of developmental outcomes, will be illustrated in the chapter through a variety of concepts and examples.

HISTORICAL CONTEXT

Dynamic systems theory has roots in several fields. Systems theory, which explores the dynamic interrelationships among components of a system, was first elaborated by Ludwig von Bertalanffy in his book, *General System Theory*, in 1968. Von Bertalanffy acknowledged his historical debt to philosophers of the 1600s as well as to scientists working in the field of cybernetics in the 1940s and '50s. One of the key concepts of dynamic systems theory is self-organization, the idea that the organization of an open system will transform itself into a more complex, effective system without guidance by outside forces. This idea was first presented by Descartes, who suggested that the ordinary laws of nature tend to produce organization. The concept was expanded by naturalists of the 18th century and revived by modern scientists who noted that there are laws of physics and chemistry that guide the form and growth of biological systems. The term *self-organizing* was introduced by W. Ross Ashby in 1947 and became linked to general system theory as a way of characterizing how systems emerge from simpler to more complex forms or patterns of behavior. The process of self-organization has been noted in physics, chemistry, mathematics, and in both the biological and social sciences (Kauffman, 1993). Within the study of development, Esther Thelen has been recognized as explicitly applying dynamic systems theory to the analysis of motor development, particularly in her analysis of infant stepping and walking. This work then led to a consideration of principles from dynamic systems theory that could be applied to cognitive development (Smith & Thelen, 1993; Thelen & Smith, 1994; Thelen, Schoner, Scheier, & Smith, 2001).

The application of dynamic systems theory to cognitive development was also undertaken by Kurt W. Fischer and Thomas R. Bidell in the 1980s and '90s (Fischer, 1980; Fischer & Bidell, 1998). They criticized the field of cognitive science that dominated the literature at the time citing the lack of theoretical concepts to account for the wide variability in age of acquisition of certain concepts, variability in the sequence of acquisition of concepts, and the tendency to want to explain action and thought through a reductionistic focus on lower level systems including genes, neural networks, or biochemical process. Fischer and Bidell offered an alternative approach to understanding cognition as comprised of organized structures that are both active and adaptive as they manage the variability that is present in the environment. Cognition emerges like a web in which "the strands are not fixed in a determined order but are the joint product of the web builder's constructive activity and the supportive context in which it is built.... The separate strands in a web represent the various pathways along which a person develops." (Fischer & Bidell, 1998, p. 473). Thus, dynamic systems theory offers a view of cognition as at once structured and variable, a product of action adapted to the constraints and affordances of the environment.

At present, many subfields in human development are looking to dynamic systems theory to provide an overarching explanatory framework to help organize disparate observations about developmental change. Beyond the areas of motor development and cognition, the perspective has been applied to language, emotion and personality development, temperament, and developmental psychopathology (Lewis, 2000).

KEY CONCEPTS

In this creative new approach to understanding development, three big ideas are signposts that help to illuminate a highly complex framework: *systems* and the nature of open systems; *emergence*; and *self-organization*. The following section provides a discussion of these ideas and the implications of these ideas for approaching the study of development.

Systems

Any system, whether it is a cell, an organ, an individual, a family, or a corporation, is composed of *interdependent elements* that share some common goals, interrelated functions, boundaries, and an identity. The system cannot be wholly understood by identifying each of the component parts. The processes and relationships of those parts make for a larger coherent entity; the whole is more than the sum of its parts. The language system, for example, is more than the capacity to make vocal utterances, use grammar, and acquire vocabulary. It is the coordination of these elements in a useful way within a context of shared meaning. Similarly, a family system is more than the sum of the characteristics and competences of the individual family members. Families are a composite of a sense of common destiny and the genetic heritage of the spouses and then of their developing children. As spouses develop or create their own composite heritage, this "we-ness" of communication patterns and reciprocal role relationships identifies the family. Common destiny, genetic heritage, patterns of communication, and reciprocal role relationships may be modified and elaborated as a family attempts to survive and undergo transformations.

A dynamic system is one that continuously changes in order to carry out its functions and to preserve its equilibrium or balance. A goal of dynamic systems theory is to understand the many interconnected relationships within the system and between the system and other living and nonliving systems that can explain the variability and direction of change over time. Fischer and Rose (1999) described the assumptions that underlie the approach of dynamic systems theory as a lens for understanding the development of human activity.

> First, many influences come together to form the emergent properties of human action and thought. Second, a person is a self-organizing system who regulates these combinations based on feedback from both the immediate world in which the activities are embedded and his or her previous experiences and activities, especially those immediately preceding the activity to be explained. In other words, a person constructs activities, regulating the combination of influences that produce those activities through dynamic processes that centrally involve feedback from the immediate world and prior experience. (Fischer & Rose, 1999, pp. 198–199)

Taking a systems perspective on human development, one must think of the many domains that contribute to individual functioning including: biological; cognitive; personality and temperament; values, attitudes, beliefs, and expectations; and skills. One must also consider these domains as they contribute to the behavior of the other significant individuals (each also a system in his or her own right) with whom the individual interacts. These individuals are then embedded in a variety of systems, and surrounded by systems that have an impact on the individual and his or her network of relationships.

Figure 10.1 offers a developmental systems perspective for a single child–parent relationship. The individual child and the individual parent form a relationship that can be viewed as a system. The individuals and their relationship are embedded in and influenced by specific community, societal, cultural, and designed and natural environments all changing over time (Lerner, 2002, p. 211). This diagram of a child–parent system is intended to give you a glimpse of the comprehensive view of development that is implied by the dynamic systems perspective. What you cannot discern from the figure is that the individuals and the adjoining systems as well as society and culture are all changing and they are changing at different rates. What is more, they are influencing each other to varying degrees. The challenge of dynamic systems theory is to trace a pathway from one point in time, when the individual is functioning at a less mature level to a later point when the individual is functioning at a more mature level, and to identify the salient factors in this comprehensive array that play the most significant role in accounting for this change.

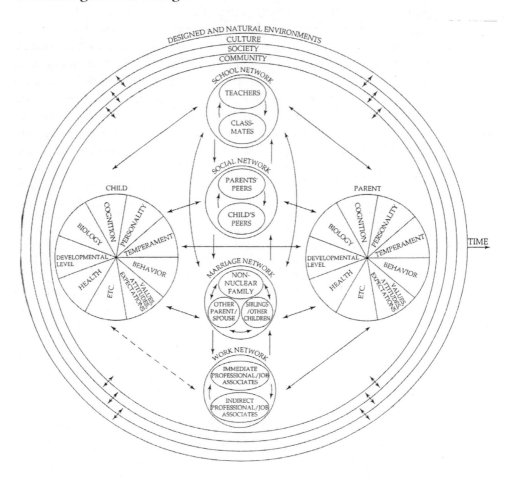

Figure 10.1.   A developmental contextual view of parent–child relations. From Lerner, R. M. (2002), *Concepts and Theories of Human Development*. Mahwah, NJ: Lawrence Erlbaum Associates. Reprinted by permission.

A system cannot violate laws that govern the functioning of the parts, but at the same time it cannot be explained solely by those laws. Biological functioning cannot violate the laws of physics and chemistry, but the laws of physics and chemistry do not fully explain biological functioning. Similarly, children's capacities for cognitive growth cannot violate the laws of biological functioning, but biological growth does not fully explain quality of thought or the nature of action. A unique consideration of dynamic systems theory is a focus on the structure that provides organization and stability among the components within a system. This theory strives to resist tendencies toward reductionism, arguing that complex human thought and action cannot be adequately understood by compartmentalizing the components and analyzing them separately. A child's attempt to engage a parent in conversation cannot be understood by looking separately at verbal skills, purposive behavior, parental identification, and attachment.

Open Systems. As we think about individuals, families, communities, schools, and societies, we are dealing with open systems. Ludwig von Bertalanffy (1950, 1968) defined *open systems* as structures that maintain their organization even though their parts constantly change. Just as the water in a river is constantly changing while the river itself retains its boundaries and course, so the molecules of human cells are constantly changing while the various biological systems retain their coordinated functions. Extending this analogy, as we think about human development, we strive to understand how it is that the psychology of the person is constantly changing, but yet development follows a patterned course and the person retains a sense of self-sameness from moment to moment.

Open systems share certain properties. They take in energy from the environment; they transform this energy into some type of product that is characteristic of the system; they export the product into the environment; and they draw upon new sources of energy from the environment to continue to thrive (Katz & Kahn, 1966). This process requires an open boundary through which energy (or information) can pass and products (or waste) can be exported. The more open the boundary, the more vigorously the process operates. Each specific system has a unique set of processes that are appropriate to the particular forms of energy, product, and transformations relevant to that system. In a family, for example, an open or permeable family boundary is responsive to stimulation and information from within and outside the family. This openness allows the family to use input for healthy adaptive growth and change. A closed family boundary does not allow for interchange and adaptive responses to the environment. In the analysis of systems, one focuses more on the processes and relationships among the parts that permit a system to survive and grow than on the characteristics of the parts themselves.

Properties of Open Systems. Systems are, by their very nature, always in a process of change. Systems move in the direction of adjusting to or incorporating more and more of the environment into themselves in order to prevent disorganization as a result of environmental fluctuations (Sameroff, 1982). System theory attempts to identify processes that help to explain how a system retains its functions while continuing to integrate new information from the environment and adjoining systems. Ervin Laszlo (1972) proposed four properties that help explain how systems balance stability and change.

The whole is comprised of relationships among component parts. The parts themselves do not comprise the whole; rather, it is the relationships and interactions among the parts that create the identifiable whole. *There is a tendency for systems to resist change and to retain their identity and functions*. The property of adaptive self-stabilization addresses the ability of a system to make internal modifications of the relationship of component parts in response to changes in the environment. *All systems exist in relationships with their environment.* Under conditions of homeostasis, the system and the environment are in balance. Changes in the environment are monitored by the system, internal relationships are modified, and the system's functions are preserved. *Systems have feedback mechanisms that allow them to reduce the impact of wide variations in the environment on the internal balance of the system's components*. The more information the system is required to monitor in the environment, for example changes in temperature, visual information, auditory information, and interpersonal communications, the more internal adjustments are required. The complexity becomes even greater when there is an interdependence among the components or subsystems—for example, when feedback from visual information, auditory cues, and olfactory cues are all needed in order to assess the safety of an environment.

Complex systems are especially vulnerable to environmental changes that might disturb the homeostasis. As a result, sensitive regulatory mechanisms, referred to as positive and negative feedback, are needed to preserve the relationship of the system and the environment. Positive feedback amplifies a variation and contributes to accelerated change in the same direct. For example, if a person is making a presentation and you say, "I can't hear you," the person will speak louder. If you say, "I still can't hear you," the person will speak even louder. Saying "I can't hear you" provides positive feedback to increase the speaker's volume. Negative feedback reduces deviations from the norm and supports stability. For example, when the oxygen level of the environment is reduced, you tend to grow sleepy. While you sleep, your breathing slows and you use less oxygen.

Some examples of adaptive self-stabilization are managed unconsciously by the organization of biological systems. Others are managed more deliberately by efforts to minimize the effects of environmental changes. Most systems have a capacity for storing or saving resources so that temporary shortages do not disrupt their operations. The process of self-stabilization allows the system to resist changes in the environment, and return to a desirable steady state.

Whereas self-stabilization describes a process of resisting environmental change, adaptive self-organization is a process of emerging changes in response to new external conditions. To the extent that the system cannot assimilate new information or buffer the subsystems from environmental changes, new subsystem relationships or new subsystem functions must emerge. Organization is essential in order to sustain life. Consider the steps involved in performing simple tasks such as getting dressed or making a meal. One plans, selects necessary resources, implements the plan, monitors the progress, and makes minor changes based on feedback. This level of organization allows for goals to be achieved with efficiency and minimal effort. Human beings are active, adaptive organisms that are able to create new forms of organization when existing structures prove to be ineffective.

Research suggests that the development of new skills depends in part on the conditions under which the reorganization occurs. For example, when a child's efforts to learn a new skill are closely monitored and stimulated with frequent, appropriate feedback, the child's learning appears to improve rapidly and shows many of the characteristics of a stage-like change in performance. However, when the same child is required to function with little support, progress is continuous and incremental. Thus, as Vygotsky pointed out, children can be functioning at several different levels depending on the conditions of support. As the child becomes familiar with the task domain and the experience of solving similar problems using different strategies, new skills and knowledge emerge (Van Geert, 1998; Fischer & Bidell, 2006).

System Hierarchy. Systems will develop in the direction of an increasingly hierarchical structure in which subsystems are organized into stable, specialized functions. The higher levels of the system have greater diversity of function, each one being comprised of subsystems that have more limited functions. One can think about spoken language as a hierarchical system that is comprised of subsystems including phonetics, syntax, grammar, and pragmatics. The system of spoken language and its subsystems work in a close interrelationship where the higher level system draws on all the sources of meaning in the subsystems to produce meaningful communication.

Dynamic systems theory uses the term *attractors* to refer to recurrent patterns or stable states that emerge through the coordination of lower-level system elements into higher-order organizations. These attractors are the organized patterns toward which change is likely to move. They are a result of many processes operating together that constrain and support each other in a given and recurring direction. Attractors are emergent processes that do not rely on a biological plan; they are likely but not fixed directions of change.

Living organisms have multiple attractors. For example, in the study of parent–child relationships, one might characterize a relationship as having four attractor states: positive playful, neutral question and answer or information sharing, negative conflictual, and disengaged. Over the course of many thousands of interactions, one could trace the amount of time spent in these four attractor states, the frequency and time spent in these states under various conditions, and the probability that time spent in one of these states at Time 1 would predict time spent in that same state at Time 2. As a relationship develops over time, some attractor states may become deeper, less vulnerable to environmental influences, and as a result, constrain future interactions (Granic & Patterson, 2006). One of the contributions of dynamic systems theory is the idea of considering an individual or a relationship system as having multiple attractor states rather than characterizing a person or a relationship as being of one type or another.

Emergence

In contrast to theories that use terms such as *learning, growth*, or *construction*, dynamic systems theory uses the term *emergence* to characterize the process of developmental change. The theory focuses on how new forms or properties come into existence as a result of ongoing processes that are found within the system itself (Lewis, 2000). Developmental change is viewed as probabilistic rather than fully predictable. Human beings are always in action and always in a dynamic relationship with a changing environment. Even in sleep, mental activity, motor activity, sensation, and perception are functioning and reactive to changing environmental conditions. Human beings also have complex capacities for memory, including motor memory, sensory memory, narrative memory, spatial memory, and memory for specific information. Finally, humans have a variety of strategies for gaining information about the environment including sensory/perceptual systems, emotional reactions, verbal and nonverbal communication, and measurement devices. In the course of planning and executing any action, there is ongoing feedback between multiple, interacting levels of information. The emergent or qualitatively new behavior is a result of the interaction of these levels over time.

The study of motor development has led the way in illustrating the usefulness of a dynamic systems model for the analysis of new motor behaviors (Metzger, 1997). Although the normative patterns of motor development suggest a sequence of stages that is heavily guided by genetics and neural structures, research on the process of motor development has challenged this view. The regularities in motor behavior are better understood as a result of a dynamic process of exploration in which infants coordinate their physical actions with the demands and opportunities of the situation. Perception and action work hand in hand, giving the infant information about the physical properties of the situation and feedback about the consequences of specific motor strategies. Over time and with practice in similar situations, the infant discovers the combination of action, intensity, direction and speed that will create the desired outcome. With additional practice, this pattern then becomes most likely and increasingly efficient (Thelen, 1995).

Principles of Change. The process of emergence is guided by three underlying observations about change (Miller & Coyle, 1999):

1. In the early phase of an emergent process, small differences or effects can have consequences that result in large difference or effects later.
2. A small change causes changes throughout the system.
3. The accumulation of small quantitative changes can lead to qualitative change as one of a number of related skills passes a certain threshold and contributes to the integration of what seems to be a qualitatively different skill.

An observational study of the emergence of infant crawling illustrates these points (Goldfield, 1989). Crawling requires coordination of head and shoulder movement, reaching, kicking, alternation of arms and legs over various types of surfaces, and ongoing feedback from each preceding action to guide the subsequent action. Fifteen infants were observed as they made the transition to crawling. Most babies reach a point when they rock in a stationary position on all fours before they can crawl. But at some point, they are able to move from a seated position to crawling. Illustrating the three ideas above, researchers found that the establishment of a strong hand preference was needed and had to occur before the system of crawling behaviors could unfold. This small change in the use of one hand over the other, which one might not intuitively associate with the emergence of a new locomotive skill, actually contributed substantially to the new behavior. This illustrates the idea that change in one component of the system will bring about changes throughout the system. When infants fell from a seated position onto their hands, they tended to fall onto their nonpreferred hand so that the preferred hand was available to reach out and begin crawling. Confidence in being able to maintain one's body weight on one arm and two legs while reaching out with the preferred hand was part of the motor sequence necessary for forward crawling. The gradual strengthening of hand preference was eventually integrated with other motor skills which resulted in the new behavior of crawling

Each new motor capacity permits exploration in a more varied environment. As a result, infants have to be able to make immediate assessments of the relationship between their physical abilities and the environmental conditions in order to decide whether to avoid action, take familiar actions, or try to invent some new, adapted action. Evidence for this flexibility can be seen in a study of ways that babies experiment with moving along a descending slope or slide. Some try going down headfirst and then roll over onto their backs; others try to go down with a crab-like crawl and then switch over to their bottoms; and others refuse to go down the slope, waiting for someone to carry them off the device (Adolph & Eppler, 2002). From a dynamic systems approach, knowing how to cope with a new environmental challenge is a convergence of perceiving, moving, and remembering as they evolve over time in response to the specific properties of the task and its match with the person's current physical capacities (Thelen et al., 2001).

Self-organization

As discussed above, adaptive self-organization is one of the central characteristics of a dynamic system, and perhaps the most essential concept relative to explaining the emergence of qualitatively new behaviors.

> Dynamic systems theorists claim that all developmental outcomes can be explained as the spontaneous emergence of coherent, higher-order forms through recursive interactions among simpler components. This process is called *self-organization*, and it accounts for growth and novelty throughout the natural world from organisms to societies to ecosystems to the biosphere itself. According to principles of self-organization, these entities achieve their patterned structure without prespecification by internal rules or determination by their environments. (Lewis, 2000, p. 36)

No single theory about how self-organization operates is accepted across disciplines or within the field of human development. However, the concept has been used to consider the spontaneous emergence of order and new levels of complexity in physics, chemistry, mathematics, biology, and the study of human social groups (Lewis, 2000; Kauffman, 1995; Kelso, 1995). When systems are in a state of extreme *disequilibrium*, or disorganization, there is a tendency for the overall organization of the system to change. The concept of disequilibrium suggests that there are circumstances when the adaptive functions of the system are not adequate to address current fluctuations either internal to the system (e.g., a breakdown in the coordination of components) or external to the system (e.g., novel conditions, or sudden depletion of resources).

Open systems have a permeable boundary that allows energy (or information) to be taken in to it in order to increase the system's order. All natural forces are expected to operate to dissipate the differences in energy between the system and its environment. When an open system is in disequilibrium, a process takes place that directs energy to the elements of the system in order to achieve a new order or relationship. When this new arrangement provides positive feedback, in other words, when it has the impact of moving the system back toward equilibrium, it is amplified and repeated at higher system levels. The overall organization of the system increases, achieving new levels of complexity and the emergence of new behaviors. New patterns at the level of the components or subsystems and new patterns at the larger system level reinforce or maintain each other, creating a condition in which the qualitatively new behavior is sustained from the "bottom up" and from the "top down" (Lewis, 2000).

Life is a process of periods of equilibrium and disequilibrium. Humans are active, goal-oriented life forms (Swenson, 1997). Disequilibrium is often produced as a result of this active, goal-striving nature, and is resolved by this same characteristic. Disequilibrium can be experienced at the physical level, as when a child's desire to ride a tricycle is incompatible with his leg length and muscle strength. Disequilibrium can be experienced at the interpersonal level when a teenager wants to be included in a group that does not offer membership. Disequilibrium can be experienced at the level of identity, when the roles that are available to the young adult are not a match with the person's values, goals, and beliefs. At each point, a process of change is set in motion in order to reestablish equilibrium in the system. Often, this results in the establishment of a new pattern of behavioral or cognitive organization.

Sameroff (1982) pointed out that as systems become more complex, they become more sensitive to environmental variations and require more finely tuned internal mechanisms in order to preserve equilibrium. For most human beings, the result of self-organization is a more flexible, efficient way of functioning. However, in some cases the new organization is not effective. It cannot be sustained by lower-level components, requires more energy or resources than are available, or may interfere with the person's ability to manage daily tasks and sustain interpersonal relationships. Over time, this may interfere with other systems and subsystems.

NEW DIRECTIONS

Dynamic systems theory lays out a complex, multidimensional framework for explaining both variability and patterns or order in the developing system. Kurt W. Fischer and his colleagues have extended the theory with a focus on examining the development of thought and action as they emerge within physical contexts and social relationships (Fischer & Yan, 2002). Over the past 30 years, their work has evolved to guide new research and application. Among the many new insights he and his colleagues have brought to the study of development three significant constructs are highlighted here: a new metaphor for conceptualizing the development of dynamic structures underlying thought and action—the constructive web; a focus on a new unit of analysis—the dynamic skill; and a way of measuring both long-term development and short term change—a scale of behavioral complexity.

The Constructive Web

Fischer and Bidell (2006) begin with a focus on the variability of human thought and action. They argue that people understand their experiences through action that has many components and occurs in a specific physical, social, and cultural context. In order to capture the variability, flexibility, and change that are characteristics of human behavior, one needs a model of psychological structures that is equally dynamic.

Fischer and Bidell (2006) suggest that in many theories of development, psychological structure is conceptualized as a ladder with a fixed set of steps arranged in a fixed sequence. Development is characterized as movement "up" the ladder from one level of organization to the next. The problem with this view is that the metaphor of the ladder does not capture the observed variability in human behavior, both within a single individual across tasks, conditions, and settings, and across individuals and cultural groups. The metaphor of the ladder also suggests that there is a predetermined series of steps with little room to account for emergent or novel structures.

In contrast to the ladder, Fischer and Bidell offer the metaphor of the web as a way of thinking about the underlying structure of development (Fischer & Bidell, 2006). The value of the web metaphor is that it helps to conceptualize the many possible trajectories for development both within and across individuals. A web is constructed through the active, goal-oriented efforts of the actor in conjunction with the supportive structure of the physical and social contexts. Just as a spider adapts its web to the convenient edges of a bench, a doorway, or a branch, the developing pattern of dynamic skills is a result of actions adapted to a specific context.

The separate strands of a web suggest different components of development, with some strands interlocking with others thereby supporting or strengthening each other. For example, the skills of reading and the skills of mathematics are distinct and develop though different trajectories. However, when children have to comprehend written instructions in order to complete a mathematics assignment or solve word problems, reading skills and mathematics skills are both required and may strengthen each other.

The strands of a web may start and end at many points in the web. The strands representing one developmental component may emerge at different times and in a different order than the strands of another component. The idea of multiple trajectories suggests that children may start out along different pathways and end up at the same point. For example, children begin crawling and pulling to a standing position at different ages and in different sequences. In some cultures, exploratory crawling is not permitted. Thus, children may arrive at upright walking through different pathways and using different motor strategies. Similarly, two children growing up in very different family and community environments, one in the suburbs and one in a very poor urban center, may arrive at the same college and be roommates.

The web metaphor also suggests diverging pathways. Two children may grow up in very similar, low-resource communities, play together and spend a lot of time together in childhood, and attend the same elementary school. Yet, they can experience very different academic pathways—one dropping out of school before graduating from high school and the other going on to college.

A strand may be fragile in its first construction, and be strengthened through repetition or adding of fibers. It may be strong in its initial construction and be weakened as a result of isolation from other related strands or build up of strands in another part of the web. This view of development helps to conceptualize the idea of *possible* selves. People can imagine possible outcomes and directions, and elect to pursue a direction by strengthening certain skills, ignoring some aspects of the self in order to enhance others, and modifying the structure in light of new opportunities or goals. The strength of the web is supported by underlying patterns of organization including the symmetry in shape, spatial relations among the strands, and effective connectivity to its context. "The web highlights integration, specificity, multiple pathways, active construction, and other central properties of skill development" (Fischer & Bidell, 2006, p. 325).

Dynamic Skill

One way that theories make their contribution to the study of human development is by focusing on specific behaviors that illustrates the processes that are central to the theory. Freud drew attention to free association, dreams and slips of the tongue as behaviors that provide insight into the unconscious. Social role theory highlights the concept of social roles as constructs that link individuals' expectations, goals, and behaviors with those of their community. Erikson described a state of tension between the competences of the developing person and the demands of the environment that led to the psychosocial crisis. Vygotsky focused on the word as a way of linking the person and the social environment, as well as thinking and speech. Following in this line of theory building, Fischer introduced the idea of *dynamic skill* as a way of integrating the many features of dynamic systems theory (Fischer, 1980). "Skill is the capacity to act in an organized way in a specific context. Skills are thus both action-based and context specific" (Fischer & Bidell, 2006, p. 321).

The study of skills provides a framework for exploring many of the principles of dynamic systems theory. Skills are actions that take place in specific contexts. One uses the skill of manipulating a fork for eating, not to type on a computer. Skills can be of varying levels of complexity, from carrying a tune to playing poker. In each case, they have a developmental trajectory—the skill begins in some rudimentary form of action which may mature to increasingly high levels of performance. Skills are both context specific and culturally guided. The skill of managing a fork for eating is valued in most western cultures, however, chopsticks are the preferred tool in many eastern cultures.

The term *dynamic skills* suggests that skills are changing as they become more advanced; they are also integrated with other skills which may permit new, more complex skills. Each skill is comprised of systems that must work together in order for the skill to be effective. For example, the use of a fork for eating requires hand–eye–mouth coordination; judgments about the consistency and size of the food; and understanding cultural practices for eating. Once the basic skill of using a fork becomes well established, it can be integrated into more complex skills such as cutting food with a knife and a fork; or the use of a fork in food preparation. The systems that contribute to one skill, such as hand–eye coordination, may contribute to more than one skill; and these contributing skills may develop at different rates, thus explaining why a skill may change slowly and then seem to advance to a new level rather suddenly.

Skills are self-organizing. Skills, by their very nature, are goal-oriented actions designed to perform specific functions in a particular environment. They depend for their effective functioning on the interpenetration or integration of several components that regulate each other. As the goals or the contexts for skill performance change, the skills may be modified or integrated with other skills to produce new behavior. For example, think about playing the piano as a skill. The original goal is to create music through the use of this specific instrument. Many components are required in order to play, including: memory, auditory perception, manual dexterity, rhythm, and the ability to read music. As one area improves, the level of playing may improve so that the notes are smoother, more rhythmic, and more "musical." At some point, simple tunes are replaced by more complex compositions requiring new fingering, more complex rhythms, faster speed, and coordinated use of right and left hands. As the technical challenges of playing the piano are mastered, the person begins to build a repertoire of pieces and introduces emotion, interpretation, liveliness, and a personal voice into the music. Now, the skill of playing the piano becomes a means of self-expression, and the entertainment of others. People gather 'round to hear the playing; the person is invited to parties to entertain others; and perhaps the person begins to think that playing the piano is a skill that could be lucrative. Piano playing is combined with other business-related skills in order to schedule gigs, advertise, and record music for sale. The person has self-organized the activity, integrating the original skill for playing the piano with other entertainment skills and entrepreneurial skills that form the basis of a musical career.

Scale of Behavioral Complexity

Fischer and Bidell point out that in order for developmental science to advance, researchers need a common scale along which to measure change. The classic examples for measurement in the physical world are the Centigrade and Fahrenheit scales for measuring temperature. These scales can be used for measuring the temperature of a wide range of substances—such as water, air, and the human body. One goal of Fischer and Bidell's (2006) was to create a scale for the measurement of behavioral complexity that could be applied across many types of skills. This common scale permits one to distinguish small continuous changes as well as growth spurts; and it suggests the direction of growth across three tiers, from action to representation to abstraction. The use of such a scale requires frequent measurements that can capture the shape of a growth curve, including the possibility of capturing both smooth growth and sudden jumps or shifts.

The scale is presented in Figure 10.2. It provides a way of thinking about dynamic skill development as comprised of 3 tiers and 10 levels. The tiers are quite similar to Piaget's stages of sensorimotor, preoperational, and for-

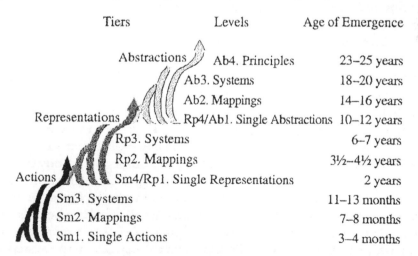

Tiers	Levels	Age of Emergence
Abstractions	Ab4. Principles	23–25 years
	Ab3. Systems	18–20 years
	Ab2. Mappings	14–16 years
Representations	Rp4/Ab1. Single Abstractions	10–12 years
	Rp3. Systems	6–7 years
	Rp2. Mappings	3½–4½ years
Actions	Sm4/Rp1. Single Representations	2 years
	Sm3. Systems	11–13 months
	Sm2. Mappings	7–8 months
	Sm1. Single Actions	3–4 months

Figure 10.2.   A scale of behavioral complexity. From Fischer, K. W., & Bidell, T. R. (2006). Dynamic development of action and thought. In W. Damon & R. M. Lerner (Eds.), *Theoretical Models of Human Development: Handbook of Child Psychology, 6th edition* (Vol. I), p. 323. New York: Wiley. Reprinted by permission.

mal operational thought. The first tier of any skill begins with actions. Within the action tier, there are three levels: single actions, mapping, and systems. As a system of action is created, it is transformed into a single representation of the action that then is mapped to other representations and forms a system of representations. This system is transformed into an abstraction which is mapped to other abstractions and forms a system of abstractions, much like the operations involved in Piaget's formal operational reasoning.

Let's look at an example. An infant uses his fingers to pick up little Cheerios from a bowl and put them in his mouth. His mother uses a spoon to put food into his mouth, and he experiments with using a spoon to pick up little Cheerios from the bowl. The action of self-feeding with fingers and spoon-feeding are mapped on each other. This leads to a system of using a spoon to feed himself. This system of self-feeding brings the action tier to a close. Now the child has a dynamic skill for self-feeding that can be represented through speech, and imaginary activities. Let's say that the child has a dog. He observes that the dog eats from a bowl on the floor without a spoon. He now pretends to eat from a bowl on the floor. He has mapped the idea of his own eating behaviors and the dog's eating behaviors. He begins to understand that he eats, his mother and father eat, and his dog eats. There is a system of representations about eating that is emerging as the child connects the actions of eating, and the representations about eating to an abstract idea about the requirement that living things must eat. This leads to observations and interests in how various living things eat, with the opportunity to read about eating behaviors among various animals and to study the ethology of eating. The young adult may even become interested in the possibility of conducting research about the conditions that influence eating behaviors. He identifies a set of interrelated domains that influence eating including sensory, perceptual, motor, cultural, and interpersonal dimensions that create a system of eating behaviors. Within this system, he recognizes the importance of the early experiences of self-feeding in infancy as a factor that guides subsequent eating behavior. He goes on to discover new principles about eating behavior, based on his own eating skills, his observational skills, and his research skills.

The behavioral complexity scale includes a three-step structure that is repeated at each tier. Skills merge with other skills or interpenetrate other skills to form new systems. One can imagine a person as having a wide variety of skills, some at the early tier of action and others more fully developed at the tier of representation or abstraction. At the tier of abstraction, a person may decide that new skills are required in order to move from the level of a single abstraction to a system of abstractions. Thus, skills can be deliberately nurtured in the service of other skills. The principle of self-organization is reflected in the transformation of the skill from a single action to a system of actions, from a single representation to a system of representations, and from a single abstraction to a system of abstractions. At each point, the system may look qualitatively distinct from the single level from which it emerged.

A RESEARCH EXAMPLE: NEWBORN STEPPING

One of the early applications of dynamic systems theory to human development was the study of infant stepping. At some point within the first 2 or 3 weeks of life, when you hold an infant upright under the arms, the infant makes stepping motions that look very much like walking. By the age of 2 or 3 months, this stepping behavior was thought to disappear. Initial explanation for this "loss" of the stepping response was that the reflex is inhibited by higher level cortical functions. The assumption was that the stepping reflex was a vestigal behavior from some earlier evolutionary primate period, and that true stepping and walking are a product of voluntary movement genetically programmed to emerge with more advanced cortical development.

The idea that a behavior that is so closely related to walking would disappear and then reappear was puzzling. Esther Thelen and Donna Fisher (1982) designed research to examine the relationship of the biomechanics of infant stepping and its relation to the infant's posture and physical growth. They were able to take advantage of video recordings and electromyography (EMG) of four muscle groups to capture data on patterns of muscle activation associated with various movements. Their first goal was to explore the similarities between infant stepping while held upright and infant kicking while the infants were lying on their backs. The former seems to disappear and the latter becomes stronger and more coordinated over time. Their second goal was to consider the biomechanical conditions that might constrain the stepping response and increase the kicking response.

The infants who participated in the study were all under 2 weeks old. Of 13 infants, 8 showed both stepping and kicking during the recording session. Both the stepping and kicking showed alternating right and left leg action. The EMG data for the two types of movement were quite similar. The timing of the flexion and extension phases of the kick and the step were also similar. Thelen and Smith argued that neonatal stepping and kicking while lying on the back are essentially the same movement patterns. The key to the "disappearance" of stepping and the increase in kicking is in the role of gravity as infants' legs gain mass. As the legs gain in fat, the muscle strength needed to lift the legs against the force of gravity is not sufficient to permit the stepping action. However, in the prone position, the kicking action is actually supported by the force of gravity. During the 1st months of life, the growth of body fat outpaces the growth of muscle mass, so the babies cannot lift their legs in the upright position. However, the action itself is not lost, and in fact is practiced actively in the prone position. When slightly older babies were submerged waist-high in water, overcoming the biomechanical constraints of body mass and gravity, the stepping pattern was observed (Thelen, Fisher, & Ridley-Johnson, 1984).

Thus, the shift from stepping to no stepping was actually a dynamic adaptation to the combination of changing physical characteristics in a particular physical context. The results of this research require a transformation in the way we think about development. In this case, walking is shown to be a product of mutually-regulating systems that self organize. The earlier way of looking at this was that the stepping motion was a primitive reflex that falls away and is eventually replaced by a genetically guided plan for voluntary walking. However, this research shows that the stepping motion remains in tact, but is not observed when the infant is in the upright position, because of a change in the ratio of fat to muscle mass. The babies' legs get too heavy to lift against the force of gravity when they are in an upright position.

Many subsystems are interacting to support the emergence of a newly integrated behavior, walking. Factors such as the ratio of body fat to muscle mass, exercise of the stepping and kicking motions, and opportunities to be in an upright or prone position may all contribute to this transformation. The results of the research illustrate that changes in one system, for example, fat content or muscle mass, prompt changes in the overall behavior.

Studies of infant care practices in other cultures, especially in Africa and Central America, find a more common practice of holding infants upright rather than lying them down in a cradle or crib. Infants in these cultures have been observed to walk at an earlier age than western infants. Thelen and Fisher suggest that infants who are given more experience in an upright position have the opportunity to strengthen their leg muscles by experiencing the resistance against gravity when they flex their legs, possibly leading to an earlier use of legs for support in standing and walking.

AN APPLICATION: A DYNAMIC SYSTEMS MODEL OF ANTISOCIAL DEVELOPMENT

An extensive literature addresses the etiology of antisocial behavior including the study of individual, family, and community contexts that give rise to aggressive and antisocial development, how antisocial behavior is maintained and transformed over time, and clinical approaches to prevention and intervention. Studies of bullying, externalizing behaviors, peer violence, peer rejection, harsh parenting, and child abuse and neglect are just a few areas that focus on the causes or consequences of antisocial development. A well-established line of research in this field is the work of Gerald Patterson on coercion theory, a model of how parents and children train each other through sequences of interactions so that the child's behavior is likely to become increasingly antisocial and aggressive, and the parents become increasingly unable to manage or regulate their child's aggressive behavior (Patterson, 1982; Reid, Patterson, & Snyder, 2002). In a recent paper Isabela Granic and Gerald Patterson (2006) applied the dynamic systems theory perspective to an understanding of the etiology of antisocial behavior, extending coercion theory and providing new ideas about how to identify young children who are at risk for the establishment of antisocial behavior patterns.

Several ideas from dynamic systems theory guided their research. First, they explore the process through which day-to-day, ongoing interactions contribute to the emergence of more complex systems of behavior. Second, they use the idea of attractors to characterize several types of stable patterns of parent–child interaction. Third, they introduce the idea of cascading constraints. This term refers to the fact that once behaviors are organized as attractors, these attractors become structured and resist change. Therefore they serve to constrain future behaviors. This idea captures the reality that an attractor is both the result of interactions that occur before the behavior has stabilized and the cause of behaviors that occur once the attractor has been formed.

You can think of parent–child interactions as creating a landscape of attractors, that is, the preferred patterns of interaction. Parents and their children typically have a variety of patterns of interaction that can be observed in different settings and for different purposes. For example, parents and children might be observed to be playful and humorous, engaged in some kind of problem solving, mutually supportive and encouraging, hostile, or disengaged. Each of these patterns is a possible attractor, depending on the specific nature of the parent–child dyad. Under normal conditions, parents and their children shift from attractor to attractor depending on the circumstances. Granic and Patterson (2006) hypothesized that interactions that were mutually hostile would be a strong attractor for children who are at risk for antisocial behavior, and that the parent–child interactions in these dyads would be more rigid than those of nonaggressive dyads.

To test these hypotheses, Granic and Lamey (2002) observed parents and their clinically referred children during 6 minutes. In their first 4 minutes, the parent and child were asked to discuss a difficult problem. Then there was a knock on the door and the parent and child were asked to use the next 2 minutes to wrap up their discussion and try to end on a positive note. The parent's and child's behaviors were marked on a coordinated grid. Every second, each partner's behavior was coded as hostile, negative, neutral, or positive. Thus, one could trace the coordinated trajectory of the discussion as the pair moved from one type of interaction to another. For example, both the parent and the child could be hostile, the child could be negative and the parent could be neutral, or both the parent and the child could be positive. This type of interaction grid allows one to characterize the trajectory of interactions as well as the most frequent types of interactions over a fixed period of time. In this study, one can also observe any shifts in the quality of interaction before the intrusion of the knock on the door and after. Granec and Lamey (2002) found that children who had been referred with externalizing problems, that is, tendencies to blame others, act aggressively to others or see the cause of their problems as due to people outside themselves, had parent–child interactions that tended to settle into two main attractors: hostile (child hostile–parent hostile) and permissive (child hostile–parent neutral or positive).

The second phase of this research linked the day-to-day quality of interactions to an emerging pattern of antisocial behavior. Researchers hypothesized that for those children who were on a path toward antisocial behavior, the hostile attractors would begin to constrain the interactions, and that parents and children would become more rigid and less able to adapt to changing environmental conditions (Hollenstein, Granic, Stoolmiller, & Snyder, 2004). This is the application of the idea of a cascading constraint to parent–child relationships.

Kindergarten children at risk for externalizing problems and their parents were observed for 2 hours in a variety of contexts including having snacks, playing games, solving academic problems, and talking about conflicts. The interactions were coded as positive engagement (humor, affection), neutral (talking, asking or answering questions), negative disengagement (sadness or fear), and negative engagement (anger or contempt) (Granic & Patterson, 2006). Interaction grids were created for each dyad and the following two indicators of rigidity were established: the number of times the dyad moved from one cell or characteristic type of interaction to another; and the mean length of time the dyad spent in each type of interaction. The more rigid parent–child dyads showed less frequent changes in their patterns of interaction and spent more time overall in specific types of interaction.

In order to link these data on moment-to-moment interactions with the emergence of developmental trends, teachers' reports of the child's antisocial behavior were collected at the beginning of kindergarten, the end of kindergarten, the beginning of first grade and the end of first grade. Children whose externalizing scores were in the top 10% of the group at each time period were compared to the remaining 90%. There were no differences in rigidity scores between the top 10% of children and the remaining 90% at the first measurement. However, at each subsequent measurement, rigidity in parent–child interactions significantly predicted which children were rated in the top 10% of externalizing problems. What is more, the children whose externalizing scores were high and remained high or whose externalizing scores increased over the 2 years of kindergarten and first grade had more rigid parent–child interactions than those whose scores declined or were low and remained low.

As predicted by dynamic systems theory, the research was able to link the microlevel analysis of patterns of rigid parent–child interaction with an increasingly stable orientation toward externalizing problems. The results demonstrated that the tendency toward antisocial behavior was not a product of genes, personality traits, bad parenting, etc. One cannot separate the child and the parent as causal factors. Antisocial behavior is a product of ongoing interactions of parents and children that rely on complex systems of behavior comprised of stable patterns of interactions, such as negative-negative or negative-neutral. Once the attractors emerge, they become increasingly structured and resist change, predisposing the child toward similar kinds of interactions in the other kinds of social relationships.

The research suggests a potential approach for early intervention. By analyzing rigid parent–child interactions, families whose children are at risk for the emergence of antisocial behaviors could be identified and involved in interventions to increase their repertoire of interaction strategies and to encourage more flexible and positive patterns of communication across contexts (Granic & Patterson, 2006).

HOW DOES DYNAMIC SYSTEMS THEORY ANSWER THE BASIC QUESTIONS THAT A THEORY OF HUMAN DEVELOPMENT IS EXPECTED TO ADDRESS?

What is the direction of change over the life span? How well does the theory account for patterns of change and continuity?   The direction of change is toward increasing complexity as higher-level systems emerge from lower-level components. One of the central contributions of the theory is its ability to account for both continuous and discontinuous change. The system has a capacity for self-stabilization that supports continuity. When the system is in an attractor state, it is buffered from minor alterations or modifications that might result in change. However, under conditions of significant disequilibrium, the system also has a capacity for self-organization through which new, more adaptive characteristics emerge. The theory assumes that the nature of development involves many systems interacting in a coordinated way all of which are changing over time. This view promises a more detailed and subtle view of continuity and change than many other theories of development.

What are the mechanisms that account for growth? What are some testable hypotheses or predictions that emerge from this analysis?   All living systems are characterized by a capacity for self-organization, the spontaneous emergence of coherent, higher-order forms through recursive interactions among simpler components. The individual person is influenced by participation in other systems including relationships, families, communities, schools, and work settings. Thus, the tendency toward self-organization in any one or more of these systems can be a factor in stimulating the process of self-organization of the individual.

A central hypothesis of dynamic systems theory is that new forms of organization can be accounted for by understanding the interactions among components of the system that are precursors or forerunners of the eventual new behavior. The combination of action and task demands, with feedback between expectancies and outcomes, brings about change. One does not need to rely on a preexisting, genetically guided plan or an environmentally orchestrated goal in order to account for change. One simply needs to identify the critical parameters along which change is taking place and the changes in essential limit-setting components that will bring about a phase shift.

One can think of a person as a maturing system with multiple attractors or organized patterns of cognitions and behaviors that change over time. Each attractor provides a model or forecast of what will happen following an action. With multiple forecasts emerging from various attractors, there is an opportunity to observe which forecasts are most accurate and which are followed by discrepancies. When the events following an expectation are discrepant from the forecast, the person experiences surprise, an emotion that can produce the energy needed to move away from one attractor and toward another attractor (Metzger, 1997). Continuous feedback among expectations, actions, and the consequences of action contributes to the process of growth and patterns of change.

How relevant are early experiences for later development? What evidence does the theory offer to support its view?   The theory assumes that complex behaviors and new patterns of behavior emerge from preexisting components which are undergoing change. Early experiences are critically relevant for later development in three different ways. First, the theory assumes that each new action is influenced in part by the memory of previous actions. If the task and the context remain the same, the preceding action will most likely be repeated. Second, early experiences provide the elements or system components from which more complex behaviors emerge. In the example of crawling cited earlier in the chapter, hand preference is an early component of infant crawling. The timing of a clear hand preference will influence the onset of crawling. Complex behaviors are a result of the coordinative interaction of many subsystems. One or more of them must reach a certain level of maturation or functioning in order for the more complex behavior to emerge.

Third, the notion of attractor states suggests that some patterns or organizations of behavior become more stable and likely than others. Whether one is focusing on language, motor behavior, concept development, or relationships, once the child or the parent–child system establishes a few stable attractor states, these states become the most likely forms of behavioral organization thus constraining subsequent behaviors. The theory does not specify which parameters or components are the critical precursors for each subsequent new behavior; nor does it specify the nature of attractors states across domains since those are not fixed, but emergent. However, it suggests that early experiences will hold the keys for understanding each step in subsequent behavioral organization.

How do the physical, cognitive, emotional, and social functions interact? How well does the theory explain these interactions?   Dynamic systems theory focuses on integrated functional organization of behavior, resisting the tendency to explain complex behaviors by analyzing their components. The theory seeks to explain the consistencies and changes in behavior by considering the coordinated integration of the physical, cognitive, emotional, and social components of behavior, recognizing that changes in one or more of these components may account for alterations in the behavior over all. Consider the infant smile, for example. Newborns, even premature infants, smile in their sleep. Thus, the smile has a physiological basis well before it is coordinated with emotional or cognitive systems. The frequency of waking smiles changes substantially some time from 2 to 3 months, and the stimuli that evoke smiles change notably from auditory and tactile to visual over this same time. By 6 months, infants use smiles to regulate social interactions and to convey intentions. Individual infants vary widely in the way they blend smiles with other facial expressions to convey surprise, excitement, coyness, teasing, and delight. The dynamic systems approach to development would consider the coordination of physiological, interpersonal, cognitive, and motivational parameters that co-vary over the first 12 months of life to understand the emergence of the changing functional organization of smiling (Fogel & Thelen, 1987).

How do the environmental and social contexts affect development? What aspects of the environment does the theory suggest are especially important in shaping the direction of development? New behaviors emerge when certain components needed for the expression of the behavior move beyond a critical value or level. The slowest or last component to reach a critical value is called the control parameter. In walking, a control parameter might be the muscle strength needed to lift one leg off the ground against the forces of gravity. In driving a car, a control parameter might be the community's decision to require drivers to reach the age of 16 before qualifying for a driver's license. According to dynamic systems theory, all actions take place in some context. Dynamic skill development, for example, is effective action that is adapted, through feedback processes, to the changing demands of the situation. The goal is to understand the control parameters, the way they are integrated and mutually constrain each other, and the key changes in the required components that result in qualitatively new actions. There is no formal difference between control parameters that originate in the individual or in the environment (Fogel & Thelen, 1987).

According to the theory, what factors place individuals at risk at specific periods of the life span? In infancy, neurological impairments, sensory and motor impairments, and lack of access to diverse sensory and motor experiences are all potential risk factors. At the same time, parents play a key role in supporting and scaffolding infant development such that factors including unresponsive, harsh, erratic, or neglectful parenting can be conditions of risk. The parent–child relationship is highlighted as a dynamic system that provides the early context for both cognitive and social development. Any factors that introduce rigidity in this relationship or that disrupt the relationship can create substantial disequilibrium for the developing child.

At each period of life, phase transitions or periods of disequilibrium are times when the person is more vulnerable to fluctuations in adjoining systems that can influence the organization or stability of behavior. These transitions include entry into child care, school transitions, moving to a new community, birth of a sibling, puberty, job change, marriage, entry into parenthood, death of a parent or loved one, or serious illness. At any of these times, existing attractors are likely to be inadequate for guiding subsequent actions, bringing the possibility for continued growth or for more rigid self-stabilization. Phase transitions offer opportunities for self-organization that can lead to new, more complex and creative levels of self understanding, new relationships, or new skills. With maturity and a lifetime of experiences of moving in and out of periods of equilibrium and disequilibrium adulthood brings new phases of brain development coupled with new ways of thinking (Cohen, 2006). However, phase transitions may result in efforts at self-stabilization in which the person resists change, minimizing the impact of the new situation or experience in order to retain the stability of the well-established patterns of organization even though they are inadequate to fully cope with the requirements of the new situation.

CRITIQUE OF DYNAMIC SYSTEMS THEORY

Strengths

Dynamic systems theory promises to advance the study of the development of patterns, change, and novelty in human behavior. Like evolutionary theory, it provides a lens or framework that links the study of human development to other fields of science including mathematics, physics, chemistry, and biology. It offers a more complex view of development than many other theories, recognizing the ongoing interactions among multiple systems as well as individual variability.

The theory focuses on the emergence of new organized patterns of behavior, acknowledging that many variables changing at different rates are required to account for these patterns. Thus, the theory offers a more authentic, nonlinear, nonreductionistic account of development. In its approach to development, the theory provides a way of explaining both continuous, moment to moment changes, and qualitatively new patterns of organization, thereby accounting for what have been observed in other theories as stages of development. At the same time, these stages are viewed as emerging directly from the integration of existing components of the system in action, which helps to account for observed variability in the timing, sequencing, and level of performance that is achieved.

The theory lends itself to simulations and mathematical modeling. This allows one to explore modifications in control parameters, the timing of perturbations in the system, variations in the parameter estimates, and unlimited replications in order to explore the likely transformation of a given behavior over time. This type of modeling permits one to demonstrate how small changes in some variables early in a sequence of events can result in qualitatively different paths or emergent behaviors later (Schöner & Thelen, 2006).

Dynamic systems theory has proven to be especially useful in accounting for changes in motor development, displacing earlier accounts of the emergence, and loss of certain motor patterns (Metzger, 1997). In the areas of cognitive development, communication, and parent–child relationships, the theory offers a promising new lens. The idea of self-organization inspires researchers to reject dualisms, such as person versus environment, brain versus behavior, perception versus cognition, or learning versus development, in order to consider the coordinated contributions of multiple processes to produce complex and changing behaviors. As research continues, it promises to provide a way of integrating neurological, psychological, and social processes as coordinated systems which account for the emergence of new behaviors.

Weaknesses

As an emerging theoretical framework, dynamic systems theory suffers from disparities in terminology, methodology, and focus that make it difficult to summarize and to apply. Many theorists who embrace the framework use different terms and different definitions for similar terms. For example, the idea of self-organization is central to the theory, however, there is no agreement about how self-organization should be defined or applied to human development across domains.

Those theorists who embrace dynamic systems theory agree that there is no hierarchical plan for development, either internal or external to the organism. They view behavior as the emerging product of the interactions of many systems and subsystems. The theory rejects a reductionist or dualistic approach to the study of development. At the same time, it does not provide guidance about which components or parameters of a system are the critical ones or how to identify these control parameters in a particular behavioral domain.

There is disagreement among researchers about the appropriate methods for investigating development. Some researchers rely largely on simulations and mathematical models; others conduct observational research; others integrate data from experiments into models. There may be a need to invent new methodologies in order to capture the dynamic nature of the theory—both new observational and experimental techniques for multiple observations over time, and new mathematical techniques for estimating parameters and modeling change.

The theory is difficult to understand, and requires advanced statistical and mathematical skills to test. This does not mean that the theory is incorrect, but it may be difficult to falsify. At the same time, these difficulties result in controversies over the correct approaches to an empirical test of the theory, and a slow integration of principles from the theory to practice.

KEY TERMS

adaptive self-organization

adaptive self-stabilization

antisocial development

attractor

behavioral complexity

coercion theory

constructive web

dynamic skill

dynamic system

dynamic systems theory

emergence

negative feedback

open system

positive feedback

system

system hierarchy

References

Abend, S. M., & Porder, M. S. (1995). Identification. In B. R. Moore & B. D. Fine (Eds.), *Psychoanalysis: The major concepts* (pp. 463–470). New Haven: Yale University Press.

Acredolo, C., Adams, A., & Schmid, J. (1984). On the understanding of the relationships between speed, duration, and distance. *Child Development, 55,* 2151–2159.

Adler, A. (1964). *Social interest: A challenge to mankind.* New York: Putnam.

Adolph, K. E., & Eppler, M. A. (2002). Flexibility and specificity in infant motor skill acquisition. In J. W. Fagen & H. Hayne (Eds.), *Progress in infancy research (Vol. 2),* (pp. 121–167). Mahwah, NJ: Lawrence Erlbaum Associates.

Ainsworth, M. D. S. (1973). The development of infant–mother attachment. In B. M. Caldwell & H. N. Ricciuti (Eds.), *Review of child development research (Vol. 3)* (pp. 1–94). Chicago: University of Chicago Press.

Ainsworth, M. D. S. (1985). Patterns of infant–mother attachments: Antecedents and effects on development. *Bulletin of the New York Academy of Medicine, 61,* 771–791.

Ainsworth, M. D. S. (1989). Attachments beyond infancy. *American Psychologist, 44,* 709–716.

Ainsworth, M. D. S., Blehar, M. C., Waters, E., & Wall, S. (1978). *Patterns of attachment: A psychological study of the strange situation.* Hillsdale, NJ: Lawrence Erlbaum Associates.

Alfieri, T., Ruble, D., & Higgins, E. (1996). Gender stereotypes during adolescence: Developmental changes and the transition to junior high school. *Developmental Psychology, 32,* 1129–1137.

Allport, G. W. (1955). *Becoming: Basic considerations for a psychology of personality*. New Haven, CT: Yale University Press.

Allport, G. W. (1961). *Pattern and growth in personality*. New York: Holt, Rinehart, and Winston.

Archer, J. (1991). Human sociobiology: Basic concepts and limitations. *Journal of Social Issues, 47,* 11–26.

Arnett, J. J. (1998). Learning to stand alone: The contemporary American transition to adulthood in cultural and historical context. *Human Development, 41,* 295–315.

Arnett, J. J. (2000). Emerging adulthood: A theory of development from the late teens through th twenties. *American Psychologist, 55,* 469–480.

Arnett, J. J. (2004). *Adolescence and emerging adulthood: A cultural approach* (2nd ed.). Upper Saddle River, N. J.: Prentice Hall.

Ashby, W. R. (1947). Principles of the self-organizing dynamic system. *Journal of General Psychology, 37,* 125–128.

Au, T. K., Sidle, A. L., & Rollins, K. B. (1993). Developing an intuitive understanding of conservation: Invisible particles as a plausible mechanism. *Developmental Psychology, 29,* 286–299.

Baillargeon, R. (2004). Infants' physical world. *Current Directions in Psychological Science, 13,* 89–94.

Bakhurst, D. (1996). Social memory in Soviet thought. In H. Daniels (Ed.), *An introduction to Vygotsky* (pp. 196–218). London: Routledge. (Original work published 1990)

Baltes, P. B. (1987). Theoretical propositions of life-span developmental psychology: On the dynamics between growth and decline. *Developmental Psychology, 231,* 611–626.

Bandura, A. (1965). Influence of model's reinforcement contingencies on the acquisition of imitative responses. *Journal of Personality and Social Psychology, 1,* 589–595.

Bandura, A. (1971) *Psychological modeling: Conflicting theories*. Chicago: Aldine–Atherton.

Bandura, A. (1977). *Social learning theory*. Englewood Cliffs, NJ: Prentice Hall.

Bandura, A. (1982). Self-efficacy mechanism in human agency. *American Psychologist, 37,* 122–147.

Bandura, A. (1986). *Social foundations of thought and action: A social cognitive theory*. Englewood Cliffs, NJ: Prentice Hall.

Bandura, A. (1989). The regulation of cognitive processes through perceived self-efficacy. *Developmental Psychology, 25,* 729 –735.

Bandura, A. (2001). Social cognitive theory: An agentic perspective. *Annual Review of Psychology, 52,* 1–26.

Bandura, A., Ross, D., & Ross, S. A. (1961). Transmission of aggression through imitation of aggressive models. *Journal of Abnormal and Social Psychology, 63,* 575–582.

Bandura, A., & Walters, R. H. (1963). *Social learning and personality development*. New York: Holt, Rinehart, and Winston.

Barbu, S., Le Maner-Idrissi, G., & Jouanjean, A. (2000). The emergence of gender segregation: Towards an integrative perspective. *Current Psychology Letters: Behavior, Brain, and Cognition, 3,* 7–18.

Barlow, N. (Ed.). (1958). *The autobiography of Charles Darwin: 1809–1882*. New York: Norton.

Barnett, R. C. (2004). Preface: Women and work: Where are we, where did we come from, and where are we going? *Journal of Social Issues, 60,* 667–674.

Barnett, R. C., Marshall, N. L., & Pleck, J. H. (1992). Men's multiple roles and their relationship to men's psychological distress. *Journal of Marriage and the Family, 54,* 358–367.

Bar-Yam Hassan, A., & Bar-Yam, M. (1987). Interpersonal development across the life-span: Communion and its interaction with agency in psychosocial development. *Contributions to Human Development, 18,* 102–128.

Beale, R. L. (1997). Multiple familial–worker role strain and psychological well-being: Moderating effects of coping resources among Black American parents. In R. J. Taylor, J. S. Jackson, & L. M. Chatters (Eds.), *Family life in Black America* (pp. 132–145). Thousand Oaks, CA: Sage.

Beere, C. A. (1990). *Gender roles: A handbook of tests and measures.* New York: Greenwood.

Belsky, J., Campbell, S. B., Cohn, J. F., & Moore, G. (1996). Instability of infant–parent attachment security. *Developmental Psychology, 32,* 921–924.

Benson, J. B. & Uzgiris, I. C. (1985). Effect of self-initiated locomotion on infant search activity. *Developmental Psychology, 21,* 923–931.

Bertenthal, B. I., & Fischer, K. W. (1983). The development of representation in search: A social-cognitive analysis. *Child Development, 54,* 846–857.

Berzonsky, M. D. (2003). The structure of identity: Commentary on Jane Kroger's view of identity status transition. *Identity, 3,* 231–245.

Berzonsky, M. & Adams, G. (1999). Commentary: Reevaluating the identity status paradigm: still useful after 35 years. *Developmental Review, 19,* 557–590.

Berzonsky, M. D., & Kuk, L. S. (2000). Identity status, identity processing style, and the transition to university. *Journal of Adolescent Research, 15,* 81–98.

Biddle, B. J. (1979). *Role theory: Expectations, identities, and behaviors.* New York: Academic Press.

Biddle, B. J. (1986). Recent developments in role theory. In R. H. Turner & S. F. Short, Jr. (Eds.), *Annual Review of Sociology, 12,* (pp. 67–92). Palo Alto, CA: Annual Reviews.

Biddle, B. J., & Thomas, E. J. (1966). *Role theory: Concepts and research.* New York: Wiley.

Bijstra, J., van Geert, P., & Jackson, S. (1989). Conservation and the appearance–reality distinction: What do children really know and what do they answer? *British Journal of Developmental Psychology, 7,* 43–53.

Blanck, R., & Blanck, G. (1986). Beyond ego psychology. New York: Columbia University Press.

Blos, P. (1962). *On adolescence: A psychoanalytic interpretation.* New York: The Free Press.

Blos, P. (1967). The second individuation process of adolescence. *Psychoanalytic Study of the Child, 23,* 162–186.

Blurton-Jones, N. (1972). *Ethological studies of child behavior.* Cambridge: Cambridge University Press.

Boesky, D. (1995). Structural theory. In B. R. Moore & B. D. Fine (Eds.), *Psychoanalysis: The major concepts* (pp. 494–507). New Haven: Yale Univeristy Press.

Bohlin, G., Bengtsgard, K., & Andersson, K. (2000). Social inhibition and overfriendliness as related to socioemotional functioning in 7- and 8-year-old children. *Journal of Clinical Child Psychology, 29,* 414–423.

Boom, J., Brugman, D., & van der Heijden, P. G. M. (2001). Hierarchical structure of moral stages assessed by a sorting task. *Child Development, 72,* 535–548.

Borden, W. (2000). The relational paradigm in contemporary psychoanalysis: Toward a psychodynamically informed social work perspective. *Social Service Review, 74,* 352–380.

Bordens, K. S. & Abbott, B. B. (2002). *Research design and methods: A process approach.* (5th Ed.). Boston: McGraw–Hill.

Bowlby, J. (1958). The nature of the child's tie to his mother. *International Journal of Psychoanalysis, 39,* 350–373.

Bowlby, J. (1988). *A secure base: Parent–child attachment and healthy human development*. New York: Basic Books.

Boykin, A. W. (1994). Harvesting talent and culture. In R. J. Rossi (Ed.), *Schools and students at risk: Context and framework for positive change* (pp. 116–138). New York: Teachers College Press.

Bradmetz, J. (1999). Precursors of formal thought: A longitudinal study. *British Journal of Developmental Psychology, 17,* 61–81.

Brainerd, C. J. (1977). Cognitive development and concept learning: An interpretive review. *Psychological Bulletin, 84,* 919–939.

Brazelton, T. B., Robey, J. S. & Collier, G. A. (1969). Infant development in the Zinacanteco Indians of Southern Mexico. *Pediatrics, 44,* 274–290.

Bretherton, I. (1990). Open communication and internal working models: Their role in the development of attachment relationships. In R. Dienstbier & R. A. Thompson (Eds.), *Nebraska Symposium on Motivation 1988: Vol. 36. Socioemotional Development* (pp. 57–113). Lincoln, NE: University of Nebraska Press.

Breuer, J., & Freud, S. (1955). Studies on hysteria. In J. Strachey (Ed.), *The standard edition of the complete psychological works of Sigmund Freud, Vol. 2.* London: Hogarth Press. (Original work published 1893–1895)

Brim, O. G., Jr. (1966). Socialization through the life cycle. In O. G. Brim & S. Wheeler (Eds.), *Socialization after childhood: Two essays* (pp. 1–49). New York: Wiley.

Brim, O. G., Jr. (1968). Adult socialization. In J. Clausen (Ed.), *Socialization and society* (pp. 183–226). Boston: Little, Brown.

Brim, O. G., Jr. (1976). Life-span development of the theory of oneself: Implications for child development. In H. W. Reese (Ed.), *Advances in child development and behavior* (Vol. 11) (pp.241–251). New York: Academic Press.

Bronson, G. W. (1973). Infants' reactions to an unfamiliar person. In L. J. Stone, H. T. Smith, & L. B. Murphy (Eds.), *The competent infant.* New York: Basic Books.

Bruner, J. (1987). In R. W. Rieber & A. S. Carton (Eds.), Prologue to the English Edition. *Vol. 1: Problems of general psychology* (pp. 1–16). New York: Plenum.

Bruner, J. (1992). Another look at New Look 1. *American Psychologist, 47,* 780–783.

Bruner, J., & Postman, L. (1947). Emotional selectivity in perception and reaction. *Journal of Personality, 16,* 69–77.

Brown, R. (1965). *Social psychology.* New York: Free Press.

Buhler, C. (1935). The curve of life as studied in biographies. *Journal of Applied Psychology, 19,* 405–409.

Buss, D. M. (1995). Evolutionary psychology: A new paradigm for psychological science. *Psychological Inquiry, 6,* 1–30.

Butterfield, E. C., Nelson, T. O., & Peck, V. (1988). Developmental aspects of the feeling of knowing. *Developmental Psychology, 24,* 654–663.

Carlo, G., Knight, G. P., Eisenberg, N., & Rotenberg, K. J. (1991). Cognitive processes and prosocial behaviors among children: The role of affective attributions and reconciliations. *Developmental Psychology, 27,* 456–461.

Carlson, V., Cicchetti, D., Barnett, D., & Braunwold, K. (1989). Finding order in disorganization. Lessons from research on maltreated infants' attachment to their caregivers. In D. Cicchetti & V. Carlson (Eds.), *Child maltreatment: Theory and research on the causes and consequences of maltreatment* (pp. 494–528). New York: Cambridge University Press.

Carr, D. (2002). The psychological consequences of work–family trade-offs for three cohorts of men and women. *Social Psychology Quarterly, 65,* 103–124.

Cassidy, J. (1999). The nature of the child's ties. In J. Cassidy & P. R. Shaver (Eds.), *Handbook of attachment: Theory, research, and clinical applications* (pp. 3–20). New York: Guilford Press.

Casteel, M. (1993). Effects of inference necessity and reading goal on children's inferential generation. *Developmental Psychology, 29*, 346–357.

Chapman, M. (1988). *Constructive evolution: Origin and development of Piaget's thought*. New York: Cambridge University Press.

Chapman, M., & McBride, M. L. (1992). Beyond competence and performance. Children's class inclusion strategies, superordinate class cues, and verbal justifications. *Developmental Psychology, 28*, 319–327.

Charlesworth, W. (1988). Resources and resource acquisition during ontogeny. In K. B. McDonald (Ed.), *Sociobiological perspectives on human behavior* (pp. 24–77). New York: Springer–Verlag.

Charlesworth, W. R. (1992). Darwin and developmental psychology: Past and present. *Developmental Psychology, 28*, 5–16.

Chavajay, P., & Rogoff, B. (1999). Cultural variation in management of attention by children and their caregivers. *Developmental Psychology, 35*, 1079–1090.

Chi, M. T. H., Feltovich, P. J., & Glaser, R. (1981). Categorization and representation of physics problems by experts and novices. *Cognitive Science, 5*, 121–152.

Chomsky, N. (1972). *Language and mind*. New York : Harcourt, Brace, Jovanovich.

Christiansen, S. L., & Palkovitz, R. (1998). Exploring Erikson's psychosocial theory of development: Generativity and its relationship to paternal identity, intimacy, and involvement in childcare. *Journal of Men's Studies, 7*, 133–156.

Clancy, S. M., & Dollinger, S. J. (1993). Identity, self, and personality: 1. Identity status and the five-factor model of personality. *Journal of Research on Adolescence, 3*, 227–246.

Cohen, G. D. (2006). The mature mind: The positive power of the aging brain. *Adult Development and Aging News, 34*, 4–6.

Cole, M. (1990). Cognitive development and formal schooling: The evidence from cross-cultural research. In L. C. Moll (Ed.), *Vygotsky and education* (pp. 89–110). Cambridge, England: Cambridge University Press.

Cole, M., & Scribner, S. (1977). Cross cultural studies of memory and cognition. In R. V. Kail, Jr. & J. W. Hagen (Eds.), *Perspectives on the development of memory and cognition* (pp. 239–271). Hillsdale, NJ: Lawrence Erlbaum Associates.

Cole, M., & Scribner, S. (1978). Introduction. In Cole, M., John-Steiner, V., Scribner, S. & Souberman, E. (Eds.), (1978). *Mind in society: The development of higher psychological processes. L. S. Vygotsky (pp. 1–14)*. Cambridge, MA: Harvard University Press.

Coles, R. (1970). *Erik H. Erikson: The growth of his work*. Boston: Atlantic–Little, Brown.

Colin, V. (1996). *Human attachment*. New York: McGraw–Hill.

Constantinople, A. (1969). An Eriksonian measure of personality development in college students. *Developmental Psychology, 1*, 357–372.

Cosmides, L., & Tooby, J. (1997). Evolutionary Psychology: A primer. Retreived Nov. 6, 2002, at http://psych.ucsb.edu

Cox, M. J., Owen, M. T., Henderson, V. K., & Margand, N. A. (1992). Prediction of infant–father and infant–mother attachment. *Developmental Psychology, 28*, 474–483.

Crain, W. C. (2000). *Theories of development: Concepts and applications* (4th ed.). Upper Saddle River, NJ: Prentice Hall.

Cramer, P. (2000). Defense mechanisms in psychology today: Further processes for adaptation. *American Psychologist, 55*, 637–646.

Crouter, A. C., & Bumpus, M. F. (2001). Linking parents' work stress to children's and adolescents' psychological adjustment. *Current Directions in Psychological Science, 10*, 156–159.

Crouter, A. C., Manke, B., & McHale, S. (1995). The family context of gender intensification in early adolescence. *Child Development, 66,* 317–329.

Currie, L. S. (1999). "Mr. Homunculus, the Reading Detective": A cognitive approach to improving reading comprehension. *Educational and Child Psychology, 16,* 37–42.

Daly, M., & Wilson, M. (2001). Risk-taking, intrasexual competition, and homocide. In R. A. Dienstbier, J. A. French, A. C. Kamil, & D. W. Leger (Eds.), *Evolutionary psychology and motivation: Vol. 47. Nebraska Symposium on Motivation* (pp. 1–36). Lincoln, NE: University of Nebraska Press.

Damon, W. (1980). Patterns of change in children's social reasoning: A two-year longitudinal study. *Child Development, 51,* 1010–1017.

Darling-Fisher, C. S., & Leidy, N. K. (1988). Measuring Eriksonian development in the adult: The Modified Erikson Psychosocial Stage Inventory. *Psychological Reports, 62,* 747–754.

Darwin, E. (1794–1796). *Zoonomia.*

Darwin, C. (1965). *The expression of the emotions in man and animals.* Chicago: University of Chicago Press. (Original work published 1872)

Darwin, C. (1979). The illustrated "Origin of species." Abridged and introduced by Richard E. Leakey. New York: Hill & Wang. (Original work published 1859)

Davey, G. (1987). *Cognitive processes and Pavlovian conditioning in humans.* New York: Wiley.

Davey, G., & Cullen, C. (1988). *Human operant conditioning and behavior modification.* New York: Wiley.

Davison, M. L., King, P. M., Kitchener, K. S., & Parker, C. A. (1980). The stage sequence concept in cognitive and social development. *Developmental Psychology, 16,* 121–131.

Davydov, V. V. (1972). *Types of generalization in learning.* Moscow: Pedagogika.

Davydov, V. V., Pushkin, V. N., & Pushkina, A. G. (1972). Dependence of the development of elementary school students' thinking on type of instruction. *Voprosy Psikhologii, 6,* 124–132.

DeAngelis, T. (1997). When children don't bond with parents. *APA Monitor, 28,* 10–12.

Deeg, D. J. H., Kardaun, J. W. P. F., & Fozard, J. L. (1996). Health, behavior, and aging. In J. E. Birren, K. W. Schaie, R. P. Abeles, M. Gatz, & T. A. Salthouse (Eds.), *Handbook of the psychology of aging* (pp. 129–149). San Diego: Academic Press.

DeLisi, R. (2002). From marbles to instant messenger: Implications of Piaget's ideas about peer learning. *Theory into Practice, 41.* Retrieved March 28, 2006 from http://findarticles

Demetriou, A., Christou, C., Spanoudis, G., & Platsidou, M. (2002). The development of mental processing: Efficiency, working memory, and thinking. *The Monographs of the Society for Research in Child Development, No. 67.*

Demetriou, A., & Efklides, A. (1985). Structure and sequence of formal and postformal thought: General patterns and individual differences. *Child Development, 56,* 1062–1091.

Denmark, F. L., Novick, K., & Pinto, A. (1996). Women, work, and family: Mental health issues. In J. A. Sechzer, S. M. Pfafflin, F. L. Denmar, A. Griffin, & S. J. Blumenthal (Eds.), *Women and mental health: Vol. 789. Annals of the New York Academy of Sciences* (pp. 101–117). New York: New York Academy of Sciences.

Denney, N. W. (1982). Aging and cognitive changes. In B. B. Wolman (Ed.), *Handbook of developmental psychology* (pp. 807–827), Englewood Cliffs, NJ: Prentice Hall.

Denney, N. W. & Pearce, K. A. (1989). A developmental study of practical problem solving in adults. *Psychology and Aging, 4,* 438–442.

Dodge, K. A., Pettit, G. S., McClaskey, C. L., & Brown, M. M. (1986). Social competence in children. *Monographs of the Society for Research in Child Development, 51,* (2, Serial No. 213).

Domino, G., & Affonso, D. D. (1990). Erikson's life stages: The Inventory of Psychosocial Balance. *Journal of Personality Assessment, 54,* 576–588.

Donald, M. (2001). *A mind so rare: The evolution of human consciousness.* New York: Norton.

Downey, G., & Walker, E. (1989). Social cognition and adjustment in children at risk for psychopathology. *Developmental Psychology, 25,* 835–845.

Dreman, S. (1997). *The family on the threshold of the 21st century: Trends and implications.* Mahwah, NJ: Lawrence Erlbaum Associates.

Dweck, C. S. (1992). The study of goals in psychology. *Psychological Science, 3,* 165–167.

Eckstein, S. & Shemesh, M. (1992). The rate of acquisition of formal operational schemata in adolescence: A secondary analysis. *Journal of Research in Science Teaching, 29,* 441–451.

Edelstein, R. S., Alexander, K. W., Schaver, P. R., Schaaf, J. M., Quas, J. A., Lovas, G. S., et al. (2004). Adult attachment style and parental responsiveness during a stressful event. *Attachment and Human Development, 6,* 31–52.

Edwards, C. P., & Whiting, B. B. (1988). *Children of different worlds.* Cambridge, MA: Harvard University Press.

Egan, G. (2002). *The skilled helper : A problem-management and opportunity development approach to helping.* (7th ed.). Pacific Grove, CA: Brooks–Cole.

Egan, S., & Perry, D. (2001). Gender identity: A multidimensional analysis with implications for psychosocial adjustment. *Developmental Psychology, 37,* 451–463.

Eibl-Eibesfeldt, I. (1975). *Ethology: The biology of behavior* (2nd ed.). New York: Holt, Rinehart & Winston.

Elder, G. H., Jr. (1974). *Children of the Great Depression: Social change in life experience.* Chicago: Chicago University Press.

Elder, G. H., Jr. (1979). Historical change in life patterns and personality. In P. B. Baltes & O. G. Brim, Jr. (Eds.), *Life-span development and behavior: Vol. 2.* (pp. 117–159). New York: Academic Press.

Elder, G. H., Jr. (1985). *Life course dynamics: Trajectories and transitions, 1968–1980.* Ithaca, NY: Cornell University Press.

Elder, G. H., Jr. (1987). War mobilization and the life course: A cohort of World War II veterans. *Sociological Forum, 2,* 449–472.

Elder, G. H., Jr. (1995). The life course paradigm: Social change and individual development. In P. Moen, G. H. Elder, Jr. & K. Lüscher (Eds.), *Examining lives in context: Perspectives on the ecology of human development* (pp. 101–139). Washington, DC: APA Press.

Elder, G. H., Jr. (1996). Human lives in changing societies: Life course and developmental insights. In R. B. Cairns, G. H. Elder, Jr. & E. J. Costello (Eds.), *Developmental Science* (pp. 31–62). Cambridge, UK: Cambridge University Press.

Elder, G. H., Jr. (1997, April). The life course as developmental theory. Presidential address presented at the biennial meetings of Society for Research in Child Development, Washington, DC.

Elder, G. H., Jr., & Caspi, A. (1988). Human development and social change: An emerging perspective on the life course. In N. Bolger, A. Caspi, G. Downey, & M. Moorehouse (Eds.), *Persons in context: Developmental processes* (pp. 77–113). New York: Cambridge University Press.

Elder, G. H. Jr., Caspi, A., & Downey, G. (1986). Problem behavior and family relationships: Life course and intergenerational themes. In A. B. Sorensen, F. E. Weinart, &

L. R. Sherrod (Eds.), *Human development and the life course: Multidisciplinary perspectives* (pp. 293–340). Hillsdale, NJ: Lawrence Erlbaum Associates.

Elder, G. H., Jr., Shanahan, M. J., & Clipp, E. C. (1994). When war comes to men's lives: Life course patterns in family, work, and health. *Psychology and Aging, 9*, 5–16.

Elias, M. J., Beier, J. J., & Gara, M. A. (1989). Children's responses to interpersonal obstacles as a predictor of social competence. *Journal of Youth and Adolescence, 18*, 451–465.

Ellenberger, H. F. (1970). The discovery of the unconscious, New York: Basic Books; London: Allen Lane, The Penguin Press.

Engels, F. (1940). *Dialectics of nature*. New York: International Publishers. (Original work published 1925)

Erikson, E. H. (1959). The problem of ego identity. *Psychological Issues, 1*, 101–164.

Erikson, E. H. (1963). *Childhood and society* (2nd ed.). New York: Norton. (Original work published 1950)

Erikson, E. H. (1968). *Identity: Youth and crisis*. New York: Norton.

Erikson, E. H. (1978). Reflections on Dr. Borg's life cycle. In E. H. Erikson (Ed.), *Adulthood* (pp. 1–31). New York: Norton.

Erikson, E. H. (1982). *The life cycle completed: A review*. New York: Norton.

Erikson, E. H., & Erikson, J. (1997). *The life cycle completed. An expanded version*. New York: W. W. Norton.

Erikson, E. H., Erikson, J. M., & Kivnick, H. Q. (1986). *Vital involvement in old age*. New York: Norton.

Erikson, J. M. (1988). *Wisdom and the senses: The way of creativity*. New York: Norton.

Farrar, M. J., Raney, G. E., & Boyer, M. E. (1992). Knowledge, concepts, and inferences in childhood. *Child Development, 63*, 673–691.

Feeney, J. A. (1999). Adult romantic attachment and couple relationships. In J. Cassidy & P. R. Shaver (Eds.), *Handbook of attachment: Theory, research, and clinical applications* (pp. 355–377). New York: Guilford Press.

Feldman, H., & Feldman, M. (1975). The family life cycle: Some suggestions for recycling. *Journal of Marriage and the Family, 37*, 277–284.

Fenson, L., Dale, P. S., Reznick, J. S., Bates, E., Thal, D. J., & Pethick, S. J. (1994). Variability in early communicative development. *Monographs of the Society for Research in Child Development, 59*, (serial No. 5).

Ferster, C. B., & Culbertson, S. A. (1982). *Behavior principles*. (3rd ed.). Englewood Cliffs, NJ: Prentice Hall.

Ferster, C. B., & Skinner, B. F. (1957). *Schedules of reinforcement*. New York: Appleton, Century, Crofts.

Field, D. (1981). Can preschool children really learn to conserve? *Child Development, 52*, 326–334.

Finley, G. E., & Schwartz, S. J. (2006). Parsons and Bales revisited: Young adult children's characterization of the fathering role. *Psychology of Men and Masculinity, 7*, 42–55.

Fischer, K. W. (1980). A theory of cognitive development: The control and construction of hierarchies of skills. *Psychological Review, 87*, 477–531.

Fischer, K. W., & Bidell, T. R. (1998). Dynamic development of psychological structures in action and thought. In W. Damon (Series Ed.) & R. M. Lerner (Vol. Ed.), *Handbook of child psychology: Vol. 1 Theoretical models of human development* (5th ed., pp. 467– 561). New York: Wiley.

Fischer, K. W., & Bidell, T. R. (2006). Dynamic development of action and thought. In W. Damon & R. M. Lerner (Eds.), *Theoretical models of human development, Handbook of child psychology, Vol. 1*. (6th ed., pp. 313–399). New York: Wiley.

Fischer, K. W., Bullock, D., & Rotenberg, E. J., & Raya, P. (1993). The dynamics of competence: How context contributes directly to skill. In R. Wozniak & K. Fischer (Eds.), *Development in context: Acting and thinking in specific environments, Vol. 1*, (pp. 93–117). Hillsdale, NJ: Lawrence Erlbaum Associates.

Fischer, K. W., & Rose, S. P. (1999). Rulers, models, and nonlinear dynamics: Measurement and method in developmental research. In G. Savelsbergh, H. van der Maas, & P. van Geert (Eds.), *Nonlinear developmental processes* (pp. 197–212). Amsterdam: Royal Netherlands Academy of Arts and Sciences.

Fischer, K. W., & Silvern, L. (1985). Stages and individual differences in cognitive development. *Annual Review of Psychology, 36,* 613–648.

Fischer, K. W., & Yan, Z. (2002). The development of dynamic skill theory. In D. J. Lewkowicz & R. Lickliter, (Eds.), *Conceptions of development: Lessons from the laboratory* (pp. 279–312). New York: Psychology Press.

Flavell, J. H. (1963). *The developmental psychology of Jean Piaget*. Princeton, NJ: Van Nostrand.

Flavell, J. H. (1974). The development of inferences about others. In W. Mischel (Ed.), *Understanding other persons*. Oxford: Blackwell, Basil, & Mott.

Flavell, J. H. (1982a). On cognitive development. *Child Development, 53,* 1–10.

Flavell, J. H. (1982b). Structures, stages, and sequences in cognitive development. In W. A. Collins (Ed.), *The concept of development* (pp. 1–28). Hillsdale, NJ: Lawrence Erlbaum Associates.

Flavell, J. H. (1996). Piaget's legacy. *Psychological Science, 7,* 200–203.

Flexner, S. B. (1987). Random House dictionary of the English language. (2nd ed., unabridged). New York: Random House.

Fogel, A., & Thelen, E. (1987). Development of early expressive communicative action: Reinterpreting the evidence from a dynamic systems perspective. *Developmental Psychology, 23,* 747–761.

Fonagy, P. (2003). The development of psychopathology from infancy to adulthood: The mysterious unfolding of disturbance in time. *Infant Mental Health Journal, 24,* 212–239.

Forman, E. A., & Cazden, C. B. (1995). Exploring Vygotskian perspectives in education: The cognitive value of peer interaction. In J. V. Wertsch (Ed.), *Culture, communication and cognition: Vygotskian perspectives* (pp. 323–347). New York: Cambridge University Press.

Freud, A. (1946). *The ego and mechanisms of defense*. New York: International Universities Press. (Original work published 1936)

Freud, A. (1965). Normality and pathology in childhood. In *Writings of Anna Freud (Vol. 6)*, (pp. 3–235). New York: International Universities Press.

Freud, S. (1892–1893). A case of successful treatment by hypnosis. In J. Strachey (Ed.), *The standard edition of the complete psychological works of Sigmund Freud*. London: Hogarth Press.

Freud, S. (1953). The Interpretation of dreams. In J. Strachey (Ed.), *The standard edition of the complete psychological works of Sigmund Freud* (Vols. 4 & 5). London: Hogarth Press. (Original work published 1900)

Freud, S. (1953). Three essays on the theory of sexuality. In J. Strachey (Ed.), *The standard edition of the complete psychological works of Sigmund Freud* (Vol. 7). London: Hogarth Press. (Original work published 1905)

Freud, S. (1955). Lecture XVIII – Fixation to Traumas – The Unconscious. In J. Strachey (Ed.), *The standard edition of the complete psychological works of Sigmund Freud* (Vol. 16). London: Hogarth (Original work published 1916–1917)

Freud, S. (1960). *A general introduction to psychoanalysis*. New York: Washington Square Press. (Original work published 1924)

Freud, S. (1964). *Leonardo da Vinci: A psychosexual study of infantile reminiscence.* New York: Norton. (Original work published 1919)

Freud, S. (1964). New introductory lectures on psychoanalysis. In J. Strachey (Ed.), *The standard edition of the complete psychological works of Sigmund Freud* (Vol. 22). London: Hogarth Press. (Original work published 1933)

Freud, S. (1967). *Moses and monotheism.* New York: Vintage Books. (Original work published 1939)

Freud, S. (1994). The social construction of gender. *Journal of Adult Development, 1,* 37–46.

Friedman, L. J. (1999). *Identity's architect: A biography of Erik H. Erikson.* New York: Scribner.

Frone, M. R. (2003). Work–family balance. In J. C. Quick & L. E. Tetrick (Eds.), *Handbook of occupational health psychology* (pp. 143–162). Washington, DC: American Psychological Association.

Funder, D. C., Parke, R. D., Tomlinson-Keasey, C., & Widaman, K. (1993). *Studying lives through time: Personality and development.* Washington, DC: American Psychological Association Press.

Galin, D. (1974). Implications for psychiatry of left–right cerebral specialization. *Archives of General Psychiatry, 31,* 572–583.

Gazzaniga, M. S. (1989, September). The organization of the human brain. *Science, 245,* 947–952.

George, C., & Solomon, J. (1999). Attachment and caregiving: The caregiving behavioral system. In J. Cassidy & P. R. Shaver (Eds.), *Handbook of attachment: Theory, research, and clinical applications* (pp. 649–670). New York: Guilford Press.

Gibbs, J. C. (1979). Kohlberg's moral stage theory: A Piagetian revision. *Human Development, 22,* 89–112.

Giedd, J., Blumenthal, J., Jeffries, N., Castellanos, F., Lui, H., Zijdenbos, A., et al., (1999). Brain development during childhood and adolescence: A longitudinal MRI study. *Nature Neuroscience, 2,* 861–863.

Giele, J. Z., & Elder, G. H., Jr. (1998). *Methods of life course research: Qualitative and quantitative approaches.* Thousand Oaks, CA: Sage.

Gielen, U. P., & Markoulis, D. C. (2001). Preference for principled moral reasoning: A developmental and cross-cultural perspective. In L. L Adler & U. P. Gielen (Eds.), *Cross-cultural topics in psychology* (2nd ed., pp. 81–101). Westport, CT: Praeger/Greenwood.

Gilligan, C. (1993). *In a different voice: Psychological theory and women's development.* Cambridge, MA: Harvard University Press. (Original work published 1982)

Glueck, S., & Glueck, E. (1950). *Unraveling juvenile delinquency.* New York: The Commonwealth Fund.

Glueck, S., & Glueck, E. (1968). *Delinquents and nondelinquents in perspective.* Cambridge, MA: Harvard University Press.

Godsil, B. P., Quinn, J. J., & Fanselow, M. S. (2000). Body temperature as a conditional response measure for Pavlovian fear conditioning. *Learning and Memory, 7,* 353–356.

Goffman, E. (1959). *The presentation of self in everyday life.* Garden City, NY: Doubleday Anchor Books.

Gold, M., & Douvan, E. (1997). *A new outline of social psychology.* Washington, DC: American Psychological Association.

Goldfield, E. C. (1989). Transition from rocking to crawling: Postural constraints on infant movement. *Developmental Psychology, 25,* 913–919.

Gopnik, A., & Meltzoff, A. (1987). The development of categorization in the second year and its relation to other cognitive and linguistic developments. *Child Development, 58,* 1523–1531.

Gopnik, A., & Meltzoff, A. N. (1997). *Words, thoughts, and theories.* Cambridge, MA: MIT Press.

Gould, R. L. (1972). The phases of adult life: A study in developmental psychology. *American Journal of Psychiatry, 129,* 521–531.

Granic, I., & Lamey, A. K. (2002). Combining dynamic systems and multivariate analyses to compare the mother–child interactions of externalizing subtypes. *Journal of Abnormal Child Psychology, 30,* 265–283.

Granic, I., & Patterson, G. R. (2006). Toward a comprehensive model of antisocial development: A dynamic systems approach. *Psychological Review, 113,* 101–131.

Gratch, G., & Schatz, J. A. (1987). Cognitive development: The relevance of Piaget's infancy books. In J. D. Osofsky (Ed.), *Handbook of infant development* (2nd ed., pp. 204–237). New York: Wiley.

Gray, W. M. (1990). Formal operational thought. In W. F. Overton (Ed.), *Reasoning, necessity, and logic: Developmental perspectives* (pp. 227–253). Hillsdale, NJ: Lawrence Erlbaum Associates.

Greenfield, P. M., & Childs, C. P. (1991). Developmental continuity in biocultural context. In R. Cohen & A. W. Siegel (Eds.), *Context and development* (pp. 135–159). Hillsdale, NJ: Lawrence Erlbaum Associates.

Greenwald, A. G. (1992). Unconscious cognition reclaimed. *American Psychologist, 47,* 766–779.

Gregor, T. (1977). *Mehinaku: The drama of daily life in a Brazilian Indian village.* Chicago: University of Chicago Press.

Hagen, K. A., Myers, B. J., & Macintosh, V. H. (2005). Hope, social support, and behavioral problems in at-risk children. *The American Journal of Orthopsychiatry, 75,* 211–219.

Halford, G. S., & Boyle, F. M. (1985). Do young children understand conservation of number? *Child Development, 56,* 165–176.

Hamachek, D. (1985). The self's development and ego growth: Conceptual analysis and implications for counselors. *Journal of Counseling and Development, 64,* 136–142.

Hamachek, D. (1994). Changes in the self from a developmental/psychosocial perspective. In T. M. Brinthaupt & R. P. Lipka (Eds.), *Changing the self: Philosophies, techniques, and experiences* (pp. 21–68). Albany: State University of New York Press.

Hamilton, W. D. (1964). The genetical evolution of social behavior. *Journal of Theoretical Biology, 7,* 1–52.

Harris, P. L. (1975). Development of search and object permanence during infancy. *Psychological Bulletin, 82,* 322–344.

Hartmann, H. (1958). *Ego psychology and the problem of adaptation.* New York: International Universities Press. (Original work published 1939)

Havighurst, R. J. (1953). *Human development and education.* New York: Longmans.

Havighurst, R. J. (1972). *Developmental tasks and education* (3rd ed.). New York: David McKay. (Original work published 1948)

Hawley, G. A. (1988). *Measures of psychosocial development.* Odessa, FL: Psychological Assessment Resources.

Haywood, H. C. (1996). Cognitive early education: A key to school success. In S. Molina-Garcia & M. Fandos-Igado (Eds.), *Educación cognitiva* (pp. 167–192). Zaragoza, Spain: MIRA.

Hazan, C., & Shaver, P. R. (1987). Attachment as an organizational framework for research on close relationships. *Journal of Personality and Social Psychology, 52,* 511–524.

Heckhausen, J., & Schulz, R. (1999). Selectivity in life-span development. In J. Brandtstadter & R. M. Lerner (Eds.), *Action and self-development: Theory and research through the life span* (pp. 67–103). Thousand Oaks, CA: Sage.

Helwig, C. C., Zelazo, P. D., & Wilson, M. (2001). Children's judgments of psychological harm in normal and noncanonical situations. *Child Development, 72*, 66–81.

Higgins, A., & Turnure, J. (1984). Distractability and concentration of attention in children's development. *Child Development, 44*, 1799–1810.

Hill, E. J., Yang, C., Hawkins, A. J., & Ferris, M. (2004). A cross-cultural test of the
work–family interface in 48 countries. *Journal of Marriage and the Family, 66*,
1300–1316.

Hollenstein, T., Granic, I., Stoolmiller, M., & Snyder, J. (2004). Rigidity in parent–child
interactions and the development of externalizing and internalizing behavior in
early childhood. *Journal of Abnormal Child Psychology, 32*, 595–607.

Hopkins, J. R. (1995). Erik Homburger Erikson (1902–1994). *American Psychologist,
50*, 796–797.

Huxley, J. (1941). *The uniqueness of man.* London: Chatto & Windus.

Huxley, J. (1942). *Evolution: The magic synthesis.* New York: Harper.

Inhelder, B., & Piaget, J. (1958). *The growth of logical thinking from childhood to adolescence.* New York: Basic Books.

Isabella, R. A., & Belsky, J. (1991). Interactional synchrony and the origins of infant–mother attachment: A replication study. *Child Development, 62*, 373–384.

Izard, C. E., & Ackerman, B. P. (2000). Motivational, organizational, and regulatory
functions of discrete emotions. In M. Lewis & J. M. Haviland-Jones (Eds.), *Handbook of emotions* (2nd ed., pp. 253–264). New York: Guilford Press.

Jackson, P. B. (2004). Role sequencing: Does order matter for mental health? *Journal
of Health and Social Behavior, 45*, 132–154.

Jacobson, E. (1964). *The self and the object world.* New York: International Universities Press.

Jacoby, L. L., Lindsay, D. S., & Toth, J. P. (1992). Unconscious influences revealed: Attention, awareness, and control. *American Psychologist, 47*, 802–809.

Jahoda, M. (1977). *Freud and the dilemmas of psychology.* Lincoln, NE: University of
Nebraska Press.

Johnston, W. A., & Dark, V. J. (1986). Selective attention. *Annual Review of Psychology,
37*, 43–75.

Jones, E. (1953–1957). *Sigmund Freud, life and work, Vols. 1, 2, and 3.* London: The
Hogarth Press; New York: Basic Books.

Jones, R. M. (1992). Ego identity and adolescent problem behavior. In G. R. Adams, T. P.
Gullota, & R. Montemayor (Eds.), *Adolescent identity formation* (pp. 216–233).
Newbury Park, CA: Sage.

Jordan, N. C., Huttenlocher, J., & Levine, S. C. (1992). Differential calculation abilities
in young children from middle and low-income families. *Developmental Psychology, 28*, 644–653.

Josselson, R. (1987). *Finding herself: Pathways to identity development in women.*
San Francisco: Jossey–Bass.

Jung, C. G. (1953). The psychology of the unconscious. In *Collected works* (Vol. 7).
Princeton, NJ: Princeton University Press. (Original German edition published
1943)

Kagan, J. (1991). Continuity and discontinuity in development. In S. E. Brauth, Hall, W.
S., & Dooling R. J., (Eds.), *Plasticity of development* (pp. 11–26). Cambridge, MA:
MIT Press.

Kalish, C. W., & Gelman, S. A. (1992). On wooden pillows: Multiple classification and
children's category-based inductions. *Child Development, 63*, 1536–1557.

Kamii, C. (2000a). Teachers need more knowledge of how children learn mathematics.
Dialogues. Retrieved March 18, 2006 from http://nctm.org

Kamii, C. (2000b). *Young children reinvent arithmetic*, (2nd ed.). New York: Teachers College Press.

Kamii, C., & DeVries, R. (1993). *Physical knowledge in preschool children*. New York: Teachers College Press. (Original work published 1978)

Kamii, C., & Joseph, L. (1988). Teaching place value and double-column addition. *Arithmetic Teacher. 35*, 48–52.

Kamii, C., Lewis, B. A., & Kirkland, L. (2001). Manipulatives: When are they useful? *Journal of Mathematical Behavior, 20*, 21–31.

Kamii, C., Rummelsburg, J., & Kari, A. (2005). Teaching arithmetic to low-performing, low-SES first graders. *Journal of Mathematical Behavior, 24*, 39–50.

Katz, D., & Kahn, R. L. (1966). *The social psychology of organizations.* New York: Wiley.

Kauffman, S. (1993). *Origins of order: Self-organization and selection in evolution.* New York: Oxford University Press.

Kauffman, S. (1995). *At home in the universe: The search for the laws of self organization and complexity.* New York: Oxford University Press.

Keating, D. P. (1990). Adolescent thinking. In S. S. Feldman & G. R. Elliott (Eds.), *At the threshold: The developing adolescent* (pp. 54–90). Cambridge, MA: Harvard University Press.

Keating, D. P. (2004). Cognitive and brain development. In R. Lerner & L. Steinberg (Eds.), *Handbook of adolescent psychology* (2nd ed., pp. 45–84). New York: Wiley.

Keating, D. P., & Bobbitt, B. L. (1978). Individual and developmental differences in cognitive processing components of ability. *Child Development, 49*, 155–167.

Kelso, J. A. S. (1995). *Dynamic patterns: The self-organization of brain and behavior*. Cambridge, MA: Bradford/MIT Press.

Kermoian, R., & Campos, J. J. (1988). Locomotor experience: A facilitator of spatial cognitive development. *Child Development, 59*, 908–917.

Kernberg, O. (1995). Psychoanalytic object relations theory. In B. R. Moore & B. D. Fine (Eds.), *Psychoanalysis: The major concepts* (pp. 450–462). New Haven: Yale University Press.

Kertzer, D. I., & Keith, J. (Eds.) (1984). *Age and anthropological theory*. Ithaca, NY: Cornell University Press.

Kihlstrom, J. L. (1987, September). The cognitive unconscious. *Science, 237*, pp. 1445–1452.

Kinder, D. R. (2006). Politics and the life cycle. *Science, 312*, 1905–1907.

Kiston, J. M. (1994). Contemporary Eriksonian theory: A psychobiographical illustration. *Gerontology and Geriatrics Education, 14*, 81–91.

Klein, M. (1948). *Contributions to psycho-analysis, 1921–1945*. London: Hogarth Press.

Kohlberg, L. (1969). Stage and sequence: The cognitive-developmental approach to socialization. In D. A. Goslin (Ed.), *Handbook of socialization theory and research.* Chicago: Rand McNally.

Kohlberg, L. (1976). Moral stages and moralization: The cognitive-developmental approach. In T. Lickona (Ed.), *Moral development and behavior* (pp. 31–53). New York: Holt, Rinehart & Winston.

Kolb, D. A. (1984). *Experiential learning: Experience as the source of learning and development.* New Jersey: Prentice–Hall.

Kolb, D. A., Boyatzis, R. E., & Mainemelis, C. (2001). Experiential learning theory: Previous research and new directions. In R. J. Sternberg & L. F. Zhang (Eds.), *Perspectives on thinking learning and cognitive styles*(pp. 227–248). Mahwah, NJ: Lawrence Erlbaum Associates.

Kroger, J. (2000). *Identity development: Adolescence through adulthood*. Thousand Oaks, CA: Sage.

Kroger, J. (2003). Identity development during adolescence. In G. R. Adams & M. D. Berzonsky (Eds.), *Blackwell handbook of adolescence* (pp. 205–226). Malden, MA: Blackwell.

Kuhn, D. (2006). Do cognitive changes accompany developments in the adolescent brain? *Perspectives on Psychological Science, 1*, 59–67.

Kwon, Y.-J., & Lawson, A. E. (2000). Linking brain growth with the development of scientific reasoning ability and conceptual change during adolescence. *Journal of Research in Science Teaching, 37*, 44–62.

Labouvie-Vief, G. (1992). A neo-Piagetian perspective on adult cognitive development. In R. J. Sternberg & C. A. Berg (Eds.), *Intellectual development* (pp. 197–228). New York: Cambridge University Press.

LaFreniere, P. J. (2000). *Emotional development: A biosocial perspective*. Belmont, CA: Wadsworth.

Lagattuta, K. H., & Wellman, H. M. (2001). Thinking about the past: Early knowledge about links between prior experience, thinking, and emotion. *Child Development, 72*, 82–102.

Laszlo, E. (1972). *Introduction to systems philosophy: Toward a new paradigm of contemporary thought*. New York: Harper & Row.

Laub, J. H., & Sampson, R. J. (1993). Turning points in the life course: Why change matters to the study of crime. *Criminology, 31*, 301–325.

Laub, J. H., & Sampson, R. J. (2003). *Shared beginnings, divergent lives: Delinquent boys to age 70*. Cambridge, MA: Harvard University Press.

Laue, J., & Wenger, E. (1996). Practice, person, social world. In H. Daniels (Ed.), *An introduction to Vygotsky*. (pp. 143–150) London: Routledge.

Lavond, D. G., & Steinmetz, J. E. (Eds.) (2003). *Handbook of classical conditioning*. Dordrecht, The Netherlands: Kluwer.

Lerner, I. M., & Libby, W. J. (1976). *Heredity, evolution, and society* (2nd ed.). San Francisco: W. H. Freeman.

Lerner, R. M. (2002). *Concepts and theories of human development*. (3rd ed.). Mahwah, NJ: Lawrence Erlbaum Associates.

Levin, F. M. (1995). Psychoanalysis and the brain. In B. R. Moore & B. D. Fine (Eds.), *Psychoanalysis: The major concepts* (pp. 537–552). New Haven: Yale University Press.

Levin, I. (1986). *Stage and structure: Reopening the debate*. Norwood, NJ: Ablex.

Levinson, D. J. (1977). The midlife transition: A period in adult psychosocial development. *Psychiatry, 40*, 99–112.

Levinson, D. J., Darrow, C. M., Klein, A. B., Levinson, M. H., & McKee, B. (1978). *The seasons of a man's life*. New York: Knopf.

Levy, G. D., (1998). Effects of gender constancy and figure's height and sex on young children's gender type attributions. *Journal of General Psychology, 125*, 65–88.

Levy, G. D., Barth, J. M., & Zimmerman, B. J. (1998). Associations among cognitive and behavioral aspects of preschoolers' gender role development. *Journal of Genetic Psychology, 159*, 121–126.

Levy, M. J., Jr., (1949). *The family revolution in modern china*. Cambridge, MA: Harvard University Press.

Lewin, R. (1987). Africa: Cradle of modern humans. *Science, 237*, 1292–1295.

Lewis, M. D. (2000). The promise of dynamic systems approaches for an integrated account of human development. *Child Development, 71*, 36–43.

Lightfoot, C., Lalonde, C., & Chandler, M. (2004). Changing conceptions of psychological life. *Jean Piaget Symposium Series, Vol. 30*. Mahwah, NJ: Lawrence Erlbaum Associates.

Linton, R. (1936). *The study of man*. New York: Appleton–Century.

Linton, R. (1945). *The cultural background of personality*. New York: Appleton–Century.

Lopez, A., Gelman, S. A., Gutheil, G., & Smith, E. (1992). The development of category-based inductions. *Child Development, 63,* 1070–1090.

Lopez, S. J., & Snyder, C. R. (2003). *Positive psychological assessment: A handbook of models and measures*. Washington, DC: American Psychological Association.

Lorenz, K. Z. (1943). Die angeborenen Formen m;auoglicher Erfahrung. Zeitschrift f;auur *Tierpsychologie, 5,* 235–409.

Lorenz, K. Z. (1981). *The foundations of ethology* (K. Z. Lorenz & R. W. Kickert, Trans.). New York: Springer–Verlag. (Original work published 1935)

Luria, A. R. (1976). *Cognitive development: Its cultural and social foundations*. Cambridge, MA: Harvard University Press.

Lyell, C. (1833). *Principles of geology* (3 Vols.). London: J. Murray. (Orignal work published 1830)

Lynam, D. R., & Henry, G. (2001). The role of neuropsychological deficits in conduct disorders. In J. Hill & B. Maughan (Eds.), *Conduct disorders in childhood and adolescence* (pp. 235–263). New York: Cambridge University Press.

Lyons-Ruth, K., Lyubchik, A., Wolfe, R., & Bronfman, E. (2002). Parental depression and child attachment: Hostile and helpless profiles of parent and child behavior among families at risk. In S. H. Goodman & I. H. Gotlib (Eds.), *Children of depressed parents: Mechanisms of risk and implications for treatment* (pp. 89–120). Washington, DC: American Psychological Association.

Maccoby, E. E. (1961). The taking of adult roles in middle childhood. *Journal of Abnormal and Social Psychology, 63,* 493–503.

MacTurk, R. H., McCarthy, M. E., Vietze, P. M., & Yarrow, L. J. (1987). Sequential analysis of mastery behavior in 6- and 12-month-old infants. *Developmental Psychology, 23,* 199–203.

Magnusson, D., & Cairns, R. B. (1996). Developmental science: Principles and illustrations. In R. B. Cairns, G. H. Elder, & E. J. Costello (Eds.), *Developmental science*. Cambridge, UK: Cambridge University Press.

Mahler, M. S. (1972). On the first three subphases of the separation–individuation process. *International Journal of Psychoanalysis, 53,* 333–338.

Mahler, M. S., & Furer, M. (1968). *On human symbiosis and the vicissitudes of individuation*. New York: International Universities Press.

Mahler, M. S., Pine, F., & Bergman, A. (1975). *The psychological birth of the human infant*. New York: Basic Books.

Marcia, J. E. (1980). Identity in adolescence. In J. Adelson (Ed.), *Handbook of adolescent psychology* (pp. 159–187). New York: Wiley.

Marcia, J. E. (2002). Identity and psychosocial development in adulthood. *Identity, 2,* 7–28.

Markovits, H., Benenson, J., & Dolenszky, E. (2001). Evidence that children and adolescents have internal models of peer interactions that are gender differentiated. *Child Development, 72,* 879–886.

Martin, C. L., Eisenbud, L., & Rose, H. (1995). Children's gender-based reasoning about toys. *Child Development, 66,* 1453–1471.

Martin, C. L., & Ruble, D. N. (2004). Children's search for gender cues: Cognitive perspectives on gender development. *Current Directions in Psychological Science, 13,* 67–70.

Martin, P., Poon, L. W., Kim, E., & Johnson, M. A. (1996). Social and psychological resources in the oldest old. *Experimental Aging Research, 22,* 121–139.

Marx, K. (1988). *Economic and political manuscripts of 1844 and The Communist Manifesto* (Martin Milligan, Trans.). Amherst, NY: Prometheus Books. (Original work published in 1844)

Marx, K., & Engels, F. (1953). *Selected works*. Moscow.

May, R. B., & Norton, J. M. (1981). Training-task orders and transfer in conservation. *Child Development, 52,* 904–913.

Mayr, E. W. (1991). *One long argument: Charles Darwin and the genesis of modern evolutionary thought*. Cambridge: Harvard University Press.

McAdams, D. P, & de St. Aubin, E. (Eds.)(1998). *Generativity and adult development: Psychosocial perspectives on caring for and contributing to the next generation* (pp. 367–389). Washington, DC: American Psychological Association.

McCabe, A. E., Siegel, L. S., Spence, I., & Wilkinson, A. (1982). Class-inclusion reasoning: Patterns of performance from three to eight years. *Child Development, 53,* 780–785.

Mead, G. H. (1934). *Mind, self and society*. Chicago: University of Chicago Press.

Meeus, W. (1996). Studies on identity development in adolescence: An overview of research and some new data. *Journal of Youth and Adolescence, 25,* 569–598.

Meeus, W., Iedema, J., Helsen, M., & Vollenbergh, W. (1999). Patterns of adolescent identity development: Review of literature and longitudinal analysis. *Developmental Review, 19,* 419–461.

Messer, S., & Warren, S. (1995). *Models of brief psychodynamic therapy*. New York: Guilford.

Metzger, M. A. (1997). Applications of nonlinear dynamic systems theory in developmental psychology: Motor and cognitive development. *Nonlinear Dynamics, Psychology, and Life Sciences, 1,* 55–67.

Miller, P. (2002). *Theories of developmental psychology*. (4th ed.). New York: Worth.

Miller, P. H., & Coyle, T. R. (1999). Developmental change: Lessons from microgenisis. In E. K. Scholnick, K. Nelson, S. A. Gelman, & P. H. Miller (Eds.), *Conceptual development: Piaget's legacy* (pp. 209–239). Mahwah, NJ: Lawrence Erlbaum Associates.

Miller, S. M. (2006). Vygotsky and Education: The sociocultural genesis of dialogic thinking in classroom contexts for open-forum literature discussions. Retrieved May 18, 2006 from http://psych.hanover.edu

Mischel, W. (1973). Toward a cognitive social learning reconceptualization of personality. *Psychological Review, 80,* 252–283.

Mischel, W. (1979). On the interface of cognition and personality: Beyond the person–situation debate. *American Psychologist, 34,* 740–754.

Mitchell, B. A. (2003). Life course theory. Retrieved January 16, 2005 from http://issues.families.com

Mitte, K. (2005). Meta analysis of cognitive behavioral treatments for generalized anxiety disorder: a comparison with pharmacotherapy. *Psychological Bulletin. 131,* 785–795.

Moore, B. E. (1995). Narcissism. In B. R. Moore & B. D. Fine (Eds.), *Psychoanalysis: The major concepts* (pp. 229–251). New Haven: Yale University Press.

Moreno, J. L. (1953). *Who shall survive?* Washington, DC: Nervous and Mental Disease Publication (Rev. ed.). New York: Beacon House. (Original work published 1934)

National Association of Cognitive-Behavioral Therapists (2005). What is Cognitive Behavioral Therapy? Retrieved October 11, 2005 from http://nacbt.org

National Center for Education Statistics. (2004). *Highlights from the TIMSS 1999 video study of eighth-grade mathematics teaching study*. Retrieved November 20, 2004, from nces.ed.gov

Neese, R. M. (2001). Motivation and melancholy: A Darwinian perspective. In R. A. Dienstbier, J. A. French, A. C. Kamil & D. W. Leger. (Eds.), *Evolutionary psychology and motivation: Vol. 47. Nebraska Symposium on Motivation* (pp. 179–204). Lincoln, NE: University of Nebraska Press.

Neimark, E. D. (1975). Longitudinal development of formal operations thought. *Genetic Psychology Monographs, 91,* 171–225.

Neimark, E. D. (1982). Adolescent thought: Transition to formal operations. In B. B. Wolman (Ed.), *Handbook of developmental psychology* (pp. 486–499). Englewood Cliffs, NJ: Prentice Hall.

Nelson, K. (1999). Levels and modes of representation: Issues for the theory of conceptual change and development. In E. K. Scholnick & K. Nelson (Eds.), *Conceptual development: Piaget's legacy* (pp. 269–291). Mahwah, NJ: Lawrence Erlbaum Associates.

Neugarten, B. L. (1963). Personality changes during the adult years. In R. J. Kuhlen (Ed.), *Psychological background of adult education* (pp. 43–76). Chicago: Chicago Center for the Study of Liberal Education for Adults.

Neugarten, B. L. (1968). Adult personality: Toward a psychology of the life cycle. In B. Neugarten (Ed.), *Middle age and aging* (pp. 137–147). Chicago: University of Chicago Press.

Neugarten, B. L. (1990). The changing meaning of age. In M. Bergener & S. I. Finkel (Eds.), *Clinical and scientific psychogeriatrics: Vol. 1. The holistic approaches.* New York: Springer–Verlag, pp. 1–6.

Neugarten, B. L., Moore, J. W., & Lowe, J. C. (1965). Age norms, age constraints, and adult socialization. *American Journal of Sociology, 70,* 710–717.

Newman, P. R., & Newman, B. M. (1976). Early adolescence and its conflict: group identity versus alienation. *Adolescence, 11,* 261–274.

Newman, B. M., & Newman, P. R. (2006). *Development through life: A psychosocial approach 9th ed..* Belmont, CA: Wadsworth.

Nickols, S. Y. (1994). Work/family stresses. In P. C. McKenry & S. J. Price (Eds.), *Families and change: Coping with stressful events* (pp. 66–87). Thousand Oaks, CA: Sage.

Norem, J. K., & Cantor, N. (1988). Capturing the "flavor" of behavior: Cognition, affect, and integration. In A. Isen & B. Moore (Eds.), *Affect and social behavior* (pp. 39–63). New York: Academic Press.

Nye, I. (1976). *Role structure and analysis of the family.* Beverly Hills, CA: Sage.

Ochs, E. (1988). *Culture and language development: Language acquisition and language socialization in a Samoan village.* Cambridge, England: Cambridge University Press.

O'Neill, D. K., & Gopnik, A. (1991). Young children's ability to identify the sources of their beliefs. *Developmental Psychology, 27,* 390–397.

O'Rand, A. M. (1996). The precious and the precocious: Understanding cumulative disadvantage and cumulative advantage over the life course. *The Gerontologist, 36,* 230–238.

Palincsar, A. S., Brown, A. L., & Campione, J. C. (1993). First grade dialogues for knowledge acquisition and use. In E. A. Forman, N. Minick, & C. A. Stone (Eds.), *Contexts for learning: Sociocultural dynamics in children's development* (pp. 43–57). New York: Oxford University Press.

Palmer, C. F. (1989). The discriminating nature of infants' exploratory actions. *Developmental Psychology, 25,* 885–893.

Parsons, T. (1951). *The social system.* Glencoe, IL: The Free Press.

Parsons, T., & Bales, R. F. (Eds.) (1955). *Family socialization and interaction process.* Glencoe, IL: Free Press.

Pashler, H. (1992). Attentional limitations in doing two tasks at the same time. *Current Directions, 1,* 44–48.

Patterson, G. R. (1982). *Coercive family processes.* Eugene, OR: Castalia.

Pavlov, I. P. (1927). *Conditioned reflexes.* (G. V. Anrep, Trans.) London: Oxford University Press.

Peterson, B. E., & Stewart, A. J. (1993). Generativity and social motives in young adults. *Journal of Personality and Social Psychology, 65,* 186–198.

Peterson, C., & Seligman, M. E. P. (2003). Character strengths before and after September 11. *Psychological Science, 14,* 381–384.

Piaget, J. (1926). *The language and thought of the child.* New York: Harcourt Brace.

Piaget, J. (1948). *The moral judgment of the child.* Glencoe, IL: Free Press. (Original work published 1932)

Piaget, J. (1951). *The child's conception of the world.* New York: International Universities Press. (Original work published 1926)

Piaget, J. (1952). *Judgment and reasoning in the child.* New York: Humanities Press. (Original work published 1924)

Piaget, J. (1952). *The child's conception of number.* London: Kegan Paul, Trench, & Trubner. (Original work published 1941)

Piaget, J. (1952). *The language and thought of the child.* London: Routledge & Kegan Paul.

Piaget, J. (1952). *The origins of intelligence in children.* New York: International Universities Press. (Original work published 1936)

Piaget, J. (1954a). *The construction of reality in the child.* New York: Basic Books.

Piaget, J. (1954b). *The psychology of intelligence.* New York: Harcourt Brace.

Piaget, J. (1955). The stages of intellectual development in the child and the adolescent. In P. Osterrieth, J. Piaget, R. DeSaussure, J. M. Tanner, H. Wallon, R. Zazzo, et al., (Eds.), *Le probleme des stades en psychologie de l'enfant* (pp. 33–42). Paris: Presses Universitaires de France.

Piaget, J. (1970). Piaget's theory. In P. H. Mussen (Ed.), *Carmichael's manual of child psychology* (3rd ed., Vol. 1) (pp. 703–732). New York: Wiley.

Piaget, J. (1971). *Biology and knowledge,* Chicago: University of Chicago Press. (Original work published 1967)

Piaget, J. (1972). Intellectual evolution from adolescence to adulthood. *Human Development, 15,* 1–12.

Piaget, J. (1985). *The equilibration of cognitive structures.* Chicago: University of Chicago Press. (Original work published 1975)

Piaget, J., & Inhelder, B. (1969). *The psychology of the child.* New York: Basic Books. (Original work published 1966)

Pleck, J. H. (1985). *Working wives, working husbands.* New York: Sage.

Postman, L., & Bruner, J. (1948). Perception under stress. *Psychological Review, 55,* 314–323.

Radke-Yarrow, M., Cummings, E. M., Kuczynski, L., & Chipman, M. (1985). Patterns of attachment in two- and three-year-olds in normal families and families with parental depression. *Child Development, 56,* 591–615.

Reid, J. B., Patterson, G. R., & Snyder, J. (2002). *Antisocial behavior in children and adolescents: A developmental analysis and model for intervention.* Washington, DC: American Psychological Association.

Rescorla, R. A. (1988). Pavlovian conditioning: It's not what you think it is. *American Psychologist, 43,* 151–160.

Ricks, M. H. (1985). The social transmission of parental behavior: Attachment across generations. In I. Bretherton & E. Waters (Eds.), Growing points of attachment: Theory and research (pp. 211–227). *Monographs of the Society for Research in Child Development, 50,* (1–2, Serial No. 209).

Ridgeway, C. L., & Correll, S. J. (2004). Motherhood as a status characteristic. *Journal of Social Issues, 60,* 683–700.

Riley, M. W., Johnson, M. E., & Foner, A. (Eds.) (1972). *Aging and society: Vol. 3. A sociology of age stratification.* New York: Russell Sage Foundation.

Ritvo, S., & Solnit, A. J. (1995). Instinct theory. In B. R. Moore & B. D. Fine (Eds.), *Psychoanalysis: The major concepts* (pp. 327–333). New Haven: Yale University Press.

Rogoff, B. (1995). Observing sociocultural activity on three planes: Participatory appropriation, guided participation, and apprenticeship. In J. V. Wertsch, P. del Rio, & A. Alvarez (Eds.), *Sociocultural studies of mind* (pp. 139–164). Cambridge, England: Cambridge University Press.

Rogoff, B., & Chavajay, P. (1995). What's become of research on the cultural basis of cognitive development? *American Psychologist, 50,* 859–877.

Rogoff, B., Mistry, J., Göncü, A., & Mosier, C. (1993). Guided participation in cultural activity by toddlers and caregivers. *Monographs of the Society for Research in Child Development, 58,* (Serial No. 236).

Rosen, A. B., & Rozin, P. (1993). Now you see it, now you don't: The preschool child's conception of invisible particles in the context of dissolving. *Developmental Psychology, 29,* 300–311.

Rosenbaum, M. (1989). Self control under stress: The role of learned resourcefulness. *Advances in behavior research and therapy, 11,* 249–258.

Rosenbaum, M., & Ben-Ari, K. (1985). Learned helplessness and learned resourcefulness: Effects of noncontingent success and failure on individuals differing in self-control skills. *Journal of Personality and Social Psychology, 48,* 198–215.

Rovee-Collier, C., Schechter, A., Shyi, G. C. W., & Shields, P. (1992). Perceptual identification of contextual attributes and infant memory retrieval. *Developmental Psychology, 28,* 307–318.

Ruff, H. A., Saltarelli, L. M., Capozzoli, M., & Dubiner, K. (1992). The differentiation of activity in infants' exploration of objects. *Developmental Psychology, 28,* 851–861.

Rumelhart, D. E., & McClelland, J. L. (1986). *Parallel distributed processing* (Vol. 1). Cambridge, MA: MIT Press.

Rushton, J. P. (1976). Socialization and the altruistic behavior of children. *Psychological Bulletin, 83,* 898–913.

Ryder, N. B. (1965). The cohort as a concept in the study of social change. *American Sociological Review, 30,* 843–861.

Sameroff, A. J. (1982). Development and the dialectic: The need for a systems approach. In W. A. Collins (Ed.), *The concept of development: The Minnesota Symposia on Child Psychology* (Vol. 15, pp. 83–103). Hillsdale, NJ: Lawrence Erlbaum Associates.

Sampson, R. J., & Laub, J. H. (1993). *Crime in the making: Pathways and turning points through life.* Cambridge, MA: Harvard University Press.

Sampson, R. J., & Laub, J. H. (2004). A general age-graded theory of crime: Lessons learned and the future of life-course criminology. In D. Farrington (Ed.), *Advances in criminological theory: Vol. 14. Integrated developmental and life course theories of offending* (pp. 165–182). Somerset, NJ: Transaction Publishers.

Sarbin, T. R., & Allen, V. L. (1968). Role theory. In G. Lindzey & E. Aronson (Eds.), *Handbook of social psychology* (2nd ed., Vol. 1). Reading, Mass.: Addison–Wesley.

Schafer, R. (1968). *Aspects of Internalization.* New York: International Universities Press.

Schaffer, H. R., & Emerson, P. E. (1964). The development of social attachments in infancy. *Monographs of the Society for Research in Child Development, 29,* (whole No. 94).

Schiff, A., & Knopf, I. (1985). The effects of task demands on attention allocation in children of different ages. *Child Development, 56,* 621–630.

Schlein, S. (1987). *A way of looking at things: Selected papers from 1930 to 1980. Erik H. Erikson.* New York: Norton.

Schneider, B. H., Atkinson, L., & Tardif, C. (2001). Child–parent attachment and children's peer relations: A quantitative review. *Developmental Psychology, 37,* 86–100.

Schulz, A. J. (1998). Navajo women and the politics of identities. *Social Problems, 45,* 336–355.

Schöner, G., & Thelen, E. (2006). Using dynamic field theory to rethink infant habituation. *Psychological Review, 113,* 273–299.

Scribner, S. (1977). Modes of thinking and ways of speaking: Culture and logic reconsidered. In P. N. Johnson-Laird & P. C Wason (Eds.), *Thinking* pp. 483–500. Cambridge, England: Cambridge University Press.

Seligman, M. E. P. (1975). *Helplessness: On depression, development, and death.* San Francisco: W. H. Freeman.

Seligman, M. E. P., Steen, T. A., Park, N., & Peterson, C. (2005). Positive psychology progress: Empirical validation of interventions. *American Psychologist, 60,* 410–421.

Selman, R. L. (1971). Taking another's perspective: Role-taking development in early childhood. *Child Development, 42,* 1721–1734.

Selman, R. L. (1980). *The growth of interpersonal understanding: Developmental and clinical analysis.* New York: Academic Press.

Selman, R. L. (1994). The relation of role taking to the development of moral judgment in children. In B. Puka (Ed.), *Fundamental research in moral development. Moral development: Vol. 2. A compendium* (pp. 87–99). New York: Garland.

Serbin, L. A., Powlishta, K. K., & Gulko, J. (1993). The development of sex-typing in middle childhood. *Monographs of the Society for Research in Child Development, 58,* (Whole No. 232).

Shibley, P. K. (2000). *The concept of revisitation and the transition to parenthood.* Unpublished doctoral dissertation, Ohio State University.

Shull, R. L., & Grimes, J. A. (2003). Bouts of responding from variable-interval reinforcement of lever pressing by rats. *Journal of Experimental Analysis of Behavior. 80,* 159–171.

Siegler, I. C., Poon, L. W., Madden, D. J., & Welsh, K. A. (1996). Psychological aspects of normal aging. In E. W. Busse & D. G. Blazer (Eds.), *The American Psychiatric Press textbook of geriatric psychiatry* (pp. 105–127). Washington, DC: American Psychiatric Press.

Siegler, R. S. (1998). *Children's Thinking* (3rd ed.). Upper Saddle River, NJ: Prentice Hall.

Siegler, R. S. (2000). Unconscious insights. *Current Directions in Psychological Science, 9,* 79–83.

Siegler, R. S., & Crowley, K. (1991). The microgenetic method: A direct means for studying cognitive development. *American Psychologist, 46,* 606–620.

Siegler, R. S., & Stern, E. (1998). A microgenetic analysis of conscious and unconscious strategy discoveries. *Journal of Experimental Psychology: General, 127,* 377–397.

Silvia, P. J. (2005). What is interesting? Exploring the appraisal structure of interest. *Emotion, 5,* 89–102.

Simons, E. L. (1989). Human origins. *Science, 245,* 1343–1350.

Sinnott, J. D., & Cavanaugh, J. C. (1991). *Bridging paradigms: Positive development in adulthood and cognitive aging.* New York: Praeger.

Skaalvik, E. M., & Hagtvet, K. A. (1990). Academic achievement and self-concept: An analysis of causal predominance in a developmental perspective. *Journal of Personality and Social Psychology, 58,* 292–307.

Skinner, B. F. (1935). The generic nature of the concepts of stimulus and response. *Journal of Genetic Psychology, 12,* 40–65.

Skinner, B. F. (1938). *The behavior of organisms.* New York: Appleton Century Crofts.

Skinner, B. F. (1987). Whatever happened to psychology as the science of behavior? *American Psychologist, 42,* 780–786.

Slee, P. T., & Shute, R. H. (2003). *Child development: Thinking about theories*. London: Arnold Publishers.

Smith, D., & Whitmore, K. F. (2006). *Literacy and advocacy in adolescent family, gang, school, and juvenile court communities*. Mahwah, NJ: Lawrence Erlbaum Associates.

Smith, L. B., & Thelen, E. (Eds.) (1993). *A dynamic systems approach to development: Applications*. Cambridge, MA.: MIT Press.

Snyder, C. R. (1994). *The psychology of hope: You can get there from here*. New York: Free Press.

Snyder, C. R. (2002). Hope theory: Rainbows in the mind. *Psychological Inquiry, 13,* 249–275.

Snyder, C. R., Cheavens, J., & Sympson, S. C. (1997). Hope: An individual motive for social commerce. *Group Dynamics: Theory, Research, and Practice, 1,* 107–118.

Snyder, C. R. & McDermott, D. (1999). *Making hope happen*. Oakland/San Francisco: New Harbinger Press.

Snyder, C. R., Shorey, H. S., Cheavens, J., Pulvers, K. M., Adams, V. H. III, & Wiklund, C. (2002). Hope and academic success in college. *Journal of Educational Psychology, 94,* 820–826.

Snyder, C. R., & Taylor, J. D. (2000). Hope as a common factor across psychotherapy approaches: A lesson from the dodo's verdict. In C. R. Snyder (Ed.), *The handbook of hope: Theory, measures, and applications* (pp. 89–108). San Diego, CA: Academic Press.

Sophian, C. (1988). Limitations on preschool children's knowledge about counting: Using counting to compare two sets. *Developmental Psychology, 24,* 634–640.

Sophian, C., & Yengo, L. (1985). Infants' understanding of visible displacements. *Developmental Psychology, 21,* 932–941.

Spelke, E. S., von Hofsten, C., & Kestenbaum, R. (1989). Object perception in infancy: Interaction of spatial and kinetic information for object boundaries. *Developmental Psychology, 25,* 185–186.

Spencer, H. (1864). *Principles of biology* (Vol. 1). London: William & Norgate.

Steinberg, L. (2005). *Adolescence* (7th ed.). Boston: McGraw–Hill.

Stevenson, H. W., Chen, C., & Lee, S. (1993). Mathematics achievement of Chinese, Japanese, and American children: Ten years later. *Science, 259,* 53–58.

Stewart, A. J., & Healy, J. M., Jr. (1989). Linking individual development and social changes. *American Psychologist, 44,* 30–42.

Stewart, A. J., & Ostrove, J. M. (1998). Women's personality in middle age: Gender, history, and midcourse corrections. *American Psychologist, 53,* 1185–1194.

Stewart, A. J., Settles, I. H., & Winter, N. J. G. (1998). Women and the social movements of the 1960s: Activists, engaged observers and nonparticipants. *Political Psychology, 19,* 63–94.

Stright, A. D., Neitzel, C., Sears, K. G., & Hoke-Sinex, L. (2001). Instruction begins in the home: Relations between parental instruction and children's self-regulation in the classroom. *Journal of Educational Psychology, 93,* 456–466.

Sullivan, H. S. (1953). *The interpersonal theory of psychiatry*. New York: Norton.

Sullivan, M. D. (2003). Hope and hopelessness at the end of life. *American Journal of Geriatric Psychiatry, 11,* 393–405.

Swenson, R. (1997). *Spontaneous order, evolution, and natural law: An introduction to the physical basis for an ecological psychology*. Hillsdale, NJ: Lawrence Erlbaum Associates.

Tattersall, I., Delson, E., & Van Couvering, J. (Eds.) (1988). *Encyclopedia of human evolution and prehistory*. New York: Garland.

Thelen, E. (1995). Time scale dynamics and the development of embodied cognition. In R. E. Port & T. van Gelder (Eds.), *Mind as motion* (pp. 69–100). Cambridge: MIT Press.

Thelen, E., & Fisher, D. M. (1982). Newborn stepping: An explanation for a "disappearing" reflex. *Developmental Psychology, 18,* 760–775.

Thelen, E., Fisher, D. M., & Ridley-Johnson, R. (1984). The relationship between physical growth and a newborn reflex. *Infant Behavior and Development, 7,* 479–493.

Thelen, E., Schöner, G., Scheier, C., & Smith, L. B. (2001). The dynamics of embodiment: A field theory of infant perseverative reaching. *Behavioral and Brain Sciences, 24,* 1–86.

Thelen, E., & Smith, L. B. (1994). *A dynamic systems approach to the development of cognition and action.* Cambridge, MA.: MIT Press.

Thomas, R. M. (1999). *Human development theories: Windows on culture.* Thousand Oaks, CA: Sage.

Thomas, W. I., & Znaniecki, F. (1974). *The Polish peasant in Europe and America (Vols. 1–2).* Urbana, Illinois: University of Illinois Press. (Original work published 1918–1920, New York: Octagon Press)

Thorndike, E. L. (1898). Animal intelligence: An experimental study of the associative processes in animals. *Psychological Review Monograph Supplement, 2,* No. 8.

Thorndike, E. L. (1911). *Animal intelligence.* New York: Macmillan.

Thomas, R. M. (1999). *Human development theories: Windows on culture.* Thousand Oaks, CA: Sage.

Tinbergen, N. (1951). *The study of instinct.* Oxford: Clarendon Press.

Tolman, E. C. (1948). Cognitive maps in rats and men. *Psychological Review, 55,* 189–208.

Tolman, E. C. (1967). *Purposive behavior in rats and men.* New York Appleton, Century, Crofts. (Original work published 1932)

Tracy, J. L., Shaver, P. R., Albino, A. W., & Cooper, M. L. (2003). Attachment styles and adolescent sexuality. In P. Florsheim (Ed.), *Adolescent romantic relationships and sexual behavior: Theory, research, and practical implications* (pp. 137–159). Mahwah, NJ: Lawrence Erlbaum Associates.

Tracy, R. L., & Ainsworth, M. D. S. (1981). Maternal affectionate behavior and infant–mother attachment patterns. *Child Development, 52,* 1341–1343.

Trends in International Mathematics and Science Study. (2004). *TIMSS results.* Retrieved November 20, 2004, from nces.ed.gov/timss

Trivers, R. (1972). Parental investment and sexual selection. In B. Campbell (Ed.), *Sexual selection and the descent of man: 1871–1971* (pp. 136–179). Chicago: Aldine.

Tudge, J. R. H. (1992). Processes and consequences of peer collaboration: A Vygotskian analysis. *Child Development, 63,* 1364–1379.

Tyson, P., & Tyson, R. L. (1995). Development. In B. R. Moore & B. D. Fine (Eds.), *Psychoanalysis: The major concepts* (pp. 395–420). New Haven: Yale University Press.

Uzgiris, I. C. (1976). The organization of sensorimotor intelligence. In M. Lewis (Ed.), *Origins of intelligence; Infancy and early childhood* (pp. 123–164). New York: Plenum.

Valsiner, J. (2000). *Culture and human development.* Thousand Oaks, CA: Sage.

van der Veer, R., & Valsiner, J. (1991). *Understanding Vygotsky: A quest for synthesis.* Oxford, UK: Blackwell.

van Geert, P. (1998). A dynamic systems model of basic developmental mechanisms: Piaget, Vygotsky and beyond. *Psychological Review, 105,* 634–677.

van Ijzendoorn, M. H., Goldberg, S., Kroonenberg, P. M., & Frenkel, O. J. (1992). The relative effects of maternal and child problems on the quality of attachment: A meta-analysis of attachment in clinical samples. *Child Development, 63,* 840–858.

Vanzetti, N., & Duck, S. (1996). *A lifetime of relationships.* Pacific Grove, CA: Brooks/Cole.

Volkart, E. H. (1951). *Social behavior and personality: Contributions of W. I. Thomas to theory and social research.* New York: Social Science Research Council.

von Bertalanffy, L. (1950). The theory of open systems in physics and biology. *Science, 111,* 23–28.

von Bertalanffy, L. (1968). *General systems theory* (Rev. ed.). New York: Braziller.

Voydanoff, P. (2004). The effects of work demands and resources on work-to-family conflict and facilitation. *Journal of Marriage and the Family, 66,* 398–412.

Vygotsky, L. S. (1962). *Thought and language.* Cambridge, MA: MIT Press and Wiley. (Original work published 1934)

Vygotsky, L. S. (1978a). Tool and symbol in child development. In M. Cole, V. John-Steiner, S. Scribner, & E. Souberman, E. (Eds.), *Mind in society: The development of higher psychological processes* (pp. 19–30). Cambridge, MA: Harvard University Press.

Vygotsky, L. S. (1978b). Internalization of higher psychological functions. In M. Cole, V. John-Steiner, S. Scribner, & E. Souberman, E. (Eds.), *Mind in society: The development of higher psychological processes* (pp. 52–57). Cambridge, MA: Harvard University Press.

Vygotsky, L. S. (1978c). Interaction between learning and development. In M. Cole, V. John-Steiner, S. Scribner, & E. Souberman, E. (Eds.), *Mind in society: The development of higher psychological processes* (pp. 79–92). Cambridge, MA: Harvard University Press.

Vygotsky, L. S. (1978d). The role of play in development. In M. Cole, V. John-Steiner, S. Scribner, & E. Souberman, E. (Eds.), *Mind in society: The development of higher psychological processes* (pp. –105). Cambridge, MA: Harvard University Press.

Vygotsky, L. S. (1984). The crisis of seven years. In L. S. Vygotsky, *Collected works: Child psychology, Vol. 4.* Moscow: Pedagogika.

Vygotsky, L. S. (1987a). Genetic roots of thinking and speech. In R. W. Rieber & A. S. Carton (Eds.), *The collected works of L. S. Vygotsky: Vol. 1: Problems of general psychology* (pp. 101–120). New York: Plenum.

Vygotsky, L. S. (1987b). The development of scientific concepts in childhood. In R. W. Rieber & A. S. Carton (Eds.), *The collected works of L. S. Vygotsky: Vol. 1. Problems of general psychology* (p. 167–241). New York: Plenum.

Vygotsky, L. S. (1987c). Thought and word. In R. W. Rieber, & A. S. Carton (Eds.), *The Collected Works of L. S. Vygotsky: Vol. 1. Problems of General Psychology* (pp. 242–291). New York: Plenum.

Walker, L. J., Gustafson, P., & Hennig, K. H. (2001). The consolidation/transition model in moral reasoning development. *Developmental Psychology, 37,* 187–197.

Waterman, A. S. (1982). Identity development from adolescence to adulthood: An extension of theory and a review of research. *Developmental Psychology, 18,* 341–358.

Waterman, A. S. (1999a). Commentary: Identity, the identity statuses, and identity status development: A contemporary statement. *Developmental Review, 19,* 591–621.

Waterman, A. S. (1999b). Issues of identify formation revisited: United States and the Netherlands. *Developmental Review, 19,* 462–479.

Waterman, A. S., & Whitbourne, S. K. (1981). The inventory of psychosocial development. *Journal Supplement Abstract Service: Catalog of Selected Documents in Psychology, 11* (Ms. No. 2179).

Weine, S., Feetham, S., Kulauzovic, Y., Knafl, K., Besic, S., Klebic, M., Muvagic, A., Muzurovic, J., Spahovic, D., Pavkovik, I. (2006). A family beliefs framework for socially and culturally specific preventive interventions with refugee youth and families. *American Journal of Orthopsychiatry, 76,* 1–9.

Weinfield, N. S., Sroufe, L. A., Egeland, B., & Carlson, E. A. (1999). The nature of individual differences in infant–caregiver attachment. In J. Cassidy & P. R. Shaver (Eds.), *Handbook of attachment: Theory, research, and clinical applications* (pp. 68–88). New York: Guilford Press.

Weiskranz, L. (1986). *Blindsight: A case study and implications*. Oxford, England: Clarendon Press.

Weiskranz, L. (1997). *Consciousness lost and found*. Oxford, England: Oxford University Press.

Weiss, J. (1990). The nature of the patient's problems and how in psychoanalysis the individual works to solve them. *Psychoanalytic Psychology*, 7, 1, 105–113.

Wellman, H. M. (1990). *The child's theory of mind*. Cambridge, MA: MIT Press.

Wellman, H. M., Cross, D., & Bartsch, K. (1986). Infant search and object permanence: A meta-analysis of the A-not-B error. *Monographs of the Society for Research in Child Development, 51* (3, Whole No. 214).

Wellman, H., Cross, D., & Watson, J. (2001). Meta-analysis of theory-of-mind development: The truth about false belief. *Child Development, 71*, 655–684.

Wentworth, N., & Haith, M. M. (1992). Event-specific expectations of 2- and 3-month-old infants. *Developmental Psychology, 28*, 842–850.

Wertsch, J. V. (1985). *Vygotsky and the social formation of mind*. Cambridge, MA: Harvard University Press.

Whitbourne, S. K., Zuschlag, M. K., Elliot, L. B., & Waterman, A. S. (1992). Psychosocial development in adulthood: A 22-year sequential study. *Journal of Personality and Social Psychology, 63*, 260–271.

White, R. W. (1960). Competence and the psychosexual stages of development. In M. R. Jones (Ed.), *Nebraska Symposium on Motivation* (pp. 97–141, Lincoln: University of Nebraska Press.

Wilson, E. O. (1975). *Sociobiology: The new synthesis*. Cambridge, MA: The Belknap Press.

Wimmer, H. M., & Perner, J. (1983). Beliefs about beliefs: Representation and constraining function of wrong beliefs in young children's understanding of deception. *Cognition, 13*, 103–128.

Wright, D. W., Nelson, B. S., & Georgen, K. E. (1994). Marital problems. In P. C. McKenry & S. J. Price (Eds.), *Families and change: Coping with stressful events* (pp. 40–65). Thousand Oaks, CA: Sage.

Yarrow, L. J., McQuiston, S., MacTurk, R. H., McCarthy, M. E., Klein, R. P., & Vietze, P. M. (1983). The assessment of mastery motivation during the first year of life. *Developmental Psychology, 19*, 159–171.

Zelinski, E. M., & Lewis, K. L. (2003). Adult age differences in multiple cognitive functions: Differentiation, dedifferentiation, or process-specific change. *Psychology and Aging, 18*, 727–745.

Zimmermann, P., & Becker-Stoll, F. (2002). Stability of attachment representations during adolescence: The influence of ego-identity status. *Journal of Adolescence, 25*, 107–124.

Ziv, M., & Frye, D. (2003). The relation between desire and false belief in children's theory of mind: No satisfaction? *Developmental Psychology, 39*, 859–876.

Author Index

Note: *f* indicates footnote.

A

Abbott, B. B., 12
Abend, S. M., 59
Ackerman, B. P., 109
Acredolo, C., 100
Adams, A., 100
Adams, G., 228
Adams, V. H., III, 231
Adler, A., 75
Adolph, K. E., 280
Affonso, D. D., 236
Ainsworth, M. D. S., 32, 33, 34, 35
Albino, A. W., 36
Alexander, K. W., 36
Alfieri, T., 171
Allen, V. L., 163

Allport, G. W., 76, 166
Andersson, K., 236
Archer, J., 22
Ashby, W. R., 271
Atkinson, L., 35
Au, T. K., 117

B

Baillargeon, R., 118
Bakhurst, D., 246
Bales, R. F., 163, 166
Baltes, P. B, 189
Bandura, A., 135, 136, 137, 139, 161
Barbu, S., 171
Barlow, N., 21
Barnett, D., 34
Barnett, R. C., 174, 175

Barth, J. M., 170

Bartsch, K., 92, 106

Bar-Yam Hassan, A., 238

Bar-Yam Hassan, M., 238

Bates, E., 14

Beale, R. L., 172

Becker-Stoll, F., 228

Beere, C. A., 170

Beire, J. J., 106

Belsky, J., 32, 34

Ben-Ari, K., 147

Benenson, J., 171

Bengtsgard, K., 236

Benson, J. B., 92

Bergman, A., 63

Bertenthal, B. I., 92

Berzonsky, M. D., 229

Biddle, B. J., 161, 162, 163

Bidell, T. R., 272, 277, 282, 283, 284,
       285, 285f

Bijstra, J., 118

Blanck, G., 62

Blanck, R., 62

Blehar, M. C., 33

Blos, P., 58, 61

Blumenthal, J., 116

Blurton-Jones, N., 27

Bobbitt, B. L., 141

Boesky, D., 61

Bohlin, G., 236

Boom, J., 104

Borden, W., 62

Bordens, K. S., 12

Bowlby, J., 28, 32

Boyatizis, R. E., 144

Boyer, M. E., 97,

Boykin, A. W., 238

Boyle, F. M., 95

Bradmetz, J., 96, 117

Brainerd, C. J., 117

Braunwold, K., 34

Brazelton, T. B., 255

Bretherton, I., 33

Breuer, J., 47

Brim, O. G., Jr., 161, 166

Bronfman, E., 34

Bronson, G. W., 32

Brown, A. L., 258

Brown, M. M., 106

Brown, R., 162

Brugman, D., 104

Bruner, J., 65, 67, 245

Buhler, C., 187

Bullock, D., 101

Bumpus, M. S., 176

Buss, D. M., 29, 30, 37

Butterfield, E. C., 108

C

Cairnes, R. B., 14

Campbell, S. B., 34

Campione, J. C., 258

Campos, J., 92

Cantor, N., 230

Capozzoli, M., 91

Carlo, G., 106

Carlson, E. A., 33

Carlson, V., 34

Carr, D., 196, 198f, 199f

Caspi, A., 187, 190, 203

Cassidy, J., 32

Casteel, M., 141

Castellanos, F., 116

Cavanaugh, J. C., 108

Cazden, C. B., 258

Chandler, M., 108

Chapman, M., 98, 99

Charlesworth, W., 28, 29, 31

Chavajay, P., 252, 253, 255, 256

Cheavens, J., 230, 231

Chen, C., 253

Chi, M. T. H., 250
Childs, C. P., 255
Chipman, M., 34
Chomsky, N., 98
Christiansen, S. L., 236
Christou, C., 141
Cicchetti, D., 34
Clancy, S. M., 229
Clipp, E. C, 190
Cohen, G. D., 294
Cohn, J. F., 34
Cole, M., 244, 252, 253
Coles, R., 213
Colin, V., 32
Collier, G. A., 255
Constantinople, A., 236
Cooper, M. L., 36
Correll, S. J., 175
Cosmides, L., 29, 30
Cox, M. J., 32
Crain, W. C., 236
Cramer, P., 67
Cross, D., 92, 106
Crouter, A. C., 176
Crowley, K., 142
Culbertson, S. A., 134
Cullen, C., 135
Cummings, E. M., 34
Currie, L. S., 110

D

Dale, P. S., 14
Daly, M., 41
Damon, W., 103, 285*f*
Dark, V. J., 68
Darling-Fisher, C. S., 236
Darrow, C. M., 215
Darwin, C., 22, 23
Darwin, E., 21
Davey, G., 128, 135

Davison, M. L., 215
Davydov, V. V., 258, 259
de St. Aubin, E., 236
DeAngelis, T., 35
Deeg, D. J. H., 237
DeLisi, R., 111
Delson, E., 24
Demetriou, A., 100, 141
Denmark, F. L., 175
Denney, N. W., 107
DeVries, R., 112
Dodge, K. A., 106
Dolenszky, E., 171
Dollinger, S. J., 229
Domino, G., 236
Donald, M., 118
Douvan, E., 165
Downey, G., 106, 190
Dreman, S., 172
Dubiner, K., 91
Duck, S., 220
Dweck, C. S., 230

E

Eckstein, S., 101
Edelstein, R. S., 36
Edwards, C. P., 171
Efklides, A., 100
Egan, G., 231
Egan, S., 171
Egeland, B., 33
Eibl-Eibesfeldt, I., 27
Eisenberg, N., 106
Eisenbud, L., 170
Elder, G. H., Jr., 186, 187, 188, 189,
        190, 193, 201, 203
Elias, M. J., 106
Ellenberger, H. F., 48
Elliot, L. B., 236, 237
Emerson, P. E., 59

Engels, F., 244, 245

Eppler, M. A., 280

Erikson, E. H., 14, 215, 216, 217, 218, 220, 221, 222, 223, 224, 227, 230

Erikson, J., 217, 221, 223, 224

F

Fanselow, M. S., 132

Farrar, M. J., 97

Feeney, J. A., 36

Feetham, S., 177

Feldman, H., 169

Feldman, M., 169

Feltovich, P. J., 250

Fenson, L., 14

Ferris, M., 173*f*, 174, 196

Ferster, C. B., 134

Field, D., 117

Finley, G. E., 194

Fischer, K. W., 89, 92, 101, 215, 272, 277, 281, 282, 283, 284, 285, 285*f*

Fisher, D. M., 287

Flavell, J. H., 98, 100, 105, 116, 215

Flexner, S. B., 1

Fogel, A., 293

Fonagy, P., 34

Foner, A., 188

Forman, E. A., 258

Fozard, J. L., 237

Frenkel, O. J., 34

Freud, A., 58

Freud, S., 49, 51, 58, 65, 76, 170

Freidman, L. J., 213

Frone, M. R., 173

Frye, D., 107

Funder, D. C., 189

Furer, M., 63

G

Galin, D., 68

Gara, M. A., 106

Gazzaniga, M. S., 65

Gelman, S. A., 97

George, C., 36

Georgen, K. E., 176

Gibbs, J. C., 103

Giedd, J., 116

Giele, J. Z., 201

Gielen, U. P., 104

Gilligan, C., 238

Glaser, R., 250

Glueck, E., 200

Glueck, S., 200

Godsil, B. P., 132

Goffman, E., 163

Gold, M., 165

Goldberg, S., 34

Goldfield, E. C., 279

Göncü, A., 256

Gopnick, A., 88, 109, 279

Gould, R. L., 43, 215

Granic, I., 278, 288, 289, 290, 291

Gratch, G., 89

Gray, W. M., 100

Greenfield, P. M., 255

Greenwald, A. G., 65, 66*f*, 67, 68

Gregor, T., 171

Grimes, J. A., 134

Gustafson, P., 104

Gutheil, G., 97

H

Hagen, K. A., 230

Hagtvet, K. A., 139

Haith, M. M., 90

Halford, G. S., 95

Hamachek, D., 236

Hamilton, W. D., 22

Hartmann, H., 61, 62

Havighurst, R. J., 215, 225

Hawkins, A. J., 173*f*, 174, 196

Hawley, G. A., 236
Haywood, H. C., 258, 260
Hazan, C., 35
Heckhausen, J., 15
Helsen, M., 229
Helwig, C. C., 103
Henderson, V. K., 32
Hennig, K. H., 104
Henry, G., 250
Higgins, A., 141, 256
Higgins, E., 171
Hill, E. J., 173*f*, 174, 196
Hoke-Sinex, L., 110
Hollenstein, T., 290
Hopkins, J. R., 235
Huttenlocher, J., 95
Huxley, J., 42, 214

I

Iedema, J., 229
Inhelder, B., 85, 89, 99, 100, 101
Isabella, R. A., 32
Izard, C. E., 109

J

Jackson, B. P., 192
Jackson, S., 118
Jacobson, P. B., 62
Jacoby, L. L., 68
Jahoda, M., 47, 48
Jeffries, N., 116
Johnson, M. A., 238
Johnson, M. E., 188
Johnston, W. A., 68
Jones, E., 48
Jones, R. M., 229
Jordan, N. C., 95
Joseph, L., 112
Josselson, R., 2387
Jouanjean, A., 171

Jung, C. G., 75

K

Kagan, J., 10
Kahn, R. L., 275
Kalish, C. W., 97
Kamii, C., 110, 111, 112
Kardaun, J. W. P. F., 237
Kari, A., 111
Katz, D., 275
Kauffman, S., 271, 280
Keating, D. P., 99, 141, 142
Keith, J., 188
Kelso, J. A. S., 280
Kermoian, R., 92
Kernberg, O., 63
Kertzer, D. I., 188
Kestenbaum, R., 91
Kihlstrom, J. L., 65
Kim, E., 238
Kinder, D. R., 193
King, P. M., 215
Kiston, J. M., 235
Kitchener, K. S., 215
Kivnick, H. Q., 217, 221, 223
Klein, A. B., 215
Klein, M., 53
Klein, R. P., 91
Knafl, K., 177
Knight, G. P., 106
Knopf, I., 141, 256
Kohlberg, L., 103, 104
Kolb, D. A., 143, 144
Kroger, J., 229, 236
Kroonenberg, P. M., 34
Kuczynski, L., 34
Kuhn, D., 108, 117
Kuk, L. S., 229
Kulauzovic, Y., 177
Kwon, Y.-J., 117

L

Labouvie-Vief, G., 107, 108
LaFreniere, P. J., 26
Lagattuta, K. H., 108
Lalonde, C., 108
Lamey, A. K., 289
Laszlo, E., 276
Laub, J. H., 196, 200, 201
Lavond, D. G., 130
Lawson, A. E., 117
Lee, S., 253
Leidy, N. K., 236
Le Maner-Idrissi, G., 171
Lerner, I, M., 24
Lerner, R. M., 274, 274f, 285f
Levin, F. M., 68
Levin, I., 215
Levine, S. C., 95
Levinson, D. J., 215
Levinson, M. H., 215
Levy, G. D., 170
Levy, M. J., Jr., 170
Lewin, R., 24
Lewis, B. A., 112
Lewis, K. L., 142
Lewis, M. D., 272, 278, 280, 281
Libby, W. J., 24
Lightfoot, C., 108
Lindsay, D. S., 68
Linton, R., 161
Lopez, A., 97
Lopez, S. J., 236
Lorenz, K. Z., 27, 28, 107
Lovas, G. S., 36
Lowe, J. C., 161, 168, 191
Lui, H., 116
Luria, A. R., 255
Lyell, C., 22
Lynam, D. R., 250
Lyons-Ruth, K., 34
Lyubchik, A., 34

M

Maccoby, E. E., 161
Macintosh, V. H., 230
MacTurk, R. H., 91
Madden, D. J., 238
Magnusson, D., 14
Mahler, M. S., 63
Mainemelis, C., 144
Manke, B., 171
Marcia, J. E., 227, 236
Margand, N. A., 32
Markoulis, D. C., 104
Markovits, H., 171
Marshall, N. L., 175
Martin, C. L., 170
Martin, P., 238
Marx, K., 238, 244, 245
May, R. B., 117
Mayr, E. W., 23
McAdams, D. P., 216, 236
McBride, M. L., 98
McCabe, A. E., 98
McCarthy, M. E., 91
McClaskey, C. L., 106
McClelland, J., 65
McDermott, D., 231
McHale, S., 171
McKee, B., 215
McQuiston, S., 91
Mead, G. H., 161
Meeus, W., 229
Meltzoff, A., 88, 279
Messer, S., 62
Metzger, M. A., 278, 292, 295
Miller, P., 83, 93, 236, 237, 267, 279
Miller, S., 258
Mischel, W., 238
Mistry, J., 256
Mitchell, B. A., 196
Moore, B. E.,
Moore, G., 34

Moore, J. W., 161, 168, 191
Moreno, J. L., 161
Mosier, C., 256
Myers, B. J., 230

N

Neese, R. M., 31
Neimark, E. D., 100, 117
Neitzel, C., 110
Nelson, B. S., 176
Nelson, K., 93
Nelson, T. O., 108
Neugarten, B. L., 161, 168, 191, 215
Newman, B. M., 96*f*, 129*f*, 167, 189, 222, 223, 226
Newman, P. R., 96*f*, 129*f*, 167, 189, 222, 223, 226
Nickols, S. Y., 172
Norem, J. K., 230
Norton, J. M., 117
Novick, K., 175
Nye, I., 166

O

Ochs, E., 256
O'Neill, D. K., 109
O'Rand, A. M., 195
Ostrove, 190, 191
Owen, M. J., 32

P

Palincsar, A. S., 258
Palkovitz, R., 236
Palmer, C. F., 91
Park, N., 147
Parke, R. D., 189
Parker, C. A., 215
Parsons, T., 161, 163, 166
Pashler, H., 256
Patterson, G. R., 278, 288, 289, 290, 291
Pavlov, I. P., 127

Pearce, K. A., 107
Peck, V., 108
Perner, J., 106
Perry, D., 171
Peterson, B. E., 237
Peterson, C., 147, 230
Pethick, S. J., 14
Pettit, G. S., 106
Piaget, J., 82, 85, 86, 87, 89, 91, 94, 98, 99, 100, 101, 102, 104, 105, 110, 249
Pine, F., 63
Pinto, A., 175
Platsidou, M., 141
Pleck, J. H., 175
Poon, L. W., 238
Porder, M. S., 59
Postman, K., 67
Pulvers, K. M., 231
Pushkin, V. N., 259
Pushkina, A. G., 259

Q

Quas, J. A., 36
Quinn, J. J., 132

R

Radke-Yarrow, M., 34
Raney, G. E., 97
Raya, P., 101
Reid, J. B., 288
Rescorla, R. A., 128
Reznick, J. S., 14
Ricks, M. H., 36
Ridgeway, C. L., 175
Ridley-Johnson, R., 287
Riley, M. W., 188
Ritvo, S., 50
Robey, J. S., 255
Rogoff, B., 253, 254, 255, 256

Rollins, K. B., 117

Rose, H., 170

Rose, S. P., 273

Rosen, A. B., 117

Rosenbaum, M., 147

Ross, D., 136

Ross, S. A., 136

Rotenberg, E. J., 101

Rotenberg, K. J., 106

Rovee-Collier, C., 90

Rozin, P., 117

Ruble, D., 170

Ruff, H. A., 91

Rumelhart, D. E., 65

Rummelsburg, J., 111

Rushton, J. P., 137

Ryder, N. B., 188

S

Saltarelli, L. M., 91

Sameroff, A. J., 276, 281

Sampson, R. J., 196, 200, 201

Sarbin, T. R., 163

Schaaf, J. M., 36

Schafer, R., 59

Schatz, J. A., 89

Schaver, P. R., 36

Schecter, A., 90

Scheier, C., 272, 280

Schiff, A., 141, 256

Schlein, S., 238

Schmid, J., 100

Schneider, B. H., 35

Schöner, G., 272, 280, 295

Schultz, R., 15

Schulz, A. J., 195

Schwartz, S. J., 194

Scribner, S., 244, 252, 255

Sears, K. G., 110

Seligman, M. E. P., 147, 230

Selman, R. L., 105

Settles, I. H., 190

Shanahan, M. J., 190

Shaver, P. R., 35, 36

Shemesh, M., 101

Shibley, P. K., 237

Shields, P., 100

Shorey, H. S., 231

Shull, R. L., 134

Shute, R. H., 127

Shyi, G. C. W., 90

Sidle, A. L., 117

Siegel, L. S., 98

Siegler, I. C., 238

Siegler, R. S., 69, 142, 254

Silvern, L., 89, 215

Silvia, P. J., 109

Simons, E. L., 24

Sinnott, J. D., 108

Skaalvik, E. M., 139

Skinner, B. F., 133, 134, 135

Slee, P. T., 127

Smith, D., 166

Smith, E., 97

Smith, L. B., 272, 280

Snyder, C. R., 221, 230, 231, 236

Snyder, J., 288, 290

Solnit, A. J., 50

Solomon, J., 36

Sophian, C., 231

Spanoudis, G., 141

Spelke, E. S., 91

Spence, I., 98

Spencer, H., 23

Sroufe, L. A., 33

Steen, T. A., 147

Steinberg, L., 223

Steinmetz, J. E., 130

Stevenson, H. W., 253

Stewart, A. J., 190, 191, 233, 237

Stoolmiller, M., 290
Stright, A. D., 110
Sullivan, H. S., 76
Sullivan, M. D., 230
Swenson, R., 281
Sympson, S. C., 230

T

Tardif, C., 35
Tattersall, I., 24
Taylor, J. D., 231
Thal, D. J., 14
Thelen, E., 272, 279, 280, 287, 288,
    293, 295
Thomas, E. J., 162
Thomas, R. M., 12, 237
Thomas, W., 187, 188
Thorndike, E. L., 132
Tinbergen, N., 27
Tolman, E. C., 137
Tomlinson-Keasey, C., 189
Tooby, J., 29, 30
Toth, J. P., 68
Tracy, J. L., 36
Tracy, R. L., 34
Trivers, R., 30
Tudge, J. R. H., 106
Turnure, J., 141, 256
Tyson, P., 55, 58, 64
Tyson, R. L., 55, 58, 64

U

Uzgiris, I. C., 85, 92

V

Valsiner, J., 170, 244, 247
Van Couvering, J., 24

van der Heijden, P. G. M., 104
van der Veer, R., 244, 247
van Geert, P., 113, 118
van Ijzendoorn, M. H., 34
Vanzetti, N., 220
Vietze, P. M., 91
Volkart, E. H., 188
Vollenbergh, W., 229
von Bertalanffy, L., 271, 275
von Hofsten, C., 91
Voydanoff, P., 174, 176
Vygotsky, L. S., 97, 243, 244, 247, 248,
    249, 250, 251, 252, 256

W

Walker, E., 106
Walker, L. J., 104
Walters, R. H., 135, 161
Warren, S., 62
Waterman, A. S., 227, 228, 229, 236,
    237
Watson, J., 106
Weine, S., 177
Weinfield, N. S., 33
Weiskranz, L., 68
Weiss, J., 58
Wellman, H. M., 92, 106, 108
Welsh, K. A., 238
Wentworth, N., 90
Wertsch, J. V., 243
Whitbourne, S. K., 236, 237
White, R. W., 215
Whiting, B. B., 171
Whitmore, K. F., 166
Widaman, K., 189
Wiklund, C., 231
Wilkinson, A., 98
Wilson, E. O., 25
Wilson, M., 41, 103

Wimmer, H. M., 106
Winter, N. J. G., 190
Wolfe, R., 34
Wright, D. W., 176

Y

Yan, Z., 281
Yang, C., 173f, 174, 196
Yarrow, L. J., 91
Yengo, L., 92

Z

Zelazo, P. D., 103
Zelinski, E. M., 142
Zijdenbos, A., 116
Zimmerman, B. J., 170
Zimmerman, P., 228
Ziv, M., 107
Znaniecki, ki, F., 187, 188
Zuschlag, M. K., 236, 237

Subject Index

Note: *t* indicates table.

A

Accentuation principle, 194
Accommodation, 86–87, 113–114, 177
Adaptation, 12, 20, 24–25, 42, 44,
        86–87, 135, 176–177, 180, 187,
        195, 212, 236
    behavioral, 26
    capacity for, 13
    cognitive, 113
    infant's, 208
    long-term species, 46
    positive, 147
    process of, 2, 38
    sensorimotor, 88
Adaptive
    problems, 29–30, 37, 39–40, 43
    self-organization, 277

self-stabilization, 276–277, 280
Adolescence, 55, 61, 216
Age
    constraints, 161
    norms, 161, 191
Agency, 2131, 238
Aggressive
    energy, 60–61
    impulses, 64
Anal stage of development, 54
Antisocial development, 288–291
Assimilation, 86–87, 113–114
Assumptions, 11
Attachment behavior system, 31–32
    formation of attachment with
            mother, father, and others,
            32

patterns of attachment, 32–33
quality of attachment, 33–34
relevance of attachment to later de-
    velopment, 35–36
the strange situation, 33
Attention, 128–129, 138, 140–141
Attentionless unconscious cognition,
    68
Attractor, 278, 289, 291–292
Autonomous reality, 102–103

B

Balancing work and family life, (*see
    also* Work-family) 36–38
Behavior guiding, 51
Behavioral complexity, 282, 285–286
Biological
    factors, 15–16
    system, 14, 82, 233, 271, 275–276
Birth cohort, 188, 196, 223
Blindsight, 68

C

Caregiver–infant interaction, 32
Causal
    relationships, 11, 94, 155–155
    schemes, 89–91
Central process, 222, 226–227, 232
Change, 14
Childhood and Society, 216
Classical conditioning, 127–133, 140,
    146–147, 149–150, 151*t*,
    152–154
Classification skills, 97–98
Coercion theory, 288–289
Cognition (*see also* Social cognition)
    82
    in adulthood, 107–108
    sociohistorical study of, 255
Cognitive
    behaviorism, 126, 138, 150, 152–153
    competencies, 138
    map, 137

Cognitive developmental theory, 2, 15,
    17*t*, 81–83, 112–115
an application of, 110-112
critique of, 115–118
    historical context of, 83–84
    key concepts of, 84–102
new directions in, 102-108
research example of, 108-110
Cognitive social–historical theory,
    241-243
    an application of, 258–260
    critique of, 264–267
    historical context of, 243–245
    key concepts of, 245–252
    new directions in, 252–255
    research example in, 256–257
Cognitive stimulation, 2
Combinatorial skills, 91, 99
Communion, 238
Concrete operational thought, 94–95
Conditioned response (CR), 127–130
Conditioned stimulus (CS), 128–131
Conscious attention, 3, 67
Consciousness, 53, 56, 65, 75,
    244–247, 264
    domains of, 50–51
Constructive web, 282–283
Continuous reinforcement, 134
Control cycle, 194
Conventional morality, 104
Conservation, 95–98, 114, 117–118,
    252
Core pathologies, 221–222
Cultural tools, 243–247, 253

D

Darwin, Charles, 11
Decentering, 101
Defense mechanisms, 56–58
Denial, 57
Development (defined), 10
    stages of, (*see* Stages of develop-
        ment)

Developmental Psychology of Jean Piaget, The, 84
Developmental stage, 215–217
Developmental tasks, 222
  integration of, 225–226
Differentiation, 61–63, 166
Diffidence, 224
Discrimination, 131
Disequilibrium, 82 –83, 87, 103, 109, 114, 280–281, 291, 294S
Displacement, 57
Dissociation, 222–223
Divided attention, 141
Domain, 10–11, 17*t*
Dreams
  logic of, 51
Drive, 49
Dynamic skill, 283–284
Dynamic system, 273, 280, 293
Dynamic systems theory, 269–271
  an application of, 288–291
  critique of, 294–296
  historical context of, 271–272
  key concepts of, 272–281
  new directions in, 281–286
  research example of, 287–288

E

Ego, 52
  development, 61, 234–238
  executive functions of, 60
  psychology, 60–62
  in relationship with id and superego, 53–54
Ego Psychology and the Problem of Adaptation, 60–61
Egocentrism, 101–102, 249
Electra complex, 55
Emergence, 278–280
Emerging adulthood, 223
Emotion of interest, 109
Empathy, 83, 104, 181
Enactive attainment, 139

Epigenesis, 1, 215
Episodic memory, 142
Equilibrium, 11–12, 49, 76, 82–83, 87, 273, 281
  biological, 63
  cognitive, 113
Erikson, Erik, 213–215
Ethology, 21, 26–29, 39, 41
  of eating, 286
Evolution, 11
Evolutionary psychology, 21, 29–30
  formation of attachments with mother, father, and others, 32
  patterns of attachment, 32–36
  research example of, 29–30
Evolutionary theory, 19-20
  an application of, 36-38
  critique of 40–41
  historical context of, 21
  key concepts of, 22-26
  new directions in, 26-31
  research example of, 31-36
Expectancies, 138, 152, 154, 201
Experiential learning, 140, 143, 145, 152
Extinction, 23, 41, 134
  and punishment, 134–135, 154
  and spontaneous recovery, 30
  versus immortality, 223

F

Father–child dyads, 41
Fitness (*see also* Inclusive fitness; Reproductive success), 22, 29, 31, 39–41, 43, 46
Focused attention, 50
Formal operational thought, 98–100
  six characteristics of, 100–101
Freud, Anna, 60–61
Freud, Sigmund, 47–48

G

Gender
  identity, 55, 59, 170–172

role, 155, 170–172, 183, 188
similarity, 197
stereotypes, 175
Generalization, 130–131, 154
Genetic information, 1
Genital stage, 55–56
Gerotranscendence, 224
Goals, 15, 31, 100 –101, 122, 138, 140,
    145, 149–150, 152, 154–156,
    161, 167, 169–170, 172, 193,
    221, 230–231, 246, 271–272,
    272, 281, 283–284
Growth
  of biological systems, 271, 275
  cognitive, 114–115, 275
  direction and nature of, 2, 26
  disruption of, 72
  in infancy, 287
  of intelligence during infancy, 88–89
  of logical thinking, 10, 84
  mechanisms accounting for, 12
  normative and pathological patterns
    of, 46
  promoting, 168
  social, 225–226
  spurts, 285

H

Habits, 89, 122, 132–134, 142, 147,
    149–150, 153–154
Hamlet, 243
Heteronomous morality, 102–103
Higher mental processes, 243
Higher order conditioning, 128
Historical time, 186, 188, 190, 195, 199
Homonculous, 1
Human
  agency, 122, 195, 200–203, 205
  development (defined), 9–10
    challenges to understanding,
      13–15
    what to expect from theory of,
      12–13

I

Id, 51–52

  in relationship with ego and super-
    ego, 53–54
Identification, 50, 53, 55, 59–60, 62,
    64, 70, 73, 168, 227, 275
Identity, 96, 108, 117
Identity: Youth and Crisis, 227
Inclusive fitness, 23
Information processing, 29, 106,
    140–141, 143, 151–153, 256
Innate
  behaviors, 27, 29, 85
    of infants, 28, 63
  drives, 72
  physical reflexes, 152
  theory of development, 2
Inner speech, 249–250
Insight, 91, 98, 102
Interdependent lives, 186, 194
Interest (*see* Emotion of interest,
    metacognition)
Intergenerational transmission,
    188–189
Intermental, 247–249
Intermittent reinforcement, 134
Internalization, 250–251
Intervening variable, 137
Interventions (*see also* Therapeutic in-
    terventions), 8, 16, 44, 258,
    278
  early, 271
  educational, 111
  medical, 14
Intramental, 247–249
Isolation (*see also* Social isolation), 57,
    62, 194

K

Key constructs, 11

L

Language capacity, 14
Latency period, 55

Law of effect, 132
Law of exercise, 132
Learned
    helplessness, 140, 146–147
    resourcefulness, 140, 147
Learning theories, 125–126
    an application of, 147–150
    critique of, 153–156
    historical context of, 126–127
    key concepts of, 127–140
    new directions in, 140–146
    research example of, 146–147
Libidinal energy, 61
Libido, 49
Life of Haifisch, The, 109
Life course theory, 185-186
    an application of, 199–201
    critique of, 204–206
    historical context of, 186–189
    key concepts of, 189–195
    new directions in, 195–196
    research example of, 196–199
Life history, 31, 41, 187–188
Life span, 193, 201, 203
    development, 187
    psychology, 189
Life stage, 193, 196, 205
Linked
    lives, 195, 204
    trajectories, 201–205
Lipps, Theodore, 83
Logical thinking, 10, 255
Logico-mathematical knowledge,
        110–112
Longitudinal research, 205
Long-term memory, 140–141, 143
Lower mental processes, 243

M

Mediated learning, 258
Metacognition, 108–110, 248–250, 268
Modeling, 136–137
Models, 136–137
Moral
    reasoning, 102–104, 228

    standards, 46, 53–54, 58
Mother–child dyads, 46, 63
Mother–father–child triad, 55
Motivated behavior, 48–50

N

Nativist theory of development, 2
Natural selection, 22–23, 29–30, 38–39,
        41–43
Nature of objects, 91
Nature theory of development, 2
Negative
    feedback, 276
    reinforcers, 133
Neurological
    bases of cognitive functioning, 116
    challenges, 115
    damage, 68, 152, 293
    development, 140–143
Neutral stimulus (NS), 128
Novelty appraisal, 109

O

Oakland Growth Study, 186–187
Object
    permanence, 91–93, 118
    relations theory, 62–64, 72, 75
Observational learning, 135, 140
Oedipal complex, 55
Open system, 271, 280
Operant conditioning, 11, 126,
        132–135, 137–138, 140,
        146–147, 149–150, 151*t*,
        152–153, 155
Operations, 102, 108, 110–113, 117
Oral sensory, 216
Oral stage of development, 54
Organizational strategies, 141–142

P

Pavlov, Ivan, 127–133, 155
Perceptual defense, 67
Person-role fit, 164

Personality
    three structures of, 51–54
Perspective taking, 102, 104–106, 163
Phallic stage of development, 54–55
Physical state, 139
Piaget, Jean, 83–84
Plans, 9, 13, 100–101, 138, 140, 145,
        152, 238, 277
Pleasure principle, 51
Positive
    feedback, 276, 281
    reinforcers, 133
Postformal thought, 102, 107–108
Practicing, 63
Preconscious, 50
Preconventional morality, 104
Preoperational thought, 93–94,
        101–102
Primary narcissism, 52
Primary process thought, 51–53, 71, 74
Prime adaptive ego qualities, 220–221
Projection, 57
Prospective memory, 142
Psychodrama, 161
Psychological Archives, 83
Psychological
    system, 15, 227, 233
    tools, 246
Psychosexual theory, 2, 15, 17*t*, 45-47
    an application of, 70-71
    critique of, 74–78
    historical context of, 47–48
    key concepts of, 48–60
    new directions in, 60-64
    research example of, 65-69
Psychosocial
    crisis, 218–220
        central process for resolving,
            226–227
    evolution, 42, 208, 214, 223
    stages, 222–224
Psychosocial theory, 211–212
    an application of, 229–231
    critique of, 235–238
    historical context of, 213–215

key concepts of, 215–222
new directions in, 222–227
research example of, 227–229
Puberty, 55, 60–61, 216
Punishment, 55, 64, 72, 115, 135, 153,
        200

R

Radius of significant relationships, 220
Rapprochement, 64
Rationalization, 57
Reaction formation, 57
Reality
    principle, 52
    testing, 52, 64
Reciprocal roles, 165
Reciprocity, 96
Regression, 57–58, 74, 2291
Reinforcement, 11, 133, 150–156
    conditions, 135
    continuous, 134
    intermittent, 134
    mutual, 25
    negative, 134–135
    positive, 134
    schedules of, 134–135, 150
    sensitivity to, 13
Repression, 57, 72
Reproductive
    age, 31, 38, 40
    capacity, 23, 27, 40
    functions, 46
    process, 2
    strategies, 29, 41
    success, 22, 26, 30–31, 38–41, 43
Response, 128–135, 137–138, 145–146,
        150, 152, 154
Reversibility, 96–97
Role
    conflict, 172
    enactments, 166
    expectations and norms, 165
    gain, 122, 179–180, 182–183
    loss, 122, 169, 179–180, 182–183
    models, 151, 154, 161, 180, 234

overload, 172
strain, 37, 167, 181, 183
taking, 161
Roles (*see also* Reciprocal roles; Social roles; Work–family roles), 161

S

Schedules of reinforcement, 151, 154
Scheme (defined), 85
Scientific
concepts, 258–259
observation, 7–9
Secondary process thought, 52, 72
Selective attention, 67–68
Self-control, 35, 44, 55, 1387, 145, 147, 218, 221, 250
Self-efficacy, 139–140, 150, 153–154
Self-encoding, 138, 152
Self-esteem, 52, 55, 57, 62, 64, 161, 229, 235–236
Self-love, 49, 52
Self-other system, 161
Self-regulation, 249
Self-sameness, 14, 275
Self-stimulation, 55
Semantic memory, 141
Sensorimotor intelligence, 88–88, 102
Separation–individuation phase, 63–64
Sexual
alliances, 37
conflict, 47
drives, 47–49, 55, 61, 70–71, 75–76
energy, 60–61
functioning, 15
identity, 61
impulses, 2
infidelity, 38
maturation, 2
selection, 21, 30
Sexuality, 54
Shaping, 121–122, 133–134, 152
Short-term memory, 141–142
Signs, 92–93, 247–248

Situation, 10
Situational imperative, 194–195
Skinner, B. F., 133–135, 155
Social
bonds, 40, 201–205
clock, 191
cognition, 104–106
contact, 2
isolation, 76, 182, 204, 224
learning, 8, 126, 137, 150, 152–154, 161
regulation, 192
support, 192, 201, 209, 227, 234–236, 258, 307
time, 191, 195
Social role theory, 159-160
an application of, 177–179
critique of, 182–183
definition of, 162
dimensions of, 163–164
historical context of, 160–162
key concepts of, 162–170
new directions in, 170–172
research example of, 172–177
Societal system, 15, 231, 233–234
Sociocultural perspective, 253–255, 258, 262–263
Sociohistorical perspective, 255, 260
Spillover, 172
Spiraling process, 58
Spontaneous
concepts, 258–259
recovery, 130
Stages of development, 54–56, 215–218
Stimulus, 131–133, 135, 137–138, 145, 149, 245
Storehouse, 11, 49
Sublimation, 56–57, 73, 75
Superego, 52–53
in relationship with id and ego, 53–54
Symbol systems, 243–248, 259–263
Symbolic
abilities, 15, 233–234
capacities, 26

equivalence, 60
play, 93
representation, 42, 73
rewards, 152
thought, 9, 93
tools, 255
Symbolism, 10, 52, 54
System hierarchy, 287

T

Teachable moments, 225
Technical tools, 246
Testable hypothesis, 11, 180
Theoretical learning, 258–260
Theory (defined), 10–12
    logic of, 11
    of mind, 106–107
Therapeutic interventions, 47, 75–76
Thorndike, E. L., 132–133
Thinking and Speech, 244
Thought and Language, 244
Toward object constancy, 64
Trajectories, 122, 189–195, 199–205,
    282
Transference, 50, 59–60, 75
Transforming environments, 202
Transitions, 190
Trial-and-error learning, 42, 91,
    132–133
Turning points, 195, 201, 205

U

Unconditioned response (UR),
    127–128

Unconditioned stimulus (US), 127–128,
    131
Unconscious, 51
    insights, 68–69
    rediscovery of, 65–69

V

Values, 9, 55, 59, 62, 67, 70–71, 170,
    138, 141, 149, 152, 154–156,
    164, 177, 188, 193, 214, 267,
    281
    of society, 161
Verbal persuasion, 139
Vicarious
    information, 139
    learning, 135–136
Vital Involvements in Old Age, 223
Vygotsky, Lev Semyonovich, 243–244

W

Whitest Parts of the Body, The, 109
Word use, 261–262
Work–family (*See also* Balancing work
        and family life)
    roles, 172–177
    trade-offs, 196–199
Working memory, 140–141

Z

Zone of proximal development, 241,
    250–252, 257, 261